COLLECTED PAPERS

VOLUME FIVE

COLLECTED PAPERS

VOLUME FIVE

INTERNATIONAL SYSTEMS: PEACE, CONFLICT RESOLUTION, AND POLITICS

KENNETH E. BOULDING

LARRY D. SINGELL, EDITOR

COLORADO ASSOCIATED UNIVERSITY PRESS

BOULDER, COLORADO

COLORADO ASSOCIATED UNIVERSITY PRESS

BOULDER, COLORADO

Copyright © Kenneth E. Boulding 1975
Colorado Associated University Press
1424 Fifteenth Street
Boulder, Colorado 80302

Library of Congress Card Number 77-135288

ISBN 87081-062-6

CONTENTS

INTRODUCTION

This volume reflects my lifelong interest in peace. There are two aspects of this interest: the personal commitment and the social phenomenon. This volume deals with the latter, that is, peace as an aspect or property of the social system. It is particularly concerned with international peace as a property of the international system, that is, with peace as the opposite of war. The papers in this volume, however, are not the result of mere curiosity, but arise from a strong value system and a set of priorities which hold not merely that war is bad but that in the twentieth century especially it has become the main threat to the future of the human race. There is no pretense, therefore, that these papers arise out of a value-free perspective. On the other hand, I am convinced that the problem of war cannot be solved without an accurate knowledge of the systems which give rise to it, and the presence of a strong value presupposition makes it all the more important to develop an accurate image of the social and international system, the truth of which does not depend on the values which inspired the search for it.

A volume of collected papers inevitably involves some repetition and this is particularly likely to be the case where—I confess unashamedly—the author has something to say that he thinks is important for the world to hear. I make no apology, therefore, for repeating what I think is important, but the papers in this volume inevitably have something of the air of a set of variations on a limited number of themes. These themes are also developed in my book, *Conflict and Defense* (1962), most of which was written in the wonderful year we spent in Jamaica at the University of the West Indies in 1959–1960. The theme of viability theory and the all-important conclusion that the increase in the range of the deadly missile destroys unconditional viability, even for the largest nations, comes out of that period even though it clearly derives from the economic theory of the firm and industry. A second major theme, also crystallized in that year in Jamaica, is that of the three-fold genetic structure of the social system: threats systems, exchange systems,

vii

and integrative systems. The basic article on "The Relations of Economic, Political and Social Systems" (1962) is published in the fourth volume of the *Collected Papers*, but its implications appear again and again in the present volume, leading up to the identification of three major categories of power in social systems: threat power, exchange power and integrative power.

A third major theme is the search for the parameters of international systems, arms races and the like, as developed, for instance, in Paper 18. Much of this derives from the pioneering work of Lewis F. Richardson, who, together with Quincy Wright, must be regarded as the founder of "Peace Science," as Walter Isard now calls it. The concept of the coefficient of reactivity (page 206) is of the utmost importance in systems of this kind. The demonstration that this must be less than one if two-party conflicts are to have equilibrium, and much less than one if many-partied conflicts are to have equilibrium, is perhaps the most important theorem of this volume.

A fourth major theme is that of the phase structure of the international system or indeed of any conflict systems, with four major phases of stable war, unstable war, unstable peace and stable peace. If we can understand the dynamics of the system through its phase space, this gives us the best hope of intervening with the object of assisting the system to move towards stable peace.

Underlying all the themes of this volume is peace research and the peace research movement, in which I have been active for at least twenty years. It was indeed the year I spent at the Center for Advanced Study in the Behavioral Sciences at Stanford (1954–1955) that brought me into the peace research movement. Only the first paper in this volume predates that year and suggests that I was ready for this new direction. It was a group at the Stanford Center, headed by Herbert Kelman, working on the problem of how to mobilize the social sciences into the study of peace and war that really drew me into the peace research movement. I recall indeed that two young men at the University of Michigan, William Barth and Robert Hefner, both of them influenced by Theodore Lentz at St. Louis, who has good claims to be the father of peace research in the United States, had approached me at the University of Michigan a few months before I went to Stanford with the suggestion of a peace research program, but nothing came of it at the time.

After the year at Stanford, I went back to Michigan in the fall of 1955. With Robert Angell, Anatol Rapoport and others, and with Barth and Hefner as our constant gadflies, we founded the *Journal of Conflict Resolution*, which led soon afterwards to the establishment of the Center for Research on Conflict Resolution at Michigan, an important focus of the peace research enterprise. I recall one dramatic moment in my office at the University of Michigan after we had published about two issues of the *Journal of Conflict Resolution* and had completely run out of money. The editorial board decided to abandon the enterprise and had just left my office when the telephone rang and a lady's voice at the other end said, "Could you use a thousand dollars for the new journal?" I ran to the head of the stairs and called the committee back as they were going out of the building, and the journal continued. The financial precariousness of the peace research movement, however, has continued. The Center for Research on Conflict Resolution has now been disbanded, though the *Journal* continues at Yale University. Apart from the Stockholm International Peace Research Institute and the United States Arms Control and Disarmament Agency, only minute sums have ever been forthcoming for an activity on which the whole future of the human race may depend.

The papers on peace research at the end of this volume reflect some changes within the peace research movement since 1968 when the summary article (Paper 25) was published. On the world scene a somewhat ideological split developed, particularly between the Americans and the Europeans, at the meetings both of the International Peace Research Association and the Peace Research Society (International). This is described in Paper 32. The divisions are still evident, though they are not as acrimonious as they were in 1969 and there is some fruitful communication among the various parties.

In North America, the Consortium on Peace Research, Education and Development (COPRED) was formed in Boulder in 1970, with the expectation that research would be its major interest. What happened however, is that with the sudden quiet on the campuses there was a great upsurge of interest in peace education, especially as reflected in peace studies programs at the undergraduate level. This should not have been surprising. After twenty years of peace research it was found that there was something to teach, that there was a literature and that students could read it and be examined in it. This is what gives any program of studies validity on a college campus. Peace research itself, however, has rather stagnated since 1970, even though the general field of international relations or international studies, as reflected in the extraordinary vitality of the International Studies Association, indicates that the larger field is still very active.

I still think there is a great deal to be done in peace research even in the narrow sense—for instance, in continued studies of problems of disarmament and of integrative dynamics and the general dynamics of the social system—that can lead the international system towards stable peace. Oddly enough, it is the "broad school" of which I was somewhat critical in "The Philosophy of Peace Research" (Paper 32) which has increasingly engaged my attention in the past two or three years under the heading, however, of "justice research," which I still think is something rather different from peace research, though closely related to it. I hope perhaps a subsequent volume of papers may concentrate on this theme.

As in the other volumes, the papers are arranged in chronological order so that the reader may observe some development in my thinking as the years go on. In this volume the estimate of the dollar value of the world war industry increases strikingly as we go from the earlier papers to the later ones, reflecting partly inflation and also the long, continued arms race.

As always, my thanks are due to many people who made this volume possible. I am grateful to Hanna and Alan Newcombe for their constant example and stimulation, and for permission to include Paper 25, which is largely their work. A special thanks again is due to Professor Singell for the job of editing. As a careful reader may deduce from the bibliography, this volume is in fact a selection from a large number of published papers on this theme. The selection has been judicious. Even where there is some duplication, as there is, for instance, in Papers 19 and 27, and Papers 30 and 31, each of these was written for a different audience and in a somewhat different style; a certain amount of repetition therefore seems justified.

Finally, no formal thanks would do justice to the extraordinary job which Vivian Wilson has done in putting together the bibliography. She, with the assistance of Sheryl Kipnis, has discovered writings which I had forgotten. In completeness and accuracy it is a bibliography beyond praise. No thanks that I could express could possibly be adequate.

The papers themselves of the last four or five years are perhaps the best expression of my gratitude to the Ford Foundation, for a grant which has supported my work.

Kenneth E. Boulding

Boulder, Colorado 1975

ECONOMIC ISSUES IN INTERNATIONAL CONFLICT

Kyklos, 2, 6 (1953): 97-115

ECONOMIC ISSUES
IN INTERNATIONAL CONFLICT*

I

International conflict, particularly in its most extreme form, war, has become not merely the major political issue but the major economic issue of our time. It absorbs an ever-increasing proportion of national incomes everywhere. It creates a sense of insecurity so profound as to put civilization itself in danger. In every city of the world those who are sensitive to the present world situation have constantly at the back of their minds the nightmare question "when?"—how long will it be before this thriving city, with all its monuments of culture, will be laid waste and thousands of its inhabitants subjected to death or injury.

For the mass of men this situation may not be a new one. Civilizations have always been built on the edge of social and political volcanoes and time after time throughout the course of history they have been swept away in eruptions of violence. Tyre and Carthage, Babylon and Rome all repeat the pattern of rise and fall. After reading any book on the history or archeology of the Middle East, for instance, one goes around America in amazement, saying to oneself "Astounding! This is the first city ever built on this site!" If there were nine Troys why should we expect there to be only one New York? Nevertheless, for Americans especially, the feeling of utter insecurity which has characterized most human lives and human history is a strange one. For most Americans, war has always been a peripheral rather than a central experience, something which could be regarded as an accident of history, to be dealt with by *ad hoc* measures, rather than as a permanent and deep-rooted element in the life of society. Until the twentieth century this was also true of Great Britain and of many parts of Europe.

Today, however, we seem to be entering upon a period in which war has become the central institution around which all our lives revolve. All over the world young men are condemned to spend the formative years of early manhood in the acquisition or the practice

* The substance of this article was given as a lecture in Vanderbilt University, Nashville, Tennessee (USA) in December 1951.

of the arts of killing their fellows. War now reaches down into every family and threatens the security of every home, either by the claims it makes upon the individual members or by aerial destruction. Nobody who has seen the ruins of the German cities, once so beautiful, can avoid picturing, in every city he visits, the dreadful vision of a possible, even a probable, future of rubble and ruins.

It is important to inquire into the reasons for this strange worsening of man's position. Paradoxically, the basic reason lies in the very increase in man's power which the technical revolution has brought about. The immense improvement in the techniques of production and social organization which has been accomplished in the past two hundred years, and which has in so large a measure lifted the curse of Adam from those societies that have benefited by it, and has showered us with refrigerators, automobiles, telephones, television, central heating and the other luxuries and conveniences of modern life, has also created the overshadowing fear of destruction. The technical revolution has not been and could not be, confined to the production of more abundant life; it inevitably spills over into the production of more abundant death. It is the profound change in the techniques of warfare resulting from the scientific and technical revolution—a change of which the atom bomb is merely a culminating and perhaps overemphasised symbol—that has produced this total insecurity of man, and the transfer of the institution of war from the periphery to the centre of man's activity.

II

The economist can offer considerable clues to the reasons for this deplorable turn of events. The theory of economic conflict, as it has been developed, for instance, in the theory of oligopoly (competition among the few), throws a great deal of light on the theory of the competition of states (war). Similarly the theory of the "viability" (the conditions of survival) of firms is relevant to the theory of the viability of states. I do not propose to give in this place a detailed exposition of these theories: their conclusions, however, may be summarised in the following series of propositions.

1. The first proposition may be expressed simply as "the further the weaker": that is, the further from the home base any organiza-

tion is operating, the weaker will be its competitive position. In the case of the firm, this is reflected in increasing transportation costs as it sells its products further and further from the point of production. In the case of the state, its power of destruction is an inverse function of the distance from the source of supplies of both men and materials.

2. The second proposition follows from the first. It is that, if there are two competing organizations located at different points, there will be a "boundary of indifference" between them, the location of which depends on what might be called the "home strength" of the two organizations. In the case of the firm the "home strength" may be conveniently measured by the lowest price of the product—reckoned at the point of production—at which the firm can survive. Thus a firm which lowers the cost of production of its product is increasing its "home strength". If we have two firms located at different points but possessing equal home strengths, the boundary of indifference will be half-way between them. As one firm increases its home strength *relative to the other*, the boundary of indifference moves towards the weaker firm and away from the stronger firm. In the case of the nation-state the "home strength" is determined by the absolute amount of resources which it can devote to defence, and also by the efficiency of their use. The boundary of indifference between two states is that point at which their military power is approximately equal. Thus, when the German armies advanced into Russia in 1942, they became progressively weaker as their lines of communication became more extended, while the Russian armies became progressively stronger as they were pushed back towards their home bases. At Stalingrad the boundary of indifference was temporarily reached. In military situations the boundary of indifference may be subject to a good deal of instability during the course of time, owing to the fluctuating efficiency of military operations. Apart from these dynamic qualifications, however, the principle of the boundary of indifference applies as much to the competition of states as to the competition of firms.

3. The third proposition is that the distance of the boundary of indifference from the centre of an organization (which is in some sense a measure of its "security") depends not on its absolute strength but on its relative strength, relative, that is, to its competitors. Thus, if a firm lowers its home price in the hope of pushing its boundary

of indifference further away from it and thereby attracting customers and expanding its operations, the advantage remains only as long as the competing firms keep their prices up. If the competing firms retaliate by cutting their prices, the boundary of indifference shifts back towards its original position. The same phenomenon may be observed in the competition of states: an increase in the armaments of one state contributes to its security only as long as the other states do not reply in kind. The "illusion of absolute strength" is one of the most widespread popular illusions concerning national defence. There is no meaning whatever in a nation's "being strong": the only meaningful phrase is "being stronger than potential enemies".

4. The fourth proposition follows from the third: that the competitive equilibrium of a *few* competitors, and especially of two competitors, is highly unstable if the competitors are close together. If the competitors are far apart, and if there is no great concentration of population in the neighbourhood of the boundary of indifference, a system of competition, whether of firms or of states, can be stable simply because neither competitor has any particular inducement to attempt to shift the boundary of indifference, either by cutting prices in the case of the firm or by increasing armaments in the case of the state. Each competitor is "secure", because each is stronger than the other in his home territory (from proposition one), and neither feels any obligation to challenge the existing boundary of indifference. If, however, the competitors are close together, and if the neighbourhood of the boundary of indifference matters for them, in the sense that it contains a large number of customers in the case of the firm, or important strategic resources in the case of the state, then the equilibrium will be unstable, and a price war or an armaments race will result. One of the organizations will try to improve its position (security) at the expense of the other, and this will force the other to follow suit in order to restore the old position of the boundary of indifference. The only answer to such a situation is "monopoly", *i.e.* the establishment of a super-organization which replaces the direct competitive relationship by an organic relationship of some kind. The super-organization may be extremely tenuous; it may be a "gentlemen's agreement" like the Concert of Europe; it may be a loose cartel like the League of Nations or the United Nations. Gentlemen's agreements and cartels, however, are notoriously unstable, and

there seems to be a considerable tendency for super-organizations to grow into fully-fledged organisms (the merger or Federal Union).

5. The fifth proposition is that the home strength of organizations is a function of their size; up to some optimum magnitude, strength increases with size: there are economies of scale. Beyond a certain point, however, what might be called the "Brontosaurus principle" (named after its most distinguished victim) begins to operate, and increasing size brings clumsiness, lack of adaptability, and other weaknesses. In the case of states the optimum size for defence probably exceeds the optimum size for governmental efficiency, as it is not the per capita efficiency of defence that is the competitive factor, but the absolute amount of defence "output". Thus sheer size gives large states a competitive advantage in defence, in spite of the fact that their per capita efficiency, in defence as in other functions of government, may be lower than that of smaller states. One has a general impression, which it is difficult to verify, that for governmental efficiency the optimum size of the modern state is from five to twenty million people: countries like Switzerland, Canada, Sweden and Uruguay seem to make a better technical job of governing themselves than their more Brontosaurian neighbours. Even in the field of defence, however, the Brontosaurus principle eventually triumphs, and history is strewn with the wrecks of great empires which fell apart from mere size.

6. The sixth proposition is that the optimum size from the point of view of defence (or survival) is itself a function of the "state of the arts", and that, as an empirical fact, economic development has resulted in a great growth in the optimum size of the unit of defence. This is a reflection of the fact that one of the main results of technological improvement is the diminution of the obstacle of space. It is not merely that we can now span the earth in less time than it used to take to go thirty miles—with the result that the earth has shrunk to the size of a neighbourhood. The more subtle obstacles of "social distance" have also been whittled away by progress in the skills of organization and communication, so that we can now contemplate a state comprising hundreds of millions of people, whereas Plato could not conceive of a state larger than a few thousand. In the days of the bow and the spear, a city-state was a viable unit of defence; the city could be walled and the basic condition of defence estab-

lished—the creation of an area of internal peace surrounded by a "skin" of war. Even as early as Alexander's time, however, the defensibility of the city-state had become dubious, and the invention of gunpowder made that unit wholly indefensible. Walls were useless against the new weapons, and defence had to be made so deep, that it absorbed the whole body of the city state—much as if the skin that defends the living body against invasion should itself become a cancerous growth invading the whole body. The Roman Empire was clearly too big for the techniques of its day: it grew and survived for a time merely because of its uniqueness—because there was no other empire of like magnitude to challenge it. Its size made for instability, however, and in the ensuing collapse the city-state reappeared, as it always tends to do if techniques fall back to a certain level. Gunpowder created the eighteenth-century state—states of the size of France, Britain, Germany and Italy, though some of these only appeared at a moment in history when their type was already becoming obsolete. The airplane and high explosives have clearly made the typical European state as obsolete as the city-state. This was probably the case even at the beginning of the twentieth century, though it took two world wars to demonstrate it beyond doubt. Consequently we are now left with only two "viable" centres of power—the two giant states of America and Russia. The disturbing question now arises whether the amazing rush of technical development has not rendered even these states obsolete, just as gunpowder made the city-state obsolete. In the days of the H-bomb and the rocket plane there is real doubt as to whether even countries as big as the United States and Russia can be defended in the traditional sense, unless, like the Roman Empire, they exist in an environment without rivals.

7. My seventh proposition is that, in the case of the rivalry of two close and approximately equal powers, the demands of national defence are inherently insatiable, and hence the proportion of national income devoted to defence rises until it absorbs most or all of the "economic surplus". In primitive economies the economic surplus is a small proportion of the total output of the society—almost the whole manpower and equipment capacity of the society have to be devoted to the task of keeping the economy running. On the other hand, a society in which the technical revolution has enabled men

to produce the necessities of life with the labour of a quarter of the population might conceivably be able to devote three-quarters of its resources to defence, and under a condition of political duopoly it may be forced to do so. It is for this reason that war has been reaching further and further down into the lives of the mass of the people. It is doubtful whether any of the wars of the eighteenth century absorbed as much as five per cent of any nation's income. Indeed, Adam Smith says, "Among the civilised nations of modern Europe, it is commonly computed that not more than one hundredth part of the inhabitants of any country can be employed as soldiers without ruin to the country which pays the expense of their service"[1]. In the second world war the United States and Britain put at least 50 % of their national incomes into the war effort, and it is clear that the United States, at any rate, did not even then exhaust her economic surplus—people could have had their consumption squeezed much further and would still have produced about as much. It is the rise in the economic surplus, therefore, coupled with the tendency for an unstable system of national defence to absorb a large proportion of this surplus, that has changed war from a peripheral to a central activity of our society.

The *sociological effects* of this change are profound. Its economic impact is perhaps less important—it simply involves a sacrifice of the potential benefits of the technical revolution, consumed in the insatiable maw of national defence; but it may still allow a substantial increase in standards of personal consumption, as has been the case so far in the United States. The Germans, however, through their reliance on national defence in a period when, for countries as small as Germany, it has essentially become obsolete, have succeeded in reducing their standard of living very substantially, in spite of great technical progress. After a third world war the same may be true even of the United States, hitherto immune from this disadvantage. More serious than the economic effects, however, are the effects on the internal order and fabric of society. This is a topic about which we actually know very little, and any propositions are highly tentative. Nevertheless, it seems reasonable to suppose that

1. ADAM SMITH, *The Wealth of Nations*, Book 5, ch. I, Pt.I (p.678, Modern Library Edition).

a society for which war is a peripheral phenomenon, carried on for the most part by specialists under the ultimate control of civilian authority, will be less subject to internal violence, disorder and break up than a society for which war has become a central phenomenon, participated in by the mass of the population. The rise of Marxism, for instance—a religion of internal violence, seeking to disrupt existing society from within—seems to me not unconnected with the rise of conscription. When the whole youth of a nation is trained in the techniques of violence, we must not be surprised if some confusion arises as to the potential victims, and if the violence is applied within as well as without. When war becomes central, therefore, the state itself is in danger of disintegrating. Democracy, with its reliance on discussion and communication rather than on violence, is in grave danger, and the acids of national defence, which are intended to protect the delicate structure of the state against the outside invader, turn inward and eat away the moral and psychological tissues which hold society together[2].

It is no exaggeration therefore to say that we are facing an acute crisis of national defence, perhaps the most acute which mankind has ever faced. Not even the largest countries now possess enough depth in defence to protect their civilians. On the other hand, our skills of organization do not seem yet to permit us to construct the world state which is the only adequate answer to the problem of defence. For the remainder of this paper, therefore, I propose to look at the old problem of the *economic causes of war*, in order to see whether anything can be learned from the economist which may help in alleviating the intensity of international conflict.

III

1. At the very outset we find a divergence of view which abruptly symbolizes the basic conflict of our age. The "classical" view of the matter, of which the principal earlier exponent was Mill, and which is represented today by Robbins, is that economic conflict is un-

2. Switzerland and the Scandinavian countries may appear at first sight, to be an exception to this rule. If they are, in fact, an exception, this seems to be due to their unique situation as weak powers in strong geographical positions. Because of this circumstance, war is still peripheral in the lives of these nations.

important as a cause of war, and that trade is everywhere a prelude to peace. By contrast we have the Marxist-Leninist view, which is that economic conflict or exploitation is the fundamental cause of war and imperialism, and that war cannot be eradicated except in a socialized world.

The classical view is based primarily on the observation that free exchange is always of mutual benefit to the parties, for unless both parties benefit the exchange will not take place. Thus trade is the very antithesis of war. In the language of the Theory of Games, war is a "negative-sum game". Because the resources devoted to it must be withdrawn from other uses, war, unless it is to be regarded as desirable in itself, reduces the total available for distribution between the two parties. Even if it were a zero-sum game one party could only benefit at the expense of the other; since it is a negative-sum game this tendency is accentuated, and if the winning party is not to lose by the war, he must take a large amount from the loser to compensate him for the cost of winning. There may have been times in history when the sporting aspect of war more than counterbalanced its economic cost, and so turned it into a positive-sum game. Nobody, I imagine, would contend that such is the case today. Trade, on the other hand, as long as compulsion is not involved, is of necessity a positive-sum game in which the result of the activity is that there is more to be divided than before. This is true not only because a simple exchange shifts commodities towards parties who value them most highly, so that there is a net gain in utility even though the exchange itself merely redistributes an existing quantity of physical goods. It is true also because trade facilitates and encourages specialization, which in turn increases the total productivity of human endeavour in the production of goods. Thus trade is thrice blessed: it not only blesses him who buys and him who sells, but it results in an actual increase in the product which is bought and sold. It is not, therefore, a game of beggar-my-neighbour, in which what I gain you lose, but an occupation which binds us all together into a comprehensive system of increasing mutual benefit. In the classical view these propositions are as true of international trade as of individual trade, and the theory of comparative advantage is an elaborate exercise on this theme of mutual benefit, even where one party is "strong" and the other "weak". And just as the robber-baron eventually saw the error of his ways and became the Improving Landlord, to the benefit of all, so the extension of trade should lead to the abandonment of the beggar-my-neighbour type of behaviour on the part of nations—represented by wars of varying degrees of coldness and heat, from protectionist commercial policy to the murder of cities—in favour of a general free-trade paradise in which competition takes the benevolent form of rivalry in the promotion of mutual benefit and in service to mankind.

At the other extreme we have the Marxist-Leninist view, in which economic life is regarded almost as a Hobbesian war of all against all, and the class struggle, expressed largely in economic terms, is the principal feature of all historical landscapes. Labour produces everything, but the capitalist takes away most of what the labourer produces and reduces him to a level of bare subsistence. As capital accumulates, however, the capitalist finds it more and more difficult to dispose of the ever-increasing product (the consumption of the proletariat being kept at subsistence level, and the consumption of the capitalist class not rising in proportion to its income). If capitalism is to be kept going, therefore, there must be an ever-increasing amount of investment. When opportunities for investment in the capitalist's homeland are no longer adequate, it becomes necessary to seek them overseas. Hence the scramble for colonies and the clash of rival imperialisms, which is the principal cause of modern war. This tenet is Lenin's special contribution to Marxist theory.

Neither the bland optimism of the extreme classical position nor the self-righteous pessimism of Marxism stands up very well under examination. Of the two the Marxist position is by far the weaker, based as it is upon a naive moralistic view of social science and an interpretation of history so oversimplified as to be almost useless, except as a corrective to earlier still more oversimplified views. Nobody is going to deny that conflicts of economic interest exist. As an explanation of war, however, they are for the most part irrelevant. The web of economic conflict nowhere coincides with national boundaries, still less with the lines of international conflict.

2. War, whether cold or hot, represents a breakdown in the body politic, a breakdown in the processes of communication and adjustment. A break may occur either because the strain is great or be-

cause the link is weak. International conflict is much more readily explainable in terms of the weakness of the links than in terms of the magnitude of the strains. Within the body of a nation the links are strong and there are political processes for the resolution of conflict; hence the internal conflicts—although equalling, if not exceeding, in severity the conflicts which happen to cross national boundaries—seldom result in war. Where political bonds are weak or nonexistent, as between vigorously independent nations alien in thought and culture, even very small conflicts can lead to political rupture. It is only a slight exaggeration, therefore, to say that war is not a function of conflicts but of independence or, to use its grander but less shocking name, sovereignty. Even if we admit that conflicts of interest are of some importance among the causes of war, conflicts of economic interest probably must take a place far down the list. War, like marriage, does not belong to the "economic" aspect of man's activity but to the "romantic" sphere. It is not something we enter into with cool calculation, carefully balancing the chance of gain against the chance of loss. We enter into it because of sentiment, because of love and hate, because some symbol dear to our emotional security has been outraged. It is the ideational and symbological conflicts, therefore, much more than the economic conflicts, that are important for an assessment of the strains put on the tenuous cords of international relationships.

Nevertheless there is a certain sting in the tail of the Marxist scorpion. A United States Senator has been reported as saying that the American economy would not last sixty days without war, or war preparations. If the Senator believes this, then he is as good as a Marxist, and should be denounced as such. The fact that it apparently took a war to pull the American economy out of the doldrums of the 'thirties, and that we have apparently kept the economy at approximately full employment since 1942 by means of extensive war preparations, seems to support the Marxist hypothesis that capitalism will seek war in a desperate attempt to save itself from unemployment. If this is indeed true we might as well all go off and join the communist party. Fortunately it is not *necessarily* true. The Marxists have mistaken a political accident for an economic necessity. Nevertheless there are conditions under which it might be true. Marxism is best understood as a highly special case of a more general social science. The conditions under which the Marxist system corresponds in its entirety to reality are fortunately very rare, though they can conceivably exist. For the most part these conditions do not exist in the western world—capital is not becoming more concentrated, the proletariat is not becoming worse and worse off, the middle class is not disappearing, and so on. Where Marxist conditions do not exist, however, it is frequently because they have been deliberately done away with as a matter of social policy, through anti-trust laws, inheritance taxes, social-security measures and the like.

The drive of capitalism towards armaments and war as a remedy for unemployment is likewise one of the conditions that can be done away with. This is not the place to elaborate, or even to outline, a full-employment policy which shall be independent of war and war preparations. It must suffice to say that there is a reasonable consensus among economists that within rather broad limits a peaceful full-employment policy is possible. A "governed capitalism" in which the excessive instability of ungoverned capitalism is replaced by orderly progress, with the minimal loss of personal liberty and freedom of enterprise, is clearly conceivable, and what is both conceivable and desirable should not, in an intelligent democracy, be politically impossible!

With the instability of the market economy removed, the optimism of the classical school would rest on a much firmer foundation. With the threat of deflation removed, the case for protective and restrictive economic policies practically falls to the ground. Protection, whether by tariffs, cartels, agricultural policy or valorization schemes, is essentially a child of deflation and depression. It is mainly an attempt to insulate some sector of the world economy, whether a nation or an industry, from the tides of world deflation. If these tides can be abolished, we may hope that the protective dykes will fall from sheer neglect. This is not to overlook the possibility of genuine monopolistic exploitation. Monopoly and protection, however, must be sanctioned by the general interest before they can be made presentable, and outright, barefaced monopoly is notoriously unstable unless it is supported by the authority of the state.

3. There is, however, a further limitation on the classical optimism, and one which is of peculiar importance in the world of to-

day. This is the problem of short-run versus long-run interests in regard to economic development. There may be a real conflict of economic interest between industrially developed areas and their sources of food and raw materials, especially if these sources are in politically independent but socially backward countries which benefit from internal redistributions of income (for example, by progressive taxation) on the part of the industrial power. The problem here is one of economic development from a low-level equilibrium towards a high-level equilibrium. It is related to what economists have called "external economies"—a term denoting a situation in which development in one part of an economy improves the other parts, through the increasing specialization which it permits and through the cultural change which development of any kind encourages. Thus, as Adam Smith himself observed, "the commerce of the towns contributed to the improvement of the country"[3]. An undeveloped area, therefore, which is an outlying part of a world economy, and which supplies raw materials and foodstuffs to distant industrial areas, may find it immediately profitable to continue in that condition, having a present comparative advantage in raw produce. In the longer run, however, such an area would do better by encouraging industry, even at the cost of denying itself some of the immediate benefits of international specialization. At first sight, therefore, it might seem as if there is a serious conflict of interest between the developed and the underdeveloped parts of the world, in that it would be to the advantage of the developed areas to keep the underdeveloped areas in their present position as suppliers of cheap raw materials and food, and hence to prevent their development. If this were true the relation of the developed to the underdeveloped areas would be one of exploitation indeed, and the appeal of communism to these areas would be based on more than blind emotion.

Fortunately, further analysis reveals that the conflict is more apparent than real. It can safely be asserted that, in the long run, economic development anywhere benefits, if not everybody, at least all reasonably heterogeneous groups everywhere. Rich countries do not, in general, get poorer as poor countries get richer. Indeed, quite the reverse is the case. By far the greatest volume of world trade, for instance, is not between the developed and the under-

3. *op. cit.*, p. 13.

developed countries, but among the developed countries. We find, furthermore, that even when we come to consider the long-run specialization between industry and agriculture, the world is not divided into "industrial" and "agricultural" regions so much as into "productive" and "unproductive" regions. It is the industrial (i.e. productive) regions that are *also* the agricultural regions. By far the largest proportion of the food supply of the industrial areas comes from industrialised regions or from areas immediately adjacent to industrialised regions. This is because it is, for the most part, only industrialised agriculture that can produce much in the way of an agricultural surplus. The agriculturalist of the underdeveloped areas produces barely enough to keep himself and his family alive, and has little to spare for trade with anyone else. Thus it is certain that the long-run interest of the developed areas will be served by a rise in productivity in the underdeveloped areas.

A strong case can be made out also for the contention that it is to the short-run interest of the developed areas to participate actively, by means of investment, in the development of the rest of the world, not only as a means of raising the world economic level, but also as a means of maintaining full-employment at home. This may seem to give some support to the Marxist criticism. If, however, an adequate domestic full-employment policy can create a situation in which foreign investment is auxiliary to, but not a necessary part of, such policy, much of the sting of the Marxist criticism is removed. What foreign investment means in real terms is a surplus of exports from the investing region and a surplus of imports in the recipient region. Such a surplus of imports may be a critical factor in getting economic development *started*. The problem of economic development is twofold: it involves reorganization of resources, and it also involves accumulation of capital. If a region is very poor, internal capital accumulation may be almost impossible, for consumption continually presses on the heels of the scanty production. The region, therefore, is caught in a trap—poverty preventing accumulation, and the lack of accumulation perpetuating poverty. I include in accumulation here not only the building-up of physical capital, but what is even more important, the acquisition of skills and character. If the poor region is, for a period, in a position to import more than it exports, it will be able to accumulate without lowering its level of consumption. Even a few years of such accumulation may give it sufficient impetus to get off the dead-centre of stagnation, and, once economic development has begun to run its course, the process of accumulation will become easier and easier.

IV

Economic development is such a central problem in the present world situation that some further comments may be justified. It has a critical character not only because it is by far the most important strictly economic problem in the world today, but also because it is the most acute problem of international relations. The difficulty of creating a two-power equilibrium, noted in the first part of this paper, is intensified enormously in the case of the United States and Russia by the fact that the "boundary of indifference"—if such a boundary actually exists—runs, for almost all its course, through underdeveloped areas: Eastern Europe, the Near East, India, Burma, Indo-China, China, and Korea. In this vast perimeter of conflict, containing well over half the population of the globe, the political alignment may well be ultimately determined by the ability of the two great competing systems to satisfy the desperate need for economic development. I propose, therefore, to conclude this paper, by considering briefly the nature of the task to be accomplished, and the relative abilities of the American and the Russian system to assist in its accomplishment.

The task is gigantic. It is that of creating a whole new culture. It nvolves setting more than a billion people on the upward path from their present low-level economy towards a stable high-level economy. The low-level economy is characterized by high birth and death rates, low expectation of life, dense population, low levels of literacy and mechanical skills, and only minute quantities of capital equipment per head. What all this adds up to is a population held in check only by starvation, the vast majority of people at or below the physical subsistence level, and a small ruling group, minute in size compared with the mass of the people, and separated from them by a vast cultural gulf. At the other extreme is the high-level economy, characterized by low birth and death rates, high expectation of life, a population not too great for the resource base, high levels of literacy and skill and large quantities of capital equipment per head—all of which adds up to average levels of income high enough to destroy poverty, to give every family at least adequate diet, housing, and convenience, and to create a highly mobile society, without sharp class distinctions, enjoying a highly integrated and widely diffused culture based on rational rather than on traditional patterns of behaviour. The terminus is clear enough: the question is, where is the railroad that runs to it? A universal high-level economy is conceivable. It is a long-term goal towards which rational steps can be taken. Nevertheless, the almost insoluble problem is that of the first step. This is perhaps the most critical point at issue between the West and the East today.

Communism says, in effect, to the underdeveloped areas: "You will never get anywhere until you dispose of the present effete, ineffective, idle, pleasure-loving ruling class and replace it by an elite of hard-working communists, devoting their lives to the task of economic development. If this involves violent revolution, so be it: if it involves the suppression of individual liberties and the establishment of a police state, one cannot make an omelette without breaking eggs. Economic development cannot take place without breaking up the old culture—based as it is on superstition and ignorance—with a new culture based on technology. And the break-up of an old culture requires ruthlessness, requires a police state, requires the suppression of individual liberties, requires, too, that you pull yourself up with your own bootstraps by internal reorganization and without foreign investment, which will involve you in political subservience to the investing power." I have deliberately put the best face possible on the communist claims. The actual level of communist propaganda is, of course, much below the above argument. In Asia communist success is due to a very simple "Robin Hood" appeal to the poor peasant: "You are poor; you see the landlord, the banker and moneylender are rich, and have become rich off your labours; take away from them what is rightfully yours, and you will be rich too!" The speciousness of this claim is immediately apparent. The dividing up of the land and the murder or exile of the tiny landowning or moneylending class does practically nothing to relieve the poverty of Asia. Indeed, it usually intensifies it through the decline in productivity which so frequently accompanies the division of land into uneconomically small holdings. The more astute communists of course know this; land reform is just a bait to catch the peasant, and once he is caught it is not long before he is collectivized and finds the state a harder taskmaster than any old landlord, bent, as it is, on extracting the last ounce of food from him and giving him as little as possible for it in the desperate endeavour to built industrial capital. It is not the bait, however, but the catch that is going to be important in the long pull. If, in fact, communism can set off a real program of economic development in the underdeveloped areas which it touches, it may capture the allegiance of the people in spite of the terror, the chicanery, the dictatorship, the nightmare of untruth and the sabotage of all simple, decent, friendly human relations which it represents.

What is the answer of the West to these claims? It is not as clear as one could wish. The main lines are something like this: "You underdeveloped areas should establish stable political regimes friendly to us; then we will undertake foreign investment in your areas. We will build dams and roads, set up factories, establish plantations. Send your young people to us and we will educate them, so that they can expand your own educational facilities. New ideas and new products will seep down towards your masses: a middle class will develop under the incentives of private property and will form a bridge between your old aristocracy and the masses, at the same time undermining the aristocracy's exclusive privileges. Develop your free labour movements, and they will take care of incidental exploitation. Be patient with inequalities: they are part of the price of progress; some among you will rise more quickly the higher levels of income, but they will not depress the rest; rather will they pull all the rest of you after them." This may not sound too convincing on paper. The best argument of the West, however, is simply that of example: look at us; we are the pioneers of economic development. We must know how it is done, for after all we did it! Follow our example, imitate our constitutions and our institutions, allow freedom of enterprise, minimize government intervention, make property secure, and watch your national income grow!

Here again I have put the best face on the claims of the West. In practice, we, like the communists, fall short of our best insight. In practice, all too often we use the threat of superior force: we say, in effect, "stay with us, or you will become another Korea; we will bomb your homes to pieces, destroy your cities, desolate your country, roast you and blast you!" The threat is a potent one, but it is likely to exact an unwilling compliance, and bodes ill for future relationships. We may find that the policy of ruthless aerial warfare in Korea has lost us Asia.

It is the great tragedy of the present situation that neither of the present solutions offered is really satisfactory. The communist solution has the virtue that it recognizes the problem with some clarity, in spite of the handicap of a thoroughly obsolete social science. But the taboos and inhibitions of Marxist social science are a great handicap indeed to realistic programs of economic betterment; its materialism, its labour theory of value, its "gigantomania", its obsession with the grandiose and the spectacular, and above all its absurd definition of exploitation are immense handicaps to realistic appraisal of the true springs of desirable social change. The great test here is China: Russia was a semi-developed country, with a fair transportation system and the beginnings of an industrial system when the communists took over. The "forced draft" economic development of Russia under the communists is not, therefore, a decisive case; for once economic development is well under way it takes a great deal to stop it! I shall be surprised, however, if communism is as successful in developing China, with its much more difficult problem, with immense pressure of population, without a frontier to expand beyond, and without an adequate social science to counteract the inevitable urge to take the short cuts of violence, which in fact lead nowhere.

On the other hand, what the West has to offer makes economic sense, but it is neither psychologically nor politically adequate. The communists offer the people bread, and in fact give them a stone. We, with bread—at least long-run bread!—to give, offer the people who are crying out for it abstractions like liberty and democracy. There is a curious illusion abroad that communism offers economic security whereas we offer political liberty. Nothing could in reality be further from the truth. In fact, the West is a thundering economic success and a resounding political failure. As a method of conducting economic life, communism is a grotesque brontosaurus with one paw tied behind its back. As an instrument of political strategy, communism is as wise as serpents, without, alas, being as harmless as doves. As a method of conducting economic life, capitalism, properly tempered by charity and control, results in a rapid rate of economic development towards a high-level economy. By comparison with our originality and inventiveness in the economic sphere, however, our military and political ideas and practices are primitive and unimaginative, and our philosophical basis is unorganized and unconvincing.

The *conclusion* of this argument is that the economic issues in international conflict, while important, are not fundamental, in that it is not economic conflict which prevents a solution of the present world crisis. In the technical language of welfare economics, we do not lie on a "contract curve" in which every movement makes one party better off and one party worse off. There are large numbers of conceivable positions in which *everybody* is better off than they are today. The trouble is that all the lines of dynamics of the world society lead *away* from betterment, towards arms races, world war, and universal catastrophe. We are not far from the top of the mountain of betterment; indeed, the summit can be seen fairly plainly. But, from where we are, all the roads run downhill.

SUMMARY

1. International conflict has become a major issue of our time. Hitherto for Americans especially war has been a somewhat peripheral experience. Now war is increasingly becoming the dominant institution in our society.

2. The basic reasons for this change lie in the technical revolution in the past 200 years. In the first place the change in the techniques of war seems to have greatly increased the minimum size of the independently defensible nation. This has lead to a situation similar to oligopoly or even to duopoly in economic relations. The inherent instability of a system of national defense, particularly under conditions of oligopoly, leads to an increasing absorption of the national product by defense, up to the limit of the economic surplus. The increase in the economic surplus, as a result of technical revolution has therefore led to a great increase in the proportion of the resources devoted to defense. The sociological and political consequences of this change have been profound.

3. In view of this situation the old problem of the economic causes of war takes on a new interest. There are two sharply contrasting views: the «classical» view

that trade and especially free trade is an instrument of peace leading nations to work together in a community of economic interest. The second is the Marxist-Leninist view that war is caused by imperialism which is in turn caused by the need of capitalism for new markets and fields for investment.

4. The situation has been sharpened in our own day by the existence of two competing philosophies of economic life and by the existence of a vast area of unstable allegiance—the underdeveloped areas. Here there is a great demand for revolutionary change of some sort and the question is which revolution offers the most hope of progress. The problem of these areas is how to change from a low level economy to a high level economy. The Communist solution is the displacement and liquidation of the obstructionist ruling class, plus rigid economic planning. The West's solution is that of slow progress under the security of existing property rights plus technical aid and foreign investment. Neither of these solutions may be particularly satisfactory. The Communist world suffers from a hard and unrealistic economic dogma, the West suffers from lack of understanding of its own philosophy and of the reasons for its economic success.

TWENTY-FIVE THESES ON
PEACE AND TRADE

The Friend (Philadelphia), 127, 18
(Mar. 4, 1954): 290-292

Twenty-Five Theses on Peace and Trade

Kenneth Boulding is uniquely qualified to suggest some of the important connections between economic policies and world peace.

I

1. Peace is government: War is the breakdown of government. Government is an organization, an apparatus, or a ritual whereby decisions may be reached on behalf of a group within which there are conflicting interests or beliefs. Government may be formal or informal.

2. Government breaks down when the tensions and divergences of interest and belief get too great for the existing apparatus to resolve in a group decision. This breakdown always results in the formation of *sub-governments*—organizations which represent only a part of the total interacting population.

3. All national governments are sub-governments. They are organized for two purposes: (i) to preserve peace within their boundaries (ii) to wage war against other sub-governments.

4. The relations of sub-governments can be peaceful only if there is a formal or informal government which transcends and includes them.

5. The possibility of establishing government depends on two things. It will be less easy to establish it the more intense are the conflicts which have to be resolved. It will be more easy to establish it the greater is the community of feeling ("we-feeling") among its members.

6. The spiritual basis of government is the "we-feeling" or sense of community. Without this no government can be organized except on a basis of pure coercion. Pure coercion is very unstable, as it is difficult to maintain the consent of the coercers in the face of the inevitably rising opposition of the coerced.

II

7. *Exchange* is a social act involving two parties in which definite quantities of goods, services, securities or moneys (exchangeables) are transferred from each to each. In so far as there is no coercion exchange is beneficial to both parties, though both parties may not benefit equally.

8. Trade, including international trade, which is merely trade that happens to cross national boundaries, consists of a set of exchanges, and therefore all parties benefit from trade, again assuming no

coercion and assuming that people act in their true interest.

9. Although there is a strong community of interest in the existence of trade, there may be a conflict of interest about the *terms* of trade—that is about the ratio of exchange or the *price* at which the trade is carried on. Buyers prefer low prices, sellers high prices.

10. The *intensity* of the conflict about the terms of trade depends on the width of the range over which the terms of trade can be varied. When this range is small there is little to fight about and the conflict is not intense.

11. The range over which the terms of trade can be varied in any particular transaction depend on the alternative opportunities to trade of both buyer and seller. Where there are many alternative opportunities the range of possible values of the terms of trade is small, as if the seller tries to get too high a price the buyer will simply go elsewhere and if the buyer tries to get too low a price the seller will go elsewhere.

12. The more alternative opportunities for exchange, therefore, the less will be the extent of conflict, and the easier it will be to establish government. This is why on the whole free and wide markets make for peace.

13. Alternative opportunities are limited, and therefore conflict is increased, by *monopoly,* which is the organization of exchange opportunities into a sub-government and the suppression of exchange opportunities outside the sub-government (e.g. a cartel or a closed-shop union).

14. Alternative opportunities are also limited, and therefore conflict is increased by *unemployment,* which is a general breakdown of the system of exchange. The solution of the unemployment problem will make for peace.

III

15. Any unilateral trade restriction, whether a tariff, quota, or immigration restriction, is an act of war on the part of one sub-government against other sub-governments, in so far as it is directed towards improving the terms of trade of the group imposing the restriction and thereby worsening the terms of trade of those with whom this group trades.

16. The *effects* of trade and immigration restrictions, however, are so diffuse, especially over long periods of time, that these restrictions are not very important as occasions or as causes of military war. Thus a tariff on, say, wool, may cause temporary benefit to domestic producers of wool and to foreign consumers of wool, and temporary injury to foreign producers and domestic consumers. As time goes on, however, any abnormal profits in the domestic wool industry will be eaten away by new producers and the expansion of the industry, any abnormal losses to foreign producers will be rectified by withdrawals from the industry, and the end result is a diffuse general loss caused by the fact that more wool is now produced in less suitable places.

17. Trade and immigration restrictions may be regarded as artifical increases in the cost of transport of goods or men (Bastiat called tariffs "negative railroads," as a railroad lowers the cost of transport between two places and a tariff increases it).

18. This does not mean, however, that all restrictions will or should disappear under government, though there is a strong tendency for this to happen (e.g. the removal of internal tariffs in Federal Unions and unitary states).

19. There is a case even at the level of World Community or World Govern-

ment for certain restrictions both on trade and immigration.

20. World free trade might lead to too much *specialization* both on an occupational and a geographical level. This is likely to happen if the trade network is more extensive than the commnications network. One-crop regions and assembly-line nut screwers may each represent a dangerous degree of specialization where the specialist is cut off from the general network of communication, ideas, techniques, and advancement, and loses the flexibility which is necessary in an uncertain world. (Even Adam Smith denounced the Division of Labor as a producer of dolts and dullards.)

21. Where there is a genuine "Malthusian situation" in any area, emigration is no permanent help in raising the standard of life of the people, and may serve only to depress standards in the areas receiving the migrants. If the only factor limiting population is starvation, emigration by releasing food supplies simply permits more babies to survive and does nothing to relieve the population pressure. There is a strong case, therefore, at the level of world community for restriction of emigration from areas where poverty is the only thing that keeps the population in check until such time as other checks are found.

22. *Existing* restrictions on trade and migration imposed by national governments greatly exceed the "ideal" amount of restriction outlined above. Almost any movement towards freer trade and migration, therefore, is a movement towards the ideal.

23. The reason for the excessive restrictions of national governments is that they are universally ruled by the interests of small organized minorities. Hence a restriction which is profitable to a small

domestic minority (e.g. beet growers) is imposed in spite of the fact that it causes a net loss even to the nationals of the country imposing it. The gain is concentrated and obvious: the loss is diffuse and widespread.

24. Restrictions which are made by multilateral agreement are a step in the direction of government: multilateral action is Peace, unilateral action is War. Even agreed restrictions, however, (e.g. International Commodity Agreements) generally represent the attempt of some economic group to capture the machinery of informal world government in its own interest.

25. Ideological rather than economic conflicts constitute the greatest present threat to world peace, mainly because of the competition between two different philosophies, backed up by the United States and by Russia respectively, for the underdeveloped areas. Removal of trade or migration restrictions will do little in itself to solve this problem.

———————

CONTRIBUTIONS OF ECONOMICS TO THE THEORY OF CONFLICT

Bulletin of the Research Exchange on the Prevention of War, III, 5 (May 1955): 51-59

CONTRIBUTIONS OF ECONOMICS TO THE THEORY OF CONFLICT

Students of conflict, especially those raised in psychology, are generally apt to overlook the important models of conflict which arise out of economic theory. It is not suggested of course that these models are wholly adequate or completely general. Nevertheless they provide an important part of the framework around which a general theory of conflict might be erected.

The first generalization arises out of the theory of exchange as developed by Edgeworth, Pareto and others. In the simplest case we postulate two exchangers and two exchangeables. We suppose that there is an initial distribution of the exchangeables among the exchangers. Then exchange represents essentially a <u>redistribution</u> of the exchangeables among the exchangers, each giving up some quantity of one and acquiring some quantity of another of the exchangeables. If there are two exchangers A and B and two exchangeables X and Y, we start with a position P in which A has a_x of X and a_y of Y and B has b_x of X and b_y of Y. Any movement to a position P' in which A has a'_x of X and a'_y of Y and B has b'_x of X and b'_y of Y is a redistribution. If $a'_x - a_x = b_x - b'_x$ and $a_y - a'_y = b'_y - b_y$, that is if B gets what A gives up and A gets what B gives up the redistribution is an <u>exchange</u>. Redistributions can be divided into two important classes: (i) those in which both parties are better off than before the redistribution, or "trading" redistributions, and (ii) those in which at least one party is worse off than before, or "conflict" redistributions. This distinction can be made quite clear if a preference function for each exchanger can be postulated to cover the field of possible positions, so that for any two points P and P' we can say that for each marketer one is superior or equivalent in desirability to the other. Then if, say, P' is "better than" or at least "not worse than" P for both marketers the movement represents "trading" ; if P' is worse than P for one marketer but better for another the movement represents "conflict." If the movement is worse for both marketers it is simply "negative trading" as a movement in the opposite direction makes them both better off.

It can be shown that under reasonable assumptions about the nature of the preferences of the marketers there is a <u>line</u> in the field (called by Edgeworth the "contract curve") which is the locus of all points in the field at which "trading" in the sense defined above is impossible. [1] That is to say there will be a set of points in the field from each of which it is impossible to move in any direction without making at least

one party worse off. The converse of this proposition is that from any
other point in the field - that is, any point not on the contract curve or
set - there are some directions in which it is possible to move (that is,
effect a redistribution) which will make both parties better off. This
"trading" movement always carries the position towards the contract
curve; as we approach the contract curve the range of "trading" possibilities becomes more and more restricted until it disappears when the
contract curve is reached. Movement along the contract curve always
implies that one party is getting better off and the other worse off.

These constructions can now be generalized to cover the theory
of negotiation. In negotiation we can again postulate a set of variables
which constitute the "agenda"of negotiation - for instance, the hourly
wage, the working day, length of vacation, and so on in a labor-management contract. A "position" in the field of negotiation is any particular set of values of these variables, and a "movement" in the field
is a change from one such position to another. Then in the "agenda-
field" we can again postulate preference or welfare functions for each
of the two negotiating parties, ordering the various positions in the
field according to a scale of "better or worse". Thus in a field, say,
with the hourly wage on one axis and length of paid vacation on the other
a movement from lower to higher hourly wage and from lower to higher
length of paid vacation is likely to move labor to "better" positions and
management to "worse" positions. Again it can be shown that there will
be a set of points at which "trading" is impossible, in the sense that no
movement can be made which will not make at least one party worse off
than before. At all other points trading is possible, that is, movement
is possible in some direction which will make both parties better off.
Thus in the above example if we are not on the contract curve (or more
generally the contract set) some combination of, say, an increase in
the hourly wage with a decrease in the length of paid vacation can be
found which moves both parties to a "better"position. It is one of the
principal skills of the negotiator to discover opportunities for "trading"
-that is to detect when a proposed position is not in the contract set and
hence movement is possible which is of benefit to both parties. One
proposition which has not, I think, been proved formally but which is
highly plausible is that the larger agenda - that is, the more variables
there are in the field of negotiation - the more chance there is of finding opportunities for trading. This perhaps explains the noticeable
tendency for labor-management contracts to proliferate clauses, for the
more clauses there are in the contract the greater the opportunity for
finding "exchange movements" which will leave both parties feeling
better off, and the less chance there is of reaching a deadlock on the
contract curve. It frequently happens in negotiations that agreement
is prevented by the absence of certain items from the formal agenda
which could be used as "trading variables". If the number of variables
in the agenda is too limited "false" contract curves are reached - that
is, positions which seem to offer no opportunity of mutually beneficial

movement as long as the field is restricted, but which would offer these opportunities if the field were to be expanded by the introduction of new variables. This principle is as important in international as in labor-management negotiations: indeed, the relative rigidity of the agenda in international negotiations may be one reason for their relative lack of success.

Suppose now, however, that all possibilities of "trading" are exausted and the parties finally reach a position on the ultimate contract curve from which no movement is possible which does not involve conflict. This still does not mean that agreement cannot be reached. In the field of positions there will be some "settlement set" A such that party A will prefer a settlement within this set to no settlement at all, and there will be a similar set B for the other party. If these two sets intersect, so that there are some positions common to both sets, the intersection represents a part of the field where agreement is possible. If the two sets do not intersect, then of course agreement is not possible. Another important function of the negotiator or "peacemaker", then, is that of discovering these possible areas of agreement. Frequently the parties to a negotiation are not well informed about their opponent's "settlement set" and frequently, indeed, each party is hazy in regard to its own interests and willingness to conclude settlements. Generally speaking the more costly is the failure to reach settlement (e.g., in terms of strikes or wars), at least in the opinion of the parties, the wider the "settlement sets" are likely to be and the more likely is their intersection in an area of potential agreement. Another function of the negotiator therefore may be to bring vividly before the parties the costs of a failure to effect settlement.

So far we have dealt merely with what might be called the "statics" of conflict. Economics has also something to contribute in the much more difficult area of the dynamics of conflict. Merely because a "trading" move is statically possible does not mean that it is dynamically possible. Thus it seems quite clear at the present time that there is a position of the international power field in which both the United States and Russia would be much more secure and better off in every way than they are now; this is the position of universal policed disarmament. All the dynamics of the situation however lead the other way, to positions in which each party is worse off and less secure. This is highly characteristic of a situation known to economists as "imperfect oligopoly" where a few competitors are operating under circumstances which give a temporary but marked advantage to the first competitor who makes an aggressive move, such as cutting price or increasing selling activity.

To take a simple example, suppose there are two firms A and B 100 miles apart, and that all potential customers are on the line that goes through the location of both firms. Suppose that each customer always patronizes the firm which sells cheapest at the place where he lives, and suppose that the price charged by each firm is equal to its "mill price" at the plant plus cost of transport. If then the mill price

of both firms is equal there will be a "boundary of indifference" half
way between them, at which their prices to the customer are equal:
all customers on A's side of this point will buy from A and all customers
on B's side will buy from B. The boundary of indifference thus divides
the "market space" between the two competitors.[1]

Now suppose A lowers his mill price, say by a cents. The boundary of indifference will be pushed over towards B by $\frac{a}{2c}$ miles, where
c cents per mile is the unit cost of transportation of the commodity, to
the new point where the customer's price of the two firms is equal. A
will then capture from B all the customers who live between the old and
the new boundaries of indifference. A will then be "larger" and B
"smaller" as a result of A's aggressive move. If at any point A and B
are content with their respective sizes, an equilibrium even under these
conditions is possible; neither aggression nor retaliation will take place
if both parties feel satisfied with their present size. This may occur,
for instance, if there are sharply diminishing "returns to scale" - that
is if the internal efficency or security of the enterprise is diminished by
expansion to larger size. If each firm however feels that it would be
better off if it were larger the situation is highly unstable. A's aggression will result in B's retaliation, as B feels too uncomfortable at its
reduced size. B retaliates in this case by cutting his mill price, thus
pushing the boundary of indifference back towards A. Both firms now
however are worse off than before. A may still feel however the need
to expand and may cut its prices further; B may retaliate with a match-
ing or even greater cut. This process may go on until both firms are
ruined, or until one firm is absorbed by the other to form a monopoly,
or until the firms come to an agreement of a monopolistic nature to
refrain from price cutting.

A similar model can be applied directly to the problem of international competition in armaments. Suppose we have two nations A
and B. We suppose that each has a "center" of power, located at A
and B respectively in Fig. 1. We will suppose further that some measure of military strength can be devised, and that this is measured in
the vertical direction in the figure, the horizontal dimension measuring
geographical or "militarily significant" space. Military strength is
greatest at the center of power (i.e., at "home") and diminishes for each
nation the further away from home it operates. This is the analogue of

---

1.   On a uniform plane the boundary in the above case will be a line
bisecting at right angles the line between the two firms. If there are
many firms the "market space" can always be divided by boundaries
of indifference into "regions of dominance" each of which can be assigned
to one of the firms. The market space need not, of course, be literal
geographical space- any continuous property or quality of the product
can be regarded as constituting a "space" which can be divided up into
regions of dominance.

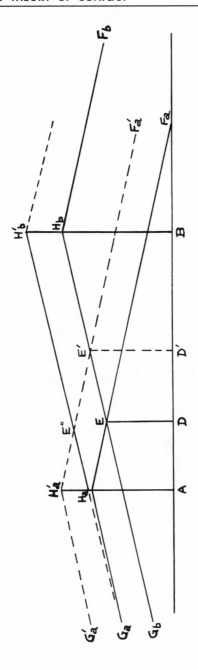

cost of transport in the oligopoly problem. Thus the military strength
of nation A at home we suppose is the length AH_a, and at other points
is given by the ordinate of line $G_aH_aF_a$. This strength-distance function
does not have to be linear, but is drawn so for simplicity. Similarly
the military strength of B at home is BH_b, and its strength-distance
function is given by $G_bH_bF_b$. There is a point E in the figure at which
the two strength-distance curves intersect. At the geographical position corresponding to this point, D, the two nations are of equal strength.
A is stronger than B at all points to the left of D, B is stronger than A
at all points to the right of D.

Now let us suppose that A is not content with his "security" and
increases his armaments. This corresponds to the price-cut in the
oligopoly example. His "home strength" increases from AH_a to AH'_a,
his strength-distance curve rises to $G'_aH'_aF'_a$. The new "boundary of equal
equal strength" is at D', the place at which the new strength-distance
curves intersect at E'. A is "more secure" and B is now "less secure".
If B is not satisfied with this situation it will raise its armaments to a
home strength of BH'_b, which will push the boundary of equal strength
back towards A again, say at E". This situation can clearly be highly
unstable, and will result in an "arms race" which can cease only when
the countries coalesce to form a political monopoly, or when one country conquers the other. The sole possibility of equilibrium in this situation is the case in which the countries are so far apart relative to the
gradient of the strength-distance curves that neither feels threatened
by the other. The case of "unquestioned stability" is shown in Fig. 2,
where the strength-distance curves H_aF_a and H_bF_b reach the point of
zero strength before intersection. For all practical purposes the countries are not in military contact, and we suppose that no practicable
increase in arms expenditure will bring the strength-distance curves
into intersection. Even if there is a point of intersection of the strength-
distance curves the position may still be stable if each nation feels that
this point of equal strength is far enough from its home base so that no
practical increase of home strength on the part of the other nation will
push the point of equal strength close enough to home to be threatening.[2]

We cannot clearly differentiate situations into stable and unstable.
What we can state with confidence, however, is that the likelihood of
instability increases with every diminution of the "effective distance"
between the national centers. A useful measure of effective distance
is geographic distance divided by the slope of the strength-distance
curves and by the sum of the absolute home strengths of the two nations.

The absolute home strength of any nation is a function of three
variables. We have first its "economic surplus"-S;that is,the amount of
resources which are "available" in the sense that they are the excess of

2.   The situation between the United States and Japan in the 1920's
may have been something like this, and is reflected in the Washington
Naval Agreement.

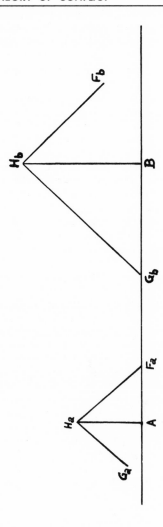

actual resources over that amount which must be devoted to the maintenance of the system. To fix ideas, let us think very crudely of resources as manpower and maintenance as food supply. A nation must use 90% of its manpower in raising food for the 100% cannot devote more than 10% of its resources to "surplus" uses, such as the arts and sciences, pleasures, display and war. A nation which can feed its people with only 10% of its manpower can devote 90% of its resources to these "surplus" uses.

The second variable which determines home strength is the degree of militarism of the people, M as reflected in the proportion of the surplus which they devote to armaments and war a highly militaristic people will devote a large proportion of the surplus to war and little to other uses. The third variable is the efficiency of military expenditures E, as determined by the particular kinds and techniques of arms and military organization. The absolute home strength H then may be described by the product $H = SME$. This formula points up the extreme importance of general economic development in the growth of absolute home strength. Historically the rise in S has probably been more important than changes in M and E. Thus a nation which increases its surplus from say 10% of national income to 20%, even without any change in M and E will double its home strength. This probably accounts for a frequently observed paradox that it is not the most militaristic nations but the commercial nations which are most successful in war. Raising H by raising M is very difficult, as it involves sharp sacrifice of other uses of surplus and may even diminish the rate of growth of S. Raising S on the other hand almost automatically increases at least the potential H without apparent sacrifice.

These considerations throw some light on the problem of the military viability of nations. A nation may be said to be militarily viable if its home strength at its center of operation is greater than the strength which can be exerted by any other nation at that point. Thus in Fig. 1, if B has a home strength of BH_b' and A of AH_a, B is actually stronger than A on A's home ground. This means that A is not under these circumstances militarily viable: it cannot, that is to say, defend itself against B because there is no area in which it is superior. It should be observed that military viability and political viability are not necessarily the same thing. Countries which are not viable militarily may continue to exist as independent nations because it is convenient to their military superiors that they should do so. Buffer states, and what might be called "tolerated" states which nobody feels it worth while to take over, are in this position.

From these considerations it is possible to develop a theory of the viable size of nations. We have seen that what determines relative viability is the absolute magnitude of home strength and the effective distances of the power centers. The absolute magnitude of the home strength is however within limits an increasing function of the size of the nation. If it were an increasing function without limit, and if a

nation by conquering another simply added the strength of the conquered
to its own, a many-nation equilibrium would be highly unstable. Any
nation which grew relative to others would be able to absorb its weaker
neighbors: the more it absorbed, the stronger it would get, and the more
countries it would be able to absorb. The end of such a system can only
be the world-state. In fact history exhibits a strong tendency in this
direction. There are, however, possible limiting factors which counteract the tendency for increased size to lead to increased absolute strength.
The larger any organization grows the more it runs into "diminishing
returns to scale"- that is, internal difficulties of organization and communication which diminish its effectiveness. This is particularly true
of nations where internal heterogeneity is a great handicap. These considerations would lead to the conclusion that with given techniques of
economic life and of warfare there is some optimum size for a nation,
"optimum" in the highly restricted sense of permitting a maximum absolute home·strength. If the nation grows beyond this size its internal
difficulties more than counterbalance the effect of sheer numbers, and
its home strength is reduced. The size of this optimum is a critical
factor in the interpretation of history, and in understanding the crisis
of our own times. Generally it may be said that the progress of knowledge and skills, especially skills of organization, tends to increase the
optimum size, and hence to increase the minimum militarily viable size
of the nation. We have seen this in the supplanting of the city state by
the modern nation. We see the principle of the optimum size reflected
also in the collapse of the "premature giants"-Babylon, Rome, and so
on- which grew beyond the optimum size for their day. Today it seems
clear that the eighteenth century national state, such as France, Britain,
and the nineteenth century "great powers", are not militarily viable by
comparison with the giant states, Russia and the United States. Germany
and Italy are good examples of "postmature" states- states which grew
to their present size only after the period had gone by in which that size
was viable. It may be that with the rapid increase of technology even
the giant states are too small to be viable, and this fact is the source
of the peculiar crisis of our times.

    I may seem in these last pages to have wandered far beyond the
confines of economics. I offer these considerations however as an example of how the economist's way of thinking and model-building pro-
pensities can be applied to the interpretation of these difficult problems.

References

1. F. Y. Edgeworth, Mathematical Psychics, London, 1881 (Reprinted
   by Augustus M. Kelley, New York,) p. 21. A geometrical discussion
   will be found in K. E. Boulding, Welfare Economics, in A Survey of
   of Contemporary Economics, Vol. II, p. 1-39 (Irwin, 1952).

DEMOCRACY AND ORGANIZATION

Challenge, VI, 6 (Mar. 1958): 13-17

Democracy and Organization

IN THE PAST 75 years there has occurred a rise in the scale of organizations of all kinds which is of such magnitude and importance that it can be called an organizational revolution. It is reflected not only in the rise of the giant business corporation; it is characterized also by the concomitant rise of labor unions, professional organizations, farm organizations, trade associations and even churches, where it takes the form of the ecumenical movement. It is reflected perhaps most importantly in the increasing scale of government operations, both civilian and military—a movement which reaches its conclusion, and indeed overreaches itself, in the brontosaurian organizations of Communist states that cover almost all fields of human activity.

Organizations have a strong tendency to grow as long as they are successful. This is not an absolutely necessary "law"; there are examples of organizations which are both successful and deliberately static. These, however, are rare examples of self-control.

However, they eventually run into obstacles because of certain "diseconomies of scale," or internal and external inefficiences of size. The internal inefficiencies are related mainly to the difficulties of maintaining two-way communications between the decision-maker and those who are affected by these decisions, or who are in contact with their effects. As an organization grows larger, it must have more stages in its hierarchy. More bottlenecks begin to develop in the flow of information from bottom to top, and top to bottom. Thus, there are more distortions in the information which reaches the responsible decision-maker, and important decisions are more often based on false images of reality. The result is more frequent "bad" decisions which injure, or may even destroy the organization.

Modification of purpose

The external inefficiencies are related to the increasing pressures of the environment as an organization expands into it. A manufacturing firm exhausts the easy market for its product and finds that it can only expand its sales at some cost, either in selling effort or in price reduction. A labor union or a religious or political sect expands easily for a while until it has attracted all those who are easily convinced; then it can only expand at the cost of increasing effort or modification of its purpose.

If, then, there has been a rise in the scale of organization, there must have been some outward movement of what might be called the "size barrier" at which inefficiencies and lack of success begin to become apparent. The origin of this action upon the size barrier is naturally complex, but most of it derives from a series of technical improvements, first in the machinery of communication, like the telephone and typewriter, and secondly in the skills

of organization itself—particularly in the development of specialization within the executive structure. The vice president is perhaps the most important invention of the 19th century.

The first "wave" of the organizational revolution came roughly from 1880 to 1900: this was the period that saw the rise of the giant corporation and the first successful organizations in labor, professional and farm groups. It is an important question whether we are not now encountering a second wave, based on electronic computers, new methods of information processing, organization theory, public relations and survey research. Certainly, many of the developments of the past 10 years have a revolutionary air about them, and may lead perhaps even to the point where internal inefficiency alone could not prevent a single corporation from expanding to take over the whole American economy. That would mean something very much like a Communist state!

Long before this point, however, the external barriers to growth come into play. The growing organization bumps into other growing organizations of like size and power. In the idyllic world of the 18th century, the internal barriers to growth of organization were so great that external barriers seldom came into play. Imagine running a big corporation, or the U.S. Army, with hand-written correspondence, no filing systems, no telephones, no typewriters and no vice presidents.

Once the internal barriers are removed, however, there is nothing to prevent the growth of organizations to the point where they impinge directly on each other, and where, therefore, the conflict between them becomes at least potentially intense. This intensification of conflict may be avoided if there is an equal growth in terms of bigger markets in the "field" into which the organizations are expanding, or if there are effective institutional frameworks for resolving the conflicts, like mediation boards, arbitrators, courts, governments and United Nations organizations.

External legal barriers

The growth in the scale of organizations has a certain inevitability about it: given the underlying changes in the techniques of communication and organization, it is almost impossible to prevent the growth of organizations short of imposing drastic external legal barriers, as we did to some extent in the United States in discouraging national branch banking.

The organizational revolution poses some difficult questions for both the theory and the practice of democracy. Historically, representative democracy has been closely associated with the "Jeffersonian ideal" of a society of small, familial organizations coordinated through the instruments of the free market and representative government. In one sense, the opposite of democracy is hierarchy—that is, the organization of men under a "boss," or a succession of bosses.

The democratic ideal is that there should be neither bosses nor bossed, that no man should be inferior in status to another, or unduly dependent on the favor of a superior. Hence it is the independent craftsman or farmer who embodies the ideal democratic type, dependent for livelihood on giving service to many customers, but beholden to no one of them. The democratic political ideal likewise sees the politician as the servant of many voters, much as a craftsman is the servant of his customers, or the writer the servant of his many readers. To have many bosses is to have none. We seek liberty, therefore —freedom, that is, from the domination of man by man—in the impersonal and atomistic operations of the free market for commodities, for votes and for ideas: free enterprise, free ballots and free speech.

The rise of large-scale organizations plays havoc with what might be called the "naive" democratic ideal outlined above. In the first place, organizations inevitably involve hierarchy. From commander-in-chief and general to private, from pope and cardinal to communicant, from the president of the corporation or the university to the operative, instructor or janitor, the line of command ramifies downward.

Along with hierarchy comes impersonality and bureaucracy. A large organization cannot be a "big happy family." In order to establish the communications system of a large organization, it is necessary to formalize, simplify and depersonalize the messages, activities and relationships of the people who form the organization. An organization consists not of "persons" but of "roles" connected by lines of communication. The building blocks of organizations are not the rich, complex behavior systems capable of almost infinite variety and unexpectedness, like you and me, but little pieces of personality like a die cutter, a foreman, or a vice president in charge of public relations.

Mechanical vice president

The role or position is not dependent on the person. It is occupied by a succession of persons, and when one leaves, another takes his place. The behavior of the occupant is determined more by the nature of the position than by his own personality. A role is thus an input-output machine, which is fed certain inputs and produces certain outputs. Indeed, machines are frequently better role-occupants than persons. As machines become more clever, we shall see them replacing persons in the more executive roles also, and a completely mechanical vice president is not outside the realm of possibility.

The picture I have drawn above is, of course, a caricature. In all organizations there is an informal structure of communication, based on more complex personal relations than the formal structure allows. This informal structure is often very different from the formal organization chart, and it is frequently the only thing which prevents the organization from grinding to a standstill in a thicket of formal misunderstanding. It does matter who occupies a role, and the personality of the occupant frequently changes the role itself. Role creation, indeed, is one of the most creative acts of the human personality; without it, organizations would die of sheer rigidity.

These qualifications, however, do not prevent the world of General Motors, the Soviet Union, the AFL-CIO, NATO, the United

Nations and the World Council of Churches from being very different from the ideal world of Thomas Jefferson. The basic values of democracy, however, are more important than the particular institutions which embody them, and one of the greatest tasks of our own day is that of the creation of institutions which can embody these basic values in a world of large organizations.

Formidable list

This means defenses against hierarchy, against the power of the superior over the inferior. It means defenses against the fragmentation of the person into roles, against other-directedness, against being all things to all men, against the loss of that inner core of personal integrity which democratic theory assumes every man to possess. It means also defenses against ruinous and meaningless conflicts, the major one being a large-scale international war, and against organizations which are specialized for conflict—defenses against militarism in the state and against militancy elsewhere.

The list is formidable; defensive institutions are few. Nevertheless, the situation is not hopeless. The skills of organization can also include skills of defending the individual against organization. One answer is the development of such institutional defenses as academic tenure, seniority, grievance procedures under collective bargaining and the legal recognition of civil rights. Opposition can take the form of "countervailing power" organizations like labor unions, farm groups, civil liberties organizations and pressure groups of various kinds. All this might be described as defense of the individual by "constitutionalization."

The maintenance of active labor markets, for instance, through full employment policy is also part of the answer. The freedom to quit, which implies the ability to find another job, is still perhaps the most powerful defense of the individual against his organizational superiors.

The ultimate defense of the individual must lie, however, in the integrity of the individual himself, and in his willingness to suffer rather than conform. The largest and most powerful organization is helpless before the individual who will die rather than serve it on unacceptable terms. The Thoreaus among us defend the liberty of all. ■

NATIONAL IMAGES
AND INTERNATIONAL SYSTEMS

Journal of Conflict Resolution,
III, 2 (June 1959): 120-131

National images and international systems

An international system consists of a group of interacting behavior units called "nations" or "countries," to which may sometimes be added certain supra-national organizations, such as the United Nations.

Each of the behavior units in the system can be described in terms of a set of "relevant variables." Just what is relevant and what is not is a matter of judgment of the system-builder, but we think of such things as states of war or peace, degrees of hostility or friendliness, alliance or enmity, arms budgets, geographic extent, friendly or hostile communications, and so on. Having defined our variables, we can then proceed to postulate certain relationships between them, sufficient to define a path for all the variables through time. Thus we might suppose, with Lewis Richardson,[2] that the rate of change of hostility of one nation toward a second depends on the level of hostility in the second and that the rate of change of hostility of the second toward the first depends on the level of hostility of the first. Then, if we start from given levels of hostility in each nation, these equations are sufficient to spell out what hap-

---

[1] This paper was presented to a meeting of the American Psychological Association in Washington, D.C., on August 30, 1958.

[2] See Anatol Rapoport, "Lewis F. Richardson's Mathematical Theory of War," *Journal of Conflict Resolution*, I (September, 1957), 249, for an excellent exposition.

pens to these levels in succeeding time periods. A system of this kind may (or may not) have an *equilibrium* position at which variables of one period produce an identical set in the next period, and the system exhibits no change through time.

Mechanical systems of this kind, though they are frequently illuminating, can be regarded only as very rough first approximations to the immensely complex truth. At the next level of approximation we must recognize that the people whose decisions determine the policies and actions of nations do not respond to the "objective" facts of the situation, whatever that may mean, but to their "image" of the situation. It is what we think the world is like, not what it is really like, that determines our behavior. If our image of the world is in some sense "wrong," of course, we may be disappointed in our expectations, and we may therefore revise our image; if this revision is in the direction of the "truth" there is presumably a long-run tendency for the "image" and the "truth" to coincide. Whether this is so or not, it is always the image, not the truth, that immediately determines behavior. We act according to the way the world appears to us, not necessarily according to the way it "is." Thus in Richardson's models it is one nation's image of the hostility of another, not the "real" hostility, which determines its reaction. The "image," then, must be thought of as the total cognitive, affective, and evaluative structure of the behavior unit, or its internal view of itself and its universe.[3]

Generally speaking, the behavior of complex organizations can be regarded as determined by *decisions,* and a decision involves the selection of the most preferred position in a contemplated field of choice. Both the field of choice and the ordering of this field by which the preferred position is identified lie in the image of the decision-maker. Therefore, in a system in which decision-makers are an essential element, the study of the ways in which the image grows and changes, both of the field of choice and of the valuational ordering of this field, is of prime importance. The image is always in some sense a product of messages received in the past. It is not, however, a simple inventory or "pile" of such messages but a highly structured piece of information-capital, developed partly by its inputs and outputs of information and partly by internal messages and its own laws of growth and stability.

The images which are important in international systems are those which a nation has of itself and of those other bodies in the system which constitute its international environment. At once a major complication suggests itself. A nation is some complex of the images of the persons who contemplate it, and as there are many different persons, so there are many different images. The complexity is increased by the necessity for inclusion, in the image of each person or at least of many persons, his image of the image of others. This complexity, however, is a property of the real world, not to be evaded or glossed over. It can be reduced to simpler terms if we distinguish between two types of persons in a nation—the powerful, on the one

hand, and the ordinary, on the other. This is not, of course, a sharp distinction. The power of a decision-maker may be measured roughly by the number of people which his decisions potentially affect, weighted by some measure of the effect itself. Thus the head of a state is powerful, meaning that his decisions affect the lives of millions of people; the ordinary person is not powerful, for his decisions affect only himself and the lives of a few people around him. There is usually a continuum of power among the persons of a society: thus in international relations there are usually a few very powerful individuals in a state—the chief executive, the prime minister, the secretary of state or minister of foreign affairs, the chiefs of staff of the armed forces. There will be some who are less powerful but still influential—members of the legislature, of the civil service, even journalists, newspaper owners, prominent businessmen, grading by imperceptible degrees down to the common soldier, who has no power of decision even over his own life. For purposes of the model, however, let us compress this continuum into two boxes, labeled the "powerful" and the "ordinary," and leave the refinements of power and influence for later studies.

We deal, therefore, with two representative images, (1) the image of the small group of powerful people who make the actual decisions which lead to war or peace, the making or breaking of treaties, the invasions or withdrawals, alliances, and enmities which make up the major events of international relations, and (2) the image of the mass of ordinary people who are deeply affected by these decisions but who take little or no direct part in making them. The tacit support of the mass, however, is of vital importance to the powerful. The powerful are always under some obligation to represent the mass, even under dictatorial regimes. In democratic societies the aggregate influence of the images of ordinary people is very great; the image

---

[3] See K. E. Boulding, *The Image* (Ann Arbor: University of Michigan Press, 1956), for an exposition of the theory on which this paper is based.

of the powerful cannot diverge too greatly from the image of the mass without the powerful losing power. On the other hand, the powerful also have some ability to manipulate the images of the mass toward those of the powerful. This is an important object of instruments as diverse as the public education system, the public relations departments of the armed services, the Russian "agitprop," and the Nazi propaganda ministry.

In the formation of the national images, however, it must be emphasized that impressions of nationality are formed mostly in childhood and usually in the family group. It would be quite fallacious to think of the images as being cleverly imposed on the mass by the powerful. If anything, the reverse is the case: the image is essentially a mass image, or what might be called a "folk image," transmitted through the family and the intimate face-to-face group, both in the case of the powerful and in the case of ordinary persons. Especially in the case of the old, long-established nations, the powerful share the mass image rather than impose it; it is passed on from the value systems of the parents to those of the children, and agencies of public instruction and propaganda merely reinforce the images which derived essentially from the family culture. This is much less true in new nations which are striving to achieve nationality, where the family culture frequently does not include strong elements of national allegiance but rather stresses allegiance to religious ideals or to the family as such. Here the powerful are frequently inspired by a national image derived not from family tradition but from a desire to imitate other nations, and here they frequently try to impose their images on the mass of people. Imposed images, however, are fragile by comparison with those which are deeply internalized and transmitted through family and other intimate sources.

Whether transmitted orally and informally through the family or more formally through schooling and the written word, the national image is essentially a *historical* image—that is, an image which extends through time, backward into a supposedly recorded or perhaps mythological past and forward into an imagined future. The more conscious a people is of its history, the stronger the national image is likely to be. To be an Englishman is to be conscious of "1066 and All That" rather than of "Constantine and All That," or "1776 and All That." A nation is the creation of its historians, formal and informal. The written word and public education contribute enormously to the stability and persistence of the national images. The Jews, for instance, are a creation of the Bible and the Talmud, but every nation has its bible, whether formed into a canon or not—noble words like the Declaration of Independence and the Gettysburg Address—which crystallize the national image in a form that can be transmitted almost unchanged from generation to generation. It is no exaggeration to say that the function of the historian is to pervert the truth in directions favorable to the images of his readers or hearers. Both history and geography as taught in national schools are devised to give "perspective" rather than truth: that is to say, they present the world as seen from the vantage point of the nation. The national geography is learned in great detail, and the rest of the world is in fuzzy outline; the national history is emphasized and exalted; the history of the rest of the world is neglected or even falsified to the glory of the national image.

It is this fact that the national image is basically a lie, or at least a perspective distortion of the truth, which perhaps accounts for the ease with which it can be perverted to justify monstrous cruelties and wickednesses. There is much that is noble in the national image. It has lifted man out of the narrow cage of self-centeredness, or even family-centeredness, and has forced him to accept responsibility, in some sense, for people and events far beyond his face-to-face cognizance and immediate experience. It is a window of some sort on both space and time and extends a man's concern far beyond his own little lifetime and petty interests. Nevertheless, it achieves these virtues usually only at the cost of untruth, and this fatal flaw constantly betrays it. Love of country is perverted into hatred of the foreigner, and peace, order, and justice at home are paid for by war, cruelty, and injustice abroad.

In the formation of the national image the consciousness of great *shared* events and experiences is of the utmost importance. A nation is a body of people who are conscious of having "gone through something" together. Without the shared experience, the national image itself would not be shared, and it is of vital importance that the national image be highly similar. The sharing may be quite vicarious; it may be an experience shared long ago but constantly renewed by the ritual observances and historical memory of the people, like the Passover and the Captivity in the case of the Jews. Without the sharing, however, there is no nation. It is for this reason that war has been such a tragically important element in the creation and sustenance of the national image. There is hardly a nation that has not been cradled in violence and nourished by further violence. This is not, I think, a necessary property of war itself. It is rather that, especially in more primitive societies, war is the one experience which is dramatic, obviously important, and shared by everybody. We are now witnessing the almost unique phenomenon of a number of new nations arising without war in circumstances which are extremely rare in history, for example—India, Ghana, and the new West Indian Federation, though even here there are instances of severe violence, such as the disturbances which accompanied partition in

India. It will be interesting to see the effect, if any, on their national images.

We now come to the central problem of this paper, which is that of the impact of national images on the relations among states, that is, on the course of events in international relations. The relations among states can be described in terms of a number of different dimensions. There is, first of all, the dimension of simple geographical space. It is perhaps the most striking single characteristic of the national state as an organization, by contrast with organizations such as firms or churches, that it thinks of itself as occupying, in a "dense" and exclusive fashion, a certain area of the globe. The schoolroom maps which divide the world into colored shapes which are identified as nations have a profound effect on the national image. Apart from the very occasional condominium, it is impossible for a given plot of land on the globe to to be associated with two nations at the same time. The territories of nations are divided sharply by frontiers carefully surveyed and frequently delineated by a chain of customs houses, immigration stations, and military installations. We are so accustomed to this arrangement that we think of it as "natural" and take it completely for granted. It is by no means the only conceivable arrangement, however. In primitive societies the geographical image is not sharp enough to define clear frontiers; there may be a notion of the rough territory of a tribe, but, especially among nomadic peoples, there is no clear concept of a frontier and no notion of a nation as something that has a shape on a map. In our own society the shape on the map that symbolizes the nation is constantly drilled into the minds of both young and old, both through formal teaching in schools and through constant repetition in newspapers, advertisements, cartoons, and so on. A society is not inconceivable, however, and might even be desirable, in which nations governed people but not territories and claimed jurisdiction over a defined set of citizens, no matter where on the earth's surface they happened to live.

The territorial aspect of the national state is important in the dynamics of international relations because of the *exclusiveness* of territorial occupation. This means that one nation can generally expand only at the expense of another; an increase in the territory of one is achieved only at the expense of a decrease in the territory of another. This makes for a potential conflict situation. This characteristic of the nation does not make conflict inevitable, but it does make it likely and is at least one of the reasons why the history of international relations is a history of perpetual conflict.

The territorial aspect of international relations is complicated by the fact that in many cases the territories of nations are not homogeneous but are composed of "empires," in which the populations do not identify themselves with the national image of the dominant group. Thus when one nation conquers another and absorbs the conquered territory into an empire, it does not thereby automatically change the culture and allegiances of the conquered nation. The Poles remained Polish for a hundred and twenty-five years of partition between Germany, Austria, and Russia. The Finns retained their nationality through eight hundred years of foreign rule and the Jews, through nearly two thousand years of dispersion. If a nation loses territory occupied by disaffected people, this is much less damaging than the loss of territory inhabited by a well-disposed and loyal population. Thus Turkey, which was the "sick man of Europe" as long as it retained its heterogeneous empire, enjoyed a substantial renewal of national health when stripped of its empire and pushed back to the relatively homogeneous heartland of Anatolia. In this case the loss of a disaffected empire actually strengthened the national unit.

The image of the map-shape of the nations may be an important factor affecting the general frame of mind of the nation. There is a tendency for nations to be uneasy with strong irregularities, enclaves, detached portions, and protuberances or hollows. The ideal shape is at least a convex set, and there is some tendency for nations to be more satisfied if they have regularly round or rectangular outlines. Thus the detachment of East Prussia from the body of Germany by the Treaty of Versailles was an important factor in creating the fanatical discontent of the Nazis.

A second important dimension of the national image is that of hostility or friendliness. At any one time a particular national image includes a rough scale of the friendliness or hostility of, or toward, other nations. The relationship is not necessarily either consistent or reciprocal—in nation A the prevailing image may be that B is friendly, whereas in nation B itself the prevailing image may be one of hostility toward A; or again in both nations there may be an image of friendliness of A toward B but of hostility of B toward A. On the whole, however, there is a tendency toward both consistency and reciprocation—if a nation A pictures itself as hostile toward B, it usually also pictures B as hostile toward it, and the image is likely to be repeated in B. One exception to this rule seems to be observable: most nations seem to feel that their enemies are more hostile toward them than they are toward their enemies. This is a typical paranoid reaction; the nation visualizes itself as surrounded by hostile nations toward which it has only the nicest and friendliest of intentions.

An important subdimension of the hostility-friendliness image is that of the stability or security of the relationship. A friendly relationship is frequently formalized as an alliance. Alliances, however, are shifting; some friendly relations are fairly permanent, others change as the world kaleidoscope changes, as new enemies arise, or as governments change. Thus a bare fifteen or twenty years ago most people in the United States visualized Germany and Japan, even before the outbreak of the war, as enemies, and after Hitler's invasion of Russia, Russia was for a while regarded as a valuable friend and ally. Today the picture is quite changed: Germany and Japan are valuable friends and allies; Russia is the great enemy. We can roughly classify the reciprocal relations of nations along some scale of friendliness-hostility. At one extreme we have stable friendliness, such as between Britain and Portugal or between Britain and the Commonwealth countries. At the other extreme we have stable hostility—the "traditional enemies" such as France and Germany. Between these extremes we have a great many pairs characterized by shifting alliances. On the whole, stable friendly relations seem to exist mainly between strong nations and weaker nations which they have an interest in preserving and stable hostile relations between adjacent nations each of which has played a large part in the formation of the other.

Another important dimension both of the image and of the "reality" of the nation-state is its strength or weakness. This is, in turn, a structure made up of many elements—economic resources and productivity, political organization and tradition, willingness to incur sacrifice and inflict cruelties, and so on. It still makes some kind of sense to assess nations on a strength-weakness scale at any one time. Strength is frequently thought of in military terms as the ability to hurt an opponent or to prevent one's self from being hurt by him. There are also more subtle elements in terms of symbolic loyalties and affections which are hard to assess but which must be included in any complete picture.

Many arrays of bristling armaments have been brought low by the sheer inability of their wielders to attract any lasting respect or affection. No social organization can survive indefinitely unless it can command the support of its members, and a continuing sense of the significance of the organization or group as such is much more durable a source of support than is the fleeting booty of war or monopoly. The Jews have outlasted an impressive succession of conquerors. These questions regarding the ultimate sources of continuing strength or weakness are difficult, and we shall neglect them in this paper.

In order to bring together the variables associated with each nation or pair of nations into an international system, we must resort to the device of a matrix, as in Figure 1. Here the hostility-friendliness variable is used as an example. Each cell, a_{ij}, indicates the degree of hostility or friendliness of nation I (of the row) toward nation J (of the column). For purposes of illustration, arbitrary figures have been inserted on a scale from 5 to −5, −5 meaning very hostile, 5 very friendly, and 0 neutral.[4] A matrix of this kind has many

----

[4] The problem of the measurement of hostility (or friendliness) is a very interesting one which we cannot go into extensively here but which is not so hopeless of solution as might at first sight appear. Possible avenues are as follows: (1) A historical approach. Over a period of years two nations have been at war, threatening war, allied, bound by treaty, and so on. Each relation would be given an arbitrary number, and each year assigned a number accordingly: the average of the years' numbers would be the index. This would always yield a symmetrical matrix—that is, the measure of I's relation to J would be the same as J's relation to I, or $a_{ij} = a_{ji}$. (2) An approach by means of content analysis of public communications (official messages, newspaper editorials, public speeches, cartoons, etc.). This seems likely to be most immediately useful and fruitful, as it would give current information and would also yield very valuable dynamic informa-

interesting properties, not all of which can be worked out here but which depend on the kind of restraints that we impose on it. If we suppose, for instance, that the relations of na-

----

tion about the *changes* in the matrix, which may be much more important than the absolute figures. The fact that any measure of this kind is highly arbitrary is no argument against it, provided that it is qualitatively reliable—that is, moves generally in the same direction as the variable which it purports to measure—and provided also that the limitations of the measure are clearly understood. It would probably be advisable to check the second type of measure against the more objective measures derived from the first method. The difficulty of the first method, however, is the extreme instability of the matrix. The affections of nations are ephemeral!

tions are reciprocal, so that I's attitude toward J is the same as J's toward I, the matrix becomes symmetrical about its major diagonal—that is, the lower left-hand triangle is a mirror image of the upper right-hand triangle. This is a very severe restriction and is certainly violated in fact: there are unrequited loves and hates among the nations as there are among individuals. We can recognize a *tendency*, however, for the matrix to become symmetrical. There is a certain instability about an unrequited feeling. If I loves J and J hates I, then either J's constant rebuff of I's affections will turn I's love to hate, or I's persistant wooing will break down J's distaste and transform it into affection. Unfortunately for the history of human relations,

	A	B	C	D	E	Totals
A		−5	+3	0	+2	0
B	−3		−2	−1	−2	−8
C	+2	−4		0	+1	−1
D	−1	−1	0		0	−2
E	+4	−3	+2	0		+3
Totals	+2	−13	+3	−1	+1	−8
X	2	−5	4	+1	−2	0
Y	1	−10½	1	−1½	2	−8

Fig. 1

the former seems to be the more frequent pattern, but the latter is by no means unknown.[5]

The sum totals of the rows represent the over-all friendliness or hostility of the nation at the head of the row; the sum totals of the columns represent the degree of hostility or friendliness *toward* the nation at the head of the column. The sum of either of these sums (which must be equal, as each represents a way of adding up all the figures of the matrix)

feeling hostile toward everyone and receiving hostility in return; *D* is a "neutral" nation, with low values for either hostility or friendliness; *E* is a "friendly" nation, reciprocating *B*'s general hostility but otherwise having positive relations with everyone. In this figure it is evident that *A*, *C*, and *E* are likely to be allied against *B*, and *D* is likely to be uncommitted.

In the matrix of Figure 1 no account is

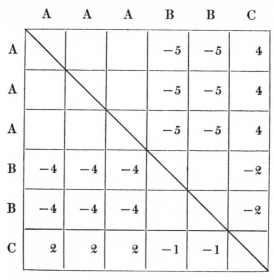

FIG. 2

is a measure of the over-all friendliness or hostility of the system. In the example of Figure 1, *B* is evidently a "paranoid" nation,

----

[5] George F. Kennan once said: "It is an undeniable privilege of every man to prove himself in the right in the thesis that the world is his enemy; for if he reiterates it frequently enough and makes it the background of his conduct, he is bound eventually to be right" ("The Roots of Soviet Conduct," *Foreign Affairs*, July, 1947). If for "enemy" we read "friend" in this statement, the proposition seems to be equally true but much less believed.

taken of the relative size or power of the different nations. This dimension of the system can easily be accommodated, however. All that is necessary is to take the power of the smallest nation as a convenient unit and express the power of the others in multiples of this unit. Then in the matrix we simply give each nation a number of places along the axes equal to the measure of its power. Thus in Figure 2 we suppose a system of three nations, where *B* is twice as powerful as *C* and *A* is three times as powerful as *C; A* is then allotted three spaces along the axes, B two, and C one. The analysis of the matrix proceeds as before, with the additional constraint that all the figures in the larger boxes bounded by the lines which divide the nations should be the same, as in the figure.

The difference between the sum of a nation's column, representing the general degree of support or affection it *receives*, and the sum of a nations row, representing the sum of support or affection it *gives*, might be called its *affectional balance*. This is shown in the row X in Figure 1. It is a necessary property of a matrix of this kind that the sum of all these balances shall be zero. They measure the relative position of each nation in regard to the degree of support it can expect from the international system as a whole. Thus in Figure 1 it is clear that B is in the worst position, and C in the best position, vis-à-vis the system as a whole. Another figure of some interest might be called the *affectional contribution*, shown in the line Y. This is the mean of the column and row totals for each nation. The total affectional contribution is equal to the total of all the figures of the matrix, which measures the general hostility or friendliness of the whole system. The affectional contribution is then a rough measure of how much each nation contributes to the general level of hostility of the whole system. Thus in the example of Figure 1 we see that nation B (the paranoid) actually contributes more than 100 per cent to the total hostility of the system, its extreme hostility being offset to some extent by other nations' friendliness.

One critical problem of an international system, then, is that of the *dynamics* of the hostility matrix. We can conceive of a succession of such matrices at successive points of time. If there is a system with a "solution," we should be able to predict the matrix at t_1 from the knowledge we have of the matrix at t_0 or at various earlier times. The matrix itself will not, in general, carry enough information to make such predictions possible, even though it is easy to specify theoretical models in which a determinate dynamic system can be derived from the information in the matrix alone.[6]

The difficulty with "simple" systems of this nature is that they are very much more simple than the reality which they symbolize. This is because, in reality, the variables of the system consist of the innumerable dimensions of the images of large numbers of people, and the dynamics of the image are much more complex than the dynamics of mechanical systems. This is because of the structural nature of the image; it cannot be represented simply by a set of quantities or variables. Because of this structural nature, it is capable occasionally of very dramatic changes as a message hits some vital part of the structure and the whole image reorganizes itself. Certain events—like the German invasion of Belgium in 1914, the Japanese attack on Pearl Harbor in 1941, the American use of the atom bomb at Hiroshima and Nagasaki, the merciless destruction of Dresden, and the Russian success with Sputnik I—have profound effects and possibly long-run effects on reorganizing the various national images. The "reorganizing" events are hard both to specify and to predict; they introduce, however, a marked element of uncertainty into any dynamic international system which does not exist, for instance, in the solar system!

----

[6] As a very simple example of such a system, let $(a_{ij})t$ be a cell of the matrix at time t and $(a_{ij})t + 1$ be the corresponding value at time $t + 1$. Then if for each cell we can postulate a function $(a_{ij})_{t+1} = F(a_{ij})_t$, we can derive the whole $t + 1$ matrix from the t matrix. This is essentially the dynamic method of Lewis F. Richardson, and in fairly simple cases it provides an interesting way of formulating certain aspects of the system, especially its tendency toward *cumulative* movements of hostility (arms races) or occasionally of friendliness.

In spite of this difficulty, which, oddly enough, is particularly acute in short-term prediction, one gets the impression from the observation of history that we are in the presence of a true system with a real dynamic of its own. We do observe, for instance, cumulative processes of hostility. If we had some measures of the hostility matrix, however crude, it would be possible to identify these processes in more detail, especially the "turning points." There is an analogy here with the business cycle, which also represents a system of cumulative stochastic processes subject to occasional "reorganizations" of its basic equations. Just as we can trace cumulative upward and downward movements in national income, the downward movements often (though not always) culminating in financial crisis and the upward movements often leading to inflation and a subsequent downturn, so we can trace cumulative movements in the hostility matrix. We have "prewar" periods corresponding to downswings, in which things go from bad to worse and hostility constantly increases. The total of all the hostility figures (e.g., −8 on Fig. 1) is a striking analogue of the national-income concept. It might be called the "international temperature." Just as there is a certain critical point in a deflation at which a financial crisis is likely to ensue because of the growing insolvency of heavily indebted businesses, so there is a critical point in the rise of hostility at which war breaks out. This critical point itself depends on a number of different factors and may not be constant. Some nations may be more tolerant of hostility than others; as the cost of war increases, the tolerance of hostility also increases, as we see today in the remarkable persistence of the "cold war." A deflation or downturn, however, *may* reverse itself without a crisis, and a "prewar" period may turn into a "postwar" period without a war. Indeed, in the period since 1945 we might identify almost as many small international cycles as there have been business cycles! The "upturn" may be a result of a change of government, the death of certain prominent individuals, or even a change of heart (or image!) on the part of existing rulers. The catharsis of a war usually produces the typical "postwar" period following, though this is often tragically short, as it was after the end of World War II, when a "downturn" began after the revolution in Czechoslovakia. The downturn is often the result of the reassertion of a persistent, long-run character of the system after a brief interlude of increasing friendliness. There seems to be a certain long-run tendency of an international system toward hostility, perhaps because of certain inescapable flaws in the very concept of a national image, just as there also seems to be a long-run tendency of an unregulated and undisturbed market economy toward deflation.

In considering the dynamics of an international system, the essential properties of the image matrix might be summed up in a broad concept of "compatibility." If the change in the system makes for greater compatibility the system may move to an equilibrium. The "balance-of-power" theory postulates the existence of an equilibrium of this nature. The record of history, however, suggests that, in the past at least, international systems have usually been unstable. The incompatibility of various national images has led to changes in the system which have created still greater incompatibility, and the system has moved to less and less stable situations until some crisis, such as war, is reached, which represents a discontinuity in the system. After a war the system is reorganized; some national units may disappear, others change their character, and the system starts off again. The incompatibility may be of many kinds, and it is a virtue of this kind of rather loose model that the historian can fill in the endlessly various details in the special situations which he studies. The model is a mere dress form on which the historian swathes the infinite variations of fashion and fact.

In the model we can distinguish two very different kinds of incompatibility of images. The first might be called "real" incompatibility, where we have two images of the future in which realization of one would prevent the realization of the other. Thus two nations may both claim a certain piece of territory, and each may feel dissatisfied unless the territory is incorporated into it. (One thinks of the innumerable irredenta which have stained the pages of history with so much blood!) Or two nations may both wish to feel stronger than, or superior to, each other. It is possible for two nations to be in a position where each is stronger than the other *at home*, provided that they are far enough apart and that the "loss of power gradient" (which measures the loss of power of each as we remove the point of application farther and farther from the home base) is large enough. It is rarely possible, however, for two nations each to dominate the other, except in the happy situation where each suffers from delusions of grandeur.

The other form of incompatibility might be called "illusory" incompatibility, in which there exists a condition of compatibility which would satisfy the "real" interests of the two parties but in which the dynamics of the situation or the illusions of the parties create a situation of perverse dynamics and misunderstandings, with increasing hostility simply as a result of the reactions of the parties to each other, not as a result of any basic differences of interest. We must be careful about this distinction: even "real" incompatibilities are functions of the national images rather than of physical fact and are therefore subject to change and control. It is hard for an ardent patriot to realize that his country is a mental, rather than a physical, phenomenon, but such

indeed is the truth! It is not unreasonable to suppose, however, that "real" incompatibilities are more intractable and less subject to "therapy" than illusory ones.

One final point of interest concerns what might be called the impact of "sophistication" or "self-consciousness" on national images and the international system. The process of sophistication in the image is a very general one, and we cannot follow all its ramifications here. It occurs in every person in greater or less degree as he grows into adult awareness of himself as part of a larger system. It is akin almost to a Copernican revolution: the unsophisticated image sees the world only from the viewpoint of the viewer; the sophisticated image sees the world from many imagined viewpoints, as a system in which the viewer is only a part. The child sees everything through his own eyes and refers everything to his own immediate comfort. The adult learns to see the world through the eyes of others; his horizon extends to other times, places, and cultures than his own; he learns to distinguish between those elements in his experience which are universal and those which are particular. Many grown people, of course, never become adults in this sense, and it is these who fill our mental hospitals with themselves and their children.

The scientific subculture is an important agency in the sophistication of images. In the physical world we no longer attribute physical phenomena to spirits analogous to our own. In the social sciences we have an agency whereby men reach self-consciousness about their own cultures and institutions and therefore no longer regard these as simply given to them by "nature." In economics, for instance, we have learned to see the system as a whole, to realize that many things which are true of individual behavior are not true of the system and that the system itself is not incapable of a modicum of control. We no longer, for instance, regard depressions as "acts of God" but as system-made phenomena capable of control through relatively minor system change.

The national image, however, is the last great stronghold of unsophistication. Not even the professional international relations experts have come very far toward seeing the system as a whole, and the ordinary citizen and the powerful statesman alike have naïve, self-centered, and unsophisticated images of the world in which their nation moves. Nations are divided into "good" and "bad"—the enemy is all bad, one's own nation is of spotless virtue. Wars are either acts of God or acts of the other nations, which always catch us completely by surprise. To a student of international systems the national image even of respectable, intellectual, and powerful people seems naïve and untrue. The patriotism of the sophisticated cannot be a simple faith. There is, however, in the course of human history a powerful and probably irreversible movement toward sophistication. We can wise up, but we cannot wise down, except at enormous cost in the breakdown of civilizations, and not even a major breakdown results in much loss of knowledge. This movement must be taken into account in predicting the future of the international system. The present system as we have known it for the past hundreds or even thousands of years is based on the widespread acceptance of unsophisticated images, such as, for instance, that a nation can be made more secure *merely* by increasing its armaments. The growth of a systems-attitude toward international relations will have profound consequences for the dynamics of the system itself, just as the growth of a systems-attitude in economics has profound consequences for the dynamics of the economic system.

If, as I myself believe, we live in an international system so unstable that it threatens the very existence of life on earth, our main hope for change may lie in the rapid growth of sophistication, especially at the level of the images of the powerful. Sophistication, of course, has its dangers also. It is usually but a hair's-breadth removed from sophistry, and a false sophistication (of which Marxism in some respects is a good example) can be even more destructive to the stability of a system than a naïve image. Whichever way we move, however, there is danger. We have no secure place to stand where we are, and we live in a time when intellectual investment in developing more adequate international images and theories of international systems may bear an enormous rate of return in human welfare.

THE DOMESTIC IMPLICATIONS
OF ARMS CONTROL

Daedalus, 89, 4 (Fall 1960): 846-859

The Domestic Implications of Arms Control

THE DISCUSSION of the domestic implications of arms control, for the United States or for other countries, depends greatly on the concept of arms control which is in the mind of the discussant. The very discussion of arms control is an indication that unilateral national defense is unsatisfactory and that some substitute is to be sought. The nature of the dissatisfaction, however, and the nature of the substitute, is subject to wide variation even among the authors of this group of essays. The concept of arms control as "military co-operation with potential enemies" seems to me the most fruitful, especially as extended to include the concept of organization for all kinds of cooperation with potential enemies designed to produce mutual security and to reduce enmity.

This concept is clearly shocking to those who are emotionally committed to the ethic of unilateral national defense, or those whose hatred of the potential enemy is so intense that they cannot bear the thought of cooperation. It is, however, a concept which is being forced upon us by the nature of modern war. So little serious intellectual attention has been given to the problem, however, in comparison with the enormous effort devoted to unilateral national defense, that we find ourselves on the threshold of doomsday unprepared to spell out even the larger framework of the changes which are now necessary in the world social system if man is to survive.

We do not even know, for instance, whether arms control will in fact lead to less government spending on defense, including the costs of inspection or of inter-armed-force or inter-nation organization. There are those who argue that arms control might lead to a larger military budget, especially if control were confined to the weapons of mass destruction. In the absence of adequate information on this point, any discussion of domestic implications must be highly speculative. It is important, however, not merely to speculate but also to build theoretical and statistical models of the domestic social system which can accommodate a number of different possibilities, even quite extreme cases. The economic system is that part of the social system in which such model building is most highly advanced, and where therefore the effects of various patterns of arms control can be most clearly followed. The economic system, however, is highly dependent on political decisions and on psychological attitudes, and we cannot be content with a mere economic analysis. Economic analysis, however, is a good place to begin, not only because in the present state of knowledge it offers the best chance of success, but also because in the minds of many people, and especially noneconomists, the economic consequences of arms control, and especially of disarmament, are a source of real anxiety.

The anxiety stems from the association of disarmament with depression and with extensive economic dislocation. The prosperity of the 1940's and 1950's, by contrast with the misery of the 1930's, is associated, whether the association is justified or not, in the minds of many people with the high level of war and defense expenditures in the former periods, and with the low level in the latter. The memories of the Great Depression are still strong in the minds of the middle-aged and the powerful, and the fear of another such experience, though by now driven down into the unconscious, is an active determinant of our value system. Nobody wants to suggest that the United States would deliberately sabotage an attempt at arms control because of this fear of depression; the frivolity and hypocrisy with which the subject of disarmament was treated in official circles in the pre-sputnik era was due almost entirely to an emotional and intellectual commitment to unilateral national defense, not to any fear of economic consequences.

Nevertheless, it is important to examine, and if possible to remove, this economic anxiety. Arms control is going to be a very difficult road to find, beset with legitimate anxieties and risky decisions. The advance clearing away of minor obstacles, illegitimate and unnecessary anxieties, and falsely imagined risks is an important part of the pathfinding process. It would be unspeakably tragic if the great moment in history arrived at which opportunity presented itself for a transition from the present system (the road to doomsday) to a system which offered at least a chance of human security and decency, and if we then found that illusions about economic systems caused us to stumble and take the wrong road.

There are, then, three major domestic economic problems which arms control may represent, summarized as *conversion, stabilization,* and *growth.* These are all general problems of the economy and are not peculiar to arms control. Conversion is the problem of how to adjust the structure of production in the economy—that is, the commodity mix of total output—to shifts in the structure of total demand, public and private. Stabilization is the problem of how to control the vicious dynamic processes of deflation, depression, and unemployment, on the one hand, or inflation on the other, which may be initiated by these shifts in the structure of total demand. Growth is the problem of achieving a structure of total demand which will give the society an optimum rate of economic growth; the latter might be defined as the maximum rate of growth which is subject to the constraints of its basic value system.

Conversion is a problem that is always with us. The movement of technology, trade opportunities, and public and private demand, constantly imposes on any economy the necessity for altering its product mix and the occupational distribution of its labor force. In the course of the past two hundred years, for instance, the United States has shifted the proportion of its labor force engaged in agriculture from about 90 percent to 10 percent under the impact of a great technical revolution, which has resulted in a more than tenfold increase in output of food and fibers per man-hour. Agricultural policy testifies both to the magnitude of the conversion problem involved and also to the ability of governments to hamper it.

To come closer to the immediate topic, the United States has suffered enormous fluctuations in the proportion of the gross national product allotted to national security (defense) in the past twenty years; at present, the latter is a little less than 10 percent of the gross national product, and the recent trend is illustrated in Table 1.

The rise in national security expenditures from the almost negligible levels of the 1930's to the heights of the mid-1940's (World War II) was, of course, accompanied by a sharp rise in GNP and a dramatic fall in the percentage of unemployment. Here we have the origin of the myth of defense-inspired prosperity. It is a myth which derives its power from the fact that it is not wholly untrue and is rooted in the personal experiences of millions of people. Nevertheless, it *is* basically only a half truth. The outstanding fact is the remarkable stability and success of the American economy under the impact of the massive armament and disarmament of the 1940's, when, for instance, in one year (1945-1946) we transferred an absolute amount of manpower and resources from war to civilian employments more than twice as much as would be involved (in real terms) in total and complete disarmament at present. The post-Korean disarmament was less well managed: unemployment rose to a disquieting 5 percent in 1954, but subsided again in later years in the face of a continued fall in the real defense burden.

TABLE 1

United States Gross National Product (GNP) and National Security Expenditures (NSE) in real terms (billions of dollars) at 1959 prices, selected years.

YEAR	GNP	NSE[1]	NSE/GNP (%)	UNEMPLOYMENT AS % OF LABOR FORCE[2]
1939	211.5	3.2	1.5	17.2
1944	366.3	164.7	45.0	1.2
1945	359.4	139.8	39.1	1.9
1946	316.0	26.7	8.4	3.9
1947	315.7	15.3	4.8	3.6 (3.9)
1953	417.1	60.1	14.4	2.5 (2.9)
1954	408.8	49.5	12.2	5.0 (5.6)
1959	478.8	45.5	9.5	(5.5)

Source: *Economic Report of the President,* 1960.

1. NSE figures are net of government sales, hence may be a little too small. There has been a substantial revision of these figures in recent years.
2. The figures in parentheses are according to the new definition.

Some of the problems of conversion do not show up in the aggregate data. Even within the defense program itself there are continual shifts involving conversion problems of the same order of magnitude as those which would be involved in substantial disarmament or even in conversion to "expensive" arms control. The shift which has taken place in the past few years from the wheel to the whoosh as the basis for military hardware, for instance, has created a substantial conversion problem within the defense industry of the same order of magnitude as that which might be expected in the shift-over from the present system to a plausibly expensive arms-control system. The current change-over temporarily created some mildly depressed areas, such as Michigan, but the economic impact of conversion has not presented itself as more than a minor national problem.

I am not arguing, of course, that conversion is costless, painless, and creates no problems, and least of all am I arguing that there should be no national policy about it and no organization to deal with it. I would argue indeed that this is a perennial problem, that even though the American economy is remarkably flexible and deals fairly well with this problem even in the absence of any governmental organization, there is a strong case for more positive social organization to deal with depressed areas and industries, whether these result from tariff changes, exhaustion of natural or human resources, shifts in technology or tastes, or changes in the defense industry. I argue also, however, that this is a manageable problem, and that it can be solved well within the limits of toleration which our value system imposes.

The ease with which the problem of conversion can be solved depends in no small measure on our ability to prevent depressions. It is dangerously easy for a free market economy with low levels of government expenditure to get into a vicious spiral of declining investment, resulting in declining incomes and profits, which lead to still another decline in investment, and so on. The remarkable resiliency of the American economy since 1945 by comparison with the 1930's can be attributed to the development of a number of "built-in stabilizers," as well as to a general expectation that government would intervene quickly to prevent a serious depression. Of these built-in stabilizers the sheer magnitude of the Federal budget is an important element. With a large over-all budget amounting to about one-fifth of the gross national product, with tax receipts amounting to an even larger proportion of disposable income, and with a tax system that is at least moderately progressive, general deflationary or inflationary forces in the private economy call forth an automatic counterforce in the public sector. Thus a deflationary movement in the private sector, due, say, to a decline in private investment expenditure or to a "buyers' strike" of consumers trying to increase their cash balances, is reflected in a decline in taxable income. With a system that is largely pay-as-you-go, this results in an immediate decline in tax receipts at both Federal and local levels.

There is also likely to be an increase in over-all governmental expenditure on unemployment insurance benefits, relief payments, agricultural price-support purchases, and so on. Government cash budgets rapidly become unbalanced: this results in an increase in the cash balances held by the public, and this is in itself an inflationary factor. It may not be enough to counteract the initial deflationary movement entirely, but it will slow down the deflation and hence tend to eliminate certain dynamic aggravations of the deflationary process. If in addition there are some deliberate policy measures, such as credit relaxation or tax reduction, a spontaneous deflationary force can easily be offset in principle, though in practice there are difficult problems involved in the timing of these changes. Similarly, if there is a spontaneous inflationary movement in the private sector, taxable incomes rise, government receipts rise and expenditures fall, and government runs a surplus which drains money out of private balances, thus reducing the inflationary pressure.

Thus, the critical question here is whether arms control will result in a sizable reduction in the over-all government budget. If we have what I have called "expensive" arms control, which seems most likely at the moment, with elaborate inspection systems and even an increase in conventional forces, the problem may not arise. The movement toward arms control, however, is more fundamental than a mere attempt to put back the clock of technology to the point where we can once more indulge ourselves in the luxury of war without the fear of annihilation. At some point in the development of a viable world social system, as we proceed from arms control to close organizational connections between opposing armed forces, or even as we proceed to a system of "absolute weapons" in which defense collapses altogether and unilateral disarmament begins to pay off, there may come a point where there is no payoff in the maintenance of expensive national armed forces and they will be dismantled. This may seem absurd to historians and political scientists who are not students of general social systems and who cannot usually imagine any social system beyond the present.

We know too little about social systems to predict their course, and there may be many possible dynamic paths to the world society—conquest, unions, agreements, tacit agreements, unilateral behavior, and so on. The possibility of "cheap" arms control must not, however, be left off the agenda, even though this is almost certainly not the next move. The problem of the reaction of the American economy to "cheap" arms control (for instance, total disarmament) is a question of more than academic interest, even though it is at the moment an "academic" question. It is important not only because it may someday happen and we should be prepared for it, but because the assertion that the American economy could not maintain its health without a large arms program is a widely held belief, not only by Communist propagandists (though this line seems at the moment to have been abandoned) but what is more important, by many Americans themselves, some of them in high places.

Suppose then, we look at a model of an American economy in, say, 1959, in which the national security budget has been virtually eliminated. The total government budget is still about 10 percent of the GNP. This is a situation surprisingly similar to that of 1929, as is shown in the following table:

TABLE 2

United States Nonmilitary Government Expenditure in Real Terms (in billions of 1959 dollars)

	TOTAL		AS PERCENT OF GNP	
	1929	1959	1929	1959
Federal nonmilitary expenditure	3.4*	8.1	1.8*	1.7
State and local government expenditure	17.4	44.3	8.9	9.2
Total nonmilitary government expenditure	20.8	52.4	10.7	10.9
GNP	203.6	478.8		

Source: *Economic Report of the President*, 1960.

* This figure is for total Federal expenditure, as military expenditure is not available separately. It would be of the order of 1.0 billion.

It may come as a shock to many people to learn that apart from national defense, the proportion of real product actually absorbed by government in the late 1950's was almost exactly the same as in the late 1920's, in spite of a more than doubled real GNP. Creeping socialism does not seem to have crept very far, outside the Pentagon, which is in terms of GNP the world's third largest nonmarket economy, with only Russia and possibly China exceeding it. There may even be something in Galbraith's thesis that the public economy needs to expand, arms control or no arms control. The question needs to be raised, therefore, as to whether a nonmilitary American economy in 1960 would be any safer from depression than in 1929 without the introduction of organizational machinery which we do not now possess. No definite answer could be given to this question without a good deal more study. There are many important differences between now and 1929. The national debt is larger. We have pay-as-you-go taxes, which are a great stabilizer (before this, income taxes were paid on the previous year's income and so went up as a percentage of income when incomes were falling). We have social security, and also agricultural price supports, which for all their vices are also built-in stabilizers. Nevertheless, it is a moot question whether these devices are quantitatively adequate to deal with a sharp deflation. We may not expect anything like 1929-1932, but something like 1937-1938 would not be beyond the bounds of possibility.

It must be emphasized, however, that the purely economic problems involved in an adequate stabilization policy have been solved at the level of first approximation. We know roughly what to do, and still more roughly how much to do and when to do it. It would be possible, for instance, to increase the sensitivity of the built-in stabilizers at a lower level of government expenditure by such devices as automatic tax-rate reduction when national income fell, and a similar increase when it rose. It would be possible also to pursue more vigorous monetary policies. I am personally against this step, but this is an internal row among the economists. The important thing is that there are many ways of stabilizing (within limits of tolerance) the gross national product. There is an important unsolved problem regarding the extent to which this can be done without long-run inflation, and how the answer to this question is related to noncompetitive labor, capital, and commodity markets, but this, in a sense, is a secondary problem. To put the matter in a rather crude form: if we take 40 billion dollars of defense production out of the gross national product, where can we find another 40 billion dollars' worth of goods and services which can be absorbed without causing deflation? The answer is partly in increased household purchases as a result of tax decreases, partly in increased investment by businesses, partly by increased government expenditure in civilian uses, and partly by an export surplus created by foreign investment or foreign aid.

It is easy to find four numbers that add up to 40 billion. The trouble may be that it is too easy: there are too many alternatives, and we may be paralyzed for want of ability to choose among them, for the choice will involve political decisions which we are not well set up to make. Furthermore, the choice involves a mixture of technical and political decisions which are hard to unscramble. Thus the decision to take steps to stabilize the GNP and so expand other forms of product absorption by roughly the amount of decline in government military expenditure would be almost nonpolitical in the sense that there would be wide agreement and little conflict of interest about the objective. When it comes to allocating this increase among the various alternative methods of achieving it—tax reduction, debt increase, shifts in the tax structure, additional government expenditure on various competing activities (health, education, social security, conservation, public works, roads, flood control, and so on) and finally foreign aid and public investment abroad—the battle of interests is on, and there is no machinery to insure that the sum total of these various decisions adds up to just the right amount. I have sometimes thought of a device like a "government dollar," in which taxes shall be collected and budgets reckoned, and a variable rate of exchange (set by an economic policy agency analogous to the Federal Reserve Board) between government money and private money: the interests could fight out the truly political problems of allocation in government dollars, and then the stabilization agency could from time to time determine the aggregate amounts by setting a rate of exchange with private money as stabilization policy demanded. The suggestion may be quite impracticable: it is offered only as an example of the kind of change in our existing economic institutions which a stabilization policy on a small government budget might require.

Perhaps the greatest immediate threat to a rational stabilization policy is the still common attitude toward the national debt which sees it as a great burden and wants to strain to reduce it. There is sometimes a case for monetizing part of the national debt (paying it off with newly created money). There is hardly ever any case for paying it off by running a budget surplus, except in periods of strong inflation of private origin. A sharp reduction in the total government expenditure will be seized on by the economic puritans as an opportunity to pay off the national debt by not reducing taxes and so producing a substantial budget surplus. Such a policy would almost certainly be ruinously deflationary, and would cause depression and prevent conversion.

The problem of designing an optimum rate of economic growth is even more difficult than that of stabilization, and arms control may well raise serious questions—questions, however, which again are capable of serious answers. Economic growth is maintained by devoting resources to the accumulation of things, skills, and knowledge, and of these knowledge is the greatest. National security expenditure generates, as an important by-product, all three of these forms of accumulation. It results in the accumulation of buildings, roads, installations, and stocks of many commodities, many of which have potential civilian uses. It results also in the accumulation of skills in the population by dragging men out of their homes and teaching them crafts, trades, and professions, as well as the arts of dealing death and destruction. Finally, and this is becoming an increasingly important aspect of military expenditure, it organizes research on a scale of expense unknown to the civilian world. The Pentagon and Hollywood seem to be the only two places in our society where extravagance is cultivated as a virtue. Therefore, when research is hitched to the military rocket, it proceeds at a pace far beyond that of the civilian and merely peripatetic philosopher. I am quite willing to deplore this fact, but I am forced to acknowledge it. Perhaps the biggest social invention of the mid-twentieth century was the RAND Corporation, which perpetually makes obsolete the institution that fathered it.

Here again the economic problem is almost trivial. If we spent as much on research and training for human welfare as we spend for defense, it is hard to believe that the results would not be even more dramatic. If all science could be pursued without the smell of brimstone, and if all secrecy were abolished, how much more quickly, and joyfully, would knowledge grow. The problem is essentially one of the political consciousness: can we organize, through both private and public organization, the same kind of effort, or an even greater effort, for pure knowledge, useful skill, and human betterment than we can for the road to doomsday? If we cannot, it can only be because of a failure of the imagination, of a lack of clear purpose, and a poverty of symbols. But if we lack these things, we do not deserve anything better than doomsday.

In spite of the fact that the main theme of this paper is the domestic implications, we should take a brief glance abroad, for several reasons. One is that the domestic implications of arms control for other countries may be different from what they are in the United States. In Russia, for instance, though exact information is not available, the proportion of the gross national product going into national security is considerably larger than in the United States—though in an economy that is substantially poorer. National security is correspondingly a much greater economic burden. In the United States the marginal significance of the arms dollar is in the realm of a little more or a little less luxury; in Russia it is much closer to basic comfort, and in India it is close to sheer necessity. The Russians correspondingly have a greater incentive than we do toward "cheap" arms control, and this may explain something of their (and our) attitudes. In really poor countries like India, Pakistan, and China, arms expenditure literally snatches life from the starving: there is an enormous economic interest in cheap security.

Indeed, economic development is such a tender plant in its early stages that a heavy arms budget may condemn a poor country to stagnation. The problem is complicated, however, by the fact that at least in its early stages arms control will probably not operate as a world system, and there will be sub-systems within it (such as the rivalries between India and Pakistan, Israel and the Arab world, Cuba and the Dominican Republic) which may escape the general system of arms control and yet may be very costly to the participants.

Another reason for looking at the world economic scene is that one of the domestic implications of arms control (at least, of "cheap" arms control) for the United States may be a release of resources for investment and development abroad. This has implications for the reduction, or increase, of world tensions which may be relevant to the success or failure of arms control itself. It is important, too, in the moral mythology of disarmament: the plea that disarmament would release large resources for economic development and for raising standards of life in the poor countries is a powerful part of the motivation which drives ordinary decent people toward it, even if it does not have much appeal for political realists and those who direct the destinies of states.

Like other myths, this also embodies an important half truth. It is true that disarmament (or cheap arms control) would release resources which could indeed be used for this purpose. They do not have to be used for this purpose, however, and there is no guarantee that they would be. If we assume that no method of domestic stabilization is acceptable, other than manipulating the export surplus, then of course the stabilization program which followed cheap arms control would involve extensive gifts and investments abroad. It is perfectly possible, however, to draw up a domestic stabilization plan which involves no increase in the export surplus and no con-

tribution to the development of the rest of the world. The plain fact
is that, beyond a certain point of profitable investment abroad, the
increase in the American export surplus involves a real cost to
Americans, in terms of consumption foregone, or what may be more
serious, domestic growth impaired. Empire, whether political or
economic, has frequently involved a high cost to the imperial power.
In terms of per-capita income, for instance, the countries that stayed
at home and minded their own business (like Sweden and Switzerland) have frequently done better than those who have spread their
flag and their subsidies around the globe, like Portugal and Spain.
The history of the technological revolution shows that man may
squeeze a hundred dollars out of nature with the effort that he
spends on squeezing one dollar out of conquest. The polite struggle to abandon empire, which is so characteristic and almost embar-
rassing a phenomenon of the modern world, may not be unconnected
with a half-conscious realization that whatever may have been the
case three hundred years ago, empire does not pay today. There
may be exceptions to this rule: the Russians have probably got
something out of East Germany, though it will be surprising if they
get anything out of Cuba and Guinea. The whole subject needs
much more careful study than has been given to it.

The impact of aid programs, both on the development of the
recipients and on the level of world tensions, needs careful study.
On the one hand, we must avoid the naïve expectation that progress
and peace can be bought by the indiscriminate shoveling out of
billions. On the other hand, we must equally avoid the niggardly
naïveté of the xenophobes and economic isolationists. Without some
acceptance of world responsibility on the part of the rich and powerful countries, it is difficult to visualize a successful system of world
peace. Yet there is also a trick of being able to accept gifts, advice,
and support without a collapse of internal morale and self-respect.
It may be more blessed to give, but it is often a lot harder to receive.
Nevertheless, this skill can be learned, as Japan has shown in regard
to knowledge and Puerto Rico shows in regard to both things and
knowledge. The problem of how to make the poor countries rich
requires a degree of serious research and attention at least com-
parable to that put into the road to doomsday. If arms control can
release this kind of resource, in the long run this may be its most
important contribution.

The economic consequences of arms control are perhaps the
easiest to trace of all the consequences for the social system. The
impact of arms control on the other institutions and patterns of

behavior in society may eventually be even more significant, but we have hardly begun to think about these deeper implications. Nevertheless, they exist—for religion, for family life, for ethics, for art, for culture in all its many dimensions, and for politics. This is true because arms control is the beginning of a great revolution in human affairs. It may look like an attempt to get national security cheap, or to safeguard the institution of limited war, or to prevent a nuclear holocaust—and it is all these things. However, arms control is only the beginning of a process of evolution of social institutions which leads to the abolition of war and the establishment of the institutions of permanent peace, even though we cannot now foretell in detail what these will be. A specter is haunting the chancelleries and the general staffs, more frightening perhaps than that which Karl Marx invoked in 1848; it is the specter of Peace— that drab girl with the olive-branch corsage whom no red-blooded American (or Russian) could conceivably warm up to. She haunts us because we cannot go back to Napoleon, or to Lee, or even to MacArthur: the military are caught in an implacable dynamic of technical change which makes them increasingly less capable of defending the countries which support them, except at an increasingly intolerable cost. The grotesque irony of national defense in the nuclear age is that, after having had the inestimable privilege of losing half (or is it three quarters, or all?) our population, we are supposed to set up again the whole system which gave rise to this holocaust!

We are, however, totally unprepared for peace. We have never had peace, and it may be forced upon us before we really want it. One can only, in the spirit of Newton's *Opticks*, raise some queries. What, for instance, can hold society together in the absence of an external threat? What are the institutions which can embody "conflict control"—that general social system of which arms control is only a special case? How do we catch the disintegrating dynamic processes in society—the epidemics of hatred, the infectious images of falsehood, the powerful symbols which lead to destruction—and stop them, by education, by quarantine, by counter-eloquence, before they spread too far? How do we give the individual an image of self-respect, of identification with some larger group, without permitting the development of images of hatred and intolerance? How do we preserve the richness and variety of cultural differences in a world of rapid communication and peace—how, in other words, do we preserve the very real virtues of nationalism in a warless world? How do we prevent the great latent social processes (population growth, emotional hysteria, charismatic leadership, mistaken images of social fact) from carrying societies to poverty, factionalism, and decay? More difficult perhaps, how do we prevent boredom, how do we preserve danger, excitement, and a sense of high purpose? How do we deal with sadism and masculinism, masochism and femininism, the strut and the swagger, the cringe and the death wish? How do we release people from the crippling "binds" of ambivalence, and release their creative potential? How do we raise children in a warless world? What kind of ethic do we inculcate, and what are our defenses against its corruption? What rituals shall we have, and what heroes? How can we prevent the corrupting influence of wealth, luxury, and the treacherous ability to satisfy the flesh? Peace, it is clear, insinuates her soft fingers into every nerve of life. We have dreamed of utopia, and secretly been thankful that it is only a dream. Now we are going to be compelled to think about it, and think hard and long, for we may be forced into it by the absence of any alternative but doomsday.

BIBLIOGRAPHICAL NOTE ON RECENT LITERATURE

The recent literature on this subject is almost entirely confined to pamphlets and journals; there is a startling absence of formal or academic studies. Many of the peace groups have published pamphlets relating to the economics of disarmament: see, for instance, *If the Arms Race Ends* (two papers by Albert L. Gray, Jr., and Byron L. Johnson, Board of World Peace of the Methodist Church, 740 Rush Street, Chicago 11, Illinois); *Fact Sheet: Economic Consequences of Disarmament* (Committee for World Development and Disarmament, United Nations Plaza, New York, October 1959); see also publications by the Friends Committee on National Legislation, 245 2nd Street N.E., Washington 2, D.C., and by the Women's International League for Peace and Freedom, 2006 Walnut Street, Philadelphia 3, Pennsylvania.

Some of the more "neutral" policy research groups have also published pamphlets: the National Planning Association (1606 New Hampshire Avenue N.W., Washington, D.C.), Joint Statement, *Can the American Economy Adjust to Arms Reduction* (4 January 1960); and the Committee for Economic Development (711 Fifth Avenue, New York 22, New York), *The Defense We Can Afford*, by James F. Brownlee. The Senate Subcommittee on Disarmament of the United States Senate Committee on Foreign Relations published *Hearings* (1957), of which Parts 8, 9, and 13 are particularly relevant.

Periodical and newspaper articles include: Emile Benoit, "Will Defense Cuts Hurt Business," *Michigan Business Review*, March 1957; Seymour Harris, "The Economics of Disarmament," *Current History*, October 1957; and "Can We Prosper Without Arms," *New York Times Magazine*, 8 November 1959; Senator Hubert H. Humphrey, "After Disarmament—What?" *Think*, January 1960. *The Nation* had a special issue, "Economic Hazards of Arms Reduction," 28 March 1959.

A PURE THEORY OF CONFLICT
APPLIED TO ORGANIZATIONS

In: *Conflict Management in Organizations.*
Ann Arbor, Mich.: Foundation for Research
on Human Behavior, 1961, pp. 43-51

A PURE THEORY OF CONFLICT
APPLIED TO ORGANIZATIONS

The Organization as a Social System

An organization is a social system, hence it must be studied as a
social system. Social systems, however, are very complex. They consist
of certain aspects of the input, output and interaction of persons. The person himself is like a complex ten-billion unit computer plus, and the interaction of persons is correspondingly more complex. In order to understand
these processes at all, therefore, we must have adequate theoretical models.
Models are simplified abstract images of social systems which can guide
our decision processes and make sense out of the information input, which
is our experience. We must be careful, of course, that the models are not
over-simplified. An over-simplified model is one that usually gets us into
trouble because of the fact that in the process of abstraction by which the
model has been created certain essential elements in the real system have
been thrown away. Unfortunately, there is usually no real way of finding
out whether a model is over-simplified until we get into actual trouble. The
important thing, however, is whether we can learn to make the appropriate
modifications in the model as a result of the trouble we get into.

Social systems are compounded of at least three elements which I
have called necessity, chance and freedom. Purely mechanical models
like that of the solar system, which have nothing in them but necessity,
are never adequate to describe social systems. Social processes are
always in some sense stochastic; this means they have chance elements
built into them and hence their future course cannot be predicted in detail

although it may be possible to calculate the probability of future events.
Social systems, however, have still a third element in them which I have
called the element of freedom. This is because social systems are composed of persons, and persons are capable of knowledge and in particular
are capable of holding in their minds images of the future. When the image
of the future is a plan, that is, an image of the social system which the individual believes he can by his action bring about, then the system includes
the element of freedom. No social system, of course, is absolutely free
in the sense that any image of the future can be realized. The images of
the future cannot violate the laws of necessity and the future itself is always
subject to chance. The more we know about social systems, however, the
more free we are; that is, the more plans it is possible to have and the
better the chance of them being realized.

Just as economic theory built itself around the abstract concept of
exchange, so conflict theory has built itself around certain abstract concepts of conflict. What the theory tries to do is to abstract out of the be-
wildering variety of actual conflict situations in industry, economic organizations, international relations, race relations, family life, etc., a set of
concepts of conflict relationships which is common to all the situations.
Such a theoretical model of conflict processes should then be able to assist
us in understanding why it is that some conflict processes seem to be creative and have built into them a continuing process of resolution--that is, a
process by which all parties seem to benefit whereas some other conflict
processes get out of hand and become clearly destructive and pathological.
Development of a general theory of conflict processes and conflict control
of this kind is one of the major interests of the Center for Research on
Conflict Resolution at the University of Michigan, not only because we
believe that the development of such a theory is a necessary prelude to the
building of institutions in international life which can give us a stable peace,
but also because we believe these processes are important to almost all
aspects of human life in organizations.

Four Basic Concepts of Conflict Theory

Four basic concepts of conflict theory can be outlined. There are
the parties to the conflict, the field of conflict, the dynamics of the conflict situation and the management and control of conflict.

(1) The Parties. There must, of course, be at least two parties
to conflict. Conflict also takes place between certain aspects of the person-

ality, or factions within the organization. Conflict, therefore, must always be visualized as a relationship between two parties, but the parties can be either persons, groups, or organizations, which gives us theoretically nine types of conflict ranging from the conflict of person against person to the conflict of organization against organization. There is some tendency for conflicts involving groups to pass over into conflicts involving organizations, as one of the impacts of conflict on an unorganized group is to push it towards organization. Thus, the group-organization conflict of, say, unorganized labor against a business firm, easily tends to pass over into an organization-organization conflict as the labor group becomes organized into a union.

(2) The Field of Conflict. The next concept is that of the field of conflict. This is an attempt to describe abstractly what conflict is about. The field of a conflict may be defined simply, for the sake of explanation, as the whole set of relevant possible states of the social system. (A relevant state, of course, is any state of the social system which either of the parties to a conflict considers to be relevant.) In the case of an industrial conflict relevance might consist, for instance, of all possible labor contracts in the given situation. We must now suppose that each party can order the field according to his own preferences, that is, that he can say of any two points in the field which one he prefers. This principle is illustrated in Table I.

Table I

Choices for Parties to a Conflict

	X_1	X_2	X_3	X_4	X_5
Party A	1	2	3	4	5
Party B	5	3	4	1	2

We suppose that X_1, X_2, X_3, X_4, X_5, are points in the field; that is, each one of them represents a specific position in the social system. We are assuming here, for purposes of explanation, that each party visualizes the social system in the same way. Under actual conditions people usually see such systems differently. To each of these points in the field we suppose that each party allocates a number as in Table I, the number being a

measure of preference for a position. We will also suppose that the
higher the number assigned the more preferable the position will be to
the party. For example, in Table I, Party A prefers the position X_5
to all others, B prefers the position X_1 to all others. Any set of numbers
would do here as long as they preserve the same rank order showing preference. We now define a move as a change in the social system from
one position to another. Inspecting Table I, we see that there are two kinds
of moves which can be made. One we shall call trading moves in which both
parties are better off. Thus, the move from X_2 to X_3 or the move from X_4
to X_5 moves both parties from a lower to a higher number, indicating that
both parties are better off. These are trading moves. By contrast a move
from X_1 to X_2 or from X_3 to X_4 may be called conflict moves in which one
party is better off and the other party is worse off. We may notice that a
conflict move may be transformed into a trading move by means of what
the game theorist delicately calls a "side-payment" or bribe. Thus if the
system is at X_2, B would like to go to X_1 but A would not. If B's gain in
going to X_1 is large enough, however, B may be able to bribe A to move to
X_1 as well. The bribe thus changes the conflict into a trading move. The
whole process of bargaining and negotiation involves the exploration of the
field of the social system in order to find what are the trading moves. Once
all trading moves are exhausted, however, we may be left with an irre-
ducible minimum of conflict. Whether under these circumstances a settlement is possible and whether, even if it is possible, it will be arrived at
depends on a great many subtle factors which involve a rather different
type of analysis.

(3) Dynamics of Conflict Situations. The third set of concepts involved in the theory of conflict relate to the dynamics of conflict situations.
In the simplest model we suppose that the field consists merely of the combination of the position of the two parties and we then suppose that each
party simply adjusts its own position to what it believes the position of the
other party to be.

Thus, let us suppose in Figure 8 that the only significant variable in
the conflict situation is the hostility of one party toward the other. We
measure A's hostility on OA and B's hostility along OB. We then suppose a
line $A_1 A_2$ which shows the level of A's hostility for each level of B's. We
similarly have a line $B_1 B_2$ which shows B's hostility for each level of A's.
In this case both parties are xenophobes because even when one party has
a zero hostility, the hostility of the other parties is positive. If the two
lines $A_1 A_2$ and $B_1 B_2$ intersect as they do in the Figure at E, there is a
position of equilibrium. If we suppose the system to move discontinuously,
then starting at O with B's hostility O, A will move to A_1 whereupon B will

Figure 8

Combination of the Hostility Position
of Two Parties

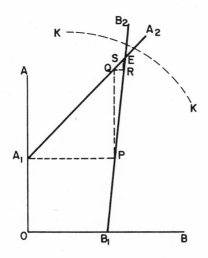

move to P, whereupon A will move to Q, whereupon B will move to R
and A to S and so we go on, approaching E all the time. I have called
these processes Richardson processes after Lewis F. Richardson who
first developed the systematic theory. They are to be observed in
many aspects of social life, in children's quarrels, in the estrangement of
husband and wife, in the buildup of mutual hostility in industrial relations
and, of course, in arms races in international relations.

These dynamic processes can often move the system in directions which might be called "negative trading," that is, to positions in which both parties are worse off than before. This is particularly likely to happen if the parties are short-sighted in their reactivity so that each reacts to the position of the other without reflecting how the other is going to react in turn. This is all too frequently the case in international relations. There is no necessity, of course, for dynamic conflict processes of this type to have any equilibrium at all. Thus, in Figure 8, if we bend the line $A_1 A_2$ towards A and the line B_1 to B_2 towards B we see that the point of equilibrium B will move outward and upward to higher and higher levels of hostility; that is, the more reactive the parties, the more hostile the equilibrium system. If the lines $\widehat{A_1 A_2}$ and $\widehat{B_1 B_2}$ become parallel or if they go beyond this and diverge, then no equilibrium is possible, for the parties simply become increasingly hostile until there is some kind of a breakdown in the system.

The notion of a system break is common to many forms of conflict. Thus verbal sparring sometimes leads to fisticuffs, family quarrels lead to separation or divorce, industrial conflicts lead to strikes, and international conflicts lead to war. This phenomenon can be represented in Figure 8, by a boundary such as the line KK. Between this boundary and the origin O, we have one kind of system; beyond the boundary we have another kind of system altogether. If, as in the figure, there is an equilibrium within the boundary, the system is stable. If, however, the equilibrium lies beyond the boundary the system is unstable and will proceed to the boundary and then transform itself. We have a good many interesting examples of what might be called alternating conflict systems. Occasionally married couples divorce and remarry, industrial relations proceed as a series of strike periods alternating with work periods, and in international relations we have what I have called elsewhere a diplomacy-war cycle which alternates between diplomacy and war and back again. This is the case where each system has an equilibrium on the other side of its boundary. Sometimes on the other hand the systems do not alternate and are thus simply destroyed. A couple divorces and never see each other again, the result of a strike is the bankruptcy of the firm or the destruction of the union, or the result of a war is the destruction of one or more of the warring nations.

(4) Conflict Management. The fourth set of concepts involves the management, control or resolution of conflict. A conflict system exhibits control if it has some sort of machinery for avoiding "pathological" moves. It is not always easy to define what is meant by a pathological move. An

"anti-trading" move is clearly pathological. The distinction, however, between pathological and non-pathological conflict moves is harder to draw. We cannot even assume that all moves which cross the system boundary are pathological or even that all alternating systems are pathological. A case can be made for some divorces and some strikes as being beneficial to both parties, though in these days it becomes harder and harder to make a case like this for war, which has become increasingly pathological. In any conflict field, however, it is not unreasonable to suppose that there is some boundary on the far side of which the system becomes pathological. A conflict system then exhibits control if it has an apparatus somewhere in the system which can "perceive" that the system is approaching the boundary of pathology and can then set forces in motion to reverse the movement of the system and pull it away from the boundary. This is an example of a familiar mechanism known as a cybernetic or homeostatic mechanism. Thus, in Figure 8, if we suppose that KK is the pathological boundary so that anything to the right and above this is pathological and anything below and to the left of it is not, then in the system as it stands there is no particular reason why the position of equilibrium E should be on one side of the boundary or on the other. With a control mechanism in the system, however, if E approaches the boundary, forces will be brought into play to bring it back into the non-pathological sector again.

Generally speaking these control mechanisms may be of two kinds, unilateral or organizational. We have unilateral conflict control when one of the parties deliberately manipulates its reaction processes in order to control the position of mutual equilibrium. This is the secret actually of a good deal of conflict control at the personal level. This is "peaceableness" in personal conduct. One suspects, indeed, that this lies at the bottom of a good deal of personnel management. In this world to a surprising extent the quarrelsome are manipulated into peace by the peaceable simply because the peaceable control their own reactions where the quarrelsome do not and the final position of equilibrium is determined by the reactivity of both the reaction functions.

Unilateral peaceableness may not always be adequate, however. As a machinery of conflict control it may become too costly for the peaceable, especially in the face of genuinely pathological behavior on the part of the non-peaceable. Under these circumstances organizational solutions must be found which in effect unite the two parties in a larger organization. This might be described as a political solution. This frequently involves the organization in a series of "side-payments" both positive and negative, which have the object of subsidizing virtue and penalizing vice, virtue and vice being defined in this connection as behavior leading towards or away from conflict resolution. The whole vast machinery of law, police and government can then be seen simply as an arrangement to implement this very simple rule.

A further aspect of the organization of conflict control is mediation. This essentially involves operating on the image of the field of the two parties in such a way that in the first place opportunities or trading moves are perceived which otherwise might not have been perceived and in the second place solutions might be given an acceptability simply by being suggested by the mediator and hence acquiring a degree of saliency which is important in making them mutually acceptable. One party often finds it difficult to accept a proposal suggested by an opposing party, whereas if the same proposal is suggested by a neutral mediator, it can be accepted without difficulty.

Applications of Conflict Theory to Organizational Theory

The theory of conflict as outlined above has important applications to the theory of organization and to the management of organizations. In the first place organizations exhibit within their own structure all types of conflict processes which have been outlined above. Organizations always contain subgroups and suborganizations, divisions and departments which are likely to exhibit conflict processes between them. The hierarchical structure of organizations can largely be interpreted as a device for the resolution of conflicts, with each grade of the hierarchy specializing in resolving the conflicts of the grade beneath it. The very structure of an organization can be regarded as a "constitution," a constitution being defined as a previously agreed method of resolving conflicts which have not yet arisen. We can go even further and argue that virtually all organizational decisions are the end product of a process of conflict resolution between the points of view of various sections and departments. Thus, in a business the production department, sales department and the finance department often have very different points of view, and when final decisions have to be made they must reconcile these various positions, that is, be at least satisfying enough to the various parties so that they will continue to work and to cooperate.

The conflict resolution aspect of organizations underlines the extreme importance of what might be called "integrative" function, especially at the top-most levels of the hierarchy. This is the function of creating an atmosphere in which there is a will to resolve conflicts. Inside organizations as between organizations, the successful resolution of conflict almost always involves a combination of unilateral and organizational methods. Unless an

organization has "peacemakers" inside it, that is, persons who are capable
of unilateral conflict resolution, it is unlikely to operate successfully. On
the other hand an organization which has no adequate organizational apparatus
for resolving conflicts will find itself placing too much burden upon the peacemakers, and may easily destroy itself by factional dispute. It will be extremely interesting to study the extent to which the failure of organizations is a
result of their inability to provide for the essential function of conflict resolution, either through organizational machinery or through the development
of a general high morale and integrated spirit through the encouragement of
peacemaking personalities. It is clear that theory of conflict has an important
role to play, both in the theoretical and empirical study of the organization,
and it should be of particular interest to the student of the business firm.

THE U.S. AND REVOLUTION

In: *The U.S. and Revolution*. Santa Barbara,
Calif.: Center for the Study of Democratic
Institutions, 1961, pp. 4-7

THE U.S.
AND
REVOLUTION_____

THE American attitude toward revolution has all the ambivalence, so beloved of the psychologist, of our attitude toward our mothers. This, of course, is because the United States as a nation was born in a revolution, which one might describe, I suppose, as an adolescent revolt. Consequently, we feel a certain obligation to like revolution on principle, having been born in one ourselves. On the other hand, we are also afraid and suspicious of revolutions. This, no doubt, can be traced back to a suppressed guilt feeling about the treachery to a parent culture which any revolution implies. Our attitude toward revolution, therefore, is a compound feeling of both love and hate, affectionate regard for the infants toddling in our early footsteps and unresolved guilt about our own breakaway.

The explanation of this ambivalence does not, of course, necessarily have to be psychoanalytic, for there are perfectly sober, rational reasons both for welcoming revolutions and for fearing them. Revolutions may get out of hand and they may turn out to be the wrong revolution. The world is haunted today by the specters of past revolutions, like past noises echoing through the corridors of the present. The French Revolution, which consists essentially in the dispossession of large landowners and the division of land among small peasants, and which, in one of its aspects at least, has been called the "green revolution," continues to explode in countries which have not yet relieved themselves of the feudal landlord and the large estate. The American Revolution, which represents the breakaway of the colonies from a metropolitan power, continues its interesting, if erratic, course, and is at the moment exploding in Africa. The Russian Revolution, which represents the dispossession of *all* capitalists and the seizure of political and economic power by a small and determined group of Communists, continued to roll pretty vigorously just after the end of the second World War, and although it has been temporarily checked it remains a constant threat.

The tendency for one kind of revolution to pass into another is at least great enough to make it hard to select the precise revolution which one wants. Under these circumstances, there is a tendency to shore up the *status quo* and to prevent *any* revolution on the grounds that no revolution is better than the wrong revolution. This, however, is a rearguard action, almost certain to lead to ultimate defeat. Once revolutions are on the march, they have to be dealt with one way or another. And in one sense the only answer to the wrong revolution is the right revolution.

A further source of confusion is that it is not always easy to tell when a real revolution has occurred. Revolution is a "system change"; a social system with certain dynamic processes of its own reaches a boundary at some date and a new social system with new laws and a new dynamic takes over. Sometimes these boundaries are dramatic and visible. The French, American, and Russian revolutions are examples of such. Sometimes, however, the boundaries are not observable. The revolution, like the turn of the tide, is unnoticed at the moment but carries with it a profound reversal of the great tide of history. The industrial and technical revolution in which we are now living was one such. It is practically impossible to put a date on it. It was inaugurated by no violence and no fanfare. We can trace its origins perhaps as far back as the Benedictines of the sixth century A.D. The movement is slow and uncertain, however, until the seventeenth and eighteenth centuries. Then it becomes clear that man is caught up in a new tide which is carrying him he knows not whither. The three types of political revolution may perhaps ultimately be seen as mere eddies in this vast tide. Nevertheless, they are still important in the small time perspective in which most human decisions have to be made.

W E can neither perceive nor judge change in systems unless we have some theory about the dynamics of social systems. There are a good many such theories around, some of them explicit, some of them largely implicit and unformulated. Two such implicit theories guide a good deal of American thinking.

The first of these might be the cowboy theory. This is the theory that people are divided into good guys and bad guys, and that the business of a revolution is to get the bad guys out and the good guys in. It is not always easy to tell the good guys from the bad guys, but, of course, if any guys happen to be on Our Side, they are obviously good, and any guys that happen to be on the Other Side are obviously bad. A good revolution is one in which the good guys beat up the bad guys and a bad revolution is one in which the bad guys beat up the good guys. If there is a good deal of shouting, shooting, and running around going on, preferably on horses, the scenario is regarded as all the more satisfactory.

A somewhat more sophisticated version of the cowboy theory is the Liberty Bell or Independence Hall theory. This is the theory that the dynamics of a society depends upon its political constitution and that if only the right political constitution can be established all will be well. Societies are divided into those which have good constitutions (like ours) and those which have bad constitutions (unlike ours). A good revolution, then, is one that substitutes a good constitution for a bad one and a bad revolution is the reverse. Unfortunately for this theory, the slavish copying of the American constitution, especially by South American republics, does not seem to have resulted in uniformly satisfactory development either economic or political. And one suspects that more variables in the social system have to be taken into account.

At the level of sophisticated, explicit social theory, we seem to have two main contenders. On the one hand, there is the Malthusian theory of the classical economics which Baumol has described as the "magnificent dynamics." This states, in effect, that in the long run the only revolution that is really worth having is one that nobody has yet succeeded in accomplishing. This is establishment of a genuine population control. In the absence of this all revolutions will lead ultimately to the same ruin and the "dismal theorem" casts its long shadow over history. The dismal theorem is the proposition that if the only thing that can prevent the indefinite expansion of population is starvation and misery then all populations will expand until they are miserable and starve. A corollary is what I have called "the utterly dismal theorem." This is the proposition that if misery is the only ulitmate check on the growth of population, any improvement in man's capacities, whether in the form of technological inventors or in the form of social inventions, merely has the ultimate result of enabling a larger population than before to live in misery. Improvement, therefore, leads to more misery not to less. We should not be deluded by temporary food surpluses into thinking that the Malthusian specter has been allayed. At present rates of increase it only takes about 700 years before we have standing-room only. Long before this time either the Malthusian revolution will have been accomplished or mankind will have sunk into a world of inconceivably teeming poverty.

The other system of explicit social dynamics is that of Marx, which perhaps we should designate out of respect for its New Testament as Marxism-Leninism. The theory is elaborate and fairly familiar and I will not outline it here. It contemplates the establishment of a rich and classless society by the expropriation of the capitalist and socialization of all property in the means of production. The actual predictions of Marx have, of course, been largely falsified by subsequent events, but this does not destroy the power of the theory. It has a peculiar fascination for poor countries which see in it a dream of controlling their own economic destiny. Its political and human costs, however, are high. It involves a gross centralization of power and is constantly exposed to the danger of tyranny.

B UT there is a type of revolution which does not fit comfortably into any of the above categories and which may be the most important of all in the long run. I call it the "Fomentarian revolution" in honor of a remarkable institution in Puerto Rico which embodies it, known as "Fomento." The Fomentarian revolution has four aspects. Its prerequisite is some kind of political consensus in the society. It cannot develop if a society is wracked with internal conflicts and factional fights, whether these are between races, cultures, classes, or political groups. There must be some widely shared vision of the future and an image of the way in which the society can move towards its future. This usually has to be the work of a charismatic leader who can inspire large numbers of people with a vision of the future. Sometimes a succession of leadership is required. The charismatic but unrealistic leader may awake the people out of their apathy and give them a sense of identity and purpose. For the revolution to be accomplished, however, a new type of leadership may be necessary—more sober, less dramatic, and with a clearer and more realistic vision.

The second pillar of the Fomentarian revolution is the stress that it lays on education and the development of human resources. If necessary, a society must be prepared to accept some sacrifice of quality in education in the interests of quantity. The developing society not only requires literacy of the mass of the people, it requires a certain type of moral education in inculcating a favorable attitude toward work and austerity and it requires technical education appropriate to the modern world. Higher education of the right kind occupies a key position in this process.

The third pillar of the Fomentarian revolution is the skill to strike clever bargains with foreign capitalists. Genuinely bootstrap development is possible, as the history of Japan showed. The development of Japan came almost wholly from internal reorganization and by the acquisition of knowledge rather than capital from abroad. For this recipe to be successful, however, a fairly authoritarian social structure seems to be necessary. Whether this is feudal as in the case of Japan, or Communist as in the case of China, bootstrap development means holding down consumption, holding down real wages, and squeezing the farmer as hard as he can be squeezed in order to extract every last ounce of subsistence for capital accumulation. In looser and more democratic societies this is hard to achieve. It is hard to resist the clamor of the people for a present share of future benefits. Under these circumstances it is hard to keep real wages from rising, which means it is hard to keep consumption from rising, which means it is hard to keep production ahead of consumption, which means it is hard to accumulate. Under these circumstances a

careful use of foreign investment seems almost necessary. If the investor can be rewarded with friendly attitudes and with long-term security, the recipient society will not have to pay so much hard cash. With an unfriendly and querulous attitude, on the other hand, foreign investment can only be attracted at a high price. The ability to make good bargains with foreign investors is a very important element in the success of the Fomentarian society.

The fourth pillar of Fomentarianism is the most difficult of all to establish. This is the ability to effect a sufficient cultural change at the level of the individual, the family, the neighborhood, and the small group so that the gains of development can be reasonably permanent and acceptable to the society. This brings us back to Malthus, for unless the revolution encompasses some kind of control of the population the revolution is doomed to failure. The control may simply be the ability to emigrate in the case of Puerto Rico. This, however, is a solution which is not open to the world at large, and it cannot be regarded as permanent. Nevertheless, the ability to emigrate from an already over-populated area may be the key, paradoxically enough, to a process of development which will eventually enable it to support a much larger population.

If a society is to enter the modern world, there must also be changes in the attitudes toward the family, toward work, and toward income and saving. All these changes, perhaps, may be summed up by saying that the transition from the traditional culture to what we call an "economic culture" will have to be made. In this process something inevitably is lost. One hopes that the gains are worth the cost.

WHEN we ask where is the Great Revolution taking us, the revolution that is science and technology, the answer may emerge that the end product of this revolution does not depend as much as we thought on the means which are used or the road which is followed. If one presses the Communists on what they mean by communism—that is, that ideal state of society toward which they hope they are moving, and which they do not now claim to have—the pat answer is, of course, that communism is a society in which we have "from each according to his ability and to each according to his needs." If they are pressed further on who is to be the judge of need and ability, the answer seems to be that, subject to the socializing forces of the society, the individual is to be his own judge. Certainly no dictator can judge either the need or the ability of the innumerable variety of men. This means, therefore, that in this ideal world people will decide what standard of life they wish to adopt and then go out and earn the kind of income which enables them to support it. We are getting closer and closer to this in the United States. What the Communists mean by communism, therefore, turns out to be surprisingly like that affluent society which is also the end of capitalist development.

The situation is somewhat confused at the moment by the fact that while we have examples of both successful and unsuccessful capitalist development, there are, as yet, no clearly unsuccessful examples of socialist development. This, I suspect, is because socialism is young. Given time, it will have no lack of failure. The crucial long-run question, therefore, for any community may not be whether it takes the capitalist or the socialist road to development. The question is whether its development is suc-

cessful or unsuccessful in either system. The good revolution, whatever it is, is that which leads to a successful process of development. The bad revolution is that which does not. It may be, therefore, that we should be more relaxed about the political form under which development takes place, and more concerned that, under any form, the development should be successful.

The great case for Fomentarian development where circumstances are such that it can be successful is that it can also be fairly cheap. Socialist development is obtained at a terrible cost. Capitalist non-development likewise has a high cost in benefits foregone. We should look carefully at those social processes, as exemplified in Puerto Rico, that seem to make the best of both worlds, that use both government and private enterprise, both domestic reorganization and foreign investment, and that foment rather than whip. These are the kinds of revolution that one would like to see us encourage.

IS PEACE RESEARCHABLE?

Continuous Learning, 1, 2 (Mar.-Apr. 1962): 63-69

IS PEACE RESEARCHABLE?

In the last few years there has developed in the United States, and to a smaller extent in Canada and some other countries, something which might be called a peace research movement. It is still very small though its pace is accelerating. It may turn out to be one of the most significant movements of our day. It is reflected in the work of such institutions as the Center for Research on Conflict Resolution at the University of Michigan, the Institute for International Order in New York, the Center for World Peace Through World Law at Duke University, the programs in international relations at Northwestern and at Stanford, the work of a handful of individuals up and down the country and finally, the new Peace Research Institute headed by Ambassador Wadsworth in Washington. The break in the clouds is no bigger than a man's hand, but it is a break and it may grow.

The crucial question, however, which confronts this movement is the title of this paper: is peace researchable? Research has become a catchword for this generation. We spend enormous sums on it, especially for war. It sometimes seems as if we believe that research can solve all things and answer all questions. If we define "research" as the organized search for knowledge, the question of the limits of this search and the limits of human knowledge may be important. There may be some things which by nature are not researchable; there may be other things which we feel it is indecent or immoral to research, and there remains, of course, the large area where knowledge can be pursued fruitfully and without shame. In a day when peace is a matter of life or death for most of us, it is a crucial question as to which of these three categories the problem of peace belongs.

We must admit, I think, that there are areas of human life which are almost by definition not researchable. A good example of this would be the Catholic doctrine of the transubstantiation of the elements in the Mass. The doctrine is, we recall, that it is the substance, not the accidents, or physical properties of the elements that are transformed, and that it is only the accidents that are subject to empirical test. Hence, by very definition, the doctrine itself cannot be tested empirically. It might be possible, of course, to test certain effects on human life and behavior of belief in the doctrine, but then we would be testing the belief, not the doctrine. Peace is clearly not in this category of the unresearchable by definition, unless we define "peace" in *Newspeak* as equivalent to war, or as equivalent to anything which our own country does.

There may be some who would argue that peace falls in the second category, of things that should not be researched. They may argue with Bismark that perpetual peace is a dream and not even a beautiful dream. Because stable peace may involve social costs, that is, the giving up of institutions, ideas, and habits to which we are attached and to which, perhaps, we attach some absolute value, it may be argued that even to investigate the conditions of stable peace is improper and that such an activity threatens morality and patriotism and perhaps even religion. Against this argument it is sufficient to point out that war has completely changed its character because of the development of the new weapons. The classical concepts of national defense and of a system in which, by increasing the resources devoted to defense, a nation might increase its security, has collapsed about our ears. Defense has passed into deterrence which is a totally different and much less manageable system. In a very real sense peace has become the only national defense that makes any sense. Under these circumstances the moral arguments against peace research fall to the ground.

There remains a more subtle argument. It may be admitted that the problem of stable peace belongs to the empirical world and that in theory, therefore, it can be researched. In practice, however, it may be argued that the social systems of which stable peace is a property are so complex and their parameters change so rapidly that it is not possible to find out enough about them to make it worthwhile inquiring into them. It may be argued, then, that even though peace is in theory researchable, in practice we do not have the methods by which we can advance our knowledge in this direction. The criticism is not entirely pointless. It is true that peace is a property of social systems and especially of international systems, and that these are unstable in the sense that the parameters which guide their movement are subject to rapid change. We can find out about the physical world because its parameters are extraordinarily constant; at any one spot on the earth, for instance, the gravitational constant obligingly remains at about thirty-two feet per second, day in and day out. If the gravitational constant were subject to rapid and unpredictable change, we would have great difficulty in adjusting ourselves to it. We would find it extremely difficult to learn, for instance, how to perform such a simple act as getting out of bed in the morning. On Monday morning g might be very small and our effort to get out of bed would send us flying through the opened window. On Tuesday morning g might be large and, in trying to get out of bed, we would merely fall with a dull thud on the floor. It would not only be hard to learn how to behave under such circumstances, it would be extremely hard to develop scientific knowledge. In social systems it can be argued that we are in precisely this fix. The instability of the parameters makes it extremely difficult not only to obtain practical knowledge of how to operate in social systems, with the result that we constantly make appalling mistakes, but also makes it virtually impossible to attain scientific knowledge of them.

This, however, is a counsel of despair. If we do not have an adequate methodology, and we do not, the answer is not to abandon the problem but to search for new methods. To return to our gravitational analogy, if man were in the fix mentioned above, he could, perhaps, devise a little device by his bedside which would inform him as he started to get out of bed roughly what to expect. He could then summon all his forces for a flying leap when his gravimeter told him that g was high and he could coordinate his muscles with extreme delicacy and lightness when the same instrument informed him that g was low. Similarly with social systems, it is the inconstancy of these systems which demands research, that is, which demands refinements in the rapid gathering, processing, and interpretation of information about them. When social systems are apt to be changing, we cannot learn to operate them simply by the knowledge acquired from our past crude experience or "common sense." Only when social systems are reasonably stable, can we rely on common sense, just as we learn to operate in a world with a constant gravitational constant without most of us having the slightest idea of what that gravitational constant is. In stable systems science is not necessary for human behavior; in unstable systems it is.

I am not arguing that we can know everything about social systems; indeed, I think we cannot know everything even about physical systems, especially when our knowledge and information processes become part of the system itself. The Heisenberg principle which plagues the physicist only in very small systems like the electron where the information process is of the same magnitude as the system itself, plagues the social scientist in all his work. A reputable economist can hardly make a prediction without changing the future. A good questionnaire changes the person who answers it. A theory about international relations will change international relations itself. We do not have to know everything about a system, however, to know how to operate it. It is possible to obtain practical knowledge of complex and indeterminate systems and it is possible to know a great deal more about social systems than we now know. There is a great deal here that we don't know that does hurt us.

The first requirement of peace research, therefore, is the identification of the system of which peace is a property. We shall find, of course, that there are many concepts of peace and that there are many systems that have these properties. Roughly, however, we may say that peace is a property of conflict systems and that it is a homeostatic or cybernetic property which enables the system, in the course of its dynamic path, to remain in some stated boundary. Where the boundary is drawn is not so important as the machinery by which the system stays within it wherever it is drawn. Most conflict systems exhibit what might be called a "Break boundary" at which the system suddenly changes into another or passes some point of no return in its dynamic processes. Thus, marital conflict may lead to separation or divorce, industrial conflict may lead to strikes, personal conflicts may lead to fisticuffs at the lower end of the social scale or to litigation at the upper end, and international relations may degenerate into war. One concept of peace would be that of a conflict system in which an approach towards the break boundary was registered somewhere in the system, whether by the parties in the conflict themselves or by a third party, and in which this perception set in force processes by which the dynamic course of the conflict might be deflected from the boundary. This may be too narrow a concept of peace; we may feel that some divorces, some strikes, and some wars are allowable within the framework of the system and, hence, we draw the peace boundary somewhere beyond the break boundary. Wherever we draw the boundary, however, there is no peace unless there is an apparatus to draw the dynamic course of the conflict away from the boundary once it begins to approach it dangerously. In this sense, peace is a perfectly definable property of social systems and there are many social systems which do not possess it in which the dynamics of the conflict process possesses no boundary-avoiding element and in which, therefore, the conflict process sooner or later must go over the boundary. It is the peculiar urgency of our present social system that, while in most countries internal conflicts possess fairly adequate-boundary control, in international systems we do not have anything of the kind that is at all adequate. Hence, we find ourselves today running like the Gadarene swine to destruction without any apparatus for calling halt or reversing the process.

Once the concept has been defined, the next step is the development of an information-processing system which is adequate to tell us at least the direction in which the conflict system is moving and roughly how far it is from the boundary that we wish to avoid. In the economic system we have achieved something like this in the form of national income statistics; whereas, in 1931, it was still possible to argue whether or not there was a depression; today, if a downturn lasts, for even two or three months, this information is obtained by an elaborate process of condensation of great masses of economic information and the condensed and significant information is rapidly available to the policy-makers. In the international system we have no such apparatus; we have instead a process of information collection and condensation which has corruption built into it. The diplomat, by reason of the restricted circles in which he moves and the imperfect nature of his sampling, is almost guaranteed to develop misinformation about the country in which he is stationed and he faithfully transmits this misinformtaion back to his headquarters where it then becomes the basis of policy. Intelligence agencies, likewise, by reason of their secrecy and their value systems are virtually designed to produce misinformation. Under these circumstances, it is not surprising that the international system works so badly. Actions designed to produce a certain effect abroad may produce quite opposite effects and we therefore easily work ourselves into dynamic processes from which there seems to be no escape and in which we all move from situations that are better to situations that are worse. International relations is a magnificent example of what might be called "anti-bargaining" dynamics. In a bargain we move from one situation into another in which all parties are better off than they were before. In anti-bargaining dynamics we move from one situation into another in which all parties are worse off than they were before. In economics we do this in depressions and in international relations we do it in the movement towards war. In an international system which has the property of stable peace, it is necessary to be able to perceive movements towards war in their early stages and to reverse them before they get too far to be reversed. One of the first priorities of peace research, then, is the development of an information-processing system in the field of international relations which can perform somewhat the same role that the Department of Commerce does in its development of national income statistics. This information-processing agency would proceed mainly by statistical analysis of economic and political data; it would devote itself to the content analysis of the world press and radio and it would undoubtedly also use the method of survey research. The operation would be expensive but it would have an enormous rate of return.

At the level of the individual scholar and researcher or the small research group, there is an enormous amount that needs to be done. There is great need, for instance, for the further development of theoretical systems in this field. A beginning has already been made in the work of men like T. C. Schelling and Morton Kaplan. The theory of conflict systems and especially of what might be called "threat systems" which are highly characteristic of military relations, and indeed, the theory of military relations in general, is still in its infancy. Its Copernicus, its Newton, or its Keynes are still to come. If the best minds of our day are not engaged in this task, this is simply evidence of our total lack of a sense of intellectual priority.

Around the main intellectual task there are a great many subordinate tasks which can support it and work towards it. Stable peace, fortunately, is not an unknown system; it is not something which lies wholly in the future. In a great many sub-systems of the world society, it already exists and it can be studied with all the methods of empirical research. Studies of industrial peace already exist and it is, perhaps, in industrial relations that the study of conflict processes and of stable peace has proceeded the furthest. There are many instances of stable peace, however, in international relations; there are, for instance, the relations of the Scandinavian countries among themselves and the relations of the United States and Canada. Here we have an example of sovereign states in stable peace. This is the world system which, at the moment, it seems most feasible to work towards. If stable peace cannot be bought at a price less than world government, our case is probably desperate. For this is coin that the human race, in its present divided state, does not seem to have. If stable peace can be found consistent with national sovereignty, its price is much less and we may be able to bargain for it. It is desperately necessary, therefore, to study these cases to see what exactly they entail. I suspect that we shall find that in each case what has happened is that a threat system, in which peace is almost of necessity unstable and which has virtually no dynamic apparatus for preventing the crossing of the war boundary, has slowly given place to another kind of system of complex trade and communications in which the threat becomes buried so far beneath the other relationships that it ceases virtually to have any significance. The problem of how we move from threat systems into stable peace systems is, I think, the number one problem of our day; indeed, the solution to this is the prerequisite to all our other problems. We can, I think, learn a great deal about this process by the systematic study of cases in which it has occurred.

Another important element in the present difficulties which can be studied in smaller systems and in historical cases is the dynamics of ideological conflict. There are many examples in history in which an ideological conflict, which at one time had no boundary conditions, over the course of time develops these boundaries and, hence, does not threaten the stability of peace. A good example of this is the series of religious wars that followed the Reformation and which came to an end in 1648 at the Peace of Westphalia. The ideological split between Protestants and Catholics was, I suspect, just as large and aroused just as much bitterness and hatred as the present split between East and West. If the old ideological struggle could pass from a war system into a peace system, the present ideological struggle can do so too. Something which desperately needs to be done at the moment is the study of these past settlements. This is a task which for some reason neither the historians nor the social scientists seem willing to undertake.

Another line of investigation which is already going forward at Stanford under the direction of Dr North is the careful study of the dynamics of the communication process in international relations. The Stanford group is subjecting the months that preceded outbreak of the First World War to a meticulous and microscopic analysis with a view to finding out what were the processes in the international system that produced a war which was a disadvantage to all. Another line of approach is that represented by Professor Richard Snyder at Northwestern University in his studies of the decision-making process in international relations. Still another line of attack is the study of the institutions of world law directed by Dr Arthur Larsen at Duke University. Alongside with these approaches goes the study of the technical problems involved in arms control, disarmament, and inspection. We desperately need, for instance, a study of the sociology of inspection. Inspection in one form or another pervades our whole society. We have income tax inspectors, food and drug inspectors, railroad inspectors, and so on; yet no one has ever studied the impact of all this inspection on the society in which it is embedded. Until we know more about inspections as a general phenomenon, we shall probably not get very far with disarmament negotiations. Another social process which desperately needs study is the negotiation process itself. Here, again, we have a mass of data and information from almost all areas of social life which we have not yet digested and reduced to transmittable knowledge.

These are but samples of a vast field of study which is relevant to the establishment of stable peace in all our various social systems and especially in the international system where war is threatening to destroy us. How can we explain that, at a time like this, we do not pursue these studies? The answer, I think, is two-fold. First, because we are a warlike people that has established a highly successful nation by a process of aggression against weak enemies. We have a moral repugnance to a type of research which seems to be based on premises which are inconsistent with our national character. In the second place, we do not properly identify the system in which our problem lies. The problem of stable peace is a problem in social systems, yet we persist in trying to solve it as if it were a problem in physical systems, in weapons, in armament, and in things which are merely the parameters of social systems. We have a prejudice, perhaps, against scientific research into social systems because we feel that we understand them already, that all we need is the wisdom of the politician or the diplomat or the State Department official. Unfortunately, the systems have been changing too rapidly for wisdom, for wisdom is based upon the experience of earlier years, and the system of earlier years on which this wisdom is based has totally passed away. In a period of rapid system change there is no substitute for science, and in the rapid change of social system there is no substitute for social science.

THE PREVENTION OF WORLD WAR III

Virginia Quarterly Review, 38, 1
(Winter 1962): 2-12

THE PREVENTION OF WORLD WAR III

WHEN we talk about preventing something we imply two things. We imply, first, that there is a dynamic system which is now proceeding that, if allowed to proceed unchanged, will result in an event which is regarded as undesirable and which, therefore, we want to prevent. We imply also that it is possible to change the dynamic system in question and replace it by another dynamic system in which the unwanted event does not occur. Thus, suppose we find ourselves driving towards a railroad crossing and suddenly we see the red lights flashing and a train approaching. Our dynamic system at the moment consists simply of velocity and direction. We are proceeding, say at 50 miles per hour, towards the crossing. The distant early warning system of our eyes informs us the crossing is dangerous. The knowledge which we have of our existing dynamic system informs us that if it continues we will arrive at the crossing at the precise moment when the train is there. The combination of a distant information system coupled with the simple dynamics of automobiles enables us, however, to prevent the disaster. We do this by putting on the brakes long before we get to the crossing. This in effect changes the dynamic system under which we have been operating. It introduces a new variable into it, indeed a new dimension, deceleration. Because of this, we are able to prevent the disaster, as we are able to avoid simultaneous occupancy of the crossing by ourselves and the train.

We must be careful, of course, in applying the analogy of a simple psycho-mechanical system like a man driving a car to the enormous complexities and uncertainties of the international system. However, the international system is still a system, even though it has important random elements in it. Because it is not entirely random, it has elements of predictability. One of the greatest difficulties lies precisely in the stochastic nature of the system. We are driving a car, as it were, that may or may not respond to brakes according to whether dice held by the driver indicate "respond" or "fail." The situation is made all the more difficult by the fact that we face here a stochastic system with a very small universe, that is, a very small number of cases. Stochastic systems with a large number of cases can be treated by the theory of probability. We have a pretty fair idea, for instance, how many people are going to die in automobile accidents next year, although we do not know exactly who they are.

The problem of reducing the total number of automobile accidents is a very different kind of problem from the one that faces the driver of the preceding paragraph. Nevertheless, even with our present knowledge it would not be difficult to design an automobile and a road system which would kill, let us say, 20,000 people a year instead of 40,000. What we would be doing here would be to reduce the probability of disaster on the part of a single individual. It is by no means impossible to think of the international system in a rather similar way, and to talk about the things we can do to reduce the probability of disaster. What we mean by this is that if we had a very large number of planets roughly identical with our own we could postulate changes in the system which would reduce the number of cases in which disaster occurred. This would be the analogue of treating road deaths as a public health problem and seeking to reduce their probability. As far as we know, however, we do not have a large number of planets like ours and for our purposes at least there is only one. Hence, reducing the probability of disaster does us very little good if the disaster actually occurs. The problem of stochastic systems with a small number of cases has received insufficient attention in the theoretical literature. It is precisely this kind of system, however, with which we have to deal in international affairs.

I believe the present international system to be one which has a significant probability built into it of irretrievable disaster for the human race. The longer the number of years we contemplate such a system operating, the larger this probability becomes. I do not know whether in any one year it is one per cent, ten per cent, or even fifty per cent. I feel pretty

sure, however, that it is of this order of magnitude, not, shall
we say, of the order of magnitude of .01 per cent. The problem of system change, therefore, is urgent and desperate, and
we are all in terrible danger. This is largely because of a
quantitative change in the parameters of the international
system under which we now live. This is still essentially the
system of unilateral national defense in spite of the development of the United Nations and certain international organizations. Unilateral national defense is workable only if each
nation can be stronger than its potential enemies in its home
territory. This is possible under two circumstances. The first
is that the nations must be far enough away from each other,
and the extent to which their power declines as they operate
further away from their own home bases must be sufficiently
great. Then each nation can be stronger than the other *at
home* with on-the-spot forces because of the fact that in a
nation's home territory the enemy operates at a certain disadvantage. There is a second condition, however, which is
that each nation must be able to dominate an area around its
home base equal in depth to the range of the deadly missile.
Because of quantitative changes in these conditions even in
the last few years the system of unilateral national defense
has become infeasible on a world scale. No nation is now far
enough away from potential enemies to be sure that it can
dominate even its own territory. Furthermore, the range of
the deadly missile is rapidly reaching 12,500 miles, which
means that the second condition cannot possibly be fulfilled.
The condition which unilateral national defense attempts to
establish, therefore, which I call *unconditional viability,* is
now no longer possible.

The urgent and desperate nature of the present situation
is created by the universality of the disaster with which we are
threatened. The system of unilateral national defense has
never given permanent security. The rise and fall of nations
and empires is a testament to this fact. Indeed, looking with
a large historical eye, one may say that unconditional viability has never existed except perhaps for brief periods and
the best that unilateral national defense could do for any society was to postpone disaster. The situation of the individual

society, that is, is rather analogous to that of the individual, whose life, on this earth at any rate, must also end in irretrievable disaster, that is, in death. Where we have a large number of individuals, however, death for the individual is not death for the race. In fact death for the individual is necessary if the race is to survive. Where the number of individuals becomes smaller and smaller, however, there comes to be a critical point where death for the individual is also death for the race and the irretrievable disaster which the individual suffers is likewise irretrievable disaster for the species. The unilaterally defended national state now seems to me to have got to this state in its development. It is no longer appropriate as a form of organization for the kind of technical society in which we live. Its death throes, however, may destroy the whole human race. The age of civilization out of which we are passing was characterized by a large number of nationstates or independent political organizations practicing unilateral national defense. Because of the large number of these organizations there were always some being born and always some ready to rise into the places of those which suffered disaster. With the number of effectively independent nationstates now reduced to two or perhaps at most three, the possibilities of irretrievable disaster become much greater.

The problem which we face, therefore, is how to effect a system change in the international order, or perhaps we should say the world political order, sufficient to lower the probability of disaster to a tolerable level. The critical problem here might be described as that of "system perception." To revert again to the analogy of the car and the railroad crossing, if the driver of the car does not see that he is approaching the crossing, if the warning lights are not working, and if he cannot see the train approaching, he will naturally not take any steps to avert the disaster. The world problem here is perhaps psychological rather than mechanical. There is a fairly widespread sense abroad of impending doom. The doom, however, is so large that we do not really believe it and we go about our daily actions as if it did not exist. This is the mechanism, as Jerome Frank has pointed out, known to the psychologists as "denial." Up to a point this is

actually healthy. We all know that we are going to die sometime and we may die tomorrow; but we act pretty much as
if we are going to live forever. We do not spend much time in
taking tearful farewells and in writing our last wills and tes-
taments. We plan ahead for months and even for years, in
spite of the fact that these plans may never come to fruition.
This perfectly legitimate response to uncertainty becomes
pathological when it prevents us from taking steps which
would postpone disaster or make it less likely. The man who
is afraid that he has a cancer but who will not go to a doctor
because he might find out that he has one is a good example.
Where the prospect of disaster, therefore, is so vague or so
uncertain that it merely results in pathological denial, it is
necessary to bring the actor to a more realistic appraisal of the
system within which he is acting.

If the problem of "denial" is to be overcome, it is necessary
to do more than merely scare people with horrendous pictures
of the possible future. Indeed, the more horrendous the picture which is drawn, the more it is likely to result in denial
and pathological inactivity. The future which faced our
driver at the railroad crossing was also horrendous, but instead of denying this and continuing on his way he presumably applied the brakes, that is, initiated a system change. The
problem in the international system is that we seem to have
no brakes. That is, it is hard for people to visualize the nature
of the system change which is necessary for survival. This,
then, is one of the major tasks today of the political scientist,
the philosopher, the journalist, and the prophet: to give the
people an image of changes in the international system which
seems small enough to be feasible yet large enough to be successful. It is not useful to picture Utopias which seem utterly
unattainable—this perhaps is the main difficulty with the
World Federationists—even though the function of Utopias
in providing a constant driving force in social dynamics
should not be underestimated. The present situation, however, calls not for Utopia, but for political solutions. Indeed,
one of our great difficulties today is that we have too many
Utopias. We need to think, therefore, in terms of a world social contract: that is, a minimum bargain between the con-

tending parties which will give the world a sufficient system change to relieve it from the intolerable burden which it now bears. This social contract does not even have to be explicit or contractual. It can begin by being tacit; indeed, one can argue that a world social contract already exists in a tacit embryo form. We can visualize perhaps the following five stages of development.

I. The stage of tacit contract. In systems which have an inherent instability, such as duopoly in the relations of firms, or a bipolar system of mutual deterrence in the relations of states, it is often possible to maintain a quasi-stable position for a long time through tacit contract: that is, through mutually consistent unilateral behavior on the part of each party. A quasi-stable position is like that of an egg on a golf-tee—it is stable for small disturbances but not for large. For considerable periods of time, however, the disturbances may be small enough so that Humpty-Dumpty does not fall. Comes a slightly larger disturbance, however, and all the King's horses and men cannot put him together again. The international system under the Eisenhower administration exhibited this kind of quasi-stability. An important element in that stability was a tacit agreement between the United States and the Soviet Union to do nothing effective about civil defense. We agreed, in effect, that our civilian populations should be mutually exchanged as hostages, for we each had the power to destroy large numbers—at least half—of each other's civilians. This meant that the chance of deliberate nuclear war was very small, though the chance of accidental war was appreciable; indeed, the missiles almost went off on at least two occasions. A natural accident, such as a large meteor, or an electronic breakdown, or a social accident, such as a mad pilot, or a political accident, such as an unwise commitment to an irresponsible third party, could under these circumstances easily set off a mutual exchange of nuclear weapons, so that the system could not be regarded as more than a temporary expedient.

Another example of tacit contract was the mutual suspension of nuclear tests, recently broken by the Soviet Union. Here the fear, perhaps, of world opinion, and the fear also of the technical consequences of an uncontrolled race for technical development of weapons, created a temporary tacit agreement. We have had similar tacit agreements in regard to spheres of influence and intervention in third-party quarrels. The United States did not interfere in Hungary, nor the Soviet Union in Egypt during the Suez crisis. The Russians allowed themselves to be thrown out of the Congo, and are not threatening to be more than a nuisance in Cuba. The conflicts in Korea and Viet Nam were temporarily settled by latitudinal partitions. The Arab-Israeli conflict does not become an arena of the cold war. All these represent systems of mutuality of conduct which might be classified as tacit agreement.

II. The fate of the tacit agreement on nuclear testing, and what looks like the impending fate of the tacit agreement on civil defense, is a testimony to the inherent instability of the tacit agreement in the long run. It is something like the gentleman's agreement in economic competition, which suffers from the defect that not all people are gentlemen. The danger is that in the absence of organization between contending parties their only means of communication is by a "threat system." A threat system, which is characteristic of unilateral national defense, is based on the proposition, "If you do something bad to me I will do something bad to you," by contrast with an exchange system, which is based on "If you do something good to me I will do something good to you." Both systems tend to lead to consummation, but whereas the consummation of exchange is an increase of goods, the consummation of threats is an increase of "bads." War is mainly the result of the depreciation in the credibility of threats in the absence of their consummation; and hence a threat system has a basic instability built into it, which tacit contract may postpone but cannot ultimately avoid. The great problem, therefore, is how to get rid of threat systems. This, I suspect, happens historically mainly by their being overlaid with other systems of relationship—trade, communication, organization—until they fall so much to the bottom of the pile that they are no longer significant.

The essential instability of threat systems and the weakness of tacit agreements, therefore, make it highly desirable to pass into the second stage of formalized agreement, and the building of what might be called "peace-defending" organizational structures. The first of these obviously is an arms control organization designed at first perhaps only to limit the present arms race but capable of the ultimate hope of policing genuine disarmament. We could begin, perhaps, with an organization for the prevention of accidental war. This will be a joint organization of the major armed forces of the world. Once this has been accomplished, a major system change is under way. It is the organizational disunity of the armed forces of the world which constitutes the real threat to humanity. If they were united they might threaten us with a great many disagreeable consequences but they would not threaten us with extinction. An arms control organization, therefore, would be the beginning of a very powerful social change. It would constitute the formal recognition of the fact that unilateral national defense is no longer possible. Once this initial break is made, system change may be expected to take place quite rapidly. It may be that we shall have to look forward to a substantial separation of the armed forces organization from the states which they are supposed to defend, and which they can no longer defend. Just as we solved the problem of religious wars by the separation of church and state, so we may be able to solve the problem of nuclear war by the separation of the armed forces from the state. The plain fact is that today the threat which the armed forces of the world present to their own civilian populations is much greater than any conflict among the nations. Arms control will be the beginning of the recognition of this social fact.

III. Arms control must move fairly rapidly into disarmament; otherwise it will be unstable. The organization of the world armed forces will be a loose and unstable one at first, and it will always threaten to break up. It may be, of course, that the major pressure towards disarmament will come from the economic side. Once the threat of war is removed by arms control and by organizational unity of the world armed forces, the economic burden of maintaining these monstrous establishments will seem intolerable, especially in view of the fact that it is the arms burden (equal to the total income of the poorest half of the human race!) which perhaps prevents the world from really tackling the problem of economic development and which condemns hundreds of millions of people and their descendants to live in misery. One looks forward, therefore, to the third stage of rapid and total disarmament, under the arms control organization. There are many difficult problems involved in this which have not been worked out and on which research desperately needs to be done. One research program is on the way at the moment on the broad problems of the economics of disarmament, conducted by Professor Emile Benoit of Columbia University. The United Nations is about to inaugurate a similar study. However, the organizational and social-psychological problems involved are very great and quite unprecedented. Growth is always much easier than decline and the problems of adjustment involved in a rapid decline in the world's armed forces still have to be faced. These problems, however, are difficult rather than insoluble.

IV. Even universal total disarmament, however, is not enough, for this too is likely to be unstable even though disarmament itself will reduce many of the sources of conflict, especially those which arise out of strategic considerations. It will not eliminate all conflicts by any means. In a world as divided as this, ideologically and economically, we may expect serious conflicts continually to arise. These conflicts will constantly present the temptation to the losing side to resort to violence and to redevelop organized armed forces. If disarmament is to be stable, therefore, there must be a system of conflict control. Conflict control is one of the essential functions of government. It is not, however, the only function. In thinking of world government, this is probably where we ought to begin. In the early stages it is more important to establish conflict control than to establish justice or to solve all social problems. Conflict control as a function of government has been inadequately studied and identified. This is perhaps because the study of conflict systems themselves is still in its infancy. However, this is a rapidly developing body of social science and one hopes that it may be possible in the not-too-distant future to develop a substantial body of knowledge on the identification and control of conflict systems. The problem, of course, is the identification of conflict processes in early stages before they become pathological. There are very difficult problems here in the definition of the pathology of conflict, as this, of course, goes very deep into our value systems. Conflict which is regarded as pathological by one person may not be so regarded by another. If, however, we regard violence as generally a sign of pathological conflict, we may be able to identify the processes of social dynamics which lead towards it, and we may therefore be able to interpose counterweights which will correct these processes. We may revert once more to the analogy of the car at the crossing. We need to develop both perception of dangers ahead and also organizations which can act as brakes. These processes have been fairly well worked out in industrial relations, where a whole profession of mediators and conciliators and personnel experts has come to being. There is no reason why these principles should not be applied in other fields of social life and especially to the conflict of states.

V. The last stage, of course, is true world government, capable not only of controlling conflict but of expressing and developing the common concerns and aims of mankind. At the moment this seems to be a long way off. Fortunately, the prevention of war does not depend, I think, on the establishment of full world government. If the stages of development which I have outlined can be pursued rapidly enough, war may be postponed for longer and longer periods until the postponement becomes indefinite by the establishment of a true world government. We must therefore find half-way houses and quarter-way houses which are moderately habitable. We must not allow Utopian longings to deprive us of political bargains. The actual negotiation of the world social contract is going to be a long and arduous business. We need to put many more resources into this than we are now doing. Nevertheless, there is something here which can be done. There is a road which leads somewhere. If we are to break out of the apathy, irrationality, and despair which beset us, we must gain a vision of that road of escape and make at least one step along it. This is the great significance of the growing movement for peace research. Just as we no longer accept depressions as "acts of God," wholly unpredictable and uncontrollable, so we need no longer accept mass violence as unpredictable and uncontrollable. The fact that we cannot yet predict or control it should stir us to a great intellectual effort in this direction, for this way lies hope. The only unforgivable sin in the present crisis of mankind is despair.

THE ROLE OF LAW IN THE
LEARNING OF PEACE

In: *Proceedings of the American Society of*
International Law, 1963, pp. 92-103

THE ROLE OF LAW IN THE LEARNING OF PEACE

We can think of human history as an immensely complicated pattern, a kind of four-dimensional carpet extending through space and time up to the present. Each day as it passes weaves a new segment of the total carpet. The pattern is complex far beyond the ability of the human mind to grasp in its entirety. Every day there are billions of events and each of these is related to a complex network of events in the past. If we are to make any sense of the pattern we must amalgamate billions of individual events into single types and we must reject other billions as an irrelevant background noise. We then identify, as it were, the colored threads of significance which run through the pattern in the hope that as we make clearer and clearer the nature of the pattern in our own minds we may be able to influence its future course.

A very important key to the pattern is the learning process. Human history differs from natural history in that it is populated not only by natural species but by social species, that is, by social organizations and artifacts in every degree of simplicity, complexity and formality. Social organizations inhabit some kind of physical setting as the mollusk inhabits its shell. The university will have a campus, the church will have an edifice and the nation will have capitals, frontiers and government offices. These shells, however, are merely the material deposits of social beings, that is, organizations, and the organizations live mainly in the minds of the people who compose them. I have elsewhere used the convenient term "image" for the total content of the individual mind and we can define organization as a set of images tied together by lines of communication. A society, therefore, is largely the function of the images of those people who comprise it.

In man these images are largely learned. They are not constructed by the genes except in the form of incoherent potentialities. The genes give the human mind its potential and also contribute certain basic elements of the value system, such as the desire for food, affection, security, and the basic sexual desire. For the most part, however, the human image is the product of an enormous input of information from experience. It is the genes that teach the bird how to build a nest, but it is experience that teaches man how to build a house. It is this learning process, therefore, by which the experience of each day changes the images of the people who comprise society, which is the principal factor in social dynamics. The sum of all human images I shall call the body of knowledge. It is a concept akin to Pierre Teilard de Chardin's concept of the "nöosphere." This body of knowledge is almost literally the "corpus" of human society. Unfortunately, in English the word "knowledge" implies that the content of the mind is in some sense "true." This is not implied by the concept which I have outlined above. A man's image is what he thinks the world is like and what he thinks is true. We will bypass the difficult epistemological question of the correspondence between the image and reality.

The body of knowledge is constantly being eroded by death or even by senescence and forgetfulness. Knowledge potential is constantly being developed by birth, and the body of knowledge itself grows as each individual learns from day to day. The society in which what is learned each day exactly replaced the loss of knowledge due to death will be a static society, simply reproducing its body of knowledge and its culture generation after generation. There have been plenty of examples of societies, even apparently quite complex societies, which have conformed pretty much to this pattern. If what might be called the "knowledge industry" is only able to replace the depreciation in the body of knowledge due to death, the society will be stationary and there will not be any social change. This condition may be due to the sheer lack of resources which can be devoted to the knowledge industry or to a lack of productivity in this industry itself. A society where the average age of death is thirty and in which people have to learn fairly complex skills, either for ceremonial or for their economic life, may be so poor that it cannot afford to devote resources to the knowledge industry more than will simply enable it to reproduce itself. Such a society is also likely to develop a value structure which is resistant to change and which cuts the knowledge industry down to size, even if it shows signs of expansion. Where, however, there is a "knowledge surplus," that is, where the product of the knowledge industry is greater than the attrition due to death, an irreversible element of social change is introduced into the society, for each generation will know more than the last. Exactly what constitutes "more" in a structure as complex as that of knowledge is of course a very tricky question and one which, for the purposes of the present paper, we shall simply notice and pass by.

The knowledge industry does not merely consist of teachers and the institutions of formal education. The child and the adult both learn constantly in the family, in the peer group, out on the job, in the church, in every organization to which the individual belongs, as well as in formal schooling. In primitive societies, indeed, the knowledge industry is not specialized at all and the knowledge is transmitted from generation to generation by strictly informal means. It is perhaps the specialization of the knowledge industry and the development of a specialized occupation of teachers which marks the great turning point and which introduces the irreversible dynamic into human society, for it is at this point that the knowledge industry is likely to begin to show a surplus. In its early stages, the surplus may take the form of rather useless or ceremonial knowledge. With the coming of the scientific revolution, however, we now have a knowledge industry which is specialized in the production of useful knowledge and this has introduced a dynamic into society of a different order of magnitude than anything which has existed before.

With these preliminary remarks to set the stage, let us now turn to the problem of peace and war as elements in human history. We can think of these almost as colors in our four-dimensional carpet, war naturally being red and peace blue. Some points in the pattern, such as Hiroshima in 1946, will be stained a very bright red, at other points the blue and red will be mixed, at other points there may be bright blues. The distinction is certainly not a very clear one and problems of measurement are acute and unsolved. Nevertheless, the concept is clear enough to be workable. We may notice that the red pieces make fairly clear patterns of a roughly triangular or pyramidal nature, for a particular war is frequently fairly well defined in space and time. It often begins in a small area, expands to a larger one, and then ends rather suddenly. The blue, we may notice, is part of the ground rather than of the pattern. This is, as a matter of fact, a fundamental assumption in a great deal of thinking about this subject which may not be wholly justified. Many people think of peace as simply the absence of war and the establishment of peace as simply cessation of war. This is one of the reasons for the weakness of the peace movement. War seems to be something positive and active which can be planned and pursued. Peace is a negative concept, simply the absence of something and hence it seems hard to plan for it or pursue it. There is undoubtedly much truth in this concept. There is also, however, a positive concept of peace as belonging to the integrative system of society which is part of the pattern rather than of the ground. Because it is somewhat the same color as the ground, however, it is easily overlooked.

The learning process is now as crucial in the understanding of any particular part of the pattern as it is in understanding the whole. We need to ask ourselves, therefore, what is the exact process by which people learn war or learn peace? War is a set of images, skills, rôles and values which originate in the minds of man and are embodied in physical things, such as weapons, or in events, such as battles. An armed force is a social organization and it therefore depends for its existence on the presence in the image of each of the persons who compose it of an appropriate set of images of the rôle of himself and of others. The moment these images become inappropriate, the organization falls apart. Each man does what he does each day because in fact all the world's a stage and each man has his image of the rôle he has to play on it. We have to ask ourselves, therefore, how do people learn the images which are consistent with the institution of war?

We can dismiss immediately the idea that these images are innate. The genetic part of man's mental equipment is potential and little more. There may be genetic differences among individuals which may determine their potential for violence, though even this is doubtful. There are certainly genetic differences in physical strength and in potential for the development of mental capacity. Whether there are genetic origins of different value structures has never been established. If there are such genetic differences, they are probably small. By far the greater part of a man's image, especially of the adult, has been learned in the course of his experience. And the genetic potential is so large anyway and so much of it is unused that it can almost be neglected as a factor.

There seem to be two kinds of learning from experience which might be called "imprint" learning and "payoff" learning. In young children, imprint learning seems to be of great importance. The child's mind is so plastic that it simply picks up knowledge from its environment, almost as a rubber stamp transfers its pattern to the paper. Even some of the structural elements of language may be picked up in this way. At an early stage, however, payoff learning begins to appear. It may begin, perhaps, with a basic genetically constructed value system. The baby likes warmth and attention, dislikes pain and indifference. When in the course of random production of sounds it says "Mama," it is rewarded, at least in an English-speaking culture. When it says "Ugug," it is not. The acquisition of the vocabulary of a native language is clearly through payoff learning. The familiar psychological learning theory of reward, punishment, reinforcement and extinction is an elementary example of learning of this kind. In human learning, however, difficulties arise because the value system itself is learned. The "payoff" is some event which ranks high on the individual's value system. When value systems themselves change, we get a very complex dynamic process which is little understood. Some values are clearly learned by association with others. Our parents, for instance, give us payoffs in the elementary genetic value system, such as warmth and food. Because of this we may associate our parents' more complex values with the simple genetic values and hence we take on the symbolic values of our parents' culture. It is possible also, of course, that we may rebel against our parents and select another set of symbolic values simply because they do *not* belong to our parents' culture. The banker's son becomes a beatnik because he hates his father, if for no other reason.

In order to explain why people learn to practice violence, therefore, we must look for the payoffs of this activity. The payoffs may be quite simply in terms of economic goods or they may be associated with subtle value systems like patriotism and religion.

In order to understand the institution of war, therefore, we ask ourselves in what social system does violence, especially organized violence, pay off. To understand this we have to go further back and understand the rôle of the threat as an organizer of social relationships. We shall neglect here the problem of violence for its own sake, for instance in sexual gratification, not because it is unimportant but because we know so little about it. I am assuming that sexual violence (sadism) is important mainly as a reinforcement for what might be called "ulterior violence," which is violence threatened or carried out in order to achieve other ends. My reason for this is that sexual violence is inherently individual and sporadic, and is not capable of providing a sufficient motive for social organization. Unless there is some social sanction for violence for ulterior ends which can lift the omnipresent social sanction against sexual violence, sexual violence may result in individual acts of rape or torture but cannot result in war.

We can distinguish a number of social systems in which violence plays an essential rôle. The first of these is the system in which violence is used for simple extermination. The robber shoots the man down and takes his wallet. One tribe exterminates another and takes their land. This is a system of violence, often organized violence, but it cannot be called war. It is fortunately rare and the more complex the society is, the rarer it is likely to become.

The second case is that in which violence is used as a strategy and in which the threat of violence is used to organize the rôle structure of a complex society. The robber who says "Your money or your life" has created in effect a temporary social organization. This is a much more subtle and complex system than that of the robber who shoots you first. If his threat is credible and if you in fact hand over your wallet, he has created a rôle and has taught you something. This is what I have elsewhere called the "threat-submission system." A says to B, "You do something nice to me or I'll do something nasty to you." If the threat is credible to B and B complies, we have a social system established which may even be fairly stable and permanent. Slavery is a good example of this kind of system and all ancient civilizations were based on it. The recipe for civilization indeed is a simple one. We have to develop agriculture so that there is a surplus of food from the food producer. By some initial threat, which is often a spiritual one, the organizers of society take this surplus away from the food producer and with this food they feed armies and an organized threat system with which they can then threaten the food producer if he does not give up his surplus. This is intrinsically a pretty stable system, even though it has a very low horizon of development.

Submission is not the only response to threat and the subsequent history of the threat system depends much on the nature of the response of the threatened party. One important response is escape. When A threatens B, B simply runs away. Ecologically, a combination of escapism and a prolific reproduction may be a very successful response to threat, as the rabbit indicates. This is a particularly important response to economic threats in a complex society, and indeed we can think of the economist's vision of perfect competition as a perfectly organized escape system in which, if B is threatened by A, he can always go to C.

Another response is that of defiance. This often works too. It takes perhaps a certain previous learning history before it can be used successfully. When A threatens B, B simply says "go jump in the lake." The initiative in decision is now passed back to A; either he has to carry out the threat or else his credibility in the future will be much impaired and he will not be able to organize B into a social system, at least not one which is based on threat and submission. The success of defiance rests on its ability to put A in a dilemma. If he does not carry out the threat, there is no social system, and if he does carry out the threat, there may be no social system either. He may say to his slave: "You work for me or I'll kill you." If the slave defies him, he is in a serious dilemma; in effect he has no slave, whatever he does. On the other hand, defiance is dangerous to the defier because the original threatener may find the loss of credibility, which is often associated with the loss of self-respect and a decline in the value put on the image of the self, more serious than the loss which he imposes on himself by carrying out the threat. The ruins of many cities and the demise of many kingdoms are testimony that the lot of the defier is frequently hard.

Because of the high costs of both submission and defiance to the threatened party, another system frequently emerges which is the system of deterrence or counter-threat. B's response to A's initial threat may be to develop a threat capability himself. Then when A says, "You do something nice to me or I will do something nasty to you," B replies, "If you do something nasty to me, I will do something nasty to you." In the short run this often looks like a very successful response to an initial threat and, if the deterrence is successful, it may even lead to a diminution of violence. As long as each party believes in the threats of the other, neither party will carry out the threats that he makes. This, indeed, is very frequently what has been called "peace" and it is the condition in which most of the world finds itself at the moment of writing. Unfortunately, deterrence, while it may be stable in the short run, is almost certain to be unstable in the long run. The reason for this is that both the credibility and perhaps even the capability of threats depreciates if threats are not carried out, and the stability of a system of deterrence depends upon the mutual credibility of the threats of the parties. We might almost say that deterrence is unstable because it is mistaken for peace, that is, for a truly integrative relationship. Deterrence is a condition of uneasy quiet and for this reason it is easy for credibilities and capabilities to change until one party decides to call the bluff. At this point either the threats must be carried out or the whole system collapses. In this system, indeed, war is the pattern and peace is only the ground, the mere interval between wars.

If man had had to reply upon the threat system alone to organize his rôles and relationships and to create his organizations, his horizon of development would have been very limited and the societies which he would have created would have been neither affluent nor pleasant. Hobbes' famous description of man in the state of nature would apply pretty closely to societies of this kind. Fortunately there are other organizing relationships which man can learn and other teaching devices besides the threat of violence. It is only as he learns to use these other relationships, indeed, that violence tends to disappear, for violence itself never seems to be able to eradicate violence. All systems of organization which have been based on the threat system seemed to have had an inherent instability. In part this is a result of the sheer geography of the threat, the fact that the threats diminish in capability and credibility with the distance from the threatener. Hence, the threat-submission system is only possible where the parties are fairly close. Distant parties have no need to submit because the threat at such a distance is no longer credible. Furthermore, the threat-submission system often rests on an uneasy bluff and easily passes over into the system of threat-defiance. The principle of diminution of threat capability and credibility with distance also permits the development of counter-threats which in turn break down into war. The history of war and organized violence can be written largely in these terms. This, however, is not the whole of human history. Alongside the rise and fall of kings, emperors, armies, and empires, other processes have been building up, processes, furthermore, with a larger development horizon which seem destined to reduce the threat system to a place of minor importance, if not to eliminate it altogether.

The most obvious of these relationships is exchange. In exchange, A says to B, "You do something nice to me and I'll do something nice to you." If the promises are credible and the exchange is agreed to and takes place, both parties are presumably better off. Exchange has a great advantage as a social organizer over deterrence, in that when it is consummated it becomes a positive-sum game, whereas when threats are carried out, it becomes a negative-sum game in which both parties are usually worse off than they were before. It is not surprising, therefore, that the great network of trade, and of the specialized production which is based on it and which gives rise to it, has gradually extended itself over the whole earth and has been the foundation for a process of economic development far beyond the dreams of the early threat-based empires. The exchange relationship itself, however, may have a degree of instability in it, even though it makes all parties better off. This is because there is real conflict in the *terms* of the exchange, that is, in the price at which the exchange is made. Although there is a range of prices at which the exchange is profitable to both parties, the distribution of this gain depends on the level of the price itself, a high price being to the advantage of the seller, and a low price to the buyer. The attempt to exploit this conflict can easily lead to the breakdown of the exchange itself, and the existence of the conflict is a constant temptation to revert back into the threat system. We see this, for instance, in industrial relations and we see it also in international trade, especially when this becomes monopolistic state trading. Even though the growth of exchange, therefore, unquestionably lessens violence, especially at the personal and small-group level, because the payoffs for participating in the system of exchange are so much greater in the long run than those for participating in the system of violence, nevertheless it seems probable that exchange by itself is not a powerful enough organizer to eliminate violence altogether—as some of the classical economists seemed to think.

There is, however, a whole set of relationships of very diverse character which I lump together under the title of the integrative system. In this relationship, A says to B, in effect: "You do something nice to me because you yourself want to do it." This represents a shift of the value system of the individual and his image of the payoffs to his own action in the direction of what might be called the socially desirable. This system covers such an enormous variety of relationships that perhaps it is too heterogeneous to be called a system. But the general idea behind all these relationships is that of somebody doing something which is socially desirable because he actually wants to do it. The actual machinery of persuading him that he wants to do it is, of course, diverse. At one end of the scale we have love, where an individual does something for somebody else because he loves him. The appeal to love is made most importantly in the family, but it is by no means unknown in the wider society, for instance, in the appeal to the love of country or even the love of mankind in general. At a somewhat lower level, we have the prestige relationship where B does something for A because of the respect in which he holds him and because A has high prestige in B's eyes so that B identifies with him. The teacher-student relationship has important elements of prestige in it. The student obeys the teacher partly, no doubt, because of the threat system, because the teacher can threaten the withholding of certain rewards or the making of certain punishments, but also because each of the parties has an image of the student-teacher relationship which is accepted by him and which implies a certain degree of obedience to the teacher on the part of the student. The relationship of the policeman to the ordinary citizen is not very different. Most of us submit to traffic cops and to parking fines because we recognize in some way the legitimacy of the system. The whole legal system, in fact, rests on legitimacy; unless people accept the law and the institutions of law as legitimate, they cannot function. What we have here is a very interesting example of a threat-submission system which is stable because it is regarded as legitimate, and has strong integrative elements in it.

Finally, we have political and constitutional systems which likewise depend on a widespread acceptance of legitimacy for their proper functioning. In a mature democracy, the convention that an adverse electoral vote deprives people of office in spite of the fact that in their official capacity they may be able to command the means of violence is so widely accepted that it is hardly even thought about. In less mature societies, where legitimacy is less widely accepted, electoral verdicts are by no means so secure. The constitution of a state, whether written or unwritten, might almost be described as legitimacy of the second degree. That is, it is a set of rules which has achieved legitimacy about what shall be the rules by which legitimacy is granted in other areas of society.

One of the most important keys to the integrative system is rhetoric, that is, the ability of language to change images and values. The language may not merely be verbal; it may be language of ceremonial, or of clothing and other symbols. The judge's wig and the monarch's crown, the professor's gown and the minister's collar, the policeman's and the soldier's uniform, are all part of the rhetoric of legitimacy. Words, too, are important. Political speeches, Bibles, the classic documents of a people, the plea of the lawyer, the harangue of the demogogue, the slogan of the advertiser, even down to the softest of soft sells, are all part of the system of persuasion and rhetoric by which people's images of fact and of value are changed in ways that make them do things that other people want them to do because they themselves want to do them. It is precisely at the point where the rhetorical system breaks down and legitimacy cannot be established that the danger of violence is greatest. The clichés of violence illustrate the point: "Force is the only thing these people understand"; "We have to teach these people a lesson." These are sure signs that the integrative system has broken down or, what is more likely, has never been established.

The integrative system, however, is something that is learned. It is learned partly in ordinary experience, as the child learns, for instance, that he can manipulate his parents by words and symbols, and partly it is learned formally or perhaps even in part imprinted by the barrage of integrative statements which the child—and the adult—receives at almost all moments of his waking life. At home, in school and in church, at political rallies and national celebrations, as well as in the press, on T.V. and on radio, through all the media of advertising, the individual is constantly bombarded with statements which are designed to change his image and his values. Perhaps the most important and effective of all such messages are those which come from a face-to-face relationship in the peer group: "You don't want to do that because if you do you won't be one of us." The threat system is here used to create integration.

The rôle of the legal system in this whole social process is of great importance and interest. In the first place, it has a rôle as part of what might be called the legitimized threat system in changing the payoffs to illegitimate violence. This is illustrated in a famous situation in game theory known as the "prisoner's dilemma." If we identify two decisions of A and B as being "peaceful" or "warlike" then if both are peaceful, they will both be better off than if both are warlike. On the other hand, a condition in which both are peaceful is unstable because, if one is peaceful and the other warlike, the warlike one gains over the position in which both are peaceful. Then if one is peaceful and the other warlike, the peaceful one can gain by becoming warlike so that they are both warlike. The dilemma, therefore, is that the short-run dynamics of the system are continually forcing the parties into positions in which everybody is worse off than he might be, if it did not pay one party shortsightedly to resort to violence. One of the purposes of the legal system, then, is to change the payoffs of the "game" in such a way that it will not pay either party to depart from a situation in which both are peaceful. If the party that first violates peacefulness finds the whole threat system of society arrayed against him, the peaceful situation will be much more stable. For this solution to be successful, however, the threats employed by the law must be regarded as legitimate, even in some sense by those against whom they may be employed.

If the law is to be successful, then it must itself be a teaching process, developing images of the integrative system. It cannot rely upon the threat system alone. In all societies the law is in some degree the embodiment of the internal threat system by which the governing class imposes its will upon the rest of society. In dictatorial and totalitarian societies, use of the law as a part of the internal threat system is very evident. The integrative system nevertheless operates in a long, slow, but almost irreversible process to build legitimacy in the society and to diminish the use of even the threat of violence, simply because, to put it bluntly, rhetoric is cheaper than violence. There is indeed, as an early Quaker, James Nayler, said, a spirit which "wearies out exaltation and cruelty."

Next, there is a process of almost irreversible social learning by which we learn to substitute the rhetoric of integration for violence and deterrence. We can see this process operating in the small, among children. Young children easily resort to violence; they fall into prisoner's dilemmas again and again. The general pattern of their relationships is remarkably like that of international relations. Older children and adults, especially in middle-class society, learn how to handle their conflicts without personal violence simply because they all learn that the payoffs of personal violence are much less than the payoffs of other forms of conflict. This takes place also without much intervention on the part of the law, even though this may be important in the background. In other words, in the solution of the prisoner's dilemma, the development of mutual long-sightedness ·is just as effective in giving stability to the situation in which both parties are peaceful as is the alteration of the payoffs through the institutions of law and punishment. Peace will be stable if nobody decides to break it. The decision to break it rests on a belief on the part of the peace-breaker that he will be better off as a result of breaking the peace. His estimate of this depends on two things: the actual value to him of a position which would in fact result from his breaking the peace, both in the short and the long run, and on the extent to which his image of the situation exaggerates or diminishes this reality.

The learning process operates on both these factors. By learning to set up the institutions of law and punishment we change the actual payoffs. By rhetoric and by the memory of experience we change the relation between the image and the reality and improve the realism, long-sightedness, and integrative skill of the parties themselves. The law is usually regarded as operating principally on the first of these. There seems to be no reason, however, why it should also not be concerned with the second, even though this has been more in the tradition of what might be called para-legal institutions, such as conciliation services, industrial mediation, arbitration, marriage counseling, international conciliation and so on. There may indeed be a certain incompatibility between the punitive aspect of law and its teaching function. Punishment is a poor teacher because of the inner conflicts which it creates. It is for this reason, perhaps, that society has tended to separate the legal from the para-legal institutions and this may indeed be very desirable. On the other hand it is also desirable to look at the legal and the para-legal institutions as a systematic whole with the same ultimate end, that of promoting a learning process in society and toward political and social maturity.

The danger of legality and the legal point of view is that it may place too much stress on third-party intervention in conflict situations so that the essential learning process by which the parties in conflict themselves become better able to handle their own conflicts is neglected. This problem is especially acute at the international level, where the integrative system is weak and the system of third-party intervention and of legitimized counter-threat is likewise still in embryo. The problem here is one of "balanced growth" towards world community and political maturity. One of the problems here is that the counter-threat system as reflected either in international war or even in operations such as that of the United Nations in Korea and in the Congo is something which is familiar and understandable. The growth of the world community and the development of integrative skills is slow, undramatic and often unperceived. Because of its invisibility it is hard to direct resources toward it consciously. On the whole it can be said, I think, that the development of the integrative system is largely a result of latent forces rather than manifest expectations. Nobody "decided," for instance, that there should be personal disarmament, which we have now largely achieved over very large parts of the world, or that dueling should be abolished or that the softer code of manners which now prevails almost everywhere should replace the harsh, brutal personal relationships of earlier civilizations or even of the Middle Ages. All this just happened ecologically, as it were, by a slow, persistent and largely unconscious process of social learning. It is true, as many writers have pointed out, that the internal democratization of the modern state has resulted in an intensification of the problem of war. The aristocracy of the 18th century in Europe, for instance, had learned how to handle war with some finesse. With the growth of democracy this skill was largely lost, possibly because so much of the learning resource had to go in this period to learning how to resolve internal conflicts within countries. It is not too much to hope, however, that the learning process will go on and that we will be able to learn on a world scale how to manage conflicts as we have been learning how to manage them internally.

Here again, the problem of legitimacy is crucial, yet it is little understood how the legitimacy is achieved. The great danger at the moment is that there is virtually no rhetoric by which the East and the West can communicate; even the propaganda of each side is put out largely for its own consumption and it is extraordinarily ineffective as a means of persuasion of the other side. A minuscule amount of resources is put rather half-heartedly into the integrative system through such things, for instance, as UNESCO, the Peace Corps and cultural exchange. There is little feeling abroad in the world, however, of the integrative system as something with which one can operate in a conscious and rational way. All the planning and all the attempts at rationality go into the threat system and practically no intellectual effort goes into the integrative system. If the legal profession the world over can be made more self-conscious as to its rôle in building up the integrative system in both national and world society, it should be in a position to make a quite disproportionate intellectual and moral contribution to the abolition of war and the establishment of world order.

TOWARDS A PURE THEORY
OF THREAT SYSTEMS

American Economic Review, LIII, 2
(May 1963): 424-434

TOWARDS A PURE THEORY OF THREAT SYSTEMS

The world of the economist is organized fundamentally by exchange. This relationship, by which each of two parties gives up something to the other and receives something in return, is indeed a powerful social organizer. It is capable of organizing the division of labor and the allocation of resources, and it guides specialized production, as every elementary student of economics knows. In its general form it starts off as a conditional promise: "You do something nice to me and I will do something nice to you." If the other party to whom the communication is addressed accepts the invitation, the promises are fulfilled and the exchange is consummated. In this consummation we have a positive-sum game, provided that the exchange has been a free one in which both parties benefit, at least in their own opinion at the time. There may be later regrets which could turn the operation as it actually takes place into a negative-sum game, but the economist has generally assumed that these are small, and that such disappointments as may occur in exchange constitute a learning process by which everybody eventually learns to make wise choices among the opportunities which are open to him in the market. Exchange, furthermore, is the key relationship in what we might call unconscious or ecological economic development. It encourages the division of labor and this in turn encourages the increase in "skill and dexterity," and the growth, ultimately, of a specialized class of "philosophers," as Adam Smith called them, who practice research and development—all of which leads to increase in the "productive power of labor."

Exchange, however, is not the only system by means of which social organization is built up. Economists have always recognized that exchange can develop a process of social organization and growth only if certain prerequisites are fulfilled in the way of institutions of property, law and order, and so on. The economist, however, has tended to identify these other organizers as essentially static or given in nature and providing merely the preconditions or the framework within which exchange does the real work. Milton Friedman and the "Chicago School" (if there is one) represent the extreme of this point of view. This, however, would seem to be an unrealistic appraisal of the way in which the dynamics of most societies operate. Exchange is by no means the only human relationship which is capable of producing differentiation, division of labor, role structure, communication patterns, and all the other marks of organizational development. I distinguish at least two other types of human relationship which have the property of organizing social systems. The first of these is the threat, which is the main subject of this paper; the second may be called the integrative relationship, which involves a "meeting of minds" (that is, a convergence in the images and the utility functions of the parties towards each other). There is, of course, a negative of this relationship: the disintegrative relationship, in which the images move further apart. The integrative relationship is itself a complex of many different types of relationship, such as, for example, the teaching-learning relationship between the teacher and the student, the persuasive relationship between an orator and his audience or between an advertiser and his addressees, and a great variety of relationships, such as respect, affection, love, and so on, which lead towards similarity in value or utility functions over the domain of various states of the world in the minds of the parties concerned. Economists pay very little attention to these integrative systems, and indeed have generally tended to assume, what in the dynamic sense is sheer nonsense, that utility functions are given —whereas, as Veblen pointed out, they are the product of human interaction. I would add that they are especially the product of the integrative relationships in society.

It must be emphasized that threat systems, exchange systems, and integrative systems are practically never found in a pure form. All actual social systems are likely to contain all three elements. Even under slavery, for instance, which has a high proportion of threat, there are elements of exchange and even of integration. At the other extreme, in the family, the monastery, or the utopian community, where the integrative system is dominant, there are also elements of exchange and threat. Even in the most loving family or community there is a point below which the terms of trade of an individual member cannot deteriorate without causing serious trouble, and the threat of expulsion always remains an ultimate sanction. Just as economics, however, has prospered by abstracting from the complexity of the social system as a whole a single relationship and element, that of exchange, and has built an elaborate theoretical and empirical structure on this foundation, which can then throw light on the more complex processes of the real world, so the phenomena of threat systems on the one side or integrative systems on the other can be abstracted out of the social complex and developed in a pure form. It is tempting, indeed, to try to assign the threat systems to the political scientist and integrative systems to the sociologist, as we assign exchange to the economist, though this division is too neat to correspond to the untidy facts of academic specialization.

Let us then look at the threat as an abstract human relationship, as an economist might look at exchange, and consider how this might be used as an organizer of society. Like exchange, threat in its simplest form is a relationship between two parties. Exchange, however, originates in a conditional promise to do something good if something good is done in return, whereas a threat originates in a promise to do something bad. The threat relationship begins when the threatener says to the threatened, "You do something nice to me or I will do something nasty to you." The exchange-like form of the threat can be seen in the threat of the holdup man, "Your money or your life," which looks like "Give me your money and I will give you your life." There is a real difference, however, between the commodity which is offered in exchange and the discommodity which is offered in the threat. "I will give you your life" means "I will not take away your life." In order for the threat to be perceived as a threat by the threatened, the threatener must be able to create a perception of credibility; that is, of both capability and will of carrying out the threat if the threatened does not do what the threatener wants him to do. We may note that we have exactly the same problem of credibility in exchange, but it is less prominent because the information is usually more obvious. We visualize the exchanger as handing out the object which he offers to exchange. In financial exchanges, however, when what is offered is a promise to pay in the future, the problem of credibility becomes very real and takes much the same form that it does in threat systems.

The subsequent course of the system depends very much on the nature of the response to the initial threat. Four responses may be distinguished which may be labeled submission, defiance, counterthreat, and the integrative response.

Submission is a not infrequent, though seldom popular, response to threat. When the holdup man threatens us we give him our wallet. When the parent says, "Don't steal the cookies or you'll be spanked," the child refrains from stealing the cookies. When the master says to the slave, "Work for me or I will kill you," the slave frequently obeys. When the state says, "Become a soldier or I will put you in prison," the young man allows himself to be conscripted. The threat-submission system is likely to be a conflict system; that is, it is likely to move the parties to a state in which the threatener is better off and the threatened is worse off than in the initial condition. The welfare situations can be illustrated in a field such as Figure 1, in which we plot A's welfare horizontally and B's welfare vertically. Suppose P_1 represents the welfare of both parties before the threat is made. The very act of making the threat is likely to change the positions of the parties in this field. They may, for instance, move to P_2, where both parties are worse off; the threat creates a state of anxiety in the minds of both parties. On the other hand it is possible that A, the threatener, may enjoy making threats, in which case the actual making of the threat might move the parties to P_2'. When submission takes place, we may move to a position like P_3, where A is better off and B is worse off. This is a typical conflict move. On the other hand, it is not impossible that B's submission to the threat may make him better off as well as A, though this is unlikely; that is, submission might move us from P_2 to a position such as P_3'. This is the situation where A is threatening to make B do something for B's own good which B would not be motivated to do in the absence of threat. The moral justification for threat frequently revolves around this hypothesis. We threaten to spank the

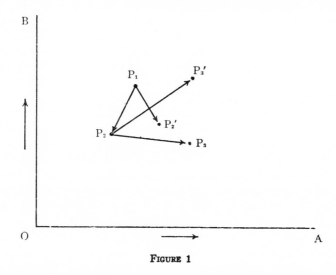

FIGURE 1

child or to fail the student or to hang the murderer strictly for his own good, even if a little skepticism as to these protestations may not be out of order.

The threat-submission relationship has been a powerful social organizer. It is, indeed, one of the major organizers of classical civilization insofar as this rests on slavery. It is also the foundation of a good deal of obedience to the law and of the authority of the state. As Baumol has pointed out in his *Welfare Economics and the Theory of the State,* we may quite rationally vote to threaten ourselves where there is something, like paying taxes, which everybody wants to do if everybody does it, but which nobody wants to do if other people do not. The possibility of nonconflictual threat-submission relationships, therefore, is not to be taken lightly. A key concept here is that of the legitimacy of threat. We submit to the traffic cop and the stoplight because we all recognize their legitimacy. The concept of legitimacy is perhaps more in the domain of integrative systems than of threat systems, but this only illustrates how intertwined these two systems may be.

Threats can be perceived as legitimate only if they are also perceived as appropriate; the threatened punishment must fit the deterred crime. Even if what we are trying to accomplish is not perceived as preventing a crime by the threatened party, that is, even if the threat is not perceived as legitimate, its credibility still depends on its appropriateness. To say to a child, "If you steal the cookies I will kill you," is only credible, and only deters, if not taken literally. This is why "massive retaliation" is impotent against "salami-slicing," to slip once more into the repulsive jargon of strategic science.

The second possible response to threat is defiance. This is somewhat analogous to the nonconsummation of exchange because of a refusal to trade. A says to B, "You give me X and I will give you Y"; B simply says, "No, it's not worth it to me," and the situation returns to the *status quo ante*. In threat systems the situation is more complicated because defiance puts a burden of response on the threatener and hence is in some sense a challenge to him. The threatener then has to decide whether or not to carry out the threat. If he does carry out the threat, this is likely to have a cost to him as well as to the threatened. We have here a very clear negative-sum game. If he does not carry out the threat his credibility is impaired; there is still a cost to him. Defiance therefore always imposes a cost on the threatener which is not found in the corresponding situation in exchange. The probability of this should presumably be taken into account by a rational threatener in deciding whether or not to make the initial threat.

The third alternative is the counterthreat; that is, "If you do something nasty to me, I will do something nasty to you." This is deterrence. This also imposes upon the original threatener a choice of whether or not to carry out the threat. If he is in fact deterred, his credibility is thereby apt to be weakened the next time he makes a threat; that is, there is a decline, as it were, in the capital value of his threat potentiality. If he carries out his original threat, there is likely to be a mutual exchange of "bads," or carried-out threats, which is very clearly a negative-sum game. This is perhaps the greatest difference between threat systems and exchange systems, for when exchange is consummated it is almost always positive-sum, whereas when threats are consummated they are usually negative-sum. This is why exchange systems have a much higher horizon of development than threat systems. This explains, I think, why in the long pull the free labor market, for instance, has always been able to outdo slavery, and why all classical civilizations have ultimately perished whereas the world of trade has grown slowly but persistently from its very origins.

Perhaps the most important single feature of systems of deterrence is their long-run instability. The whole history of threat systems is summed up succinctly in two verses from St. Luke (11:21-22): "When a strong man armed keepeth his palace, his goods are in peace; but when a stronger than he shall come upon him and overcome him, he taketh from him all his armor wherein he trusted and divideth his spoils." It is indeed a source of the basic long-run instability of all threat systems that the unilateral threat system, or the threat-submission system, which may be fairly successful for a time, almost inevitably degenerates into the bilateral threat system, or deterrence. Deterrence is successful as long as it deters, but deterrence itself seems to be unstable. The reason for this, I suspect, is that the credibility of threats depreciates with time if threats are not carried out. Hence threats occasionally need to be carried out in order to re-establish their credibility. Another reason is that threat capability declines if threats are not occasionally carried out, particularly where this capability is enshrined in complex social organizations and in apparatus such as armed forces.

For both these reasons, a state of stable deterrence is rarely stable for long. Eventually either the capability or the credibility, or both, of one of the parties will depreciate to the point where the other party will make new demands. At this point deterrence breaks down and the system slips either into submission or into defiance. Submission is particularly hard if the parties have lived under stable deterrence for a while, so the outcome of a new demand is likely to be defiance. This, then, forces on the imposer of the new demand the choice between carrying out the threat or acceptance of the defiance, which would further destroy his credibility. He is likely, therefore, to carry out the threat, which will lead to the carrying out of the counterthreat, which will result in a negative-sum game known as war. In this, it is true, one party may emerge relatively better off than the other, and indeed if the loser is very much worse off the victor may even be absolutely better off. In this case we may pass again to a unilateral threat system. This is the "successful" period of the new civilization, and this again leads to counterthreats and ultimate downfall. Thus the rise and fall of civilizations seems to be implicit in the very nature of the threat system itself—as, indeed, a pure exchange system is also likely to experience ultimate cycles of boom and collapse. It may be that, ultimately, only integrative systems can provide stability, and I am not sure even of that.

This brings us to the fourth possible response to threat, which is the integrative response. This is harder to analyze and to describe. It may take a great many different forms because of the very richness of the integrative system itself. The integrative response is that which establishes community between the threatener and the threatened and produces common values and a common interest. The integrative response may be mixed with any one of the first three responses. Submission, for instance, may be made in such a way that the threatener is eventually absorbed into a larger culture and the threat system disappears. The experience of the Negro in the United States may be such a case. By accepting and illuminating the ostensible value system of his conquerors, the Negro both made and produced an integrative response which eventually made slavery impossible. In the gandhian experience in India we have an example of defiance mixed with an integrative response; this is the essence of nonviolent resistance. The threatened party, by defying the threatener and by accepting the consequences without bitterness or complaint, eventually undermines the morale of the threatener and the threat system disintegrates. Examples of counterthreat used as an integrative response seem to be rarer, for whereas both submission and defiance, in a sense, unite the threatener and the threatened in some sort of a social system in which integrative factors may operate, the counterthreat divides the threatener from the threatened, breaks any bond which might develop between them, and hence is apt to be disintegrative rather than integrative. This perhaps is another reason for the fundamental instability of deterrence, and its ultimate certainty of failure. It is still not inconceivable, however, that a carefully controlled counterthreat might be combined with an integrative response. We may have seen something like this happen in the industrial relationship, where the threat to fire on the part of the employer may produce either the counterthreat to quit or the more organized counterthreat of the strike. In this case, however, the very nature of the relationship and the fact that if there is to be an industrial organization at all the parties have to live together, opens up the possibility of integrative solutions to counterthreat systems. Where, for instance, the threat or even the actuality of the strike is used to obtain union recognition and a contract, we see counterthreat being used as a device to establish an essentially integrative system of industrial jurisprudence. Parallel to this in international systems might be a counterthreat system used to achieve a disarmament organization or a world government.

Like exchange systems, threat systems have a geographical structure which is imposed on them by the fact that threats, like commodities, have a cost of transport. Because of this there are many striking parallels, as I have pointed out in *Conflict and Defense* (Harper and Row, New York, 1962), between the competition of states by means of threats and the competition of firms by means of exchange. Thus the theory of duopoly is very much like that of a bipolar system in international relations. Each of the competing organizations has a certain "home strength" as represented by the threat capacity in the case of the nation or the cost of production at the mill in the case of the firm. As it goes away from home it has to incur a cost of transport, so that the further from home the organization operates the smaller the threat that it can bring to bear or the higher the price it must charge. In each case this represents an application of the general principle of "the further the weaker." Between two states as between two firms there is likely to be a boundary of equal strength, with each organization dominating the area between itself and the boundary. Such a situation can easily lead to an arms race or a price war, as each organization tries to push the boundary of equal strength further from its home base, either by increasing its armaments or by cutting its mill price. This is pretty clearly a negative-sum game, from which the parties can usually only be rescued by an integrative system of some kind, for instance a merger in the case of the firms, or in less extreme forms a gentleman's agreement, and in the case of states a federation or a "security community."

These considerations lead to an interesting theory of viability which I have also expounded in some detail in *Conflict and Defense*. An organization may be said to have unconditional viability if no other organization has the capability of destroying it; that is, an organization is unconditionally viable if it is dominant over all other organizations at its home base. A system of unconditional viability is only possible if each organization is stronger than any other or any reasonable combination of others. This paradoxical result is attainable if the organizations are far enough apart and if their strength, that is, their threat capability, diminishes rapidly enough for each one as he goes away from home, that is, if there is what I call a high loss-of-strength gradient. A system of stable unconditional viability is threatened either by an increase in the number of organizations in a given field or by diminution of the loss-of-strength gradient. The less the loss-of-strength gradient, the fewer organizations can coexist in unconditional viability.

I have argued that the peculiar crisis of national defense today is a result of the loss of unconditional viability even by the largest nations in the light of the nuclear threat. If we are to exist at all, it must be on conditions of conditional viability, in which each organization can destroy the other but refrains from doing so. This is not an altogether unfamiliar system—indeed, in interpersonal relations we have had to live with it. In the age of the sword, unconditional viability for the individual was at least not inconceivable, even though one had to be a pretty good swordsman to achieve it. The crossbow and, following that, firearms ruined this system and in our personal relations we now live in a world in which we are literally all at each other's mercy. One would think that, in these circumstances, mercy would be taken seriously and studied, but this is the last thing that anyone seems to want to do. In international relations, especially, we are still living under the illusion of unconditional viability, and we may have a very rude awakening.

Concepts of liquidity and inflation which have been developed in economics have also some applicability to threat systems. The concept of generalized military capability is closely related to the economic concept of liquidity. A liquid asset is something with which anything can be bought; a military capability is something with which anything can be destroyed. It is, as it were, money for the doing of harm. Another reason for the instability of threat systems, incidentally, is that harm can be done much faster than good (I am indebted to T. C. Schelling for this observation). One might add, however, as a corollary that the ultimate victory of exchange and integrative systems over threat systems is assured by the fact that more good can be done than harm. The doing of harm has a limit of total destruction; that is, of zero good. The doing of good has no definite upper limit. The liquidity or the lack of specificity of a military capability is another factor which is likely to lead to the instability of the threat system. The military capability of A is a generalized threat directed, say, at B, C, D, and E. Each of these parties, however, perceives the threat as if it were directed wholly at him. The perception of the threat, therefore, on the part of the threatened is four times the amount of the threat on the part of the threatener at a maximum. It is not surprising that under these systems threat systems produce armament races which almost inevitably lead to the carrying out of the threat.

When threat systems become embodied in military organizations, we have problems arising which are strikingly parallel to those which develop for economics when production and exchange get to be concentrated in firms. The military organization, which I have elsewhere called the "milorg," is the equivalent in the threat system of the firm in the exchange system. It possesses many of the qualities and characteristics of the firm. It has a hierarchical organization, it is organized by a budget, it has flows of expenditures most of which are laid out in the purchase of inputs, and it has a flow of receipts. The major difference between the milorg and the firm arises from the source of the receipts: in the case of the firm, receipts are derived from the sale of a product on the market; in the case of the milorg, the receipts are derived from a government budget and ultimately from taxation or from the creation of money. The milorg, that is to say, does not produce a clearly defined product in the way that a firm does; its receipts have more the character of transfer payments than of returns from sales;

that is, exchange. In this respect it is more like a philanthropy than it is like a firm. If we ask what it produces, we would have to answer in terms of a generalized threat; that is, a capability of doing harm to unspecified persons or things.

We may go further, indeed, and distinguish a number of different "commodities" which the milorg produces. One in the currently fashionable terminology is the "counterforce." This is the diminution of a potential enemy's capacity to harm the home organization. This might take the form of a defensive work such as a wall, a buffer state, a Maginot Line, or anything which would sharply increase the potential opponent's loss-of-strength gradient as he moved towards the defended center. It might also take the form of an ability to destroy the opponent's milorg or those aspects of it which have capability of destroying the home organization. Another product of the milorg might be, again in the fashionable terminology, "countervalue." This is the ability to threaten, not the threat-makers of the opponent, but the things which he values—his cities, people, social organizations, and so on. Countervalue weapons and organizations are generally associated with deterrents, that is, with counterthreats, but they may also be used unilaterally to threaten the opponent into doing something which the threatener wants. The great difficulty of operating a threat system is that all these different threat-commodities are very hard to distinguish in practice, and hence an action which is intended to be one kind of threat may be interpreted at the other end as a totally different kind. Insofar as threats are used as instruments of persuasion to change people's opinions or behavior, they tend to suffer from a defect of all persuasion systems: that what is persuasive to the persuader is not always persuasive to the persuadee. The threatener or the persuader has an image of the other which is derived largely from his own experience, and hence is likely to be false in many important regards. Our threats, like our persuasions, tend to be directed at some imaginary person whom we have made in our own image, not at the real person at whom the activity is directed.

The analogue of inflation in threat systems is found in the arms race, in which both parties continually increase the amount of economic resources which they are putting into organized threats (milorgs) without changing their relative power position. Today, indeed, we may be approaching a hyperinflation of the threat system under the impact of military research and development, which effectively destroys any validity which the system once may have had. We can then look at arms control as an attempt at stabilizing the "price level" after a hyperinflation.

The subject could be pursued much further, and there seems to me to be no reason why a science of threat systems should not be developed at least as elaborately as economics builds from exchange. This science, perhaps, still has to find its Adam Smith, but one feels that so much development has gone on in it in recent years that its "Wealth of Nations" must be just around the corner. The need for this science, furthermore, is very urgent. Because of the development of the nuclear weapon and the consequent disappearance of unconditional viability, the whole threat system, that is, the system of national defense, is suffering a grave crisis—indeed, I would argue, a breakdown. The control of the threat system, therefore, is a matter of the topmost priority for the human race. Unless we do this we may not have a chance to develop any other systems. In order to control a threat system, however, we must understand it. It is one of the most astonishing features of human society that governments are willing to invest so much money in threat systems with only crude folk knowledge as to how these systems actually work, and without being at all interested, apparently, in finding out more about them. This is perhaps because the threat system is an important element in the integrative system of most societies. Nations are built on the solid foundations of violence and cruelty, threats and counterthreats. Our national heroes are soldiers and our national mythology is a mythology of successful threat. A threat to the threat system, therefore, is seen as a threat to the integrity of the society itself. We love making threats and it satisfies our masculine demand for "strength" to make them, and hence a threat to the threat system is seen as a threat to that which we love. To make a science of threats, however, is to threaten the threat system itself, for a system so inefficient in producing welfare as the threat system is can only survive as long as it is supported on folk ignorance. It is little wonder, therefore, that the science of threat systems has been so slow to develop.

My thesis may perhaps be summarized in the following lines of verse:

> Four things that give mankind a shove
> Are threats, exchange, persuasion, love;
> But taken in the wrong proportions
> These give us cultural abortions.
> For threats bring manifold abuses
> In games where everybody loses;
> Exchange enriches every nation
> But leads to dangerous alienation;
> Persuaders organize their brothers
> But fool themselves as well as others;
> And love, with longer pull than hate,
> Is slow indeed to propagate.

NEEDS AND OPPORTUNITIES IN PEACE RESEARCH AND PEACE EDUCATION

Our Generation Against Nuclear War,
3, 2 (Oct. 1964): 22-25

NEEDS AND OPPORTUNITIES IN PEACE RESEARCH AND PEACE EDUCATION

THE PEACE research movement is now well enough established that it can claim to be a going concern. Centers such as the Canadian Peace Research Institute, the Center for Research on Conflict Resolution at the University of Michigan, the centers at Oslo, Groningen, and Hiroshima, the programs at Stanford, San Francisco State, Northwestern University, the expansion in a certain new direction of the older institutes and centers of international relations, all point to a movement that is no longer a set of proposals but is being embodied in journals, articles, books, institutes and conferences as well as in the solid work of many individual scholars. It has now reached the point where a real "take-off", to use the language of economic development, seems well within reach. A good deal of enthusiasm has been generated but funds are still very hard to come by and in quantitative terms the intellectual effort is still miniscule.

The purpose of this paper is to ask the question: if financial resources were available on the sort of scale which they are used in the war industry, would it be possible to use them wisely, usefully and without undue waste in the intellectual, educational, and technological task of establishing stable peace? The answer which I would give to this question is "Yes". It is not difficult to envision something like a 20-year program designed to focus a major intellectual resource of the world on this problem. It would be expensive but much less expensive, of course, than war or preparations for war. I suspect, indeed, that a billion dollars is all that could be usefully used, but this might be an underestimate. This is less than 1% of the annual cost of the world war industry.

Consider first the intellectual task. We now have the beginning of something which looks like an adequate theory of peace. It is fragmentary and it comes out of a number of social science disciplines but its outline is beginning to show. It is clear, for instance, that stable peace is a property of social systems and it is a property of some social systems and not of others. Research, therefore, needs to be concentrated in the field of social systems, particularly in regard to their dynamic properties. This involves an integrated attempt on the part of economics, sociology, psychology, political science, anthropology, and so on. It is clear also that the problem of stable peace lies mainly in the province of "threat systems", that is, attempts to organize society by means of threats and counter-threats. A weapon, for instance, is only significant insofar as it is part of a threat system and the whole problem of arms races and disarmament, therefore, clearly falls into this category. The present crisis of the international system is a result of the collapse of a traditional threat system (the world system of unilateral national defense) as a further result of an extraordinary change in the technology of destruction. Threat systems, however, are very little understood even though they are widespread in social life and a concerted attack on them by theorists, mathematicians, small-group experimentalists, simulators, historians, and so on is badly needed.

The next unsolved intellectual problem is that of reality testing of images of social systems and especially, of course, of international systems. It is the absence of such reality testing that makes the cold war possible, that makes attitudes rigid, and that makes any ideological conflict difficult to resolve. As long as perceptions of social systems are ambiguous and as long as reality testing is difficult, many essentially meaningless social and political conflicts can go on. I am not suggesting, of course, that reality testing is all that is necessary to resolve social conflicts, as there may be very real conflicts in value systems. The study, however, of how value systems are created, sustained, and changed might go a long way towards managing conflicts that arise from this source as well.

Closely related with the problem of reality testing in international systems is the task of developing an adequate information processing machinery in them which will not possess the built-in corruption of existing information collection and processing (the diplomat-spy complex). We have already come a long way towards adequate information processing in economic systems with the development of national income statistics and we almost certainly now have the technical knowledge to do this in international systems.

If the threat system is to be reduced to tolerable proportions, substitutes for the threat as an organizer of social life must be found. We find these partly in the exchange system and partly in what I have called elsewhere the "integrative system". Exchange systems we know a good deal about, for this is a subject matter of economics, though even here we need to do much more reality testing, especially at the level of current ideological struggle. We know very little, however, about the integrative system, that is, how people develop such things as respect, empathy, and affection. We do not even know very much about how people develop a disintegrative system of hatred and prejudices.

There is a large area of needed research in the technology of integrative systems about which we know very little indeed. We have always tended to regard war as the "pattern" of history and peace as the "ground", that is, merely the interval between wars. There are, however, integrative systems, that is, relations and networks of love and respect in society and dynamic "peace processes" which are harder to identify than wars but which are no less real and which consist in the building up of integrative networks in the family, the school, the church, the nation, and finally the world. The building of integrative structures requires a technology of its own, not only in the form of social inventions (such as missions, peace corps, cultural exchange, etc.) but perhaps even in the physical and biological environment of the social systems. Could there be, for instance, "weapons of peace" and if there were, what would they look like ? Is there any way in which threats can be used *integratively* to replace the threat system itself by something better ?

Peace and Social Systems

Even though there is a great deal of evidence that we can solve the problem of war long before we solve most of the other problems of mankind, nevertheless peace will not be stable unless the social system also has a problem-solving apparatus which leads towards the solution of problems which are environmental to the problem of peace, such as poverty, population, symbolic and psychological disorders, political mental health, and so on. We have not put any major intellectual resources, for instance, even into economic development, much less into parallel problems of political and social development.

The Peace Movement

The world peace movement, considered as a social movement, is not to be neglected even though at the present time it is likely to be impotent and frustrated. In the socialist countries it has been captured by the prevailing "establishment" and in the Western World it has largely been manned by those so completely alienated from their own society that they can make very little impact on it. But these aspects of the peace movement may be changing. Here again, reality testing is of enormous importance, and what might be called "action-oriented research" could play a very important part in this. If every action program had a research program of equal size along with it which could give feedback to the actionists about the results of their action, even though the initial result might be a lot of disillusionment and frustration, in the long run action would be better informed and much more effective. Action movements of all kinds have a strong tendency to satisfy mainly the internal needs of the activists and as a result at times they seem almost deliberately to sabotage their own effectiveness. If a symbiotic relationship can be established between action and research, both would benefit enormously. Research would find a laboratory in which it could study the more extreme positions of social systems. The actionists could develop a process of feedback which might easily initiate a long cumulative process of social learning in the whole world society.

None of these things, of course, can be done without trained personnel and, even though we have at the moment a considerable pool of dedicated intellectual ability which could easily be diverted into this field if finances were available, under the impact of merely substantial funds the existing pool would soon be exhausted and we would be faced with the problem of training a new generation of peace researchers and educators. This process, indeed, should begin right now and part of any integrated program, therefore, should be devoted to setting up in universities, fellowships and training programs, attractive enough to divert a substantial proportion of the ablest minds into this field.

The problem of peace research must also be visualized as part of a larger problem, which is; how we acquire enough knowledge to get us through the present transition is the state of man and develop a stable high-level world society. This is a task, furthermore, at which we might fail completely, and our descendants may inhabit a ravaged, exhausted, and hopeless earth. The three major intellectual tasks of this transition are: first, peace research, to develop the knowledge on which a world social system can be developed capable of adequate conflict managements, second, general social systems research, of which economic development and population control are major, but not the only parts, and third, technological and engineering research to develop a material technology *not* based on exhaustible resources.

In achieving any new level of organization two aspects of the process must be kept in mind, first the "capital" aspect which involves the setting up of the structure of the new organization, and secondly the "income" aspect which involves the running and maintenance of the new structure. Peace research, and more generally what I would like to call "transition research" is mainly concerned with the "capital" aspect of the problem, especially in the setting up of new structures in the human mind, though it cannot be indifferent to the "running costs" which consist largely of education and the replacement of knowledge lost by death. It also is concerned, of course, with organization and even physical capital, even though the "intellectual capital" aspect is dominant.

In the light of these considerations, we may ask the question, therefore, whether the time has now come for a concerted effort on the part of those who see what needs to be done to put these proposals before those who command the resources which are needed to do it, so that the needs and resources can be brought together.

WHY DID GANDHI FAIL?

In: *Gandhi: His Relevance for Our Times,*
G. Ramachandran and T. Mahadevan, eds.
New Delhi: Gandhi Peace Foundation,
1964, pp. 129-134

WHY DID GANDHI FAIL ?

As a young man growing up in England I was enormously influenced by Gandhi and the whole idea of Satyagraha and Ahimsa, especially as interpreted, for instance, by writers such as Richard B. Gregg. Even after thirty years I can still recapture the sense of excitement, the sense that a great new idea had come into the world, an idea of enormous importance for mankind. Coming to adolescence in the aftermath of the first World War, I was conscious of the break-up of an old order, of the end of an old era. The whole world of national states and empires, which had seemed so secure and permanent in 1914, was revealed as incapable of providing a decent order and habitation for the human race. War seemed like an absolutely intolerable betrayal of the spirit of man, and the state which demanded it a monster only to be appeased by endless human sacrifice. On the other hand there seemed to be no alternative in the face of the very real conflicts of the world but a passive withdrawal, equally unacceptable to the spirit concerned with justice and the right ordering of society. In this dilemma the message of Gandhi came like a great light, indicating that it was possible to reconcile peace and justice, to reject war and at the same time participate in

a great historical process for human betterment. The idea
of a nonviolent struggle which refused to break the community
of mankind, refused to exclude even the enemy from this
community, and which rested on a view of human nature
and of the social process much deeper than the crude arguments of the advocates of violence, was like a revelation.
"Great was it in that dawn to be alive, and to be young was
very heaven!"

"That dawn" for Wordsworth was the French Revolution,
and a false dawn it turned out to be, a dawn not of liberation
but of terrible violence and tyranny. Wordsworth's disil-
lusion drove him to retreat into a barren conservatism in
later life, and one can hope not to repeat this. No doubt
all dawns are false, or rather, each dawn leads only to another
day; the great tides of human history submerge the momentary
waves of excitement and exaltation. Nevertheless it is hard
to avoid a sense of disappointment at the grey day that
followed the Gandhian dawn. The second World War
was nothing unexpected : it was implicit in the very system
of national power. The independence of India likewise
was not unexpected, for we had all looked forward to it for
years. Some of us hoped indeed that India, because of
Gandhi, would be a new kind of nation, rejecting the whole
system of threats and counter-threats which had brought the
world to disaster. What has happened since 1947 however
has been profoundly disturbing for those of us who held these
high hopes.

For what has happened? India has become a nation
like any other, and even, truth compels me to say with pain,
less mature in its foreign relations, less peaceful, less realistic, than many others. In its internal policies there is one
outstanding achievement, the maintenance of internal freedom
and democracy in the face of enormous problems and difficulties. I happened to witness the military parade in
New Delhi last January 26th, on my way to the Pugwash
Conference in Udaipur. I felt as if I was back in the Europe
of 1914, and hardly knew whether to laugh or weep. It was
as if Gandhi had never lived, or had lived in vain. I confess

I never expected to live to see girls in saris doing the goose-step! It is very hard for Indians now to see how they look to the world outside, for they are naturally preoccupied with their enormous internal problems. It is very easy, however, for India's actions to be interpreted as those of a weak and petulant bully, not hestitating to use the old-fashioned threat against a weak enemy, as in Goa, answering provocation with provocation in the case of a strong enemy, such as China, and refusing to make a desperately needed adjustment in the case of Kashmir. I am not saying that this image of India is either true or just, merely that it is a possible interpretation of India's actions. What is abundantly clear is that India's international posture is an enormous handicap in achieving economic development, a handicap so great that it may prevent development altogether, and may have in it the seeds of a human catastrophe on an almost unimaginable scale. The problem of development in a country like India, burdened with a tradition and a religion which for many centuries has produced a heroic adjustment to poverty rather than to a sober and organized attempt to get out of poverty, is so difficult in itself that it requires every ounce of human effort, of talent for organization, and of economic resources to break out of the trap. Every man, every rupee wasted in military effort is a millstone round India's neck, and may condemn billions of her unborn to poverty and misery. Economic development is like a man trying to jump out of a ten-foot hole ; it is no use his jumping nine feet eleven inches, for he will just fall back. At a certain crucial stage a little more effort may make the whole difference between ultimate success and failure. What are we to say, therefore, to a man who tries to jump out of this hole with a cannon deliberately strapped on his back—yet is not this precisely descriptive of India today !

The plain and ugly truth is that in the game of international politics India is going to be a militarily weak nation for many decades to come. In the modern world especially, with the United Nations and the increasing recognition of the illegitimacy of war, it is quite possible for a weak nation

to survive and prosper, and indeed eventually become a
"strong" one for whatever that may be worth, which is not
much. When it is weak, however, it must behave like a
weak nation, and not pretend that it is a strong one. Both
India and Indonesia—the latter much more so—seem to be
under the illusion that because they are big nations they
must, therefore, simply because of their large populations,
be powerful. Nothing could be farther from the truth—
their very size is a major source of their weakness, for in the
modern world small nations have a much better chance of
managing their internal affairs well and getting on the road
to development than large nations. It is a fatal mistake,
however, for a weak nation to behave as if it were a strong
one, which seems to me precisely what India is doing.

Quite apart from Gandhian moral standards, then, and
even judged by the low morality of international power
politics, India is behaving badly and gets a low mark. The
child born with such high hopes has turned out not only to
be no better than the average, but actually worse. There
are, of course, many extenuating circumstances. Colonial
rule is a dreadful thing, which corrupts both ruler and ruled,
and the ex-colonial countries all suffer from a well-recognised
disease of society which might be called the "post-colonial
trauma", and from which it may take several generations to
recover—indeed, I sometimes think the trouble with England
even today is that it never really recovered from the Norman
conquest, for it too exhibits many of the marks of a post-
colonial society! It takes time to learn mature international
behaviour, and the nations—including my own—are all
busy teaching each other how to be immature and childish,
and learning this lesson all too readily. Still, the nagging
question remains : India, because a new light shone into the
world there, should have been different—or perhaps one
should have expected Gandhi to suffer the fate of the
Buddha ! A prophet, as the Christian Bible says, is not without honour save in his own country !

For those concerned with the theory of nonviolence the
failure of Gandhism in India to produce a successful develop-

ment process after the "revolutionary" change raises severe problems. Nonviolence remains a powerful instrument of revolutionary change—as we see now, indeed, in the movement of Martin Luther King in the United States. It perhaps has a greater effect on those against whom it is used than on those who use it. In a very real sense Gandhi liberated Britain more than he liberated India ; when I go back to Britain I am astonished at how much richer and happier a country it seems to be than the "Imperial" England of my childhood. In spite of the damage and sufferings of the wars, and though Gandhi can hardly be given all the credit for this, the plain economic fact is that in the twentieth century empire became a burden to the imperial power, not a source of wealth or even power. It is hard, however, to cast aside even burdens willingly, as the case of Portugal (the poorest country in Europe, with the largest empire) indicates. Nonviolence indeed is only effective when it is aligned with truth—Ahimsa and Satyagraha must go hand in hand. When truth is rejected, and when an illusory view of the world clouds the judgement, as it seems to me is true of India today, of course nonviolence will be rejected. The critical problem then, comes down to how we learn to test the reality of our images of social and political systems, for the greatest enemy of nonviolence is the lack of "reality testing". Even violence can be interpreted as a crude and costly method of testing our images of the world—as, for instance, Japan and Germany discovered by violent defeat that their images of the world had been wrong.

Thus, the failure of Gandhism is not a failure of Ahimsa, but a failure of Satyagraha. The modern world is so complex that the truth about it cannot be perceived by common sense or by mystical insight, important as these things are. We must have the more delicate and quantitative sampling and processing of information provided by the methods of the social sciences if we are really to test the truth of our images of social and political systems. The next logical step, therefore, for the Gandhian movement would seem to be in the direction of the social sciences, in peace research,

and in the testing of all our images of society by the more
refined means for discovering truth which are now available
to us.   I am not suggesting, of course, that the social sciences
produce "absolute" truth, or indeed that much valid perception is not achieved through common sense and insight.
What I do suggest however, is that the problem of truth is
so difficult that ·we cannot afford to neglect any means of
improving the path towards it, and that without this, nonviolence will inevitably be frustrated.

Everywhere I went in India in my brief and inadequate
visits I heard one thing : "There is no alternative".   It
was precisely the greatness of Gandhi that he always insisted
there *was* an alternative.   Morality always implies that
there are alternatives to choose, for morality is choice.   To
deny alternatives is to deny morality itself.   To perceive
alternatives requires imagination, hard thinking, and costly
and painstaking study.   If the Gandhian movement   in
India can recapture this great vision of the alternative, India
may yet be saved from the disaster towards which she seems
to be heading.

WAR AS A PUBLIC HEALTH PROBLEM: CONFLICT MANAGEMENT AS A KEY TO SURVIVAL

In: *Behavioral Science and Human Survival,*
Milton Schwebel, ed. Palo Alto, Calif.:
Science and Behavior Books,
1965, pp. 103-110

War as a Public Health Problem: Conflict
Management as a Key to Survival

The philosophy of public health envisages man as a species in an ecological framework. This ecological framework consists not only of other species but also of man's own institutions and artifacts. His houses, sewers, weapons, corporations, nations, and churches must be regarded as species in the grand ecosystem, just as wheat, rabbits, and field mice are. We must think of this whole system as exhibiting a dynamic course through time, the future of which is a function in some degree of its existing state at the present moment. We are certainly not in anything like an ecological equilibrium, and it is hard to predict at the present time what such an equilibrium would be. The expansion of the human population has gone hand in hand with the expansion of the population of various kinds of social species, such as machines, or even biological species of man-produced plants and animals. It has also gone along with a certain dimution in other species, especially those associated with forests and wildlife.

Man's present population explosion has been compared rather gruesomely to that of a colonizing species such as, for instance, the fireweed which takes over after a forest fire. Any major shift in the ecological environment is likely to produce an enormous expansion of a few populations, but the colonizers often lose out in the long run and may even disappear from the earth altogether is not as remote these days as it used to be, and it is certainly possible that the subspecies known as civilized man might disappear, together with the world of artifacts and organizations which surround him, and man might find himself reduced to a more primitive level of culture than he now enjoys. This may happen even without nuclear war, simply by a combination of the exhaustion of natural resources coupled with unrestricted population growth. We still do not have a permanent high-level technology, although this does seem to be almost within sight. If we do not achieve this, our present achievements are merely a flash in the pan of geological time, soon to be followed by the long, sad twilight of the exhausted earth, where a small fraction of the present population scrabbles for a living on a planet devoid of ores or fossil fuels. This prospect may seem too far in the future to worry about, though it could certainly come about within a few hundred years if we are not careful.

For the immediate generation, however, the principal danger to man lies in his inability to manage conflict, especially international conflict. War, therefore, must be regarded as the major public health problem of the day. It has always been an important cause of death, though somewhat far down the list compared to most common diseases. Today we have had what has been called the "revolution of the mega-death," and war threatens to become the major source of human mortality, not only in the generation on which it actually falls but for many generations to come, through genetic mutation. It is surprising that the public health movement has been so little cognizant of this and so slow to recognize peace research as one of its major research components. In the absence of this concern, public health looks uncomfortably as if it is fattening us up for the eventual slaughter. We conquer tuberculosis and polio only to provide more people for the eventual roasting.

The ecological point of view, to which the public health movement is deeply committed, can make an important contribution to the study of war and peace itself, and to the conquest of war. The view still lingers that war is an act of God, essentially uncontrollable by man. We used to think the same about disease, and even a generation ago we thought the same about economic depressions. In the early 1930's we talked about the "economic blizzard" as if an economic depression were much the same as a depression on the weather map. Most of us now no longer accept this view, and regard the control of depressions as a legitimate function of government — and a function, moreover, of which it is perfectly capable. It has taken us longer to come to the view that war likewise is not merely a matter of the international climate, but is something which can be mastered and controlled by man. In the last resort, the epidemiology of war is not tremendously different from the epidemiology of malaria. Just as malaria is the product of a biological system that includes man and the Anopheles mosquito, so war is the product of a social system that includes independent national armed forces and certain tendencies toward infectious mental diseases without adequate institutions for checking them. War, in other words, is a product of some social systems and not of others. The systems which imply it should be identifiable, and the minimum institutions for the maintenance of stable peace should be capable of specification. Then the problem becomes one of the dynamics of social systems, by which we may be enabled to move from the present system, which does not have stable peace, to some future system which possesses this happy property.

We do not have to study the whole social system in order to find those parts of it which are peculiarly relevant to the problem of war and peace. We can identify war and peace very readily as properties of conflict systems, and, among conflict systems, only of those which involve large-scale organizations specialized for violence. Of the latter, international systems comprise by far the larger part, though the occasional existence of civil war, insurrections, or riots, and so on, within the body politic necessitates a certain broadening of the concept of war beyond that of the international system as such. The logical relations are illustrated in Figure 1, which shows that all war systems are conflict systems, some war systems are international systems, and some international systems are conflict systems.

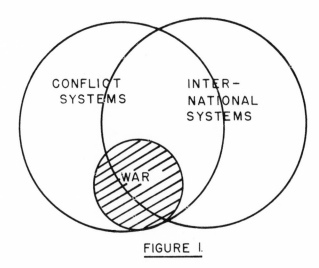

CONFLICT   INTER-
SYSTEMS   NATIONAL
                      SYSTEMS

WAR

FIGURE I.

The study of the ecology of war and peace, therefore, begins with the study of the ecology of conflict itself. Conflict is carried on typically by a reaction process in which, for example, A makes a move which changes B's perception of the state of the world and his optimum position in it, so that then B moves. This changes A's perception in turn, and he moves again, which leads to further moves by B, and so on. A conflict move is then defined as one in which one party becomes better off and another party becomes worse off. This process is illustrated in Figure 2. Here we plot A's welfare vertically and B's welfare horizontally. A move from, say, P_1 to P_2 is a conflict move because it diminishes A's welfare and increases B's welfare. We will neglect the difficult problems involved in the perception of welfare and assume for the moment that some objective measure is possible. In a field such

as this, a move in either a southeasterly or a northwesterly direction
is a conflict move; a move in a northeasterly direction may be defined
as a "benign" move, for this increases the welfare of both parties;
similarly, a move in a southwesterly direction may be defined as a
"malign" move in which both parties are worse off. An important proposition here is that a succession of conflict moves, that is, a conflict
process, may be either benign or malign depending on the exact parameters of the process itself. Thus, again in Figure 2, suppose we start

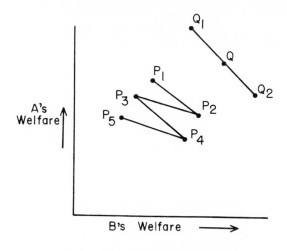

FIGURE 2.

at P_1. B makes a move to P_2, where he is better off but A is worse off,
whereupon A responds by moving to P_3, where he is better off but B is
worse off. B responds to P_4, A to P_5, and so on. The succession of
conflict moves here results in a malign process in which both parties
are getting worse off in the process as a whole. Although each time a
party makes a move he gets better off, this improvement is more than
cancelled by the next move of the other party. Suppose, however, that
we move from P_5 to P_4 to P_3 to P_2 to P_1: we would have a succession
of conflict moves in a generally benign direction. On the whole, economic competition tends to be benign in its over-all effect, though not
universally so, whereas international competition, especially arms
races, almost always tends to be malign. Interpersonal or interorgan-
izational conflict can easily be of either character. We all know families or organizations shaken to pieces by malign conflict processes,
and we also know those whom conflict has seemed to strengthen.

Neither malign nor benign processes can go on forever. A malign process, if it goes on long enough, will reach some kind of a boundary at which the process will break down. An arms race leads to a war, marital quarrels lead to divorce, industrial conflict leads to a strike. One party may be eliminated, or some drastic reorganization may take place. The existence of a boundary of this kind at which the system breaks down is highly characteristic of conflict systems. benign moves, too, are not likely to go on forever; a system of this kind is likely to exhibit some upper boundary which is imposed by the sheer scarcities of the system, such as Q_1 to Q_2 in Figure 2. When the conflict process reaches this upper boundary, further benign moves are no longer possible, and the only possible moves are conflict moves. From the point Q, for instance, we can only go either toward Q_1, in which case A is better off and B is worse off, or toward Q_2, where B is better off and A is worse off. Even these scarcities, however, are not absolute. What economic development means, in fact, is pushing out this boundary of scarcity in a generally benign direction. The more resources that are devoted to diminishing scarcity, the better chance there is of maintaining in the system benign moves which make everybody better off.

Conflict management is essentially a developmental or learning process. It has two aspects: first, the prevention of malign conflict processes, and second, the diminution of scarcity by economic, political, and social development. Both these cases have a centralized and a decentralized aspect. In avoiding malign conflict processes an important element is the development of skills in the management of conflict by the parties themselves. We see this, for instance, in the development of the child, at least in a middle-class environment, when the fist-fights of first grade are gradually replaced by the more subtle conflicts of adult life. We see this also in the "gentling" process of social learning, through which we have attained personal disarmament, the abolition of dueling, and the almost complete disappearance of personal combat in very large sections of society. Supplementary but also essential to this process has been the development of a centralized process of conflict management, such as law, arbitration, conciliation, and so on. This might be called third-party control. Ideally, it should involve two things: the first is a reserve power, as it were, on the part of the third party which can be thrown toward one or the other of the contending parties in order to prevent malign conflict processes. The second aspect is the impact of the third party on the learning processes of the parties in conflict, by means of which certain attitudes and values are legitimatized and accepted by the conflicting parties as norms of behavior. Unless the fear of the law passes over into respect for law, the power of the legal institution, or of government itself, is very limited. Unless, therefore, the payoffs, both positive and negative, actual and potential, which third-party control introduces contributes to the learning process of the other parties, third-party control is likely to be ineffective. It is hard for anyone who has grown up in a society like that of the United States, where the law is largely respected and indeed almost taken for granted, to realize how precarious this consent may be and how impotent the law is in a society where it does not command respect.

The development of decentralized control depends on the growth of three factors in the images, value systems, and behavior patterns of the parties concerned. The first of these is accuracy in the perception of the nature and intentions of the other party by each of the parties to conflict. There is a good deal of empirical work which shows that individuals can manage conflicts even when there are wide incompatibilities and possibly conflicts of interest between the parties, if each has a realistic appraisal of the character of the other. When the image that each party has of the other diverges sharply from the image which the party has of itself, each party is behaving, as it were, in an unreal world, and it is not surprising that the management of conflict becomes difficult. We see this in the most extreme form in the schizophrenic or the paranoid, for whom every act of the other party is interpreted as hostility, and benign moves become impossible.

The second characteristic is perhaps an aspect of the first, but it is so important that it deserves special mention. This is the character of long-sightedness on the part of the parties. Malign processes frequently arise because the party making the conflict move does not anticipate the reaction of the other. Thus, in Figure 2 again, if B is shortshighted, he may make a move from, say, P_1 to P_2. If A's reaction to this is to move to P_3, B is worse off than he was before. If B is longsighted, therefore, he will not make the move to P_2, but will make some less extreme move which will provoke either no response, or a less violent one, by A. The "prisoners' dilemma" in game theory is a good example of a situation in which a succession of shortsighted moves is invariably malign, but in which, if each of the parties is longsighted, a benign move can be made. The difficulty here is that benign moves frequently require both parties to be longsighted, and if one of the parties is shortsighted this may force the other one to be shortsighted too. This is one of the major reasons why decentralized control alone is not usually adequate, and why centralized or third-party control usually has to be brought in to protect society against what might be called "unilateral shortsightedness." This is done by changing the payoff in such a way that shortsightedness does not profit the shortsighted even in the first instance.

The third source of success in decentralized conflict management is empathy, or the identification of each party with the interests of the other. Parties who are friendly toward each other are likely to make benign moves, for moves which benefit both parties simultaneously will be strenuously sought after and conflict moves will be made reluctantly and with as little loss to the other party as possible. By contrast, when the parties are hostile, so that each rejoices in the misery of the other, the probability of a malign succession of moves is much enhanced.

It is one of the great weaknesses of game theory as a guide to the interpretation of social systems that it fails to take into account this factor of empathy or identification. This is the basis of much that is fallacious in what has been called "strategic thinking," which takes the existing hostilities of the international system for granted and does not inquire how to change them. Without a strong element of what I have called the "integrative system," however, no social system could possibly survive, and it is surprising that this element in the social system has been so little studied and, indeed, has been treated almost with contempt by those who fancy themselves sophisticated.

Both hostility and friendliness are essentially learned attitudes, and one of the most important contributions which the behavioral sciences could make to this infant science of conflict management would be to investigate the origin of these states of mind. What is it, for instance, in the experience of individuals which makes some people generally benevolent and eager to identify with others, while some people are malevolent in disposition and seem to need a positive hatred in order to organize their own personalities? There is a great deal of evidence which suggests that early childhood experience is a crucial factor in determining these predispositions, but we are still a long way from really identifying their causes, and there seems to be surprisingly little work specifically directed toward this problem. The study of integrative systems, therefore, would seem to me the most exciting and also the most important frontier of all behavioral science, both at the theoretical and at the empirical level.

The study of centralized conflict management, or third-party intervention in the form of law, police, judiciaries, arbitration or conciliation, and the like, has an enormous literature. Yet much of the effect of this discussion is lost by the failure to realize that third-party intervention is not a system in itself, but is merely one aspect of a much larger system of the dynamics of social conflict. There is, of course, a quite legitimate study of the formal aspects of third-party intervention in the study of law, constitutions, and so on. This covers a large part of the traditional ground of political science. Unless third-party intervention, however, is seen as part of a larger process of social learning by which the elements that lead to decentralized control are also enhanced, we will certainly fail to understand why given institutions are successful in some environments and not in others. The fallacy of much legal and political thinking is that it tends to identify the institutions of third-party control as self-contained systems, whereas in fact the significance and the success of these institutions rests to a considerable degree on the extent to which they supplement and enhance a system of decentralized control. Unless the political and legal institutions of a society create a learning process in which individuals learn to handle their own conflicts, they can easily become ineffective or possibly move toward breakdown. If democratic government, for instance, does not result in a process of social learning which accumulates over a period of time, it is almost bound to fail. The success of political and legal institutions, therefore, often depends on the existence of other, complementary institutions, through which these political and legal processes themselves are fed into the overall learning process of the society. These integrative institutions — the family, the church, and the school—provide the soil in which the dry seeds of legality can either come to life or remain barren.

Just because we claim that it is possible to learn to manage conflict, we do not mean that conflict is illusory. The world is full of perfectly real conflicts of interest and, in the great dynamics of the social system, some parties "win" and become relatively better off, and other parties "lose" and become relatively worse off. In a society with a stationary, low-level technology, conflict can be very real and very severe indeed. A high-level, expanding technology, on the other hand, is in a very real sense a substitute for conflict, because it constantly yields situations in which everybody can be better off and most moves are benign. This is why technology represents such an enormous political change. In a society with a stationary technology, almost the only way to become better off is to make somebody else worse off. In a society with an advancing technology, we can become better off without making anybody worse off, and indeed we can all get better off together.

In all societies it is important to avoid malign processes, for these are always pathological and it is to the interest of all parties to avoid them. Insofar as these processes rest on illusions and on failures of social perception, the elimination of these illusions would be an important contribution to the elimination of malign processes. It is possible that some benign processes also rest upon illusion, but this is much less likely. But in a technically developing society, malign processes become all the more intolerable simply because benign processes are so much more possible. In this fact, perhaps, lies one of the major hopes for the future of mankind.

REFLECTIONS ON PROTEST

Bulletin of the Atomic Scientists
21, 8 (Oct. 1965): 18-20

Reflections on Protest

I PARTICIPATED in what may well turn out to have been an historic occasion, the first "teach-in" at the University of Michigan. This originated as a protest movement against the escalation of the war in Vietnam by a group of Michigan faculty, mostly younger men. It developed from a simple protest into what turned out to be a unique educational experience, in which between two and three thousand students literally sat down and talked and argued all night. The movement spread rapidly to other campuses and organized a national teach-in which was held in Washington in May. It now begins to look almost a national mobilization of university teachers and students. In a way, the forerunner of this movement was the remarkable mobilization of faculty members on university campuses against Goldwater, which represented political arousement on a scale which has rarely, if ever, been seen before in these supposedly cloistered circles. The teach-in movement is clearly a response to Johnson's behaving like Goldwater, so in a way is part of this same arousal.

Nobody, unfortunately, is much concerned to study the effects of all this, some of which may be quite different from what the people who are aroused by the arousal intend. I am constantly impressed by the ironies of social systems, where action often produces quite the reverse of the consequences which are intended. On the other hand, presumably, the better our knowledge of social systems, the more likely are we to avoid any unintentional consequences. It is important, therefore, for protesters to have some theory of protest, and to be sensitive to those circumstances in which protest is effective in achieving its intended consequences, and those circumstances in which it is not.

THEORY OF PROTEST

Let me venture, then, on a few tentative suggestions for a possible theory of protest, in the form of some tentative propositions.

1. Protest arises when there is strongly felt dissatisfaction with existing programs and policies of government or other organizations on the part of those who feel themselves affected by these policies but who are unable to express their discontent through regular and legitimate channels, and who feel unable to exercise the weight to which they think they are entitled in the decision-making process. When nobody is listening to us and we feel we have something to say, then comes the urge to shout. The protester is the man in the advertisement who does not read the *Philadelphia Bulletin*, but who has something very important to say that clearly isn't in it. Furthermore, as he apparently has no access to the *Bulletin*, all he can do is to stand in the middle of its complacent readers and scream. In the present case, the State Department White Paper on Vietnam is clearly the *Philadelphia Bulletin*; the protesters are those who see something quite obvious that isn't in it.

2. Protest is most likely to be successful where it represents a view which is in fact widespread in the society, but which has somehow not been called to people's attention. The protest of the man who does not read the *Philadelphia Bulletin* is likely to be highly successful, as he is usually trying to call attention to events which obviously *ought* to be in the *Bulletin*, being intrinsically newsworthy. Societies, like solutions, get supersaturated or supercooled; that is, they reach a situation in which their present state is intrinsically unstable but it does not change because of the absence of some kind of nucleus around which change can grow. Under these circumstances, protest is like the seed crystal or the silver iodide in the cloud. It precipitates the whole system toward a position which it really ought to be in anyway. We see this exemplified in the relative success of the protest movements in civil rights. Here we have a situation, as Myrdal saw very clearly in *The American Dilemma*, in which certain fundamental images of the American society were inconsistent with its practices, and where, therefore, the protesters could appeal to an ideal which was very widely held. Wherever there is hypocrisy, there is strong hope of change, for the hypocrite is terribly vulnerable to protest. On the other hand, in the absence of protest, the supersaturated society may go on for a long time without change, simply because of what physicists call the nucleation problem.

3. Where the society is not supersaturated, a protest movement has a much rougher time. It then has to move the society towards the new position from which change can then crystallize out, and this is a much more difficult task than crystallizing change in a society that is ready for it. Furthermore, protest as a social form, which may be very effective and indeed necessary in crystallizing a supersaturated society, may be quite ineffective in moving a society

which is not saturated for change towards a point where it is saturated. That is, the techniques for creating the preconditions of change may be very different from the techniques required for crystallizing it. Where a society is divided and ambivalent, a protest movement designed to push it in one direction may easily arouse movements of counterprotest designed to resist the movement or to push it in the other direction. This is something to which protesters rarely give sufficient attention. Because they are themselves emotionally aroused, they tend to think that almost everybody must be in a similar frame of mind, which may not be true at all. It is quite possible for instance, for protest movements to arouse counter-protests much larger than the original protests, and hence the net result of the protest is to move the system away from the direction in which the protesters want it to move. The Goldwater campaign was a good example of this. Goldwater was nominated as a Republican candidate as a result of a protest movement among discontented conservatives. The result, however, was the arousal of a much larger movement of counterprotest among those who were frightened and dismayed by Goldwater, which resulted in a quite unprecedented defeat.

4. The dynamic process of social systems are not entirely random, and this means that any particular social system is more likely to go in some directions than it is in others. Obviously, a protest movement which is trying to push the social system in a direction in which it has a high probability of going anyway is more likely to be successful than one that is trying to push the social system in a direction that has a low probability. Unfortunately, it is by no means easy to assess the various probabilities of change; nevertheless, we can surely know something about it. At least we can be pretty sure, for instance, that movements toward absolute hereditary monarchies today have a pretty slim chance of success. We can identify certain cumulative processes in the history of social systems, such as the growth of knowledge, the widening of integrative systems, and so on, which have a certain long-run irreversibility about them, even if they may have short-run set-backs. Systems move, however painfully, towards payoffs. As we learn to understand the payoffs, we can identify those protest movements which have the best chance of success. On the other hand, it is not the "real" payoffs which determine human behavior, but the imagined ones, and there can often be a strong divergence between the two, at least in the short run, and this short run can be painfully long.

5. We might perhaps distinguish between protest movements and educational movements, the one designed to crystallize a change for which a society is ready, the other to push the society toward a change for which it is not yet ready. The techniques of these two movements may be very different. A protest movement needs to be shrill, obstreperous, undignified, and careless of the pattern of existing legitimacy which it is seeking to destroy in the interest of a new pattern which is waiting to emerge. Educational movements have to be low-keyed, respectful of existing legitimacies, and tying into them wherever possible, and chary of arousing counterprotest. A good example of this in race relations is the work of the NAACP, which unquestionably laid the educational groundwork for the recent protest movement in civil rights. When the moment for protest arrives, however, the educational institution is often pushed aside, and perhaps properly so, as inappropriate in the circumstances. On the other hand, protest movements for which society has not been prepared by education, or which are seeking for improbable change, are virtually doomed to failure, like the IWW. The movement for social security in this country is an interesting example of one in which the educational process dominates it almost completely, and where the role of protest is almost negligible.

6. Even when a situation is ripe for a protest movement, it can go astray and be ineffective if it takes an inappropriate form. The form of a protest should be closely related to the object of protest. This is why, for instance, on the whole, the sit-ins have been very successful, whereas marches and parades are usually less so. It can be particularly disastrous to the protest movement if the protest takes a form which arouses a counterprotest over the form itself, and not over the object of protest. Any object of protest can easily be lost in argument and counter-argument over the question as to whether the form of the protest is legitimate or appropriate.

7. Protest movements are also likely to be weakened if the object of protest is not clear, or if there are many different objects, some of them incompatible, combined in the same protest. Thus the strike in industrial conflict is usually a rather effective form of protest, particularly when it is directed toward a change that would have come anyway, because it is appropriate to the objective, and the objective itself is usually very clear. Political protest, by contrast, is apt to be diffuse; its objectives are unclear and often inconsistent. Political protest movements almost always run into the problem of strange bedfellows, and the less clear the objectives of protest, the less likely is anybody to fulfill them.

CASE IN POINT

With these propositions in mind, let us now take a look at the peace movement and the current movement of protest against the war in Vietnam. Unlike the civil rights movement, which had fulfilled almost all the conditions for successful protest, the peace movement only fulfills some of them. The condition which it fulfills is that related to the long-run payoff. There is no doubt that the payoffs of a stable peace are enormous. The $120 billion a year that the world spends on the war industry is an appalling waste which may well set back the achievement of world development by even hundreds of years, and might even prevent it altogether. The probability of long-run change toward a system of stable peace is therefore high, and the peace movement fulfills this one essential requirement for the success of a movement for social change. On the other hand, it fulfills practically none of the other conditions. Its objectives in terms of specific institutional and behavioral change are not clear. We still do not really know how to get stable peace, and what particular forms of behavior lead us toward rather than away from this goal. There is, furthermore, a great diversity of view as to immediate objectives within the peace movement.

It is clear also that American society at least is not supersaturated in regard to social change toward stable peace. In a sense, the task of the peace movement is fundamentally educational, rather than protest. Most of the communications which are received by Americans, whether in the formal educational system or in the informal contacts of face to face conversation, tend to create an image of the world in which war is a recurrent necessity, and in which, furthermore, for the United States, war has paid off pretty well. We tend to associate war with easy victories, like the war against Mexico or Spain, or with periods of economic prosperity and recovery from depression, as in the second world war. We are not and never have been a peace-loving nation; we are not only ruthless and bloody but we feel no shame about it. There is nothing in our Constitution; in our national heroes, many of whom are generals; in our national origin, which came out of a war; in our greatest single national experience, which was the Civil War; or in anything which contributes to our national image which makes war illegitimate in the way racial discrimination is felt to be illegitimate and inconsistent with our national ideals. In the case of war we have very little hypocrisy, and change is very difficult. The peace movement is not simply trying to mobilize an already existing mass feeling of sentiment; it is trying to create a radical change in the national image, against which all the forces of ordinary legitimacy seem to be arrayed. In the case of the peace movement, therefore, protest arouses counterprotest with great ease. The hawks in our society far outnumber the doves, and those who flutter the dovecotes stand in danger of arousing clouds of hawks from their innumerable nests. It will take an extensive process of education and perhaps even the grim teacher of national disaster before we learn that the prevailing national image is incompatible with our well-being or even with our survival, and we have yet to learn that we are only one people among many, that we are not the rulers of the world,

that power cannot be exercised without legitimacy, and that the costs of stable peace, significant and important as they are, are far less than the benefits.

The teach-in movement represents perhaps a partly subconscious recognition of the validity of some of the above principles. It began as a movement of pure protest and outrage. The motivations which inspired it were no doubt various. They included a genuine fear of escalation into nuclear warfare; they included also a sense of moral outrage at the use of such things as napalm and the "lazy dog," and the appalling sufferings which we are imposing on the Vietnamese in the supposed name of freedom and democracy. Coupled with this, unquestionably, were some people on the left who were politically sympathetic with the objectives of the Vietcong, though in the original movement there were few if any of these. I am inclined to think that the largest motivating factor was a sense of simple human sympathy with the sufferings of the Vietnamese, and a sense of outrage at the utterly inhuman weapons of the American air force, and a sense of outrage also that we were using Vietnamese as the guinea pigs in weapon experimentation. The method of protest first suggested by the original group at University of Michigan was a work moratorium and a one-day suspension of classes. This violated a good many of the above principles. It is a form of protest which is not related to the object of protest; it immediately aroused a large counterprotest over the means, as well as over the object of protest, and it was very strongly on the protest side of the spectrum and away from education. The teach-in, which was adopted as a substitute, was much more successful. It at least edged toward the education end of the spectrum, even though it still retained a good many of the qualities of protest, and it was appropriate to the situation. The teach-in movement, furthermore, seems to be developing more and more in the direction of dialogue rather than pure protest, and this itself reflects the fact that there is an educational task ahead rather then a task of pure protest. The basic problem here is change in the national image itself, and this is something which protest is singularly unable to do, for protest has to take the image for granted and call attention to certain inconsistencies and incompatibilities. It assumes a given national image and says, in effect, to the policymaker, "be consistent with it."

AN EFFECTIVE STRATEGY

Under these circumstances, what is likely to be the best strategy for those of us who are interested in producing social change toward stable peace? The answer seems fairly clear. It should be a strategy of limited protest and extensive education. We should not, I think, abandon protest altogether, for there are many points even now at which, for instance, the conduct of the war in Vietnam violates a widespread national image of the United States as a reasonably decent and compassionate country. Protest, I suspect, should be directed mainly at the air force; it should be directed at the use of specific weapons which certainly fall under the heading of "cruel and unusual punishments," the moral feeling against which is securely enshrined in our Constitution and history. We have paid enough lip service to the United Nations also, to render protests on this score viable. The contrast between the shred of legitimacy which the United Nations gave us in Korea and the total absence of legitimacy in Vietnam is very striking, and protest could well be concentrated on this. We also have in our national image a high value on negotiation and a willingness to negotiate, and our present interpretation of negotiation as the abject surrender of the other side can be protested fiercely and effectively. Beyond this, I suspect, protest will be ineffective, with one possible exception. Our deepest trouble in Vietnam arises out of the total failure of our China policy, and at this point it may well be that the country is ripe for change, and that, to continue this particular metaphor, protest will shake the tree. There is real danger lest in our obsession with Vietnam we forget the larger issue and we forget that the solution to Vietnam lies in our relationship with Peking.

Beyond this, social change toward stable peace can only come through education and research. The educational task is to convince people that stable peace is possible. Here we need to point to the many examples in which it has already been achieved. In the educational process, unlike in the process of protest, we want to tie in as far as possible with existing legitimacy, existing images, and familiar history. We need to play up how we got a security community with the British and the Canadians. We need to play up historical examples of peaceful coexistence, such as was achieved between Protestants and Catholics in the Treaty of Westphalia in 1648. We need to emphasize the continuing dynamic that goes on in socialist countries as well as in our own, and to emphasize the learning process and our role as a teacher. We need to emphasize also the possible role of the United States not as a great power or as a world dominator, but as a leader in a world movement for stable peace. All these things can easily be fitted into existing images and existing legitimacies. Then at some point, a protest movement may be necessary to crystallize the image as a peace leader. This may be some time off, but we should be ready for it when it comes.

CONFLICT MANAGEMENT AS A LEARNING PROCESS

In: *Ciba Foundation Symposium on Conflict in Society,* A.V.S. de Reuck and J. Knight, eds. London: J. & A. Churchill, 1966, pp. 236-248

CONFLICT MANAGEMENT AS A LEARNING PROCESS

T HE theory of conflict, like most other theories, can be divided into statics and dynamics. Statics, to be meaningful and interesting, has to be what economists call "comparative statics", that is, the comparison of two possible states of a system. If the states have some kind of equilibrium properties, this makes the comparison all the more interesting. In the case of conflict systems, equilibrium states such as, for instance, the equilibrium position of an arms race have some meaning and comparative statics has some interest, especially when it demonstrates how a very small change in the parameters of a system can sometimes cause large changes in the equilibrium position. Many conflict processes, however, do not have clear equilibrium states and for the study of these, dynamics is essential. Conflict dynamics, then, deals with the succession of states in the system and the way in which two or more successive states of the system are related in some stable or non-random fashion. Dynamics is more fundamental than statics in the sense that any equilibrium system is only a special case of a dynamic process in which the dynamic process itself results in a continuation of the present state of the system. In a simple dynamic process of the first degree we suppose that we have a succession of states of the system S_0, S_1, S_2, etc., and that S_0 produces S_1 and S_1 produces S_2 in some fairly simple and regular way. If now this dynamic system eventually produces a state S_e such that S_e produces S_e and so on indefinitely, we have an equilibrium system.

The key to both statics and dynamics in any process is the abstract description of the state of the system as it exists at any one moment. The exact description of the state of any system, and especially of any social system, is almost certainly beyond the powers of any possible human language. If communication is to be achieved at all there must be abstraction, that is, a deliberate simplification of the system to what are regarded as its essential elements. This process of abstracting the essential elements of the system is the main task of theory, and without theory of some kind, no communication is possible, even in the most commonplace conversation. Scientific theory consists merely in doing in a formal and rigorous way, taking special precautions against false inference and false perception, what we do all the time in ordinary life and conversation.

The simplest abstract description of a conflict system is shown in Fig. 1 in what is sometimes known as a welfare or utility field. Here we suppose that we have two parties; let us call them Able and Baker. We do not specify the nature of the parties; they may be persons or they may be organizations; they may even be subsystems within a person or organization. All we need to know about them is that it should be possible to derive some kind of objective or formal measure of their welfare. We shall leave the question of whether this needs to be a cardinal measure or whether we can be satisfied with ordinal measures, as for some purposes we can, and shall assume for the moment a cardinal measure. This might be something like, for instance, an index of real per capita income. We then measure Able's welfare in the vertical direction parallel to OA and Baker's welfare in the horizontal direction parallel to OB. Any point in such a field, such as P_0, then represents a combination of the welfares of Able and Baker, P_0M for Baker and P_0N for Able. Any change in state in such a field, say, from P_0 to P_1, we call a "move". If the slope of the line P_0P_1 is negative, this is defined as a "conflict move", since the move makes one party worse off and the other party better off. Thus the move from P_0 to P_I makes Baker better off and Able worse off; a move from P_I to P_0 would make Able better off and Baker worse off. Two other kinds of moves are also possible. When the line joining the two positions has a positive slope, such as a move from P_0 to P_b, I call this a "benign

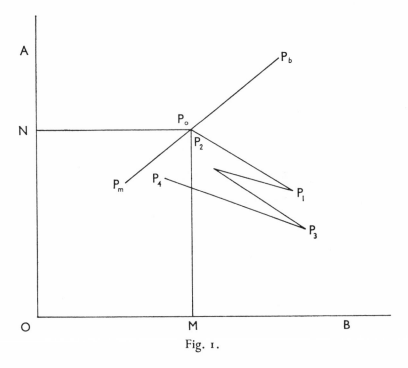

Fig. 1.

move" because it makes both parties better off. A move such as from P_0 to P_m I call a "malign move" because it makes both parties worse off.

The next step is to describe the value system and the behaviour of the parties in the field. Let us suppose first an arbitrary succession of moves and suppose that Able makes the first move from the point P_0. We may suppose that he has an image in his mind of an opportunity field, which is the shaded area in Fig. 2, surrounded by an opportunity boundary The opportunity field

consists of all the points in the welfare field which Able believes
he can reach by some act or decision on his part. Each of these
points in the utility field corresponds to one or perhaps more
points in the larger *n*-dimensional field which represents the
actual state of the system. Where Able will move, that is, what

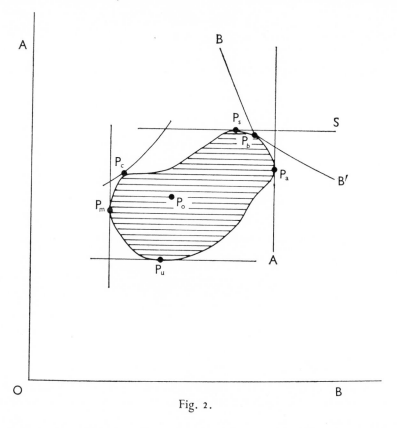

Fig. 2.

decision he will make, depends not only on his perception of the
state of the system and his perception of the relation between the
state of the system and the welfare field, but also on his personal
value function, the value function being defined as the ordering
which he gives to every point on the welfare field. Able's value
function can be described by means of indifference curves, or
lines of equal value to him, which will be the contours of a

surface in which the vertical dimension represents Able's evaluation, or the value placed by him on the situation. The slope of these indifference curves describes a very important characteristic of the value function. Four extreme cases may be distinguished. The first is pure selfishness, in which Able is indifferent to Baker's welfare and always prefers his own welfare to be higher. The indifference curves will then be horizontal straight lines parallel to P_sS and Able will take the decision which will move him to P_s, where his own welfare is maximized. Another extreme case is that of absolute altruism, in which Able is indifferent to his own welfare and always prefers an increase in the welfare of Baker. In this case his indifference curves will be vertical, such as P_aA, and he will move to the point P_a, where Baker's welfare is maximized within Able's opportunity field. Two other extreme cases may be postulated for the sake of completeness. One is absolute unselfishness, or perhaps masochism, in which Able is indifferent to Baker but prefers a lower to a higher welfare for himself (we recall that welfare is an objective, not a subjective, measure). In this case he will move to a point such as P_u. The other possibility is absolute malevolence, in which case Able is indifferent to his own welfare but always prefers to have Baker's welfare lowered. In this case he will move to the point P_m. Between these extreme positions there will be mixed cases. If for instance Able has some selfishness and some benevolence, his indifference curve will have a negative slope such as BP_bB', and Able will move to a point such as P_b, where his opportunity field boundary is touched by one of these indifference curves. It will be noted that the indifference curves do not have to be linear. The slope of such an indifference curve at any point might be called a coefficient of benevolence (mathematically negative), as it represents the amount of Baker's welfare that Able will substitute for one unit of his own and still feel equally well satisfied. If the indifference curve has a declining slope, as in the figure, it means that Able's benevolence diminishes as Able's welfare diminishes, which is not implausible. If the indifference curve has a positive slope, we have mixed selfishness and malevolence, as at P_c.

In the simplest dynamic model we simply assume a succession of moves, we assume the opportunity boundaries for each party, and we assume their value functions. In these circumstances a succession of moves can be specified in advance. Able will move to the position where his value is maximized. Baker then is able to draw an opportunity boundary around this point and moves within this to a point where his value function is maximized. Then Able repeats the process, Baker repeats the process, and so on. We then get a succession of states of the system, such as P_0, P_1, P_2, P_3, P_4 and so on in Fig. 1. Each of these moves may, of course, be either a conflict move or a benign or malign move, depending on the nature of the value systems. The succession from P_0 to P_4 in Fig. 1 has the very interesting property that even though each of the individual moves is a conflict move, the final result of the move from P_0 to P_4 is malign; that is, both parties are worse off objectively as a result of the succession of conflict moves. A benign succession is equally possible, moving, let us say, from P_4 to P_3 to P_2 to P_1 to P_0.

A succession of moves in the welfare field may reach an equilibrium, this being defined as the point where both parties visualize their opportunity boundary and their value function in such a way that they cannot increase the value by making any move at all. Thus, suppose in Fig. 2 that the actual position was P_b and Able's value function was BP_bB'. Able would not be able to make any move which would make him subjectively better off, and hence he would remain at P_b as long as the choice lay in his hands. If Baker was in a similar position, the whole system would remain in equilibrium.

It is when we come to look at what might be called the second-order dynamics of a system that the learning process becomes important. In the dynamic model already described there is no learning at all. The perceptions of the field, the perceptions of the opportunity boundary and the value functions are simply accepted as given for the two parties and we see that even in these circumstances a dynamic process can be described. In reality, of course, these things are not given; they are learned. They are learned partly through genetic processes which govern the growth of the nervous system and partly from inputs of information. As we move up the evolutionary ladder the proportion of total learning which is genetic diminishes until in the case of man it is almost insignificant, though it cannot be neglected entirely. If, then, there is a dynamics of learning from inputs into the system, we can no longer assume that the perceptions and the values of the parties are given, for these will change in the course of time, simply because every move in the process represents an input of information. These inputs take place in a number of ways. There is, first of all, direct perception and experience. If somebody hits me on the nose, I tend to "learn" that he is hostile towards me. He may not, in fact, be malevolent; he may indeed be quite benevolent and is hitting me on the nose for my own good. I am inclined to interpret this experience, however, as malevolence on his part, and I consequently learn to be malevolent towards him. One of the rules of learning in conflict situations seems to be that each party learns to become like his perception of the other. A situation of this kind can easily produce curiously unstable dynamic systems. Even an accidental act which is interpreted as a hostile one may produce malevolence in one party which may then produce malevolence in the other in a dynamic process of constantly increasing malevolence in the value systems. In terms of Fig. 2, with each move the indifference curve of each party tends to have a greater positive slope. Even a process of this kind may, of course, reach an equilibrium at the point at which no further reaction on the value systems takes place. A similar process of increasing benevolence can also take place, often again started off by a relatively random event. As Lewis Richardson himself pointed out, falling in love is a process qualitatively extraordinarily similar to an arms race, the only difference being in the mathematical sign.

The system is complicated by the fact that even in a relatively restricted conflict process we learn not only from the process itself but also from inputs from systems outside the process. Both Able and Baker in the model are continually receiving inputs from other parties. The pure dyad is a very rare social system. These inputs from other parties again may take the form of direct experiences, or they may take the form of general information inputs of a symbolic nature, such as talk, reading, plays, television and the other mass media, and so on. It is this generalized input of information which tends to teach what might be called the general structure of the images of the parties, within which they are apt to interpret their own conflict situation. Thus, if Able as a result of his input from other parties has learned that the world in general is rather hostile and malevolent towards him, he is likely to interpret even benevolent moves of Baker in a hostile and malevolent way. We see this phenomenon in the extreme, of course, in the case of the paranoid, who interprets every input of information as confirming his previous view of the universe. The difficulty here is that these views often tend to be self-confirming. A person who believes that the world around him is fundamentally hostile will tend to behave in such a way as to make it so. There is a complex interaction here between the initial value function with which we start, our perception of the world, and the dynamics of the objective reality, whatever we mean by that.

An important element of the learning process in conflict systems is the development of what might be called "long-sightedness". This is largely a question of how we learn our image of the opportunity boundary. Thus, suppose we look at the process in Fig. 1 in which Baker moves from P_0 to P_1, making himself better off objectively and Able worse off. The assumption here is that P_1 is at the highest value point of his opportunity field, as shown in Fig. 2. Able now retaliates to P_2, Baker to P_3, and Able to P_4. The result of all these processes is that Baker is worse off than he was before, at P_0. If he is long-sighted, therefore, he will never move to P_I, because this will no longer be in his perception of his opportunity field; that is, the long-sighted opportunity field will be different from the short-sighted one. A great deal of the development of what I have called mature conflict behaviour consists in the development of long-sightedness, or the realization that the taking of the short-run advantage often results in a long-term loss because of the reactions of other parties. One of the questions on which very little research has been done, however, is how people and institutions in fact develop long-sightedness, beyond the fact that this seems to be characteristic of a process of maturation. Even adolescents, for instance, tend to be more long-sighted than small children, and adults more long-sighted than adolescents; perhaps even old organizations are more long-sighted than young ones. Nevertheless, we understand extraordinarily little about the exact processes and the exact inputs that produce this change. Learning is always associated with some kind of feedback or disappointment, and it is presumably because short-sightedness gets us into trouble that we learn to change it. However, the fact remains that some people learn and some people do not, no matter how much trouble they get into, simply because it is not always easy to identify the source of the trouble in our own images, values and behaviour.

What I have called the development of long-sightedness is one aspect of a larger process, which is the formation of "realistic" images. The epistemological question of what we mean by realistic here is a difficult one and all sorts of philosophical spectres lie lurking in the bushes. If we like, we can simply define "realistic" operationally as those images of the world which give us the highest probability of benign moves, or of moves which lead to an actual increase in our own values. However, this still leaves open the question, which cannot be altogether shunted aside, of whether our values are "good" values. There is a critique of value systems itself which is the function of ethical analysis and which cannot be gone into here. It is perhaps easier to define "unrealistic" images than realistic ones. An unrealistic image is one which leads to the realization of a lower level of our own values than we expected—strictly, I suppose we should say a different level of values from the one we expected. If, however, such disappointments are to result in more realistic images there must be an efficient learning process. The most important element in conflict management, therefore, is learning how to learn. One is in some danger of an infinite regress here, for then we have to learn how to learn how to learn, and so on. We may, however, perhaps be content with identifying in the dynamic process certain elements which improve the ability to learn and which result, therefore, in the development of more realistic images.

One of the problems in the dynamics of conflict which we have hitherto neglected, but which is also intimately bound up with the learning process, is the problem of when to move, which is involved in the larger problem of the succession of moves itself. Up to now we have assumed that the succession of moves was arbitrary, and that each party moved after the other. In the real world this is often not the case. We may get a succession of moves by one party without any response at all on the part of the other, simply because there is in the system a dynamic process of change which is not dependent on the decision of the parties themselves. If the decision of the parties could alone change the system, then if we could decide which party moves first, which is often very important, the system would be determinate from then on, as each party presumably moves in each move to an optimum position and will not make a subsequent move unless the other party makes one which changes his position. Where, however, the system itself is changing because of the decisions of parties outside the particular system or because of trends and movements in the environment which are not due to any decision at all, the question of when to move becomes more difficult and the possibility of a sequence of moves by a single party without any response from the other can arise. In a dynamic system of this kind, we have to invoke something like a "threshold" phenomenon, assuming that a move takes place only when the pressure to move rises above a certain threshold. The question of what thresholds are optimum is a very difficult one, to which very little attention has been given. In the Richardson theory of arms races, for instance, an essential parameter is the reactivity of each party towards the other.* This reactivity, however, may depend much more on some generalized threshold phenomenon than on anything which is peculiar to the international system. Thus the American-Russian arms race was damped down under Eisenhower not because he was less reactive to the Russians but because he was conservative financially. A learning process in one field, therefore, easily carries over into the parameters of another. This makes for almost unbearable theoretical complexity, but it is a complexity, alas, which is all too characteristic of the real world.

Perhaps the main reason why conflict, in spite of its many generally beneficial effects, is continually tending to get out of hand and to become destructive and malign, is that the conduct of a conflict frequently results in a pathological learning process. If somebody hits me on the nose, I learn something, but I am unlikely to learn either long-sightedness or scientific method, and I am particularly unlikely to learn how to refine the learning process itself. As conflicts degenerate into violence, they are particularly likely to corrupt the learning process. It is depressingly significant of our value system today, for instance, that we use the term "escalation", that is, going up, for what is essentially a process of going down, into violence and into ever more degeneration and corruption. Conflict management, therefore, is something which does not necessarily arise out of the conduct of conflict itself. It has to be fed into it from outside. That is to say,

---

* Richardson, L. F. (1960). Arms and Insecurity: A Mathematical Study of the Causes and Origins of War. Ed. Rashevsky, N., and Trucco, E. Pittsburgh: Boxwood Press.

it is when conflict exists in a social matrix and also an organizational matrix which can lead to a lot of input into the system from outside the parties that it is most likely to result in constructive learning and benign processes. Here, again, is a field of much-needed research, especially in the family and in larger organizations. What, for instance, is the impact of parents on the conflict management and the learning processes of children? It would seem from casual observation that children do not learn the processes of conflict management from each other or from their peers, simply because the emotional trauma which results in the conflict processes is so great that it inhibits the development of long-sightedness. This, however, is a proposition capable of disproof, and it may be that there are subtle elements within conflict processes themselves which permit constructive learning from them in the process of maturation.

At the larger level of society as a whole, we also need studies of the social matrix of conflict, particularly considered as the source of the learning process. The institutions of law, for instance, have rarely been considered in this light. Nevertheless, unless the institutions of law result in a learning process on the part of those affected by them, they are likely to be ineffective. Religion likewise is a powerful instrument of outside learning in many conflict processes and the extent to which it exacerbates or resolves conflict may depend very much on the nature of the learning processes associated with its institutions and practices. There is great need for some collaborative studies between the sociologists of religion on the one hand and the students of conflict on the other. Formal education likewise is an important element in creating the matrix of conflict. It frequently tends towards the resolution of conflict within the State and the exacerbation of conflicts between them, as formal education becomes more and more an instrument of the State. The learning of nationalism, for instance, is something that has been very little studied. This perhaps is the main reason why conflict tends to be managed fairly well within a society, whereas international conflict, which has only a very primitive social matrix, is managed extremely badly and at enormously high cost.

It is my personal view that the major task facing humanity today is the reconstruction of the international system along lines which make its conflicts more manageable and less costly. The theoretical considerations of this paper should be of great importance here, for what we are facing is a learning process in the minds of the decision-makers who operate the international system. Unfortunately, the number of these decision-makers is rather few, which means that the random element in the system is very important. Nevertheless, one can hope that a general learning process can go on, that more sophisticated images of the system can become widespread, and that as formal education propagates these more sophisticated images, the external learning process in the international system can tend to dominate that internal learning process which is so destructive. The conduct of international conflict produces violence, paranoia, and pathological learning processes. It is only as we can develop inputs of information from outside the system that we can hope to change and reverse this process and develop an international system which will have the property of stable peace.

THE PARAMETERS OF POLITICS

University of Illinois Bulletin,
63, 139 (July 15, 1966): 3-21

THE PARAMETERS OF POLITICS

The simplest definition of a parameter is that it is a variable constant, but as this definition, though simple, is also absurd, some verbal bypass has to be found. My weightiest authority in this matter (about eight pounds), Van Nostrand's Scientific Encyclopedia, defines it as "(1) An arbitrary constant, as distinguished from a fixed or absolute constant. Any desired numerical value can be given to a parameter. Parametric equations are often useful, especially in the description of plane or space curves. (2) In statistics, a parameter is a constant, capable of having any one of a set of values, appearing in the specification of a probability distribution."

Other dictionaries, other circumlocutions, as the French might say. However defined, the parameter is an enormously important concept in systems theory. Any system is defined first by a set of elements, that is, whatever it is that participates in the system, secondly by a set of relationships among these elements. If there are enough relationships and of the right kinds, the system is said to be predictive, in the sense that specifying the relations also specifies all the characteristics of the system. If the relations càn be expressed by equations having parameters which can be given numerical values, the system may be said to be a parametric system. This then has the property that if the relationships are specified, the properties of the system are a function of the parameters, that is, they depend on the numerical values of the constants of the equations.

Parametric systems are common in all sciences. One of the simplest is the movement of a body with constant acceleration, as for instance under the influence of gravity in a vacuum. At a given point, the actual path of the body depends on the constant of acceleration itself; thus at the surface of the earth it will be very different from what it would be at the surface of the moon, or out in space. Coming now closer to the social sciences, equilibrium price theory is a parametric system, as represented, for instance, by the Walrasian Equations,[1] in which we postulate n equations involving the set of all relative prices and n unknowns of the relative price set itself, so that theoretically the equations, if they are well behaved, can be solved. We may note a rather tricky point here, that if the equations of a parametric system are linear, there is no problem about their solution except insofar as the solution values may not be empirically

[1] Walras, L., *Elements d'économie politique pure,* 4th ed., Lausanne, 1900.

significant. Thus, for instance, it may not be possible for the variables to have negative values. If the relationships are nonlinear, we can get into much more trouble. We may get multiple solutions, though these may in some cases be significant; or we may get solutions in terms of imaginary numbers, which represent an empirical breakdown of the system altogether. These nonempirical solutions may, of course, be significant, insofar as they represent a breakdown of the system which may correspond to empirical reality. Empirical study is always heavily biased in favor of what exists, whereas in the totality of possible systems, systems which do not exist or even which cannot exist are far more numerous than those which exist.

What might be called the crude Keynesian system is a good example of a parametric system and the parametric way of thinking, which has had a profound effect on economic policy in all countries, even more so, perhaps, than the parametric models of demand and supply. There are four variables of the system, the total national income or real product (Y), the aggregate real consumption (C), the aggregate level of accumulation or investment (A), and the amount of the desired or planned investment (A'). There are then four equations or relationships which determine the system:

$$Y = C + A \tag{1}$$

$$C = F_c(Y) = C_o + m_c Y \tag{2}$$

$$A' = F_a(Y) = A_o + m_a Y \tag{3}$$

$$A = A' \tag{4}$$

Equation (1) is an identity which simply states that everything that is produced in a given period is either consumed or it is still around, that is, it has been added to the total stock. If we put this into the form

$$Y - C = A \tag{5}$$

it becomes the famous "savings equals investment" identity, income minus consumption being aggregate saving, and accumulation being aggregate investment. Equation (2) is the consumption function, indicating that consumption is a function of total income; equation (3) is the induced investment function, indicating that the total volume of desired investment may also be a function of aggregate income; and equation (4) is the condition of equlibrium, that actual investment should equal planned or desired investment. If now we suppose that equations (2) and (3) have a linear form as shown, the equations can be solved as in equation (6):

$$Y = \frac{C_o + A_o}{1 - (m_c + m_a)} \tag{6}$$

Y is then an equilibrium value of the national income. It was Keynes' most profound insight to suggest that this equilibrium value did not necessarily represent a full-employment value, and that hence we might have under-employment equilibria which would be at least moderately stable in the short run.

Each of the four parameters of the system has a simple meaning. C_o measures the height or the magnitude of the consumption function; m_c is the famous marginal propensity to consume, or the increase in consumption which results from a unit increase in total income. Similarly, A_o, which is probably negative, measures the height or magnitude of the investment function, and m_a is the propensity to invest, or the increase in investment which will result from a unit increase in income. A simple graphic solution of the system is shown in Figure 1, where total income is measured horizontally and its various components vertically. C_oC is the consumption curve corresponding to equation (2), A_oA the investment curve corresponding to equation (3); the curve B_oB is the summation of

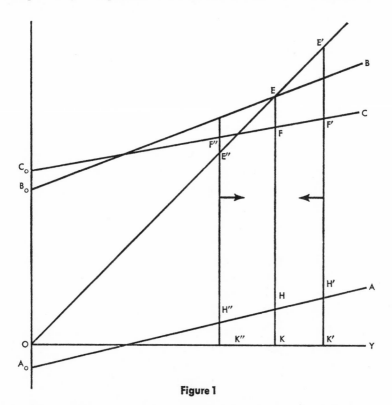

Figure 1

the two, which I have called the total absorption curve, and it shows
how much of the total product will be absorbed either in consumption or in desired investment at each level of income. The equilibrium position is at E, where B_oB is intersected by the 45° line OE,
indicating the fact that at the equilibrium point all the income or
product must be absorbed. Thus at E, the actual accumulation EF,
or the excess of income over consumption, is equal to the desired
accumulation HK, shown by the investment curve. OK is the
equilibrium level of income. At levels above this, for instance at
K′, the total actual accumulation, F′E′, is greater than that desired,
K′H′. This means there will be unwanted accumulations, and the
reaction of the system to this is a reduction of output. If output is
below OK, say OK″, the actual accumulation, F″E″, will be less
than desired, K″H″; there will be unwanted decumulations, and
output will increase. The system therefore is stable.

This system can be expanded and modified in a great many
different ways. We can introduce an acceleration principle into it
by supposing, for instance, that desired investment depends on the
rate of change of income, as well as on income itself. We can expand the system by introducing government explicitly, thus edging
closer towards the political parameters. This is shown in equations
(7) to (11):

$$Y = B + G \tag{7}$$

$$B = B_o + m_b(Y - T) \tag{8}$$

$$Y = \frac{B_o + G - m_bT}{1 - m_b} \tag{9}$$

$$D = G - T \tag{10}$$

$$Y = \frac{1}{1 - m_b} B_o + \frac{m_b}{1 - m_b} D + G \tag{11}$$

$B = (C+A)$ might be called the total private absorption. G is the
total product absorbed by government, in dollar terms equal to total
government expenditure. Equation (7) then states that the total
income must be absorbed either by the private sector or by government. Equation (8) is a behavior equation, which indicates that
private absorption is a function of what might be called private
income, $Y - T$, T being the total tax bill. Solving these two equations, we get an equation for total income (9) in terms of total government expenditure and total government receipts. If we define
the government deficit, D, as $G - T$, equation (10), then we can put

equation (9) in the form of (11), relating the government deficit and total government expenditure to total income.

The implications of equation (11) to those unaccustomed to parametric thinking are quite startling. It suggests, for instance, that an increase in government expenditure produces an equal increase in income, if the other parameters do not change. It suggests even more strikingly that an increase in the deficit without any change in government expenditure will produce a greater increase in income than the increase in the deficit. If the propensity to absorb, m_b, is about 0.8, which seems a reasonable figure, then the deficit multiplier, as it is called, $\dfrac{m_b}{1 - m_b}$, is about 4, indicating that a one dollar increase in the deficit increases income by four dollars. The model illustrates, however, one of the dangers of parametric systems. We must beware of assuming that the parameters of the system are independent of each other. In this case they may not be. An increase in G, for instance, is quite likely to produce an increase in D, especially if the increase in G is large enough, as it is in wartime. An increase in either G or D may produce a decrease in B_0, that is, may reduce the private absorption constant. The Ricardian case against attempting to increase income by government expenditure or deficits rested on the implicit assumption that any increase in D or G would produce an exactly offsetting increase in B_0.

This model can also be applied to problems of inflation. It leads directly, for instance, into what is called the "principle of overfinance," that is, if we have an increase in total government expenditures, G, and we wish to keep the total income constant in order to prevent inflation, we must diminish the deficit or increase the surplus, which is simply a negative deficit, by an amount depending on the deficit multiplier. This means that if we are at full employment and wish to prevent inflation under the impact of an expansion of government expenditure, we must raise taxes by more than the expansion of government expenditure. This is pretty hard to do in the case of a war, where G expands very rapidly, so that it is not at all surprising that war virtually always produces inflation.

This model also illustrates another principle of parametric systems, that in applying them to reality we have to be very careful that their inevitable incompleteness does not mislead us. Thus in the case of the system which results in equation (11), no explicit account is taken of the price-wage level. Y is the national income in dollar terms, and is equal to the product of the national income in real terms, Y_r, and the wage-price level, P (equation 12).

$$Y = Y_r P \qquad (12)$$

We could stabilize Y and have large fluctuations, in opposite directions, of Y_r and P, and as it is Y_r that we are really interested in, stabilizing Y is not enough. This illustrates what is in fact a major dilemma of the American economy at the moment, that as we increase Y towards a full employment level with existing prices and wages, prices and wages start to rise, and the attempt to prevent a rise in prices and wages by monetary or fiscal methods results in unemployment, not in affecting prices and wages themselves. Up to now we do not have any institutional device much more subtle than the Presidential anger institutionalized as guidelines, which is hardly a very adequate apparatus. On the other hand, nobody wants to go to detailed price and wage control, which is an administrative nightmare.

Equations (9) or (11) illustrate very beautifully the logic of the tax cut as an instrument of increasing national income. We see directly from equation (9) that a diminution in taxes, government expenditure and private absorption being constant, will increase income by an amount greater than the tax cut. The tax cut multiplier, indeed, is $\dfrac{m_b}{1 - m_b}$, which, as we have suggested, may be as large as four, so that a dollar tax cut produces a four-dollar increase in national income, other things being equal. If the tax cut makes people cheerful and encourages private absorption so that B_o increases, the effect is still larger.

The model can easily be extended to illustrate another property of parametric systems, which is the frequently unintended consequences of new policies and institutions. Suppose we recognize that the total tax bill is itself a function of the national income, and assume a simple relationship such as equation (13).

$$T = T_o + m_t Y \qquad (13)$$

Here T_o measures the general level of taxes, m_t is the propensity for taxes to increase with income. If the tax system is progressive, m_t will be greater than 1, that is, a dollar increase in income will produce more than a dollar increase in total taxes. Substituting this value of T in equation (9), we get equation (14):

$$Y = \frac{B_o + G - m_b T_o}{1 - m_b (1 - m_t)} \qquad (14)$$

Comparing equation (14) with equation (9), we see that the denominator in equation (14) is much larger than in equation (9). This means that the results on Y of changes in B_0 or G are much less in equation (14) than they are in equation (9), that is, the stability of the system is much greater; and the greater is m_t, the greater the stability of the system. Thus the introduction of a progressive deductible-at-source income tax, conceived primarily in the interests of social justice and administrative convenience, in fact turned out to be an enormously successful automatic stabilizer, and provided, as it were, a real thermostat for the economic system, with enormous political consequences. It so happened that in the '50s the thermostat was set too low, and that the system stabilized at about 6 percent unemployment. In the 1960's we have done better than that, and we have an almost certain protection against a great depression.

We might draw other illustrations from economics, but the main purpose of this paper is to ask how far the notion of parametric systems can be applied to what are political variables. The first question, of course, is what are the elements of the political system. This is by no means an easy question to answer, especially for one who has no more than doubtful amateur status as a political scientist. The political system is less sharply defined even than the economic system. I have been tempted sometimes to define it as that part of the total social system which is concerned with organizing human behavior through legitimated threat, as economics organizes it through exchange. There are, however, many elements of exchange and bargaining in what are ordinarily thought of as political institutions, and indeed a good deal of political theory in the last ten or fifteen years, by such authors as Lindblom and Dahl,[2] Buchanan and Tulloch,[3] and Anthony Downs,[4] have attempted to explain political life and institutions almost wholly in terms of an extension of exchange through bargaining procedures. Another approach to the definition of politics comes through decision theory, political decisions being those which are made on behalf of others or which affect others in such a way that there is feedback from those affected to those making the decisions. In this sense there is a political aspect of all organizations, even the family, and the bigger

[2] Dahl, R. A., and Lindblom, C. E., *Politics, Economics, and Welfare.* New York: Harper and Bros., 1953.
[3] Buchanan, James M., and Tulloch, G., *The Calculus of Consent.* Ann Arbor: University of Michigan Press, 1962.
[4] Downs, Anthony, *An Economic Theory of Democracy.* New York: Harper and Row, 1965.

the organization, the more important the political aspect becomes. There are certainly political aspects of trade unions, universities, corporations, and so on, which are just as extensive as the political aspects of national states; and the older political theory which thought in terms of politics as "government" and political institutions almost exclusively in terms of the state is seen to be only part of a much larger political aspect of the social system. It is not my business, however, and perhaps not anybody's business, to try to define the boundaries of politics, and I am only going to try a rough list of elements in the order in which they seem susceptible to parametric treatment, that is, to quantification, both in the definition of the element and in the specification of the relations between them. The list is intended to be illustrative rather than definitive, and I would be happy to receive suggestions for additions or even subtractions.

1. I would list first the size and composition of budgets, both of national states, their political subdivisions, and even perhaps the budgets of organizations which are not usually thought of as political, such as universities, corporations, trade unions, churches, and so on. A budget seems to me the prime expression of political decision. It may be arrived at, of course, by all sorts of bargaining and horse-trading among people and organizations who are affected, but the essence of the political process in any organization seems to me to reach a decision on a budget, and to make this decision effective. The budget, therefore, is the typical institution of politics as the market is of economics, and indeed the degree of politicization of a society can be measured by the extent to which the allocation of its resources is determined through budgets rather than through markets. The processes by which the size of budgets is determined are by no means clear, and they differ from organization to organization. Nevertheless, as I hope to show later, certain rather simple parametric systems may throw light on this problem.

2. Another group of elements in the political system relates to what might be called the degree of political participation. Statistics of election votes are an example of this, and studies of voting behavior already suggest that there may be parametric systems involved. The problem is complicated, however, by the fact that a vote is taken at a particular moment in time, and represents a temporal cross-section of a complex dynamic process, which seldom has a chance to reach an equilibrium. We also have here a system with fairly strong random elements, in which, again, decisions are

made at particular moments in a dynamic process, the course of which may be strongly affected by random shocks. We should not despair, of course, even of dynamic and stochastic parametric systems, but these are much more difficult to formulate and interpret, and it is very hard to find out what their parameters are. Another aspect of this part of the system would consist of various measures of political participation, party membership, attendance at meetings, arousal in regard to particular issues, and so on. Also related to these processes is the nature of the political information system, the political slants, for instance, of the mass media, the importance of political propaganda, the significance of face-to-face contacts or particular individual experiences, and so on. Here we rapidly reach an area where parametric models, though not inconceivable, have not yet had much success, though it is tempting to use certain epidemiological models in analyzing the spread of opinion, membership in organizations, or even techniques of action.

3. Budget formation, and even voting behavior, take existing political institutions and structures for granted. At the next level of theory, we must remove this limitation, and ask ourselves for instance what determines the sizes of political units. Is there an optimum size of the state, as there is of the firm; and if so, on what parameters of the social system does this depend? Are there similar rules for hierarchical subdivisions, which might determine how many provinces go to a country or how many departments to a dean? There are some parametric models, at any rate, which might throw light on this problem, even though the great intangibles of accident and history also play a nonparametric role. Related to the above question, but much more resistant to the parametric approach, are questions involving the structure of political organizations, the nature of constitutions, the democratic or dictatorial nature of the system, the presence or lack of stability of political institutions, the appropriateness of particular institutions to particular stages of economic development, the nature of legal systems, the nature and development of quasi-legal institutions such as regulatory commissions, civil rights boards, and so on. All this requires a vast amount of descriptive material, and a good deal of it is fairly resistant to quantification, but it represents an essential element of the political system nevertheless.

4. Finally, we come to what might be called the larger dynamics, the theories of history, the growth of community, the rise and sometimes the decline of legitimacies, the whole problem

of ideology, problems of the formation of nations, and their dissolution, problems of the rise of international and world organization, and so on. Here again is something which cannot be excluded from politics, but it is a field also where there are only the crudest attempts at quantification, as for instance in Toynbee's notion of optimum challenge, or Spengler's notion of a life cycle of civilization; and even these attempts are highly suspect.

Let us return, then, to the first of our categories of elements and look at one or two parametric models. We will probably not get very far in an attempt to develop models of total budgets, for these are made up from so many different elements. An interesting model can be constructed, however, of those parts of total budgets which are highly dependent on appropriations in budgets elsewhere. The most obvious example of this kind of system is that of the military budget. As a first approximation to answering the question, why are military budgets what they are, it is not unreasonable to suppose that the military budget of any one state is a function of the military budgets of all other states, even though some of the parameters of these functions may be zero. This gives us immediately a system of n equations, one for each state in an n-state system, and n unknowns, the military budget of each state; and if the equations are reasonably well behaved, an equilibrium solution can be found. We can illustrate this first with reference to a two-state or bipolar system. We suppose only two states, A and B, with military budgets in real terms, D_a and D_b. We then postulate two equations of partial equilibrium for each state, equations (15) and (16).

$$D_a = H_a + r_a D_b \qquad (15)$$

$$D_b = H_b + r_b D_a \qquad (16)$$

Each of the parameters has a clear meaning. H_a might be called the coefficient of hostility or militarism; it shows what will be the military budget of country A even if country B has no military budget at all. Similarly, H_b is the coefficient of hostility of country B. The parameter r_a is the coefficient of reactivity of A, and it shows by how much A will increase its military budget for each dollar increase in the military budget of B; r_b is the corresponding coefficient of reactivity of B. We can solve these equations and get explicit formulae for D_a and D_b, as in equations (17) and (18).

$$D_a = \frac{H_a + r_a H_b}{1 - r_a r_b} \qquad (17)$$

$$D_b = \frac{H_b + r_b H_a}{1 - r_a r_b} \qquad (18)$$

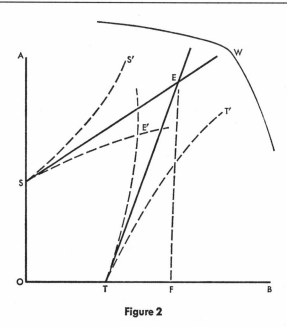

Figure 2

It is clear that the more hostile each country is and the more reactive it is, the larger the military budgets which we will end up with. This system is illustrated in Figure 2, where we measure A's military budget vertically and B's horizontally. SE represents equation (15), so that $OS = H_a$, and the slope of the line is r_a. The line TE represents equation (16), with $OT = H_b$, and the inverse slope of the line TE equal to r_b. E is the point of equilibrium, EF being the equilibrium value of D_a and OF the equilibrium value of D_b.

Those familiar with the work of Lewis Richardson[5] will recognize this as a Richardson process, as I have elsewhere called it, and in this very simple case it is clear that there will only be a position of equilibrium if the product of the reactivity coefficients is less than one. If it is equal to one, the two lines will be parallel, and if it is greater than one, they will diverge. The ever-present instability of the arms race is very clearly expressed in this model, for we might well regard a reactivity coefficient of one as "normal," and hence even for the bipolar system, we must have reactivities below normal, what we might perhaps call Eisenhower reactivities, if the system is to exhibit any equilibrium or stability.

If now we introduce a third country into the model, the situation gets much worse, from the point of view of the probability of

[5] Richardson, Lewis F., *Arms and Insecurity*. Pittsburgh: Boxwood Press, 1960.

equilibrium. If D_c is the defense expenditure of the third country, C, we now have three equations, (19), (20), and (21).

$$D_a = K_a + r_{ab}D_b + r_{ac}D_c \qquad (19)$$

$$D_b = K_b + r_{ba}D_a + r_{bc}D_c \qquad (20)$$

$$D_c = K_c + r_{ca}D_a + r_{cb}D_b \qquad (21)$$

These again can be solved. I have written out only the solution for D_a, equation (22), as the solutions for D_b and D_c are essentially similar, with corresponding changes in parameters.

$$D_a = \frac{K_a(1 - r_{bc}r_{cb}) + K_b(r_{ab} + r_{ac}r_{cb}) + K_c(r_{ac} + r_{ab}r_{bc})}{1 - r_{ac}r_{ca} - r_{bc}r_{cb} - r_{ab}r_{ba} - r_{ab}r_{bc}r_{ca} - r_{ac}r_{ba}r_{cb}} \qquad (22)$$

If we suppose that the reaction coefficients of all parties are equal and equal to r, equation (22) reduces to (23).

$$D_a = \frac{K_a(1 - r) + K_b r + K_c r}{1 - r - 2r^2} \qquad (23)$$

In order to have a solution, that is, for D_a, D_b, and D_c to be positive, we must have r less than ½. This means a very low reactivity, and it can be shown that the more parties there are in the system, the lower the average reactivity has to be to obtain an equilibrium. In Hobbes's "war of all against all" the reactivity would have to be negligible in order to get any equilibrium at all. Actually, of course, the more countries we have in the system, the better chance is there that there will be alliances, or low reactivities because of sheer distance. Thus, suppose that countries A and B are in what might be called a neutral alliance, so that $r_{ab} = r_{ba} = 0$, that is, each country regards an increase in the arms of the other as involving no change in its own security. In that case equation (22) reduces to equation (24).

$$D_a = \frac{K_a(1 - r_{bc}r_{cb}) + K_b r_{ac}r_{cb} + K_c r_{ac}}{1 - r_{ac}r_{ca} - r_{bc}r_{cb}} \qquad (24)$$

If we now suppose that all the reaction coefficients are equal and equal to r, the denominator of equation (24) reduces to $1 - 2r^2$, and the condition of equilibrium is that:

$$r < \frac{1}{\sqrt{2}} = 0.7 \qquad (25)$$

Even in the case of a neutral alliance, therefore, we see that the reactivity coefficients must average substantially less than "normal" if equilibrium is to be established.

Systems even as simple as this three-party system can often show quite unsuspected properties, which at least warn us against jumping to conclusions from models which are too simple. Thus in the above case, suppose we have what might be called a watertight alliance, in which A and B regard an increase in the armed force of the other as virtually the equivalent to an increase in its own, so that we have $r_{ab} = r_{ba} = -1$; that is, an increase in the military budget of either power of one dollar will result in the diminution of the military budget of the other by a dollar. We might think that this would reduce to the two-party case; in fact it does not, and the solution can easily break down. In cases like this the algebraic solution is often misleading, for the system operates under certain constraints. In this case, for instance, we suppose that the military budgets must be positive; hence if the algebraic solution gives a negative value for any one of them, this simply means that the system moves to the boundary, at which the value is zero. Figure 3 illustrates the difficulty in the above case. Here the field is the same as in Figure 2. The partial equilibrium curves, however, are AA' for A and BB' for B. Here we suppose that the slopes are the

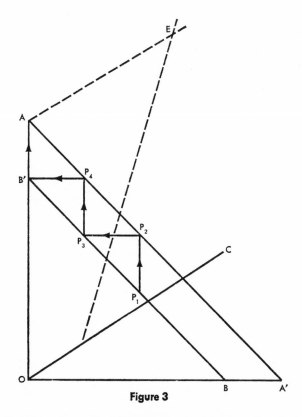

Figure 3

same, each having the same reactivity of -1. We have supposed, however, that A's index of hostility is somewhat greater than B's, OA being greater than OB. If now we suppose that the dynamics of the system involves successive moves, each party moving to its particular equilibrium curve, if we start from the point P_1, A will move to P_2, B to P_3, A to P_4, B to B', and A to A, ending up with B completely disarmed and relying entirely on A's armament. If now we measure D_c in the third dimension along OC, behind the plane of the paper, A and C may have a point of equilibrium at E, with B still disarmed and A and C in equilibrium with each other. This is not, perhaps, wholly unlike the situation of United States, Japan, and Russia in the last twenty years, with Japan, of course, playing the part of B.

These complications, of course, are merely illustrative of the complexities one may get into as one increases the number of actors. One gets into further complexities as one relaxes the assumption of linearity. In this system, indeed, it is quite probable that the functions are nonlinear. The next simplest case would be where the reaction coefficient itself was a linear function of the total level of military expenditure. If the reaction coefficient declines with increased military expenditure, as in a certain range it may do, this improves the chance for stability in the system. In this case the lines SE and TE in Figure 2 would bend toward each other with a somewhat lower equilibrium at E'. If, however, the reactivities increase with increased military expenditure, as for instance the lines SS' and TT' in Figure 2, the chances of their intersecting and producing an equilibrium are so much reduced. We could obviously increase the complexity of the model as much as we wished, but by this point we are pretty certainly running into diminishing returns. Even as simple a model as this, however, can quite materially assist our thinking about the real world. It shows, for instance, that an arms race may reach an equilibrium or may not, depending on the quantitative parameters of the system. If it does not reach an equilibrium, then the system will explode towards some kind of a boundary, which presumably in this case is war. Thus in Figure 2, we could postulate a war boundary which might be something like the line W, and if the system has an equilibrium inside this line, it will remain in stable peace; if, however, the equilibrium point is beyond this line, the arms race will proceed until war ensues. If we are interested in disarmament, it is clear that we must work on the parameters of the system, building up the integrative system, reducing hostilities, reducing reactivities, until the position of equilibrium moves down towards the zero point of the field. If this happens, we can even have a disarmament race, which has, indeed, happened occasionally in human history. A certain amount of personal disarmament, for instance, proceeded in this way; as society mellowed, personal touchiness diminished, and a rational ethic replaced the heroic. It is not inconceivable that the same thing could happen in international relations; indeed on a small scale it has already happened, as between, for instance, the Scandinavian countries or as between the United States and Canada. The great advantage of thinking in terms of a parametric system is that it forces our attention on the parameters, not on the equilibrium itself; and attempts to change the equilibrium without changing the parameters are likely to be highly unsuccessful.

The system which we have developed for the theory of military expenditure might also be applied to certain other items of budget, particularly where emulation is important. In state budgets in the United States, for instance, if one state is particularly out of line with the others on a certain aspect of its budget, for example, education or care for the mentally ill, the adverse comparison with other states can easily be used as a political weapon within the state, and pressures are generated to move the state towards the average. This tendency is much stronger for states that are below the average than states that are above; consequently, where there is emulation, this tends toward a constant increase in the average itself. Indeed, one is almost tempted to formulate a law of ever-increasing budgets, simply because the forces, both internal and external, that lead to increase always seem to be stronger than those which lead to decrease. Internally, budgets originate in the divisions and departments of the organization, and each segment always thinks it could do a much better job if it got a larger share of the budget; hence initial estimates are almost always larger in total than the budget eventually turns out to be, and as the budget-making process proceeds up through the hierarchy, external factors come to be more and more important and the total environment of the organization comes into play, and the final decision almost always cuts back the budget from the totals which originated in the lower levels of the hierarchy. Nevertheless, the combination of a certain internal pressure to increase the budget with external emulation easily results in a dynamic which seems to have no real equilibrium. I confess that this is very far from an adequate theory of budgets, but then we *are* very far from an adequate theory of budgets. This is one of the most mysterious of social processes.

Turning now to my second class of elements of the political system, those relating to political participation, we seem to have here a part of the system which undoubtedly exhibits certain crude regularities, but where no simple parametric model, up to now at any rate, has been developed which corresponds even to the grossest characteristics of the system. Thus, assuming, for instance, that under many circumstances we will have an alternation of parties in power in a two-party system, what are the parameters which determine either the amplitude or the period of the fluctuation? We really do not know. Similarly, I know of no model of a political system which predicts the number of parties. Why, for instance, does the two-party system seem to be rather stable in some countries, like the United States and Great Britain, where it has even survived the elimination of a major party and its substitution by a new one, by contrast with the many-party systems which have characterized other countries, such as the Third Republic in France, and which ultimately seem to have led to a discrediting of the system? Even under a two-party system, the parties are loose coalitions, and under a many-party system, the government is a loose coalition. Why should the coalitions be stabler in some systems than in others? Perhaps somebody knows, but I must confess that I do not. Why, indeed, is the proportion of the electorate which votes so much larger in some countries than in others? What determines the degree of political participation? Again I find myself at a loss. These look like beautiful quantitative variables, about which, furthermore, we have a great deal of information; but no clear theory seems to emerge from the collection of this enormous mass of data.

The studies of voting behavior, especially during election campaigns, suggest that we are here in the presence of a very subtle dynamic system with no real equilibria and with very strong random shocks. The closest one seems to be able to come to a system of this kind with a parametric model is in the epidemiological models which have been developed to account for the spread of disease. Lewis Richardson, for instance, who is certainly the pioneer of parametric politics, tried to use these in the explanation of the war moods of a society, but without much success.[6] The trouble seemed to be that most epidemiological models are based on contagion, in which it is contact of one person with another that either transmits or fails to transmit a certain state in one direction or the other. In

[6] Lewis Richardson, *op. cit.*

political epidemiology, however, the epidemics are airborne through the mass media, such the Kennedy-Nixon debates. The effect of these may be reinforced by what might be called local contagions of face-to-face contact, producing, say, the famous "bandwagon" effect if it goes beyond a certain point. Thus, while explicit models are very hard to construct in this field, there do seem to be certain parameters which can be identified. Such things, for instance, as party loyalty, the propensity to disillusionment, the capacity to tolerate ambiguities in the coalition, and so on, might be identified. If then certain basic variables of the system, such as the proportion of Democrats who become Republicans, the proportion of Republicans who become Democrats, the proportion of people who become neutral or apathetic, and so on, can be related to these various parameters, we might develop at least some kind of stochastic process, with random shocks at intervals, which would simulate the actual course of events. I just throw this out as a challenge to the bright young mathematical computer types, as something which looks as if it ought to be possible but has certainly not been done yet.

Moving now to my third category, involving the sizes and organization of political units, my impression is that whereas the potential for useful parametric models is perhaps less than it is in the second category, in the second category the models have not yet been developed, while in the third category, models of a limited kind have been developed which are quite useful and illuminating in spite of the enormous complexity of the system. In terms of accomplishment rather than potential, therefore, I should have exchanged my second and third categories. The model which has most application is the theory of size of organization and of the interaction of organizations, particularly as it has been developed in economics as applied to the firm and to oligopolistic relations among firms, and as this theory can be extended rather easily to other organizations, such as churches, trade unions, and to the national state, where it becomes in essence a theory of the international system. The work of Kaplan[7] is particularly noteworthy in this regard, and the reader may also wish to refer to my own *Conflict and Defense*[8] for further details. The general principles are fairly simple. Both organisms and organizations, and even ecological populations, are limited in their size, first by certain internal factors

[7] Kaplan, Morton A., *System and Process in International Politics.* New York: John Wiley and Sons, 1957.

[8] Boulding, K. E., *Conflict and Defense.* New York: Harper and Row, 1962 and 1963.

which produce the principle of diminishing returns to scale, secondly, by external factors — the principle of increasingly unfavorable environment — "returns" in this case being interpreted as survival value. In the case of the social organization, the main factor is the nature of the communication system. The key parameter, indeed, is cost of transport, whether this is of information and ideas, of threats, or of commodities. This basic parameter, indeed, applies both to external and to internal limitations. Internally, the principal limitation of the size of organization is the inability of an internal information system to cope with increased size, an increased number of steps in the hierarchy, and an increased distance from the "sensors" of the environment to the central decision makers. It is a well-known principle that all hierarchy corrupts information, simply because there are payoffs to lower members in the hierarchy in corrupting it. One rises in a hierarchy by pleasing one's superiors, which often involves telling them what they want to hear, not what is true. Hence the more levels there are in a hierarchy, the more corrupt the information system is likely to be, for information is filtered out with a value filter at each stage. The number of levels in the hierarchy, however, depends on the size of the organization and the span of control, that is, the number of people with whom one member of the hierarchy can have effective contact. If this is ten people, then in an organization of a million people there must be about ten levels in the hierarchy. Various social inventions, of course, can offset this pollution of information, for instance, the development of staff rather than line personnel, the reliance on external sources of information such as auditors and consultants and outside research firms. Even such devices as tenure, which diminish the power of the superior over the inferior, tend to diminish information pollution. At some point, however, the brontosaurus becomes extinct; eventually diminishing returns to scale set in.

In the relations *between* organizations, cost of transport again is a crucial parameter. All organizations lose in competitive power as they move away from their central location. This is as true of the state as it is of the firm. If the cost of transport is high, this "loss of strength gradient," as I have called it, is also high; and organizations will be small, as one cannot dominate another at a distance. As the cost of transport diminishes, so does the size of the organization increase, both for internal reasons and because of their power of external domination. Here, therefore, is a crucial parameter of politics as of all other relations, which explains, for instance, why classical empires were unstable, why the city-state became nonviable, and why a world state is now in slow process of formation. The theory applies not only over physical space but over social space. We can, for instance, preserve small organizations like sects by increasing social distance, cutting off communication, and by cultural segregation. The principle of returns to scale also explains a great deal about the structure of organizations. It explains why large organizations have to have quite a different structure from small ones, both in the biological and in the social system. It explains also the need for redundancy, and why efficiency is inimical to survival, why adaptation leads to death and adaptibility to life. It may not be easy to express these principles in formal models, but they unquestionably represent a parametric type of thinking.

These systems merge imperceptibly into my fourth category, what I have called the larger dynamics. Here some parametric models, such as those of the "magnificent dynamics," as Baumol has called it, of the classical economists, have unquestioned value. We have to beware, however, of false analogies like Spengler's and incomplete systems like Toynbee's. We have to admit, also, that even the long run of human history is subject to random shocks. There are what I call "watershed systems" here, in which a breath of wind at a particular point can send a system to widely divergent goals, like a drop of water on the Continental Divide. Nevertheless, one still looks for parameters, such as the constant growth of knowledge, the change in values towards larger and larger integrative systems, the long, slow revolutions in legitimacy, and on the other side, the erosion of natural resource bases or even of cultural and political resources when knowledge fails to get transmitted. The historian is apt to dismiss the search for parameters here as hopeless. I am not prepared to give up so easily, even though the search is a long way from conclusion. It may well be that as we learn how to sample and quantify human history, we will find out its more subtle parameters and will be able to direct self-conscious policies towards them. It does not seem absurd, at least, to suppose that we can develop concepts of what might be called historical health, in which perverse and destructive processes are identified and remedies are devised to rectify them. Even if the maintenance of long-run health involves occasional catastrophe, at least we may be able to see to it that these catastrophes do not get out of hand.

EVOLUTION AND REVOLUTION IN THE DEVELOPMENTAL PROCESS

In: *Social Change and Economic Growth.*
Paris: Development Centre of the
Organisation for Economic Co-operation
and Development, 1967, pp. 19-29

EVOLUTION AND REVOLUTION
IN THE DEVELOPMENTAL PROCESS

The existence of a developmental process in social systems and in the history of man can hardly be doubted, even though there are many difficulties of measurement. Furthermore, the process has a large number of different dimensions, and in some of these dimensions the difficulties of measurement are so great that we are not always certain even of the direction of change. Just as, however, we perceive a direction in the evolutionary process in the biological sphere, a direction at least in increase in complexity and in the control of the environment, similarly we can see a certain direction in social evolution. The parallels, indeed, between evolutionary development in the biological sphere and the developmental process in society are striking, and it seems quite legitimate to regard development in the social system as a continuation of the evolutionary process in the biological system.

The model which has proved most useful in the interpretation and understanding of the process of biological evolution is the mutation-selection model. In this model, mutation is supposed to occur, presumably at random, in the genetic material or the genes. The genetic material, or genotype, as it is contained in the chromosomes of the fertile egg, organises the phenotype - the flower, the tree, the animal, or the human body - and a selection takes place through the ecological equilibria in dynamic interactions of the phenotypes. Although

this model is enormously useful in interpretation of past data,
it must be admitted that it has very low predictive power,
mainly because of the enormous complexity of ecological equilibria and of the genetic material itself. We cannot really
predict what are the most probable mutations, nor can we predict, except perhaps at the extremes, what it is that gives
survival value. What we have in evolutionary theory, therefore,
is a programme for a pattern, but we do not really know the
pattern itself. A programme for a pattern, however, is better
than nothing.

In social evolution, as in biological evolution, we can
distinguish beween the genotype and the phenotype, and the mutation-selection model can be applied. Here, however, the system is looser, and has to be applied with even greather care.
Social phenotypes consist of stable patterns of social relationships or stable role structures, that is, in a broad
sense, organisations. They include such things as the family,
friendship groups, firms, churches, labour unions, clubs,
political parties, states, empires, and international organisations. All these social phenotypes exhibit homeostasis in
a greater or less degree, that is, a capacity for adapting to
and resisting changes in the external environment. They are
all in greater or less degree open systems, in the terminology
of General Systems, in the sense that they maintain a structure of roles in the middle of a through-put of persons or
role occupants. This last property is least characteristic of
the family, though widows have a certain tendency to remarry.
It is most true of formal organisations like firms, universities, and churches, where there is a formal, well-established
role structure and "organs" within the organisation whose
business it is to keep the roles occupied at all times, so
that when one man resigns or retires, another is found to take
his place. In this respect the parallel beween the organisation
and the biological body is quite strong. Both of them are
open systems, the body maintaining a certain structure in the
presence of a through-put of chemical elements, the organisation maintaining a structure in the midst of a through-put of
personnel.

The social genotypes are harder to identify and are considerably less stable than the biological genotypes; nevertheless, they exist and can be identified. They consist of such things as blueprints, plans, ideas, symbols, sacred histories, images of the past and of the future, which have the power of organising role structures, developing relationships between roles, and hence creating social organisations. Every organisation originates as an idea or image of the future in the mind of some person, which is then communicated to others and forms itself in the minds of others in a pattern that is quite reminiscent of the way in which the gene reproduces itself by "printing" its pattern on the chemical material around it. The social genes, however, are much less stable than their biological counterparts. The amino acids which form the code of the biological gene have come down unchanged for millions of years; the images of the future which are the genes of society and social organisations are constantly changed in transmission from one mind to another because of the extraordinary complexity of the process of communication between minds and the large amounts of noise in the system.

In social systems also the processes of reproduction by which the sequence genotype ——► phenotype ——► genotype ——► phenotype ——► is continued are much more complex than they are in the biological processes. In the biological world we seldom have more than two sexes; in the world of social organisations and their products, the number of sexes is almost infinite. That is, instead of the genetic material being transmitted half from a phenotype of one sex and half from a phenotype of the other, it is transmitted from many minds into many minds in the huge mêlée of social communication, education, research, conversation, mass media, and other forms of transmission, and is capable of almost indefinitely fine degrees of subdivision and addition. Nevertheless, the recurring sequences of phenotypes and genotypes can readily be perceived in the processes of development of social systems, as organisations generate ideas and images both in the interests of their own perpetuation and also, from their own point of view, at random, so that one organisation gives birth to

another. One can carry these analogies too far, but it is
certainly not absurd to regard an automobile plant as the womb
of the automobile, and the designer's office as the father,
injecting sperm into the process in the shape of blueprints.
Commodities, of course, are social organisations imprinted on
the material world; and they may be regarded as the excreta
of some organisations and the food of others, producing a material cycle which has some parallels with things like the nitro-
gen cycle in the biological world.

I distinguish three main categories of social genotypes,
that is, relationships among persons capable of organising
role structures according to some image of the future. The
first of these is the threat system, which begins by one person
saying to another, "You do something nice to me - that is,
occupy a role which I create - or I will do something nasty to
you." The second is the exchange system, by which one person
says to another, "You do something nice to me and I will do
something nice to you." If the offer is accepted, an exchange
takes place, the division of labour begins, and occupational
roles are established. The third is the integrative system,
whereby one person says to another, "You occupy this role because of what you are and what I am, because of how we visua-
lise our common relationship." This is the way in which roles
are organised in terms of status.

The threat system, whether spiritual or temporal, is the
foundation of the urban revolution and of early civilisation.
It developed such institutions as slavery and war. It is capable
of producing a moderately elaborate society such as the
civilisations of antiquity, but its developmental horizon is
limited and it cannot organise societies beyond a certain degree of complexity. It produces phenotypes in the shape of
temples, armies, states, empires, but these have a relatively
short expectation of life and are incapable of more than what
might be called a primitive complexity.

The exchange system, as Adam Smith points out so well,
develops the division of labour and increases the productive
powers of labour, and sets in motion a long process of economic
development, the end of which, indeed, is not yet in

sight. It is a process with a long horizon, though this too runs into certain limits. It produces social phenotypes in the shape of businesses, corporations, banks, insurance companies, and so on, which exist mainly in an exchange or market environment and rely only on a relatively small framework of threat to preserve property, without which, of course, exchange is impossible. Property, of course, may be either public or private, and the problem of the proper mix relative to particular cultural systems is one of the major unsolved problems of our day. Security of property of any kind, however, is essential to this kind of development. The plans for the future which are based upon exchange and exchange opportunities must not be voided by the exercise of arbitrary political power. Under these circumstances, a system of reasonably secure private property, in the absence of monopoly and arbitrary police power can, as Adam Smith points out so elegantly, produce a quite remarkable process of development.

The question of whether the kind of development which is created by exchange as such itself has certain horizons, is a very interesting one and not easy to answer. Insofar as the exchange system is always set in a matrix of threat systems and integrative systems, it may run into difficulties from the point of view of arbitrary power on the one side or a failure to achieve legitimacy on the other. The merchants may become rich and they may help to make everybody else rich, which they generally do; but their very riches excite the envy and cupidity of those who command the organised threat system, and the development through exchange is brought to an end by arbitrary seizure of persons or property. When the golden egg gets big enough, the temptation to kill the goose seems to be almost irresistible. On the other side also, it is hard to legitimate the process of exchange, mainly because it seems to involve an abstract, "inhuman" attitude of mind, and the merchant is sometimes as vulnerable to the priest and the preacher as he is to the king.

There are also technical reasons within the exchange system itself why it might under some circumstances reach a horizon of development and become incapable of creating a further

organisation. An exchange system is a profit system relying on
the difference between buying price or cost and selling price
to motivate the organisers themselves, and there are reasons,
though not necessarily sufficient reasons, for supposing, as
the classical economists supposed, that in the course of economic development profits would decline to the point eventually where they might no longer be sufficient to motivate the
system. There are also technical problems involving "secular
stagnation" of a Keynesian type, which result when an exchange
system runs into unemployment and deflation and becomes disorganised by its own failure to achieve the full employment of
resources. There may be, therefore, both recognisable "diseases" of the exchange system, which may limit its role in
development; and the horizons which this development may reach
may in turn depend on the setting of the exchange system and
the development of the other systems in which it is embedded.

The integrative system does not have the unity of the
other two. It consists of a large number of diverse social
organisers, all of which revolve around the establishment of
community, status, legitimacy, love, loyalty, benevolence,
malevolence, and so on. These integrative structures provide
the matrices within which both the threat system and the
exchange system can operate, and without some integrative structure probably no development can take place. Threats must be
legitimated, and so must exchange, before it can succeed as a
social organiser. The integrative system also provides organisers of its own, for instance in the family, the church, and
the state, which are in some ways the phenotypes of this system.
Because of the difficulties of measurement, the concept of
development in the integrative system is not much in the consciousness of the present time. Nevertheless, this concept is
a most important one, and necessary to a full understanding of
the developmental processes of society. I have suggested one
very first-approximation measure of the integrative system in
the structure and extent of what I have called the "grants
economy", that is, that part of the economic system in which
unilateral transfers of goods and services are made between
persons or organisations. A grant is a symbol of community.

We do not give grants to people unless we have some kind of
integrative relationship with them. Grants of goods and services, of course, are not the only kind. We give time, energy,
attention, love, and so on, and these things are much harder to
measure. Nevertheless, the possibility of measurement, at least
of a rough kind, undoubtedly exists, and the concept of growth
of the integrative system can therefore be established. The
increase in the number of people participating in both organisations and communities from the first hunting band or family
to the tribe, the nation, the church, and now the rapidly
approaching world society, is perhaps the best evidence of the
concept of integrative development.

Behind all these developmental processes lies one fundamental process of the growth of knowledge. Knowledge, properly
interpreted, is the only thing which can grow or develop. Matter is subject to an inexorable law of conservation, at least
in the absence of nuclear processes, and is simply moved around
from place to place. Energy is subject to an even more depressing principle, the Second Law of Thermodynamics, which is a
law of degradation. Available energy, that is, continually
declines, and entropy or disorganisation increases. It is only
the knowledge processes, therefore, which can give rise to
evolution at all, meaning by this the development of improbable
structures which have a capacity for self-reproduction. We can
distinguish here two processes, roughly analogous to the genotype and the phenotype. The first I have called "printing",
the print shop providing the best examples of it, in which a
structure simply reproduces itself by imposing a pattern on the
material world around it. The gene is a three-dimensional prin-
ter, given a suitable environment, and knowledge, likewise
reproduces itself in the teaching process, in which by a strange
miracle the learners come to know more and the teacher does
not know any less. There is also another process which I call
organisation, by which a genotype produces a phenotype and by
which it organises the environment around it into complex and
improbable forms.

Development has many aspects, of which economic development
is perhaps the most visible. Economic development itself depends

on development in other spheres, such as the capacity of the
society to resolve conflicts and organise itself politically
through the legitimation of threat as well as its capacity to
develop trust, honesty, and certain other aspects of moral
and integrative development. It is tempting, therefore, to
take the rate of economic growth, as measured for instance by
the growth in the real gross national product per capita, as
the best first approximation to the overall rate of development. We must not take this too seriously, though, because
other aspects of development may be independent of economic
development and are also important. It is quite possible, for
instance, for a society which is not growing much in wealth to
be getting "happier" by abolishing poverty through redistributions, developing a stronger sense of loyalty and affection
towards its members, and developing superior methods of organising the resolution of conflicts. It is possible also for a
society to be increasing very rapidly in real income and at
the same time to be getting increasingly disorganised politically, to have widening maldistributions, to be increasing poverty in one part at the same time as it increases wealth in
another. There are patterns of economic development, indeed,
which are self-defeating because of the fact that they are not
accompanied by a development in the other systems. A pattern
of economic development, for instance, which concentrates all
the fruits of development in a relatively small proportion of
the population, leaving the major part unaffected or even
worsening, is a developmental process that may very soon be
brought to an end by an upset in the political system. On the
other hand, it is also true that economic development makes
development in the other fields easier. In a society which is
getting richer, conflicts are less intense, for there is as it
were a fund out of which they can be resolved. Bargaining for
shares of an increase is much easier than the kind of bargaining for a static amount in which the gain of one is the loss
of another. Similarly, when a country is getting richer, it is
easier to develop an integrative system. It is tempting, indeed, though rather cynical, to regard integration as a "luxury" which can only be afforded by rather rich societies.
Certainly at the other end of the scale, poverty destroys

love and community, even though riches do not necessarily
create it.

This whole developmental process, however, is a learning
process. Economic development is not merely a matter of piling
up stocks of old commodities, it is a matter of learning how
to do new things altogether, learning a new view of the world,
new skills, scientific knowledge, and so on. Even the accumulation of capital can be regarded as a learning process imposed
on the material world, for a capital good essentially is frozen knowledge, and a tractor contains a lot more frozen knowledge than a hoe. If indeed the knowledge structure of a society remains undamaged, it can recover very quickly from the loss
of its material capital, as the case of post-war Japan and
Germany showed. If, however, the knowledge structure is nonexistent or is impaired, development will be slow. Development
outside the economy is likewise a learning process. We have
to learn how to live at peace with one another and with our
neighbours; we have to learn how to establish justice, how to
make the fruits of virtue secure and the retributions of vice
reasonably certain. We have to learn also how to organise,
how to establish the minimum degree of trust and confidence
in other people and of abstract honesty towards all which makes
a complex society possible. We also have to learn compassion,
and that expansion of self-interest to include others which
is the foundation on which all community rests.

I define an "acceleration" as an increase in the rate of
development. Sometimes this takes place rather suddenly in a
society, as it did, for instance in Japan at the time of the
Meiji Restoration or after the second world war. Sometimes the
acceleration may take a generation or more to accomplish. In
Europe, one is tempted to identify a number of such accelerations. The first is somewhat uncertainly represented by the
rise of the classical civilisations, Mycenae, Greece, Rome, and
so on, in the centuries before Christ. The second seems to
have taken place after the fall of Rome, the Roman Empire having had a zero rate of development for its last four hundred
years. After 600 A.D., however, we detect a positive rate of
development in Europe which continues as a slowly rising rate

till the eighteenth century. The third great acceleration,
which is the result of the development of science, hits the
economy about 1860. Measures, of course, are very scarce from
the earlier period. One could hazard a guess that per capita
income may have doubled in a thousand years between 600 and
1600; it almost certainly doubled again by 1800. From 1860 on,
in the more rapidly developing countries, it was doubling almost every generation, that is, every 25 to 40 years. Since
1945 it has been doubling about every eight years in Japan,
which certainly seems like a new order of development.

In this process, then, what is the role of revolution?
This is a term which is used very loosely. In a political sense,
it usually means some kind of over-turn in the power structure
by which an old elite is displaced by a new one with a greater
or less amount of violence and upheaval. Revolutions sometimes
produce an acceleration; on the other hand they usually have
a certain amount of cost. The acceleration is produced if the
incoming elite has a higher level of knowledge and organisation relevant to development than the outgoing. The classical
situation is that in which before the revolution, those who
have the will to develop do not have the power and those who
have the power do not have the will, and the society is stagnant. The revolution displaces those who have the power and
not the will by giving those who have the will the power, and
then an acceleration may be expected. On the other hand, if
the revolution is violent, if it produces a lot of emigrés,
there may be a great waste of the talents of the society and
an actual loss of the knowledge structure which it may take
even a generation or two to recover. Really violent revolutions
like the French Revolution or the Russian Revolution are apt
to cost a generation or two of growth. The ideal situation is
an acceleration without a revolution, such as happened in Japan around 1868. Under some circumstances, of course, we may
have to buy acceleration with revolution, but we should always
try to get it as cheap as possible.

The revolutionary sentimentality of the Far Left can
easily be an obstacle to development, as we see it in Indonesia and Cuba. A perpetual revolution is nonsense. A revolution

may perhaps be compared to an orgasm, but for growth we need
a womb. Sentimental revolutionism, then, of the type of Soe-
karno or Castro, can only be regarded as a handicap. Even the
American Revolution had a certain cost in terms of development.
The 40,000 or more Tories who were forced out of the country carried with them a considerable amount of knowledge and skill,
and gave a rapid impetus to the development of Ontario. The
American Revolution, however, was fortunate in having rather
non-revolutionary leaders; even Jefferson, who has some claims
in his writings to being a sentimental revolutionist, in his
pratice was much more conservative. Consequently the revolutionary regime in the United States soon developed into what
might be called a nurturing regime, and the history of all
revolutions is rather similar. That is, if a revolution is to
lead to development, it must stop being revolutionary. The
people who make a revolution are rarely fit to lead a development. In this sense, revolution is the enemy of development,
even though in some cases it may be its prerequisite.

A question of great importance in today's world is the
relative merits of capitalist free market development versus
socialist development. The well-governed free market societies
seem to have produced the highest rate of development, even in
the last twenty years, as witness Japan and West Germany.
Communism can give a society a high developmental morale in
spite of some scientific inadequacies in its ideology, and the
socialist societies have certainly been capable of fairly high
rates of development. Their failures in agriculture, however,
are likely to create a low horizon of growth beyond which they
may find it difficult to break. Unsuccessful capitalist development takes place in those countries which are not able to
liberate themselves from traditional patterns of life and
organisation sufficiently to develop an active market economy.
Many Latin American countries and the Arab world seem to fall
into this category. At the bottom end of the scale we have
what might be called unsuccessful socialist development, as
represented by Indonesia, Burma, and Ceylon, where there is
enough socialism to destroy the advantages of the market and
not enough to provide the advantages of a centrally planned
society.

THE IMPACT OF THE DRAFT
ON THE LEGITIMACY OF
THE NATIONAL STATE

In: *The Draft: A Handbook of Facts and
Alternatives,* Sol Tax, ed. Chicago:
Univ. of Chicago Press, 1967, pp. 191-196

ONE of the most neglected aspects of the dynamics of society is the study of dynamic processes which underlie the rise and fall of legitimacy. This neglect reflects, in the United States at least, not merely a deficiency in social sciences and social thought; it reflects a grave deficiency in what might be called the popular image of the social system. We all tend to take legitimacy for granted. Thus, the economist hardly ever inquires into the legitimacy of exchange, even though this is the institution on which his science is built. The political scientist rarely inquires into the legitimacy of political institutions or of the institutions of organized threat, such as the police and the armed forces. Consequently we are much given to discussions of economic development as if this were a mechanical or quasi-automatic process without regard to the conditions of legitimacy of various activities and institutions. Similarly, in our discussions of the strategy of threat we rarely take account of the legitimacy of the institutions which either make the threats or provide their credibility. To put the matter simply, we tend to regard both wealth and power as self-justifying and this could well be a disastrous error.

The truth is that the dynamic of legitimacy, mysterious as it may seem, in fact governs to a remarkable extent all the other processes of social life. Without legitimacy no permanent relationship can be established, and if we lose legitimacy we lose everything. A naked threat, such as that of the bandit or the armed robber, may establish a temporary relationship. The victim hands over his money or even his person at the sword's point or the pistol's mouth. If we want to establish a permanent relationship, however, such as that of a landlord demanding rent or a government demanding taxes, the threat must be legitimized. The power both of the landlord and of the government depend in the last analysis upon the consent of the rentpayer or the taxpayer and this consent implies that the whole procedure has been legitimated and is accepted by everyone concerned as right and proper. Legitimacy may be defined as general acceptance by all those concerned in a certain institution, role, or pattern of behavior that it constitutes part of the regular moral or social order within which they live. Thus legitimacy is a wider concept than the formal concept of law, even though the law is a great legitimator. At times, however, law it-

The Impact of the Draft on the Legitimacy of the National State

self may become illegitimate and when it does so its capacity to organize society is destroyed.

Legitimacy Defined by Sacrifice

Legitimacy has at least two dimensions which might be described as intensity and extent. Its intensity refers to the degree of identification or acceptance in the mind of a particular individual, and it may be measured roughly by the extent of sacrifice which he is prepared to make for an institution rather than deny it or abandon it. The extent of legitimacy refers to the proportion of the relevant population which regards the institution in question as legitimate. An overall measure of the legitimacy of any particular institution might be achieved by multiplying its intensity by its extent, but such a measure might easily obscure certain important characteristics of the system. A case in which an institution was regarded with intense allegiance by a small proportion of the people concerned would be very different from one in which there was a mild allegiance from all the people; the former, indeed, would probably be less stable than the latter. In considering any particular case, therefore, it is always important that we consider both dimensions.

The creation, maintenance, and destruction of legitimacy of different institutions presents many difficult problems. Legitimacy is frequently created by the exercise of power, either economic power in the form of wealth or political power in the form of threat capability. Legitimacy, furthermore, frequently increases with age so that old wealth and old power are more legitimate than new. The nouveau riche may be looked upon askance but their grandchildren easily become aristocrats. The conqueror likewise is illegitimate at first, but if his conquest is successful and his empire lasts, it eventually acquires legitimacy. All these relationships, however, seem to be nonlinear, and reverse themselves beyond a certain point. Thus, the display of wealth tends to become obscene and damages the legitimacy of the wealthy. In order to retain legitimacy they often have to diminish their wealth by giving it away, establishing foundations, or at least by abstaining from ostentatious consumption. Similarly, political power often seems to lose its legitimacy when it is apparently at its very height. It is at the greatest extent and power of a regime, nation, or empire that it often suddenly collapses through sheer loss of belief in it. Even age does not always guarantee legitimacy. After a certain point an ancient person or institution simply becomes senile or old-fashioned and its legitimacy abruptly collapses.

There have been enough examples of collapse of legitimacy of apparently large, prosperous and invincible institutions to suggest that we have here a general, though not necessarily a universal, principle at work. It is perhaps an example of another much-neglected proposition, that nothing fails like success because we do not learn anything from it. Thus in Europe the institution of the absolute monarchy seemed to be most secure and invincible at the time of Louis XIV, yet only a few decades later it was in ruins. Similarly, in the early years of the twentieth century the concept of empire seemed invincible and unshakably legitimate, yet in another few decades it was discredited, illegitimate, and the empires themselves collapsed or had to be transformed.

An Institution Must Be Transformed

It looks indeed as if there is some critical moment at which an institution must be transformed if it is to retain its legitimacy and transformed, furthermore, in the direction of abandonment of either its wealth or its power in some degree. Thus, after the eighteenth century the only way in which the institution of the monarchy could retain its legitimacy was to abandon its power and become constitutional. By abandoning his political power, that is, his threat capability, the monarch was able to become a symbol of the legitimacy of the state and hence was able to preserve his role in the society. Where the monarch did not make this transition, as for instance in France, Germany, and Russia, the incumbent frequently lost his head, and the whole institution was destroyed, and the role simply abandoned. Similarly, in the twentieth century, if any semblance of empire was to be maintained, the political power had to be abandoned and the empire transformed into a commonwealth or community based on sentiment rather than on threat. Even the church in the twentieth century has largely had to abandon the fear of hell, that is, its spiritual threat system, as the prime motivation in attracting support. In most countries, furthermore, it has likewise had to abandon the support of the state and the secular arm, that is, the secular threat system, in an attempt to enforce conformity. Here again we see an example of the abandonment of power in the interests of retaining legitimacy.

The National State Dwarfs All

At the present time by far the most wealthy, powerful, and legitimate type of institution is the national state. In the socialist countries the national state monopolizes virtually all the wealth and the threat capability of the society. Even in the capitalist world the national state usually commands about 25 per cent of the total economy and is a larger economic unit than any private corporation, society, or church. Thus the United States government alone wields economic power roughly equal to half the national income of the So-viet Union, which is the largest socialist state. Within the United States government the United States Department of Defense has a total budget larger than the national income of the People's Republic of China and can well claim to be the second largest centrally planned economy in the world. It is true that the great corporations wield an economic power roughly equal to that of the smaller socialist states; there are, indeed, only about 11 countries with a gross national product larger than General Motors. Nevertheless, when it comes to legitimacy the national state is supreme. All other loyalties are expected to bow before it. A man may deny his parents, his wife and his friends, his God, or his profession and get away with it, but he cannot deny his country unless he finds another one. In our world a man without a country is regarded with pity and scorn. We are expected to make greater sacrifices for our country than we make for anything else. We are urged, "Ask not what your country can do for you, ask what you can do for your country," whereas nobody ever suggests that we should "Ask not what General Motors can do for you, ask what you can do for General Motors."

An institution of such monumental wealth, power and legitimacy would seem to be invincible. The record of history suggests clearly, however, that it is precisely at this moment of apparent invincibility that an institution is in gravest danger. It may seem as absurd today to suggest that the national state might lose its legitimacy as it would have been to suggest the same thing of the monarchy in the days of le Grand Monarque. Nevertheless both monarchy and empire have lost their legitimacy and that at the moment of their greatest power and extent. If history teaches us anything, therefore, it should teach us at this moment to look at the national state with a quizzical eye. It may be an institution precisely filling the conditions which give rise to a sudden collapse of legitimacy, which will force the institution itself to transform itself by abandoning its power or will create conditions in which the institution cannot survive.

Individuals Must Justify Their Sacrifices

These conditions can be stated roughly as follows: An institution which demands sacrifices can frequently create legitimacy for itself because of a strong tendency in human beings to justify to themselves sacrifices which they have made. We cannot admit that sacrifices have been made in vain, for this would be too great a threat to our image of ourselves and our identity. As the institution for which sacrifices are made gains legitimacy, however, it can demand more sacrifices, which further increases legitimacy. At some point, however, the sacrifices suddenly seem to be too much. The terms of trade between its devotees and the institution become too adverse, and quite suddenly the legitimacy of the whole operation is questioned, and ancient sacrifices are written off and the institution collapses. Thus men sacrificed enormously for the monarchy, and the king was able to say for centuries, "Ask not what I can do for you, ask only what you can do for me," until the point when suddenly people began to ask. "What can the king do for me?" and the answer was "Nothing." At that moment the monarchy either died or had to be transformed.

We may be in a similar moment in the case of the national state. The real terms of trade between an individual and his country have been deteriorating markedly in the past decades. In the eighteenth century the national state made relatively few demands on its citizens, and provided some of them at least with fair security and satisfactory identity. As the nation has gathered legitimacy however from the bloodshed and treasure expended for it, it has become more and more demanding. It now demands ten to twenty per cent of our income, at least two years of our life—and it may demand the life itself—and it risks the destruction of our whole physical environment. As the cost rises, it eventually becomes not unreasonable to ask for what. If the payoffs are in fact low, the moment has arrived when the whole legitimacy of the institution may be threatened.

Has Technology Made the State Obsolete?

We must here distinguish the internal from the external payoffs of the national state. Internally the payoffs may still be quite high, though it is perhaps still a question whether governments today, like the medical profession a hundred years ago, really do more good than harm. In the external relations, however, there can be no doubt that the system of national states

is enormously burdensome and costly. It is not only that the world-war industry is now about 140 billion dollars, which is about equal to the total income of the poorest half of the human race, it is that this enormous expenditure gives us no real security in the long run and it sets up a world in which there is a positive probability of almost total disaster.

It is perfectly reasonable indeed to ask ourselves this question: After a nuclear war, if there is anybody left, are they going to set up again the institutions which produced the disaster? The answer would clearly seem to be "No," in which case we may say that as the present system contains a positive probability of nuclear war it is in fact bankrupt and should be changed *before* the nuclear war rather than afterward. It can be argued very cogently indeed that modern technology has made the national state obsolete as an instrument of unilateral national defense, just as gunpowder made the feudal baron obsolete, the development of the skills of organization and public administration made the monarchy obsolete, and economic development made empire obsolete. An institution, no matter how currently powerful and legitimate, which loses its function will also lose its legitimacy, and the national state in its external relations seems precisely in this position today. Either it must be transformed in the direction of abandoning its power and threat capability or it will be destroyed, like the absolute monarchy and the absolute church before it.

The Draft Calls All Into Question

What then is the role of the draft in this complex dynamic process? The draft may well be regarded as a symbol of a slow decline in the legitimacy of the national state (or of what perhaps we should call more exactly the warfare state, to distinguish it from the welfare state which may succeed it), that slow decline which may presage the approach of collapse. In the rise and decline of legitimacy, as we have seen, we find first a period in which sacrifices are made, voluntarily and gladly, in the interests of the legitimate institution, and, indeed, reinforce the legitimacy of the institution. As the institution becomes more and more pressing in its demands, however, voluntary sacrifices become replaced with forced sacrifices. The tithe becomes a tax, religious enthusiasm degenerates into com-

pulsory chapel, and voluntary enlistment in the threat system of the state becomes a compulsory draft.

The legitimacy of the draft, therefore, is in a sense a subtraction from the legitimacy of the state. It represents the threat system of the state turned in on its own citizens, however much the threat may be disguised by a fine language about service and "every young man fulfilling his obligation." The language of duty is not the language of love and it is a symptom of approaching delegitimation. A marriage in which all the talk is of obligations rather than of love is on its way to the divorce court. The church in which all worship is obligatory is on its way to abandonment or reformation, and the state in which service has become a duty is in no better case. The draft therefore, which undoubtedly increases the threat capability of the national state, is a profound symptom of its decay and insofar as it demands a forced sacrifice it may hasten that decay and may hasten the day when people come to see that to ask "what can your country do for you" is a very sensible question.

The draft, furthermore, inevitably creates strong inequities. It discriminates against the poor, or at least against the moderately poor; the very poor, because of their poor educational equipment may escape it just as the rich tend to escape it, and the main burden therefore falls on the lower end of the middle-income groups. As these groups also in our society bear the brunt of taxation—for a great deal of what is passed as "liberal" legislation in fact taxes the poor in order to subsidize the rich—an unjust distribution of sacrifice is created. Up to now it is true this strain has not been very apparent. It cannot indeed be expressed directly because of the enormous legitimacy of the national state, hence it tends to be expressed indirectly in alienation, crime, internal violence, race and group hatreds and also in an intensified xenophobia. This is the old familiar problem of displacement. We dare not vent our anger at frustrations upon their cause and we therefore have to find a legitimated outlet in the foreigner, or the communist, or whoever the enemy happens to be at the moment. What is worse, the frustrated adult frequently displaces his anger on his children who in turn perpetuate the whole miserable business of hatred and lovelessness.

Like compulsory chapel or church attendance, which is its closest equivalent, the draft has a further disadvantage in that while it may at best produce a grudging and hostile acquiescence in the methods of the society, it frequently closes the mind to any alternative or to any reorganization of information. The psychological strains which are produced by compulsory service of any kind naturally result in displaced aggressions rather than in any reform of the system which created them. Consequently the draft by the kind of indoctrination and hidden frustrations which it produces may be an important factor in preventing that reevaluation of the national policy and the national image which is so essential in the modern world if the national state itself is to survive. The draft therefore is likely to be an enemy of the survival of the very state in the interests of which it is supposedly involved. It produces not a true love of country based on a realistic appraisal of the present situation of human society but rather a hatred of the other which leads to political mental ill health, and an image of the world which may be as insulated from the messages which come through from reality as is the mind of a paranoid.

We Must Attack the Legitimacy of the Draft

Perhaps the best thing that can be said in defense of the draft is that the alternative, namely, raising a voluntary armed force by offering sufficient financial inducements, or by persuasion and advertising, would involve even more the whipping up of hatred of the foreigner and the reinforcement of paranoid political attitudes. The draft by its very absurdities and inequities at least to some extent helps to make the whole operation faintly ridiculous, as we see it in comic strips like Beetle Bailey or in movies such as *Dr. Strangelove,* and hence makes the operation of national defense commonplace rather than charismatic. The draft certainly represents the institutionalization of the charisma of the national state, to use an idea from Max Weber, and this may be something on the credit side. Even this merit, however, is dubious. Insofar as the draft leads to widespread commonplace acceptance of mass murder and atrocities, and an attitude of mind which is blind to any but romantically violent solutions of conflict, its influence is wholly negative. Certainly the political wisdom of the American Legion is no advertisement for the political virtues of having passed through the Armed Forces.

It seems clear therefore that those of us who have a genuine affection for the institution of the national state and for our own country in particular should constantly attack the legitimacy of the draft, and the legitimacy of the whole system of unilateral national defense which supports it, in the interest of preserving the legitimacy of the national state itself. The draft, it is true, is merely a symbol or a symptom of a much deeper disease, the disease of unilateral national defense, and it is this concept which should be the prime focus of our attack. Nevertheless, cleaning up a symptom sometimes helps to cure the disease, otherwise the sales of aspirin would be much less, and a little aspirin of dissent applied to the headache of the draft might be an important step in the direction of the larger objective. Those of us, therefore, who are realistically concerned about the survival of our country should probably not waste too much time complaining about the inequities and absurdities of the draft or attempt the hopeless task of rectifying it when the plain fact is that the draft can only begin to approach "justice" in time of major war, and a peacetime draft has to be absurd and unjust by its very nature. The axe should be applied to the root of the tree, not to its branches. An attempt to pretty up the draft and make it more acceptable may actually prevent that radical reevaluation of the whole system of unilateral national defense which is now in order. We are very close to the moment when the only way to preserve the legitimacy of the national state will be to abandon most of its power. The draft is only a subplot in this much greater drama. ∎

THE LEARNING AND
REALITY-TESTING PROCESS IN THE
INTERNATIONAL SYSTEM

Journal of International Affairs,
XXI, 1 (1967): 1-15

The Learning and Reality-Testing Process in the International System

The Aztecs apparently believed that the corn on which their civilization depended would not grow unless there were human sacrifices. What seems to us an absurd belief caused thousands of people to be sacrificed each year. The arguments by which the Aztecs rationalized this image of the world have largely been lost, thanks to the zeal of the Spanish conquerors. One can, however, venture upon an imaginative reconstruction. The fact that the corn did grow was probably considered solid evidence for such a view; and in those years when the harvest was bad, it was doubtless argued that the gods were angry because the sacrifices had been insufficient. A little greater military effort would result, a few more hearts would be torn from their quivering bodies, and the following year it was highly probable that the harvest would be better and the image consequently confirmed. Not only empirical evidence would support the doctrine, however; the great truth that it represented could easily be held to be self-evident. The seed must die if the corn is to grow. We all know, furthermore, that the spectacle of violent death arouses the seed in man and is likely to produce an increase in the population. What could be more resonable, therefore, than to assume that these two phenomena are connected?

If this is a parody, it is too close to the truth to be wholly comfortable. Arguments of this kind have often been used to justify human sacrifice and the image of the world that demands it, whether on the part of a religion or on the part of a state. The sponsors of the Inquisition thought that by roasting some people alive they would save many souls from roasting after death. The proposition that South Vietnam is a domino that has to be propped up by the dropping of napalm, the burning of villages, the torture of prisoners, and the sacrifice of American blood is a proposition that appeals to us much more strongly than these others; but it is being tested in much the same way as the Aztecs and the inquisitors tested their views of the world: by appeals to analogy, to self-evidence, and to the principle that if at first you don't succeed try more of the same until you do.

Image and Reality

The problem of what constitutes realism in our image of the world has bothered philosophers from the very beginnings of human thought, and it is certainly far from being resolved. Indeed, Hume may well have demonstrated that it cannot be resolved, simply because images can only be compared with other images and never with reality. Nevertheless, common sense leads us to reject Humean skepticism in practice; we must live and act for the most part as if our images of the world were true. Moreover, there are processes for the detection and elimination of error; so that even though truth constantly eludes us, by the progressive and systematic elimination of error, that is, false images, we may hope that we may gradually approximate it.

The elimination of error is accomplished mainly by feedback. From our image of the world we derive an expectation, that is, an image of the future. As time goes on, the future becomes present and then past. It is then possible to compare our image of the future with our image of the same period when it has become the past. In January we recall our image of December as we had it in November, and we compare this with our image of December as we have it in January. If the images do not correspond, we are disappointed and hence act to adjust one image or the other. There are actually three adjustments that can be made. We can adjust our image of the past and say that it was mistaken, that what apparently happened did not really happen and that we have been misinformed. We can adjust our past image of the future; that is, we can say that the image of December that we had in November was wrong. We can do this for two reasons, for our image of the future is derived by inference from our general view of the world. We can therefore say, on the one hand, that the inference was wrong and that our view of the world did not really imply that December should have turned out the way we expected; or, if we cannot deny the validity of the inference, then we must revise our general image of the world. The elimination of error can take place at all three of these levels.

The elimination of error, however, is only one of the results that disappointment can produce. Error exists primarily in our general image of the world. Disappointment, unfortunately, does not always force a revision in this image, for it can cause us to deny either the image of the past or the inference that gave rise to the image of the future. If a genuine learning process—the continual elimination of error in our image of the world, as well as the enlargement of this image—is to take place, there must be safeguards against rejecting inferences or rejecting the image of the past.

There are two levels of human learning-processes at which these conditions for the progressive elimination of error are met. One is the process of folk learning in everyday life, in which we learn about the immediate world around us and the physical, biological, and social systems that constitute our direct and immediate environment. Here feedback tends to be rapid; the images of the immediate past are especially hard to reject; and, because we are operating with fairly simple systems, the inferences that we draw from our general view of the world are likewise hard to reject. Consequently, disappointment causes us to make revisions in our general image of the world, and if these revisions result in further disappointments they will be further revised until disappointment is reduced to a tolerable level. People who are incapable of responding in this way to the feedbacks of ordinary life eventually find themselves in mental hospitals. Indeed, what we ordinarily think of as mental disease is the inability to perform reality-testing—the progressive elimination of error—on the folk-learning level. If a person's image of the world is entirely self-justified and self-evident, he will soon get into serious trouble. Suppose, for instance, that he is a paranoid and thinks that everybody hates him. All his experience will confirm this image no matter what the experience is. Experience that fails to confirm the image will be dismissed as due to either false inferences or mistaken images of the past. His fundamental image of the world is unshakable by any event that seems to contradict it. Such a person is incapable of learning, and it is this incapacity that really constitutes mental disease.

The other field where error is progressively eliminated and a genuine learning process takes place is in the subculture of science. Contrary to common belief, the method of science does not differ essentially from the method of folk learning. Both proceed through disappointment. (Indeed, it is only through failure that we ever really learn anything new, for success always tends to confirm our existing images.) Both methods are safeguarded against denials of the image of the past, that is, of experience, and against the denial of inferences; hence in both cases experience that does not jibe with an image prompts modifications in the image. The only difference between folk learning and scientific learning is in the degree of complexity of the systems that are involved in each image of the world. Science deals with complex systems and folk learning with simple systems; but the methods by which errors are eliminated are essentially the same. Because of the complexity of the systems with which science deals, however, it must use refined instruments and precise means of measurement in the development of its image of the past. It must likewise use highly refined methods of inference, employing mathematical and logical methods in order to derive its expectations of the future from its image of the world. It is in the refinement of perception and inference, however, not in the essential nature of the learning process, that science distinguishes itself from ordinary folk-learning.

We may perhaps illustrate the difference with reference to our image of space. The folk image of the world is that of a flat earth encased in the dome of the sky. For the ordinary business of life this image is quite adequate, and as long as we confine our movements to our immediate neighborhood it gets us into no trouble. Over a range of ten miles the curvature of the earth is quite irrelevant to the activities of ordinary life; and although the hills and valleys of the surface are much more relevant, we can learn about them through the ordinary processes of folk learning. For an astronaut, however, it would be quite disastrous to take an image derived from folk experience and to generalize it to the world as a whole. An astronaut requires the scientific image of a spherical—indeed, pear-shaped—earth. He must have very refined instruments and means of measurement. He must, at the very least, live in a Newtonian world and be capable of Newtonian inference, and as speeds increase he may even have to make Einsteinian adjustments. The folk image here would lead to immediate and total disaster. Nevertheless, this highly refined image of space has been obtained in ways that differ only in degree of sophistication from the methods by which we derive our image of how to get from our home to the post office.

The Literary Image and the International System

Between the world of folk learning and the folk images derived from it, and the world of scientific learning and the scientific images derived from it, there lies another world of images that I have elsewhere described,[1] perhaps unkindly, as the world of literary images. It is in this world that reality-testing is least effective and that the elimination

---

[1] Kenneth E. Boulding, *The Image* (Ann Arbor: University of Michigan Press, 1956).

of error either does not take place at all or is enormously costly. It is precisely in this world, however, that we find the images of the international system by which its decision-makers are largely governed, and it is for this reason that the international system is by far the most pathological and costly segment of the total social system, or sociosphere, as it is sometimes called. If we look at the various elements of the social system that are ordinarily regarded as pathological, such as crime, mental and physical disease, and economic stagnation, the international system probably costs about as much as all these put together, with the possible exception of economic stagnation, which is itself in part a function of the nature of the international system.

The direct cost of the international system must now amount to something like 150 billion dollars a year. This would include the total spent by all the nations on their military establishments, information systems, foreign offices, diplomatic corps, and so on. In addition, some estimate of the present value of possible future destruction should be included. Any figure placed on this is at best a wild guess. To be pessimistic, let us suppose that the destruction of a third world war would amount to half the present physical capital of the world, or about two thousand billion dollars, and that the chance of this happening is about five per cent in any one year; in this case we should add a kind of depreciation or discounting factor to existing world wealth of about 100 billion dollars a year. This would represent, as it were, an insurance premium for war destruction. A more optimistic assumption of, say, a one per cent chance of a major world war would reduce this to 20 billion annually. It is interesting to note, incidentally, that the size of the current expenditure on the war industry is almost certainly much larger than any reasonable insurance premium for war destruction would be. This points up a general principle that the cost of the war industry for any country in terms of resources withdrawn from the civilian economy is much larger than any insurance premium that might be conceived for a policy covering destruction by enemy forces. This is often true even in time of war. A study of the impact of the war industry on the Japanese economy[2] suggests that even during the Second World War the cost of the Japanese war industry to the Japanese economy was of the same order of magnitude as the destruction by the American war machine. One's friends, in other words, generally do more damage than one's enemies.

---

[2] Kenneth E. Boulding (with Alan Gleason), "War as an Investment: The Strange Case of Japan," *Peace Research Society (International) Papers*, Vol. III, 1965, pp. 1–17. Also in Kenneth E. Boulding Collected Papers Vol. III (Colorado Associated University Press, 1973), pp. 257–275.

If we suppose that the gross world product is roughly 1,500 billion dollars, the international system and the war industry account for about ten per cent of this. It would be extremely surprising if all the other pathological elements in the social system taken together account for more than this. Crime and disease are likely to account for no more than five per cent of it, or 75 billion dollars. Even if we include the potential loss resulting from the failure of economic development, and if we suppose that a projected annual growth rate of two per cent is not realized, this would only amount to a loss of 30 billion dollars a year, as a measure of what might be called the pathology of the world economy. Even if we raised this projection to an optimistic four per cent, the loss would only be 60 billion, far below the cost of the international system.

One may object, of course, that it is unfair to regard the cost of the international system as if it were not offset by benefits, even if it is very hard to put a dollar value on them. We get the benefits of nationality: tangible ones like protection when we go abroad, and intangible ones like the sense of identity that thrills to the flag, that expands beyond the narrow limits of family and locality, and that responds gladly to the call for self-sacrifice. The sense of satisfaction that comes from being American or German or British or whatever is certainly an important benefit, however hard it is to evaluate. It must be recognized, however, that such advantages of nationality are virtually the only advantages of the nation-state system. There are no economic payoffs to the present system; indeed, in addition to the loss of resources we should also add the cost of tariffs and trade restrictions, and of the almost universally deleterious effects on the rate of development caused by high military expenditures. There was a time, perhaps, when the international system paid off for its principle beneficiaries, the great powers, in terms of the economic exploitation of their colonial empires. Even if the international system produced little gain for the world as a whole, it could be argued that it redistributed the world product in favor of those who played the international game successfully and became great powers. Today even this argument has little validity. Empire in the last 100 years has turned out to be a burden rather than an asset, and in terms of the rate of economic growth, being a great power has not paid off. The British and French growth rates, for instance, from 1860 on were considerably less than those of many less ambitious countries, such as Sweden or even Japan. The German and Japanese attempts to become great powers were enormously costly; but their ultimate failure provides an even more striking insight into the realities of the present international system.

After total military defeat and a complete loss of their great-power status, they have both achieved absolutely unprecedented rates of economic growth, far exceeding the growth rates of the victors.

This is indeed a strange world, in which nothing fails like success and nothing succeeds like defeat, in which great powers find that their greatness impoverishes them, and in which the way to get rich is to stay home and mind one's own business well and to participate as little as possible in the international system. Of course there are also historical examples of countries for whom defeat has been disastrous, though such examples are rather scarce since Carthage, or perhaps Byzantium. It is also possible to find examples of countries that stayed home and minded their own business badly. Such examples, however, do not affect the fundamental proposition that at least since 1860, when the impact of the scientific revolution on economic life really began to be felt, we have been living in a world that is qualitatively different from that of the past, a world in which, as I have said elsewhere, one can extract ten dollars from nature for every dollar one can exploit out of man. The scientific revolution, therefore, has completely eliminated any economic payoffs that might have been available through the international system in the past. And while diminishing the system's returns, the scientific revolution has at the same time enormously increased the cost of the system. In order to justify the continuation of this costly and precarious system, we have to put an enormous value on the nation-state as such and on the national identity it confers on the individual. It should at least be asked whether the value of these things is commensurate with the risks and costs of maintaining the system.

The Pathological State of the International System

What, then, are the sources of this pathological state of the international system? A number of answers can be given. Most significantly, a system of unilateral national defense, which still characterizes the international system in spite of the small beginnings of world political organization, is a "prisoner's dilemma" system:[3] the dynamics of the system produce an equilibrium in which everybody is much worse off than in some alternative state of the system. In the two-country version of this system, let us suppose that each country has two choices: disarm or arm. They will clearly be better off economically and more secure

---

[3] Anatol Rapoport and Albert M. Chammah, *Prisoner's Dilemma: A Study in Conflict and Cooperation* (Ann Arbor: University of Michigan Press, 1965).

politically if they both disarm. If both are disarmed, however, it pays one to arm—at least it may in terms of his image of the system. And if one is armed, the other will have a powerful incentive to follow suit. Both will probably end up by being armed, in which case both will be worse off than they would have been had they remained disarmed.

Whether there is an equilibrium in the world war-industry depends largely on the reactions of the parties concerned. The fundamental parameter here is the "reactivity coefficient," that is, the extent to which one country will increase its arms expenditures for each additional dollar that it perceives being spent on arms in another country. I have shown in another paper[4] that in a two-country system the product of the reactivity coefficients must be less than one if there is to be an equilibrium; otherwise the war industry will expand explosively until the system breaks down as the result of war or of some sort of parametric change. It can also be shown that the more parties there are in the system, the smaller the reactivity coefficient must be if an equilibrium is to be attained. It must certainly average less than one. As a reactivity coefficient of one might be regarded as normal, it is clear that a system of this kind must be abnormally unreactive if it is to achieve an equilibrium. It is not surprising, therefore, in the light of existing reactivity coefficients, which are certainly close to one if not above it, that the world war-industry maintains an uneasy and continually upward-groping equilibrium at about 140 billion dollars per year. Furthermore, this equilibrium, even if it exists, is inherently precarious in that a very slight change in the reactivity coefficients even on the part of a single country can destroy the equilibrium altogether.

The reactivity coefficients are themselves functions of the value systems of the decision-makers and of their general image of the international system, or perhaps of their images of other people's reactivity. And all these in turn are related to the gathering and processing of the information on which the decision-makers depend. The pathology of the international system, therefore, is closely related to the method by which it generates and processes information and the way in which these information inputs influence the decision-makers' images of the world. The question as to what is meant by the "reality" of these images in the international system is a very difficult one. In the first place, insofar as the system itself is determined by the decisions of a relatively small number of decision-makers it inevitably contains a considerable

---

[4] Kenneth E. Boulding, "The Parameters of Politics," *University of Illinois Bulletin* (July 15, 1966), pp. 3–21. Also in this volume, Chapter 18.

random element. The image of the system, therefore, should always be an image of probabilities rather than certainties. There is no very good way, however, of finding out what the probabilities of the system are. We do not have enough cases to compute frequencies like the life tables of insurance companies, and whenever one hears the expression "a calculated risk" in international politics one tends to interpret this as meaning "I really don't have the slightest notion." The epistemological problem itself, in the case of international systems, is very difficult; and one certainly cannot come up with any perfect solution for the problem of producing truth in the image of the system, for the system itself consists in considerable part of the images about it.

Even if the truth in an absolute sense may elude us, this still does not prevent us from discussing health, or at least disease, and there are certain diseases of the information system (and the images it produces) in the international system that can be diagnosed. The basic problem, as I have suggested earlier, is that adequate images of the international system cannot be derived from folk learning, because the simple feedbacks of the folk-learning process are quite inadequate to deal with the enormous complexities of the international system. At the present time, however, the role of science is extremely limited, indeed, almost nonexistent. We do not apply scientific techniques of information gathering and processing, even those available in the social sciences, to the image-creating processes of the international system. Social science, indeed, is regarded with considerable suspicion by most of the professional practitioners in the international system, perhaps rightly so, for it represents a certain threat to their status and power. On the whole, therefore, the images of the international system in the minds of its decision-makers are derived by a process that I have described as "literary"—a melange of narrative history, memories of past events, stories and conversations, etc., plus an enormous amount of usually ill-digested and carelessly collected current information. When we add to this the fact that the system produces strong hates, loves, loyalties, disloyalties, and so on, it would be surprising if any images were formed that even remotely resembled the most loosely defined realities of the case.

Almost every principle we have learned about scientific information gathering, processing, and reality-testing is violated by the processes of the international system. Indeed, the conflict of values between the subculture of science and the subculture of the international system may well turn out to be one of the most fundamental conflicts of our age. In science secrecy is abhorrent and veracity is the highest virtue. In science there is only one mortal sin: telling a deliberate lie. In the international system, on the other hand, secrecy is paramount and veracity is subordinated to the national interest. The national interest can indeed be said to legitimate almost every conceivable form of evil: there is not one of the seven deadly sins that is not made into a virtue by the international system. Another fundamental characteristic of the scientific community is that it is basically a community of equals, for the very good reason that hierarchy always corrupts communication. A dialogue can only exist between equals. In a hierarchy there is an inescapable tendency toward pleasing the superior, and hence confirming his own ideas. Hierarchy in organizations, therefore, produces a condition akin to paranoia in individuals. The information-gathering apparatus always tends to confirm the existing image of the top decision-makers, no matter what it is. This organizational "mental illness" is nowhere better illustrated than in the international system, which is composed of numerous foreign-office and military-establishment hierarchies that thrive on self-justifying images.

Finally, in the scientific community power is supposed to have a low value and truth the highest value, whereas in the international system the reverse is the case. It is not surprising that under these circumstances the international system is so spectacularly pathological in an organizational sense. Indeed, if one were designing an organization to produce pathological results, one could hardly do better than an information system dependent mainly on spies and diplomats. This is not to say, of course, that the individuals who occupy these roles in the international system are themselves necessarily crazy, although they do suffer from certain occupational diseases. On the whole, the people who run the international system are well above average in intelligence and education and even in personal morality, for they would probably not be content to serve in a system so absurd if they did not possess high moral ideals. Economic man does not go into the international system. He can live a better life outside it. It is the moral, patriotic, and self-sacrificing individuals who are most likely to be the active participants in the international system. It is the organization, not the individuals, which is pathological, by reason of the corruption of both the information and the values that have produced it.

Can the System Be Cured?

The next question, therefore, is whether we can learn to change the organization in ways that will make the whole system less pathological.

There seem to be two general answers to this question. One is given by the advocates of world government, who feel that the defects of the present international system cannot be remedied and that therefore the only solution is to abolish it by transferring the locus of sovereignty from independent states to a world government. It is argued that this is a logical extension of the ongoing process in which smaller states have been absorbed or federated into larger ones, and that we have now reached the point where the existing international system is so dangerous and so costly that the sacrifice of national sovereignty sacrifices nothing but the dangers and costs. Only world government, it is argued, can prevent war or establish anything that even remotely resembles justice.

A somewhat less drastic view holds that stable peace is possible within the framework of an international system, given certain conditions, and that therefore world government in the strict sense is unnecessary. It is argued, in effect, that the pathological character of the international system which is so striking today is not necessary, but is rather a function of certain parameters and characteristics of the system, and that a nonpathological, healthy international system is conceivable and possible. Such a rehabilitated system, it is felt, might be more desirable in many ways than a unified world government.

These two approaches may not be as contradictory as they seem at first sight, though they do represent, in effect, two different solutions to the problem of the prisoner's dilemma, which, as we have seen, is at the root of the pathology of the international system. One solution to the prisoner's-dilemma problem is to change the payoffs of the game through the intervention of some third party. This is in effect what law, especially in its penal aspect, is supposed to do. The prisoner's dilemma in a sense governs all forms of the social contract, where each party has the choice of being either "good" or "bad." If they are all good, they will all be better off; and yet if they are all good it may pay one of them to be bad, in which case it pays all of them to be bad and they all end up worse off. The function of law and of government, in its role as the creator and sustainer of law, is that of altering the payoffs for the individual decision-maker so that it will not pay him to be bad even if everybody else is good. The business of government, then, is to define what is "bad" and to see that this kind of behavior is appropriately penalized so that the social contract is not broken.

The other approach to the problem of the prisoner's dilemma is the development of farsightedness on the part of the players themselves. This involves a learning process, and as Anatol Rapoport's experiments have suggested,[5] many people do learn after a while that "bad behavior" does not pay off in the long run. Hence they refrain from trying to gain temporary advantages that unilateral bad behavior might give them.

In the long-run development of the international system, both these processes may be observed. On the one hand, we have seen the development of supranational political institutions of slowly increasing capacity: the Concert of Europe, the League of Nations, and the United Nations. Each catastrophe apparently teaches mankind to set up institutions that might have prevented it, though they usually do not prevent the next catastrophe. Just as the generals are always supposed to be prepared to fight the last war, so the international institutions are designed to prevent it. The slow learning process nevertheless goes on, and the institutions themselves can be regarded as repositories of political skill and knowledge. Indeed, for the meagre resources that we devote to the international order, we get a remarkable return. This becomes apparent when we consider that the combined budget for all the international agencies is less than that of the Ford Foundation.

Along with this process of developing world political institutions, we have also seen the development of areas of stable peace within the international system even without supranational institutions. The two best examples are probably North America and Scandinavia, though the socialist camp may be another example and perhaps by this time all of Europe, although it is a bit early to say. Stable peace, at any rate, is a recognizable phase of the international system, which tends to pass into this phase when a certain level of maturity in national behavior has been reached. One might even suppose, perhaps a bit optimistically, that relations between the United States and the Soviet Union might develop as they have between the United States and Canada or among the Scandinavian countries.

The growth of stable peace requires a learning process on the part of the national decision-makers, a learning process that includes the accumulation of tradition and role images which are passed on from role occupant to role occupant. The process involves a change in values as well as in actual images of the system, and these are closely related in a very intricate and complex manner. The nation-state can no longer be treated as a sacred institution; there must be a deflation of the emotions and values that attach to it, a decline, if you

---

[5] Anatol Rapoport, *op. cit.*

will, in the passion with which people love their countries and an acceptance of the nation-state and the nation-state system as essentially mundane institutions designed solely for public convenience.

One great problem that the world is likely to face in this connection is that the maturation process of the nation-state takes place at different rates, so that at any one time some are much more mature than others. This, however, may give the immature ones an advantage, since they will be able to elicit more passionate devotion to the national cause from their citizens. This is perhaps one of the most persuasive reasons why the mature states, who have outgrown the adolescent disease of nationalism, should be all the more concerned to set up world political institutions that have some hope of exercising restraint on the less mature states. What might be called the "mature-conflict-behavior solution" of the prisoner's dilemma depends on both parties being mature. If only one party is mature, then a third-party alteration of the payoffs is the only solution, which in this case means world government.

The development of the social sciences and especially of a genuine social science of the international system, which is only in its infancy, is likely to have a substantial effect on the progress of the international system toward maturity. War is a crude, extremely expensive but often effective form of reality-testing, which has the added disadvantage of changing the reality to be tested. The improvement of the information system and the prevailing images of the international system that would follow from the development of a genuine social science of the international system would almost certainly have the effect of diminishing the probability of what might be called unintended war, that is, war that results from a lack of realism in the estimate of the consequences of decisions. Thus it is highly probable that the war of 1914 would not have occurred if the international system had possessed a more objective, carefully sampled, and adequately processed information system, which could have given the makers of a number of disastrous decisions a different image of the system. A more realistic image might have prevented these decisions, even without any change in ultimate values.

An improvement in the information system, however, would not leave ultimate values unchanged. The development, for instance, of a certain measure or index of success is likely to direct attention toward that aspect of the system which the index measures and to cause a high value to be placed on it. Thus the development of a way to measure the rate of economic growth has profoundly affected the valuation that many political decision-makers now place upon economic policy.

Similarly, a measure of, shall we say, the general level of hostility in the international system, which would be quite within the present capability of the social sciences, might have a very profound effect not only on the image of the world held by the international decision-makers but also on the values they apply to it.

One word of hesitation and warning is worth making here, along the lines of Alexander Pope's admonition about a little learning. The image of the international system even in the best informed minds is subject to a large amount of uncertainty, and the decisions that are made in it should reflect the real uncertainties of the system. In a system of great uncertainty, he who hesitates is frequently saved. There is a danger that the techniques of the social sciences might be used to give an illusion of certainty where none exists. There is some evidence that war-gaming has had this effect, which could easily be disastrous. There is danger also that value systems are moved too easily in the direction of what is measurable and apparently known. Decision-making in systems as complex as the international system inevitably requires the operation of the unconscious as well as the conscious mind. The wisdom in decision-making that comes from wide experience and an almost unconscious appreciation of reality is not as good as explicit knowledge. Nevertheless when knowledge lingers, as it inevitably must, wisdom will have to do; and an attitude of mind that rejects wisdom in favor of imperfect knowledge may easily be disastrous. In this connection, the present tendency to try to develop rational modes of behavior in decision-making must be looked upon with a great deal of suspicion as well as some enthusiasm. Nevertheless, to reject knowledge where it exists in favor of a doubtful wisdom is no wisdom at all. The development of improved methods of collecting and processing information from the international system by such techniques as sample surveys, content analysis, correlation and factor analysis of complex systems, and the whole expansion of information processing and indexing that the computer makes possible is almost bound to have a maturing effect on the national images, both in regard to realism of content and humaneness of values.

The one possible cause for optimism about the international system is that there exists what might be called a "macro-learning" process, which seems to be cumulative in much the same way as science. It is only within the last 200 years, for instance, that we have achieved something that could be called a security community or stable peace in segments of the international system. During that period, we can trace something that looks like a progression from stable war into unstable war into unstable peace and finally into stable peace. As experience accumulates and as the memory of disastrous feedbacks affects present images of the system, these more mature images become a kind of folk wisdom that is transmitted from generation to generation, however precariously; and with the rise of genuinely scientific images of the international system we may expect this cumulative learning process to accelerate. It is reasonable to hope, therefore, that we may be fairly close to that key watershed in which the international system passes from a condition of unstable peace, albeit with enclaves of stable peace, into one in which stable peace becomes a property of the general system, which still however may have enclaves of unstable peace within it. At the moment, it must be admitted, the enclaves of stable peace appear as figures upon a ground of unstable peace. However, a little expansion of the figures to include, let us say, all of Europe, the United States, the Soviet Union, and Japan, and the ground will become the figure and the figure the ground. Quantitatively this change may be very small; yet it will be a watershed, and the system will never be the same again. One may then expect the enclaves of unstable peace to diminish as the learning process continues, until finally the vision of a world in stable peace, which has haunted mankind so elusively for so long, will finally be realized. When it is realized it will be the result of a long process of learning, in which cheap methods of learning such as science and perhaps even accumulated folk wisdom are substituted for the expensive methods of learning such as war.

THE ROLE OF THE WAR INDUSTRY IN INTERNATIONAL CONFLICT

Journal of Social Issues, XXIII, 1
(Jan. 1967): 47-61

The Role of the War Industry in International Conflict

President Eisenhower, in his famous farewell address, made a classical allusion to the "military-industrial complex". The expression "the war industry" has also been used to describe the same phenomenon, and as this is somewhat more in line with the general terminology of economics, I propose to use it. What I mean, then, by the war industry is that segment of the economy which produces whatever is bought by the defense budget. This includes, then, the armed forces themselves and all those segments of the economy, such as the armament industry, which supply goods and services to the armed forces. There are some tricky problems here of measurement which arise mainly because a considerable part of the labor force of the war industry are conscripts, not free labor. If we were to reckon the cost of the war industry at shadow prices equal to the market price of the labor involved, it would almost certainly be considerably larger. Conscription, however, like any other form of involuntary servitude, distorts the price system and leads to some false accounting of human capital. The situation is further complicated by the fact that the income of members of the armed forces is to a considerable extent in kind, that is, they are fed, housed and clothed at government expense and without much personal freedom of choice.

The question at issue in this paper is that of the reciprocal relations between the war industry on the one hand and the other elements of the international system on the other. It may be objected that the war industry is such a large part of the international system that this relationship is almost too one-sided to discuss. Nonetheless, even though the war industry is quantitatively by far the largest sector of the international system, if we look at it for instance in terms of the total labor force devoted to it or the total product imputed to it, it is frequently in a somewhat dependent relationship to other elements in the system. At the decision-making level it is frequently the tail (that is, the civilian politicians, legislatures, opinion makers and diplomats) that wags the dog of the war industry. On the other hand, there have been sufficient cases in which the dog wagged his own tail, or perhaps we should reverse the metaphor and say has run his own head into a wall, that the problem of the reciprocal interaction between the war industry on the one hand and the rest of the international system on the other becomes enormously important.

The Threat System

The war industry differs from the rest of the economy mainly because it is a component of a threat system rather than of an exchange system. In an exchange system goods are produced and exchanged one against the other. The farmer produces food and exchanges this with the industrial sector for industrial goods. In the threat system threat capabilities are produced, that is, the ability to produce "bads", a bad being the destruction of somebody else's good (Boulding, 1963, 424-34). Even though there are certain parallels between the exchange system and the threat system, the differences are highly significant. Thus if a bandit says, "Your money or your life", we give him our money, he gives us our life, and this looks superficially like exchange. What he is giving us, however, is not a good but an abstention from doing bad, that is, a negative bad; and for society at large at any rate, a negative bad is by no means the same thing as a positive good. Furthermore, if the threat system is to be capable of achieving a stable and recurrent change in the social system, it must be legitimated. A bandit can take away your money once; if he wants to do it every year, however, he has to turn himself into a tax collector, who is a sort of legitimated bandit. Legitimation, of course, is done in all sorts of ways, through the pomp of princes, the blessing of religion or the rituals of democracy.

The problem of the legitimation of the threat system in the international arena is particularly complex. The national armed force is neither quite a bandit nor is it a policeman. It occupies an uneasy limbo between these two extremes. It has a great deal more legitimacy, of course, in its own country than it does outside. On the other hand, armed forces cannot really even fight each other unless there is some kind of overriding legitimacy given to the general procedure. There is a curious paradox here, that the various armed forces, and especially the armed forces of countries which threaten each other, are in a symbiotic relationship in the sense that each depends on the other for its own justification. One notices a somewhat parallel symbiotic relationship between the police and the criminals, though here perhaps it is truer to say that the police are parasitic upon criminals (the more criminals, the more police; the more police, the fewer criminals; the more dogs, the more fleas, the more fleas, the fewer dogs). The relationship of armed forces, somewhat by contrast, is more like that of two mutually cooperative species: the bigger the Russian armed forces, the bigger will be the American; the bigger the American armed force, the bigger will be the Russian.

The symbiotic nature of the system makes its equilibrium, if it exists at all, highly sensitive to changes in the parameters of the system. Let us suppose, for the sake of simplicity, two countries A and B, and suppose that the decision of each about the size of its defense budget depends only on the defense budget of the other. If D_a and D_b are the defense budgets of the two countries respectively, we then have two equations, assumed for the moment to be linear:

$$D_a = K_a + m_a D_b \qquad (1)$$

$$D_b = K_b + m_b D_a \qquad (2)$$

Solving these two equations, we get:

$$D_a = \frac{K_a + m_a K_b}{1 - m_a m_b} \qquad (3)$$

$$D_b = \frac{K_b + m_b K_a}{1 - m_a m_b} \qquad (4)$$

The parameters of these equations can be given fairly simple meanings. K_a and K_b might be called the *absolute militarism* of the two countries, these representing the expenditures on the armed forces even in the absence of any external threat. The parameters m_a, m_b may be called the *reactivity coefficients* of the two countries, and measure how much each country will increase its own defense budget for each unit increase of the defense budget of the other. Thus if m_a is small, it means that country A is unreactive to a change either up or down in the defense budget of country B. Equations (3) and (4) indicate that the equilibrium level of the defense budget is highly sensitive to the reactivity coefficient of the countries concerned. If $m_a m_b$ is greater than 1, no equilibrium is possible, and the system is explosive. Defense budgets will expand continually as each country reacts to the other until finally some boundary is reached, at which the system changes. Usually this boundary is war.

If we think of a reactivity coefficient of unity as in some sense "normal" (if he increases his budget by a million dollars, I'll do the same), it is clear that if the reactivities are normal, there is no equilibrium. If the reactivities of both countries are below normal, there is an equilibrium; if one is below normal, the other may be correspondingly above and there still might be an equilibrium. The geometric mean of the reactivities of the two countries must, however, be below normal if there is to be an equilibrium. It is not surprising, therefore, that this system is so rarely stable, and that systems of deterrence (which is what this is) in the past have almost inevitably led to war.[1] If nonlinearity is allowed, it is clear that if the reactivity coefficients diminish with increased defense budgets, the possibility of equilibrium is enhanced. On the other hand, if high defense budgets lead to higher reactivity coefficients, the probability of an equilibrium position is diminished. The above model I have elsewhere called the Richardson model, as it was first developed in a somewhat different form by Lewis Richardson (1960).

The introduction of a third country into the model, as always, increases its complexity enormously; and the n-country model is very difficult indeed. As soon as we get three parties, we have to consider the possibility of coalitions; and if these are unstable, the probability of achieving equilibrium in a system of this kind declines very sharply. Let us take, for instance, the 3-country case without coalitions. Using the notations as before where D_a, D_b and D_c represent the defense expenditures of the three countries, we postulate three equilibrium conditions, as in equations, (5,a), (5,b) and (5,c), signifying that the defense expenditure of each one depends on the defense expenditures of the other two. The reaction coefficients, such as a_b, show how much the defense expenditure of one country, (A), will increase for each dollar increase in the defense expenditure of another, (B). The solution of these three equations for D_a is shown in equation (6).

$$D_a = K_a + a_b D_b + a_c D_c \qquad (5)(a)$$

$$D_b = K_b + b_a D_a + b_c D_c \qquad (b)$$

$$D_c = K_c + c_a D_a + c_b D_b \qquad (c)$$

$$D_a = \frac{K_a(1 - b_c c_b) + K_b(a_b + a_c c_b) + K_c(a_b b_c + a_c)}{1 - a_c c_a - b_c c_b - a_b b_a - a_b b_c c_a - a_c b_a c_b} \qquad (6)$$

The solutions for the other countries, of course, are similar, with proper substitution of coefficients. The denominator in each case is

---

[1] A more extended graphical analysis of systems of this kind, extending to nonlinear functions, will be found in K. E. Boulding, *Conflict and Defense* (New York: Harper and Row, 1963), Chapter 2.

the same. If then there is to be a finite solution, the coefficients must conform to the inequality (7):

$$S = a_c c_a + b_c c_b + a_b b_a + a_b b_c c_a + a_c b_a c_b < 1 \qquad (7)$$

If there is to be an equilibrium solution, the expression on the left hand side of the inequality, which we call the *solution coefficient*, S, must be less than 1. If there is mutual hostility among all three countries, all six reaction coefficients will be positive, and they must, therefore, be quite low if S is to be less than 1. Even if we suppose that there is normal reactivity, so that each of the coefficients is 1, we then have $S = 5$, and there is no solution. If all the coefficients are equal and equal to m, then we have equation (8):

$$S = 3m^2 + 2m^3 \qquad (8)$$

Then if $S = 1$, $m = \frac{1}{2}$; and the condition therefore for any stable equilibrium is that the reaction coefficients should be less than $\frac{1}{2}$, which means a pretty low reactivity. The more countries we include in the system, the lower must the coefficients of reactivity be in order to achieve any equilibrium at all.

Alliances and Coalitions

The situation is further complicated, of course, if there are alliances or coalitions. Suppose, for instance, that in the situation of equation (5), countries (A) and (B) are allied against country (C). We can then suppose that the coefficients a_b and b_a will be negative; that is, if either (A) or (B) increases its defense budget, the other country will diminish its budget, as the defense is regarded in some sense as mutual. This would involve a very close alliance. If the allies are rather suspicious of each other, a_b and b_a may still be positive, though they may be small. If $a_b = b_a = 0$, which is the case we might call a neutral alliance, we still have:

$$S = a_c c_a + b_c c_b \qquad (9)$$

and even under these circumstances, if we have the normal reaction coefficients of 1, $S = 2$ and the system will have no equilibrium. In this case, if we suppose that the remaining reaction coefficients are all equal and again equal to m, we have:

$$S = 2m^2 \qquad (10)$$

and in order to obtain an equilibrium position, we must have:

$$m < \frac{1}{\sqrt{2}} = 0.7 \qquad (11)$$

We need not pursue these complexities further at this point, for it is clear that the more nations there are in the system, even if they have alliances, the less chance is there of any equilibrium of unilateral national defense.

Formation of Military Budgets

Up to this point, I have not made any distinction in the model between the nation and its armed forces. I have assumed that a single decision-making process applies to both. When we look at what determines the coefficients, however, which are so crucial in determining whether there will be an equilibrium or not, the organizational structure and the decision-making process within the nation is of enormous importance. Decisions as to the amount of the defense budgets in any nation emerge as a result of a long and complex process of political compromise, proposals and counter-proposals, rising up through the hierarchy of decision making until some final decision is made at the top. The checks and balances involved in this process are of enormous significance. By and large it is fair to assume that as in any budget-making process, those who are the principal and immediate beneficiaries of budget increases will press for them, and those who are concerned with large issues and larger agendas will tend to cut them down. This seems to be a practically universal principle of budget formation; and as the size of the war industry, unlike that of industries serving consumers, is determined almost entirely by a budget process and not by a market process, budget formation is obviously the key to the overall dynamics of the situation.

There is great need for empirical study of the process of budget formation in military budgets, for as far as I know there has been practically no work, at least of an objective character, in this field. The most one can do is to suggest some hypotheses which might be tested by such studies. One such hypothesis is that there are two large constellations of forces affecting a total budget. One consists of the forces of the internal environment, which almost continuously make for budget increase. Every department within any organization always feels that it could do a much better job if it had a somewhat larger budget. Hence the first step in budget making, which is the collection of proposals from departments and units of an organization, always results in a total budget proposal which will almost certainly be larger than that finally arrived at; and it will almost always result in an increase in budgets over last year, or whatever is the budget period. As these budget proposals move up through the hierarchy of the organization, they are met by another set of forces representing the external environment. At the lower levels of the organization and in its smaller units, these external forces are likely to be weak, though there may be some exceptions to this, in the case of units which are specialized in contact with the external environment, such as, for instance, staff units. Even where the external environment is perceived, however, at these lower levels, there is likely to be distortion of perception which gives a bias towards budget increases rather than budget decreases. As the budget moves up through the hierarchy of the organization from departments to divisions to larger and larger units and aggregates, the external environment becomes more important, and in the final decision the external environment may dominate.

Thus in the case of a state university, the external environment of the legislature is remote at the level of the department, highly salient to the level of the President. Similarly in the case of the defense budget, the external environment may not be very important at the lower levels but becomes extremely important at the top. Generally speaking, therefore, we can suppose that there is an upward bias in budget formation in all organizations, including defense organizations, and that it takes rather an unusual perception of the external environment to bring about budget cuts. In the case of defense establishments, this happens, for instance, at the end of a war, particularly a victorious war, when the international system is suddenly perceived as being much less threatening; decisions to reduce the establishment drastically are made at the top, perhaps in response also to a perception of the internal domestic environment of the country (the "bring the boys home" mood); and the lower echelons of the organization are quite defenseless against the overall budget reduction. Circumstances of this kind, however, are unusual, and in normal circumstances the structure of budget formation, in defense as in other organizations, tends to give an upward bias towards a constant increase.

In terms of our equations, this means that the coefficients of militarism, K_a, K_b, etc., under ordinary circumstances tend to rise year after year, which leads further to diminishing the chances of stability in the system. The one factor which tends to counteract this is stinginess on the part of civilian government, in response either to the personal prejudices of the decision makers or in response to political pressures from the civilian population. An increase in military budgets must result either in increased taxation, in inflation or in reduction of civilian budgets. There will be political pressures against all these three reactions, and if the ultimate decision-maker is highly sensitive to these pressures, the forces making for increase in military budgets will be correspondingly damped. A study of the Eisenhower period, 1952-1960, for instance, indicates that one of the major factors in damping the arms race in this period was the "stinginess" in President Eisenhower, who had strong personal prejudices against increasing public expenditures in general, and who therefore held down military budgets out of sheer parsimony. This substantially increased the stability of the international system, and almost certainly gave us a kind of equilibrium which a more spendthrift, energetic President could easily have destroyed. It is an indescribably tragic commentary on the nature of a system of unilateral national defense that almost the only way in which it can be workable is through the major decision makers being rather stingy, insensitive and unreactive.

One of the crucial factors in the decision-making and the budget-making process here is the extent to which the defense establishment is under civilian political control or the extent to which the defense establishment itself makes the final decisions about the government budget. By and large, the hypothesis may be put forward that civilian control strengthens the damping forces on budget formation and is likely to result in smaller coefficients and to increase the possibility of an equilibrium of the unilateral defense system; whereas under military control of final budgets, we are likely to see a much greater sensitivity to increase in the budgets of other countries, that is, high reaction coefficients, and we are also likely to see an insensitivity to civilian demands on the budget, which is likely to result in high coefficients of militarism.

Industrial-Military Complex

The role in a society of what might be called the private sector of the war industry, that is, the industrial part of the industrial-military complex, may also be relevant to the fundamental coefficients of the international system. In the 1930's, the view that war was mainly a product of the armament manufacturers was very popular. One recalls, for instance, the Nye investigations and the Johnson Acts. This, however, seems now to be a gross oversimplification. It is certainly true that armaments manufacturers represent, as it were, an upward pressure in the formation of military budgets. Under most circumstances, however, this pressure is fairly small compared with the enormous pressures imposed by the external military and political environment and the rest of the internal political environment, as represented by the competing claims on the overall budget. There is, indeed, a dangerous change in this respect in the United States, as we have become a relatively militarized nation. Before the Second World War there was really nothing that could be called a specialized armaments industry. Most of the suppliers of the Department of Defense, such as Dupont, General Motors, and so on, were primarily engaged in the production and sale of consumer goods, and were what might be called consumer-oriented organizations. Since the end of the Second World War, we have seen the rise of firms like General Dynamics and most of the airframe companies, which are not consumer-oriented at all, and which make almost their entire sales to the Department of

Defense. There is a recognition among these firms that the defense industry is an unstable customer and that in the interest of their own survival, it would be advisable for them to diversify their activities into civilian markets. Many of them, however, have had some unfortunate experiences with this activity, simply because the kind of organization which is well adapted at selling things to government, which is, shall we say, an understanding and sympathetic customer, is not well adapted to selling things on the hard cold world of the civilian market. Even so, there is not much evidence that as a political pressure group, especially in Congress, the private sector of the war industry in any way dominates defense decisions.

Defense Industry and Depressions

There is a more subtle problem in this connection, which may be of more importance. In the economic folklore of the United States especially, there is a widespread belief that it is only the defense industry which saves us from depression. We were half grateful to Hitler and the Japanese for getting us out of the Great Depression of the '30's, and this memory is still strong in the minds of the generation of powerful decision-makers today. The association of peace with unemployment is particularly strong in the labor movement, which accounts at least in part for its almost total loss of idealism, and the fact that it is the principal drum-beater for the Cold War. The problem of economic adjustments to disarmament, or even to changes within the war industry, is a real one. Nevertheless, with the resources which we now have, it is soluble, given reasonably sensible economic policy.[2] Indeed the American economy is quite astonishingly flexible and adjustable, provided it does not run into deflation; and as deflation can very easily be avoided by monetary and fiscal policy, the association of war with prosperity has now been broken. A good example of this adjustability can be seen in the experience of Michigan. In 1958 the war industry largely moved out of Michigan to California. Temporarily, the results were almost catastrophic. Unemployment in Michigan, for instance, rose from about 5% of the labor force in the summer of 1957 to 16% of the labor force in the summer of '58. By the late summer of '59, however, it had recovered almost to its 1957 level, and after a secondary recession in 1961, under the stimulus of the tax cut it fell to around 3% by the summer of 1965, in spite of the fact that the overall size of the defense industry was fairly stable.

I am not suggesting, of course, that this problem is unimportant. If, for instance, there was a drastic reduction of defense expenditure in the United States, there would be serious local depressions, especially

2 See the Report of the Committee on the Economic Impact of Defense and Disarmament, U.S. Government Printing Office, July, 1965.

on the West Coast. Unless the reduction in defense expenditure was accompanied by a substantial budget deficit and an easy monetary policy, these local depressions might easily cumulate into an overall deflation. If the overall level of demand, however, is taken care of, the evidence suggests that local adjustments, even without much in the way of government assistance, can be made in about the period of a year. The extraordinary ease with which economic adjustment was made to the great disarmament of 1945-46, which was by far the greatest disarmament in history, is further evidence of the extraordinary flexibility of the American economy.[3] Nevertheless, it is not the reality but the image which dominates behavior, and as long as there is a prevailing folk image of the war industry as a source of prosperity, this is an important factor operating to resist a reduction in military budgets. Furthermore, in order to justify military budgets, we almost have to be reactive, and we have to interpret the messages which come from abroad as hostile. All this increases both the coefficients of militarism and the coefficients of reactivity, and even if it leads to an equilibrium position, the equilibrium has large military budgets.

When one looks at the long run and takes a perspective which may extend over decades or even centuries, the relations of economic power to military power and the equilibrium of the war industry become subtle but enormously interesting. One might attempt to sum up the situation in the aphorism that wealth creates power, and power destroys wealth. Like all aphorisms, this is a half-truth; but it is at least a place to start. The first half of it will generally be accepted without much question. If we want to get a rough measure of the relative power of nations, their gross national product is at least a place to start. The absolute magnitude of the war industry of any nation is, of course, equal to its gross national product multiplied by the proportion of gross national product devoted to the armed force; this is simply a truism. As the variance, however, in the proportion devoted to the armed force is much less than the variance in the gross national product itself, the gross national product is the dominant variable in this equation. The proportion of the gross national product devoted to the war industry does not, with one or two exceptions, exceed 10% (the only exceptions according to Bruce Russett are Jordan, 25.70 and Taiwan, 12.30), and there is a very heavy concentration between about 2% and 7%. The gross national product, on the other hand, varies from well under a billion for the smaller countries to five or six hundred billion for the United States. The conclusion of this is that as we look at the long run dynamics of the system, the relative position of nations on the power scale is going to depend on their sustained rates of economic growth, in terms of overall gross national

---

[3] In a single calendar year National Defense purchases fell from 35.5% of the GNP in 1945 to 8.9% in 1946, and then to 4.9% in 1947.

product. A critical stage in the international system occurs when one nation overtakes another in its economic growth as measured, say, by the GNP; for even though this may not represent an immediate reversal of power positions, at some point, if this process continues, the power positions will soon be reversed. If there is, as indeed there usually is at this point, a serious lag in the image of the world of the decision makers, unrealistic decisions can be made which easily lead into war, even unintended war. The First World War was probably an example of this, in which France and Britain underestimated the growth in the power of Germany and Germany underestimated the growth in the power of the United States.

Power Destroys Wealth

The second proposition, that power destroys wealth, is likely to be received with more skepticism, though the rise, fall and succession of empires may be adduced as rough evidence. As further evidence, I adduce the following table. It will be noticed here that in the period

TABLE 1
RATE OF GROWTH OF OUTPUT PER HEAD OF POPULATION

	1870-1913	1913-50	1950-60
Belgium	1.7	0.7	2.3
Denmark	2.1	1.1	2.6
France	1.4	0.7	3.5
Germany	1.8a	0.4	6.5
Italy	0.7	0.6	5.3
Netherlands	0.8b	0.7	3.6
Norway	1.4a	1.9	2.6
Sweden	2.3	1.6	2.6
Switzerland	1.3c	1.5	3.7
United Kingdom	1.3	1.3	2.2
Canada	2.0	1.3	1.2
United States	2.2a	1.7	1.6
Average	1.6	1.1	3.1

Source: Angus Maddison, *Economic Growth in the West,* page 30.
a 1871-1913.
b 1900-13.
c 1890-1913.

from 1870-1913, the imperial powers, France, Belgium, the Netherlands and the United Kingdom, developed at a slower rate than the nonimperial powers such as Denmark, Sweden, Canada and the United States, even in terms of rate of growth of output per head of the population. It is true that Italy, which was not a particularly imperial power in this period, did not do very well; neither did Switzerland. Nevertheless, the relationship is a striking one, and the inference would seem to be that the road to rapid economic development is to stay home and mind one's own business well. Italy, presumably, stayed home and minded it badly. The cost of war involvement is clearly seen in the period 1913-50; and the period 1950-60 shows the remarkable results of getting rid of empire, becoming minor powers, and concentrating on getting rich rather than on being powerful.

There certainly seems to be a good deal of evidence that the obsession with being a world power, following the Second World War, has seriously hampered the economic growth of the United States. In the 1950's, for instance, there were actually 45 countries with a higher rate of growth of per capita income than the United States. By way of dramatizing this situation, I have calculated, in Table 2, what would

TABLE 2

PROJECTED "OVERTAKE DATES" AT WHICH VARIOUS COUNTRIES WOULD
OVERTAKE THE U.S. IN PER CAPITA GNP

Country	Per Capita GNP, 1957 $ U.S.	Rate of Growth, 1950-1960 %	Year in Which Country Overtakes U.S. in Per Capita GNP
United States	2577	1.6	
West Germany	927	6.5	1979
Switzerland	1428	3.7	1986
Japan	306	8.0	1992
Italy	516	5.2	1999
France	943	3.5	2011
Netherlands	836	3.6	2014
Sweden	1380	2.6	2020
Norway	1130	2.6	2040
Denmark	1057	2.6	2047
Belgium	1196	2.3	2069
United Kingdom	1189	2.2	2086
Canada	1947	1.2	Never

Sources: Bruce M. Russett, *World Handbook of Political and Social Indicators,* page 155; Angus Maddison, *Economic Growth in the West,* page 30.

be the "overtake dates" at which various countries would overtake the United States in per capita GNP if we start at 1950 and project growth at the rate which these countries followed from 1950 to 1960. It will be seen that these dates are suprisingly close to the present. A table such as this, of course, is in no sense a prediction; indeed it is no more than an arithmetical exercise, and it is already obsolete, for in the '60's, the rates of growth of the United States have increased substantially and of many other countries have declined. It is an illustration, however, of the rapidity with which change in the relative structure of the international system can take place under rather divergent rates of economic growth.

The gross national product itself, of course, is a product of two variables, the gross national product per capita and the total population. As it is the overall gross national product which is the dominant variable in determining the position of a nation in the relative power structure, we have to look both at increase in productivity, which is reflected in the per capita GNP, and increase in the population itself. Thus the rise of the United States to the position of the dominant power in the world is associated not only with its economic development, but also with its enormous population increase in the last hundred and fifty years, as it expanded into a virtually empty continent. There are now, however, no empty continents to expand into, and population increase in many parts of the world can easily result in an offsetting diminution in the per capita GNP. Actually, the differences in per capita GNP are sufficient to offset quite wide divergences in population. Thus Japan still probably has a larger gross national product than the People's Republic of China, in spite of the fact that it only has a seventh of the population.

These considerations actually give rise to a modest optimism about the stability of the international system in, say, the next fifty years. Assuming that the United States has emerged from the doldrums of the '50's, and assuming also that the socialist countries, because of their failures in agriculture, are going to find their overall rates of development slowing down, the prospects for any radical revisions in the order of national power are unlikely for at least a couple of generations. If Chinese development is successful, of course, China may be in a position to challenge the United States in the 21st century. This will certainly not happen, however, for fifty or perhaps a hundred years. The current detente between the United States and the Soviet Union is probably connected with a perhaps unconscious recognition on the part of the Russians that they are going to be second fiddle for a long time, and that if they accept this position, the second fiddle is an instrument on which a lot of beautiful music can be played. A nuclear war, of course, would change the whole world picture quite unpredictably, and would probably lead to the reduction of the present great powers to minor status.

Arms Race and Poor Countries

A danger which seems very real at the moment is the development of arms races among the poorer countries, to the point, indeed, where it can seriously hamper their development or even prevent it altogether. This can happen partly because the arms races themselves absorb resources which are desperately needed for development, which is the case, for instance, in most of South and Southeast Asia; but there is a secondary consequence, that unstable military governments do not produce the kind of economic policies which are favorable to development. One has to be careful of generalizing here; there are military leaders who have succeeded in acquiring what might be called a political personality, once they have achieved national power as head of a government. Ataturk in Turkey, Nasser in Egypt, and, one might even add, Eisenhower in the United States, are perhaps cases in point, though even the record of these men in terms of development is by no means encouraging. The fact that the military are accustomed to a threat system, are accustomed to command rather than influence, and usually have very poor feedback from their decisions, generally unfits them for the leadership of a development program. In this sense an ideology of power can easily result in a failure to develop wealth, and from the point of view of the poor countries this could easily be an unspeakable tragedy. There is real danger at the moment, for instance, that Africa, which stands roughly today where Latin America did, shall we say, in 1820, will pursue a path of military dictatorships, local arms races, expropriations with subsequent destruction of credit ratings, and hence will be a developmental failure. The evidence at this point, however, is somewhat conflicting, and there is an enormous need for better information.

Future of International System

One can only permit oneself a modest optimism regarding the future of the international system, for the forces which make for catastrophe are very strong. Nevertheless, a modest optimism is perhaps better than no optimism at all, and there are certain elements in the present situation which can at least save one from total despair. There is undoubtedly a growth in the strength of the world integrative system, as reflected in Dr. Angell's paper in this issue, which should lessen the coefficients of militarism and reactivity, and hence make for a more stable international equilibrium and a lower level of the war industry. The demographic crisis is unfortunately likely to raise these coefficients, especially in the poorer countries, which increases the danger for the whole world. Certainly within the next hundred years, and perhaps much sooner, effective control of population growth must be achieved or no stable international system can be expected. The international corporations may play an important role in holding the world together, if they can solve the problem of their own legitimacy. One would like to see them explore the possibility of United Nations charters, for the United Nations is the only official source of world legitimation at the moment, and even this is pretty inadequate.

Finally, it may be possible to develop what might be called a "national image policy" deliberately directed towards changing national images in directions which are consistent with a stable international order at a low level of the war industry. The nations are beginning to try these integrative policies, through such things as cultural exchange, and efforts of this kind might reduce the reactivity coefficients very substantially and have enormous payoffs in terms of a reduction in the size of the world war industry. Perhaps the most important contribution to this end, finally, will be the increased awareness that the world war industry does constitute a total system, and that every national act must be judged by its effect on the total. The more realistic the image of the world which the decision makers in the international system have, the better chance we have of reducing the enormous burden which the operation of this system now places on the human race.

REFERENCES

BOULDING, K. E. Towards a pure theory of threat systems. *Journal of the American Economic Association,* May 1963, 53, 424–434. Also in this volume, Chapter 12.

RICHARDSON, LEWIS. *Arms and Insecurity.* Pittsburgh: Boxwood Press, 1960.

AM I A MAN OR
A MOUSE—OR BOTH?

Review of Konrad Lorenz, *On Aggression* and Robert
Ardrey, *The Territorial Imperative: A Personal
Inquiry into the Animal Origins of Property and
Nations. War/Peace Report, 7,* 3
(March 1967): 14-17

AM I A MAN OR A MOUSE—OR BOTH?

Is man's aggressiveness instinctive or acquired? Two recent and widely-noted books suggest this trait is instinctive, as is the case with many animals, but this reviewer calls that thesis "scientific humbug." ON AGGRESSION. By Konrad Lorenz. 306 pp. Harcourt, Brace & World. $5.75. THE TERRITORIAL IMPERATIVE: A Personal Inquiry into the Animal Origins of Property and Nations. By Robert Ardrey. 390 pp. Atheneum, $6.95.

Two recent books by Konrad Lorenz and Robert Ardrey have aroused a great deal of discussion and have raised at least by implication some important questions. Lorenz is a very distinguished Austrian ethologist who has made a life-long work out of studying animal behavior. His earlier book, *King Solomon's Ring,* is a classic in the field. I am not professionally equipped to assess his scientific contributions, but to judge from some of the scientific reviews, Lorenz is a pioneer in the field of the study of animal behavior, that is, ethology, but like many pioneers he is now regarded as somewhat old-fashioned by the rising generation striding forward into the field. But whatever may be the scientific merits of Lorenz, the literary merits are unquestionable. He writes with great vigor and charm and opens up new and exciting worlds to the reader. The animal world is never the same again after one has read Lorenz; he opens one's eyes to its richness and complexity.

Ardrey is not a scientist but a playwright and a moralist, though it would be legitimate to describe him as a popularizer of science. He has both read and listened widely. Nevertheless, he almost literally has an axe to grind and enters the courtroom of the mind, as it were, with a brief. His style, while it is readable and has a superficial charm, often seems to me to weaken itself by straining for effect, and does not have the effortless grace of Lorenz. His works, furthermore, betray a life-long love affair with himself which gets rather tiresome, and he can be irritating enough to make one want to throw the book across the room. However, he has something to say, and his brief at least deserves to be examined carefully and judged in the light of further evidence.

There are many things common to these two books, which is not surprising, as they both deal with essentially the same subject of animal
behavior. Both deal with aggression in animals, although neither of them
defines it. Both are concerned with territoriality, that is, the tendency that
many animals have either as individuals, as pairs or as groups, to stake out
a territory in the environment, mark it with some distinguishing odor or
disfigurement, and defend it against intruders of the same species. Where
the theme of territoriality is central to Ardrey, to Lorenz it is merely part of
a much larger problem of conflict management within a species, having
many other aspects. Both the authors are naturally concerned with the
processes of evolution, especially of genetic or biologic evolution, and
neither of the authors hesitates to make a great leap from animals to man or
from genetic evolution into cultural evolution, and to draw conclusions
about man from the behavior of animals. It is this last aspect of the work
which has aroused most of the controversy and to which I propose to devote
most attention, though it should be noted that the strictly ethological
material of these works is by no means immune from criticism, for
ethology is a young and rapidly advancing science and has still explored
only a very imperfect and probably biased sample of its field.

What Can We Learn?

Let me begin then by raising the central question of what we can learn
about man and the social system by the study of animals and animal
society, before we examine in detail the conclusions which these authors
have drawn. There is no doubt, of course, that a man is a physiological
organization produced by a growth process which is largely organized by
characteristics coded into the total genetic structure of the fertilized egg.
The characteristics contained in man's genetic code are accumulated over
billions of years and are the end result of a very complex process of
mutation and selection. We could in theory postulate an unbroken genetic
chain from the primordial amoeba or whatever it was that started life to any
individual person existing today. The further back we go in this sequence of
genetic structures, presumably the simpler they get in terms of the
characteristics they code. Presumably the genetic structure of an amoeba is
much simpler than that of a fish, a fish simpler than that of a monkey, a
monkey simpler than that of a man.

There are probably no representatives around today of organization of
the identical genetic composition of man's ancestors. Even the amoeba
today is probably a little different from the one-celled organism of two
billion or more years ago from which we sprang, but nevertheless there are
parallels. Some branches of the great tree of evolution have changed less
than others. The amoeba today, therefore, is probably a good deal like
man's one-celled ancestors, the fish of today may resemble man's fishy

ancestors and the monkeys of today have some similarities with man's simian ancestors. This is one conceivable justification for the belief that the study of animal behavior will throw light on human behavior. By studying the behavior of simpler living organisms, we may be able to perceive patterns which may have been present in our ancestors and which may therefore also be present in the complex system of man himself.

We can see immediately, however, how dangerous the method of analogy may be. None of man's direct genetic ancestors are any longer around. Their behavior cannot be studied, though their bones may be. The monkeys of today may have diverged almost as much from their ancestors of two million years ago as man has diverged from his. In jumping from monkeys to man, therefore, we are really making two leaps in the dark, one from the monkey back to man's common ancestor, and again from this ancestor to man. A leap in the dark, of course, may land us on the right side of the pit, but it has to be scrutinized with unusual care to be sure that we have not fallen into serious error. The greatest danger here is from leaping from the simple to the complex, for it is precisely what is not in the simple system that may constitute the essential character of the complex. Hence, even if the simple system is itself embodied in the complex one, this fact only carries us a very little way toward understanding the nature and behavior of the complex.

We could perhaps draw a parallel here from the evolution of man's artifacts, which follow a course of mutation and selection not unlike that of biological evolution. There is a kind of genetic chain in man's imagination and skill leading from the flint knife to the metal axe to the pneumatic drill to the modern coal-mining machine. Also, shall we say, from the wheelbarrow to the cart to the automobile to the jet plane. The problem with deducing the nature of the artifacts of primitive times from those which are around today is not so difficult, especially as primitive artifacts have left a good many traces. The critical question is how much we could learn about the jet plane from studying the wheelbarrow or even from studying the automobile; if the jet plane is man, the automobile perhaps is the mammal, the wheelbarrow the fish, in terms of relative complexity of system.

Nobody would deny that we could find out something about the jet plane by studying the wheelbarrow. We could find out perhaps about metals and about wheels, but we certainly would not find out about flight. An even better comparison would be between a one-task machine like a loom and the modern computer that is capable of learning and can be programmed to innumerable tasks. Because a loom has a shuttle are we to say a computer must also have a shuttle, or some analog of it? Similarly, if displaced aggression in the goose leads to love, as Lorenz says it does, or if territoriality is a characteristic of the Uganda kob, as Ardrey describes, does this mean either that man's ancestors possessed these qualities and attributes or that man today does? It is clear that a great leap has been made in the dark but it is by no means clear that our feet have landed on firm ground.

The crux of the matter, of course, is the old argument about nature and nurture, heredity and environment, instinct and learning. There is little doubt that the oriole's genes build into the bird itself both the knowledge and the desire to build an oriole nest and that this knowledge comes from the information in the gene rather than information coming into the bird through its senses. It is the great peculiarity of man, however, differentiating him from all the other animals, that what his genes endow him with is an enormous nervous system of some 10 billion components, the informational content of which is derived almost wholly from the environment, that is, from inputs into the organism from outside. The genetic contribution to man's nervous system is virtually complete at birth. Almost everything that happens thereafter is learned. It is this consideration which inspires the modern anthropologist to declare that man has virtually no instincts and that virtually everything he knows has to be learned from his environment, which consists both of the physical world in which he lives and moves and the social world into which he is born. It is this characteristic that differentiates cultural evolution from biological evolution. The time seems to be approaching, indeed, when cultural evolution will dominate biological evolution because man will acquire power to manipulate the gene pool directly. Up to now he has not been able to do this, but even so, in at least the last ten thousand years the cultural evolution has dominated the scene, transmitting information through the learning process and not through the information coded in the genes.

The critical question here is the extent to which the genetic composition of the human body limits and determines what it can learn from its environment. That such limits exist there can be no doubt, for no man has an indefinite capacity for learning. Furthermore, it is clear that genetic defects which, for instance, produce the mongoloid or the idiot, result in a very serious limitation of the potential field of learning, even though there is a good deal of evidence accumulating that this limitation itself is a function of the culture into which the child grows and may be less confining than we now think. We are pretty sure that it is genetic constitution which prevents a dog or a chimpanzee from learning to talk; we are not quite so sure about the dolphin. What does seem to be clear, however, is that for the normal human being the limits on learning imposed by the physiological constitution of the human nervous system are very far out, and that most of the limits come from a dynamic failure of the learning process in experience rather than from any limitations imposed by the physiological nature of the human nervous system, the capacity of which seems very far from having been exhausted. It is, indeed, the existence of large excess capacity in the human nervous system which it seems to me vitiates the arguments of those who seek to find in "instinct" any explanation whatever of human behavior beyond the most elementary and primitive acts of the newly born.

The argument is complicated, however, by the fact that environments themselves can breed. Culture is a body of coded information which is passed on from generation to generation, suffering mutation and selection, just as the coded information in the gene is passed on, except that cultural evolution is much more subject to mutation and proceeds at a much more rapid rate than the evolution of the genetic structure. Consequently, the concept of a cultural instinct is by no means absurd, even though the genes of culture are much less stable and much more subject to mutation than the biological genes. We have not learned aggression, however, from our remote biological ancestors, nor have we learned territoriality from them. Insofar as aggression or territoriality play a part in human culture — and they do — each generation learns them from the previous generation and perhaps in a lesser degree from its own physical environment and random events.

A change in human affairs comes hardly at all from changes in the gene pool and its distribution in mankind, though this cannot be wholly excluded. Genetic changes do take place slowly as previously isolated gene pools intermingle through the breakdown of concepts of caste and race, as aristocracies fail to reproduce themselves, and as peasants multiply, but it would be surprising if these factors accounted for more than a fraction of one per cent of social change and social evolution. It is new inputs of information into a culture that constitute mutation in social evolution and these inputs can affect either the image of the world or the value systems, according to which decisions are made. Human aggression and human territoriality are products of social systems, not of biological systems, and they must be treated as such, even though concepts and analogies which are derived from biological systems may occasionally be helpful. The naive analogizing, therefore, even of Lorenz and especially of Ardrey will not stand up to a moment's serious criticism.

An Ideological Need

In light of the fact that these works have been rejected by the scientific community almost without exception as serious scientific documents, at least in regard to the conclusions which they draw about society, it is important to ask why they have received so much attention and why they seem to meet an ideological need, especially in the United States. This is a question, unfortunately, to which a fairly clear answer can be given out of the analysis of social systems. I say unfortunately, because the answer is a disagreeable one, but I see no way of escaping it. By a very complex series of events the "establishment" of American society, that is, those people who are either important decision-makers or close to them or identified with them have "learned" that the international system is primarily a "threat system" and that threats must be made credible by occasionally carrying them out, even though this involves inflicting appalling suffering upon innocent people.

The war in Vietnam can only be interpreted as an attempt to make the American threat system credible by demonstrating our willingness to be cruel and merciless so that people will believe the threat implicit in our enormous military establishment. To be effective, however, it is not enough that threats should be credible; they also should have to be legitimate, especially in the minds of the threatener himself, for unless he feels that his cruelty is justified he will find it hard to continue in it. The rise of Hitler and of Pearl Harbor in the 1930s and early '40s taught this country that naive idealism did not pay so we decided to throw away the idealism.

On the other hand, idealism of some sort is necessary for justification and legitimation, for no line of policy can be pursued for very long without self-justification. A line of argument like that of Ardrey's, therefore, seems to legitimate our present morality, in regarding the threat system as dominant at all costs, by reference to our biological ancestors. If the names of both antiquity and of science can be drawn upon to legitimate our behavior, the moral uneasiness about napalm and the massacre of the innocent in Vietnam may be assuaged. Dr. Lorenz, I am sure, who is a gentle, humane soul, still, one would judge, living in the afterglow of Franz Josef, would be horrified by this suggestion. Nevertheless, one cannot altogether absolve even Dr. Lorenz (to whom I owe some of the most delightful hours of my reading life), from the sin of using the prestige of one science to jump to unwarranted conclusions in another, and hence to bring the weight of scientific authority behind essentially unproven propositions. In Ardrey's case the need for legitimation is more obvious, and there are real dangers of a pseudo-science used to bolster and legitimate an otherwise untenable moral position. Even Ardrey, however, I am sure, is a decent fellow at heart, and is on the side of man. Nevertheless, the pit that he is leaping over in the dark is very wide and destruction lurks at the bottom, and those who have the interests both of science and mankind at heart at least need to turn on their flashlights.

We have seen in the Nazi movement how appallingly dangerous a pseudo-science can be in the legitimation of an absurd and evil system. I am not suggesting that either Lorenz or Ardrey is a racist theorist like Gobineau or Houston Chamberlain. However, one could imagine their superficially attractive neo-social-Darwinism applied to very ill uses indeed, and the fact that it is scientific humbug does not unfortunately detract from its attractiveness.

THE UNIVERSITY AND
TOMORROW'S CIVILIZATION

Journal of Higher Education
38, 9 (Dec. 1967): 477-483

The University and Tomorrow's Civilization

Its Role in the Development of a World Community

A UNIVERSITY is already an agent and an example of that growing uniform world culture which has been called the "super-culture." The super-culture is the culture of airports, automobiles and throughways, television stations and newspaper offices, and of course, universities. Just as all airports are the same airport with very minor variations, whether in Detroit, Brussels, Bangkok, Tokyo, or even Moscow, so all universities are in a very real sense the same university. Certainly all departments of chemistry are local congregations, as it were, of a world-wide chemical church, the devotees of which all speak much the same scientific language, have the same view of the universe, use much the same symbols, have the same table of elements on the walls of their classrooms, and read the same journals. There is no such thing as American chemistry or Russian chemistry, capitalist chemistry or communist chemistry, Protestant chemistry, Catholic chemistry, or Buddhist chemistry. There are ninety-two natural elements and hydrogen is the first, no matter what nation the chemistry department happens to be in or in what local culture it is imbedded.

Chemistry, perhaps, is a strong case. The same would undoubtedly be true of mathematics, physics, and in large part the biological sciences. As we move toward the social sciences and the humanities we would find more local differences. What is taught in the economics department in Moscow University is rather different from what is taught at the University of Michigan, though the mathematical economics which is taught in the mathematics department at Moscow in no way differs from the mathematical economics which is taught at Michigan. It is not surprising, however, to find that as we move into the humanities, in the English-speaking countries there are very large departments of English, in Russian universities there are large departments of Russian, in Japanese universities there are large departments of Japanese. Even this can be regarded as local color, somewhat analogous to the gift shops in the airports. No great university today can be without departments which represent all the major languages and literatures of the world. This was not true even a generation ago, when it was possible, for instance, at Oxford to regard the study of Greek and Latin and their respective literatures as "standard," whereas the study of Sanskrit, Hindi, or even Russian was regarded as exotic. What we have seen in the last generation, however, is the virtual disappearance of the concept of the exotic. All the great universities, wherever they are in the world, are in fact world universities, whoever supports them or whatever is taught. Their curriculum is nothing less than the universe, as their name indicates. Nothing that can be known is alien to them.

THE universality of the university is in fact a creation of very recent times. Most existing universities, especially those which are sanctified by age, originated as trade schools, studying only a particular part, and a useful part at that, of the total universe of knowledge. The medieval universities were trade schools for the church, the land-grant colleges were trade schools for agriculture and engineering. It is the logic of the epistemological process itself, however, which has forced universities to become universal, often against their will. The logic is the logic of unboundedness. It is the fact that in the kingdom of the mind there are no natural boundaries, which has forced the university to become universal. Anyone who says, "Knowledge must stop here," soon finds that he has drawn an arbitrary line which the flood of increasing knowledge will soon wash over.

The universality of the university, however, does not come without a struggle, often a severe struggle. A university as an institution is set in a local, not a universal setting. It is supported and financed out of a local culture, not out of the universal culture. It is not surprising therefore that constant tension arises between the universality of the university and the local and particular nature of the culture in which it is set. A local culture, whether it is a religious sect, an ideological party, a state, or a nation, sets up a university in order to further its own ends.

It is under the illusion that it can provide the values and the objectives, and that the university provides the means of carrying them out. What I have called the "Pinocchio principle," however, soon comes into play. The university, because it is universal, begins to develop values of its own, which may not be consistent with the local culture which set it up. A sect finds that a college or university which it establishes to perpetuate its own doctrines becomes, as it were, a traitor in the camp, and undermines the very doctrines which it was set up to propagate, simply because the dynamic of epistemology and of increasing knowledge is more powerful than the defenses of conservatism can handle. What happens to the church-related college also happens to the university which is set up by the national state or by an ideologically committed party. Truth turns out to be the enemy of all existing forms of power, because all existing forms of power are based solely on partial truths. In all societies, therefore, the universities become centers of revisionism simply because of the dynamics of the learning process. Learning *is* revisionism. It means revising our view of the world as new evidence comes in. Insofar as the universities are committed to a learning process, therefore, and particularly committed to that learning process which we call science, they will inevitably come into conflict with all the dogmatisms of the world and with all systems of "unrevisable" truth.

THE university, therefore, can well be regarded as a focal point of that conflict between the super-culture and the folk-culture which is one of the most striking phenomena of our age. This is a conflict, however, which is much more complex than might appear at first sight. It is not a conflict, for instance, between the super-culture, which is always right, and the folk-culture, which is always wrong. It is not a conflict, furthermore, in which the super-culture will always and necessarily win. This is because the super-culture is still primarily a culture of means rather than of ends, of techniques rather than of goals, of instrumental rather than of fundamental values. The super-culture, therefore, cannot be a complete culture. It must be supplemented by folk-cultures of various kinds within the total life of the individual and the society. While he is in the chemistry department the chemist may be very much part of the super-culture and is a citizen of the great republic of science. Once he takes off his lab coat, however, and goes outside he becomes an American, a Russian, a Communist, a Catholic, or whatever other identity he may happen to have. Furthermore, insofar as his work is concerned with the applications of chemistry, it may well be the folk-culture which dominates. He may be concerned with the production of a toothpaste, with the production of napalm, with the development of chemical warfare, rather than with the propagation of pure science as such. In this sense, even though the pure science of chemistry is universal, chemists may be American chemists or Russian chemists, and this makes a great deal of difference in their behavior. Similarly, the university may be an

American university or a Russian university, and this will also make a difference in its behavior and in the behavior of the faculty.

There are very good reasons for all this. The super-culture does not provide many of the essential elements necessary for the creation of human personality. The production and rearing of children, for instance, is largely in the hands of the folk-culture. What we learn from our mothers and grandmothers is of enormous importance in determining the kind of people we are and the kind of identities we will assume. The corollary of this proposition is that the super-culture does not provide an adequate identity. In our world there is no way for a man to be a human being. He must have a national identity, he must be an American or a Russian or something like that. He may also have a political or a religious identity, he may be a republican or a Communist, a Baptist or a Buddhist, he may have an identity in a peer group or in a work group, he may have an occupational identity, and almost all of these belong to the folk-culture rather than to the super-culture. It is not surprising, therefore, that the conflict between the super-culture and the folk-culture is not only intense and prolonged, it is not resolved, and it constantly tends to be denied and suppressed, simply because it is so painful. It would be unbearably painful for any of us to have to admit that our identity as a scientist was incompatible with our identity as a husband, as a Mormon, or as a Communist, or as an American. Consequently we tend to suppress this conflict by compartmentalizing our minds in our various systems. As scientists and as members of universities we believe in veracity at all costs, and in the universality of truth. We believe in the necessity of testing and revision. We believe in the separation of beliefs from identity so that to discover one's self in error is supposed to be a matter for rejoicing rather than for anxiety. As Americans or Russians, however, we have very different value systems. In the international system, for instance, veracity is not highly regarded. We defend our old errors with tenacity because our identity is deeply bound up with them and we condone violence, deceit, secrecy, and threats in a way that we would never dream of doing in the scientific community.

The critical question here is that granted that the super-culture because of its incompleteness will not supersede the folk-cultures in which it is embedded, can it modify these local folk-cultures? The answer to this question is undoubtedly yes, as it has modified folk-cultures very substantially already. We see this for instance in the transformation of medicine in the last hundred years. It is a relatively short time ago that medicine belonged essentially to the folk-culture and it is highly doubtful whether it did more good than harm. The conquest of medicine by the super-culture began only in the mid-nineteenth century and was resisted strenuously by the medical profession itself. Nevertheless, its results have been spectacular as measured, for instance, by the expanding expectation of life. The impact of the super-culture on the family, though it has been less spectacular than its impact on medicine, is nonetheless profound. When parents begin to learn more from books about how to rear their children than they do from their own parents, an enormous change in society is underway, and it may well be that Dr. Spock will have a greater influence on American society than any other man of the twentieth century, part of which, at any rate, represents the impact of the super-culture on the family. On the church likewise the super-culture has made great impact in forcing a long retreat from super-stition and unquestioned traditional authority as the foundation for religious community.

THE one aspect of the folk-culture which is most resistant to the impact of the super-culture is the national state itself. Here, indeed, we see the phenomenon of the national state attempting to take over the super-culture. This is what has been called the "Constantinization of science," using the parallel of the takeover of the Christian Church by Constantine in the late Roman Empire. The power and legitimacy of the national state are so enormous today that it seems to have no serious competitors, not even in the super-culture itself. Consequently we have found the national state turning the power of science to its own ends in the making of weapons and in the manipulation of minds. Never-theless, the conflict between the super-culture and the national state is just as real as it is between the super-culture and any other aspect of folk society, even though in our day it is almost entirely suppressed.

The record of universities in the struggle between the super-culture and the national state has been ambiguous, to use the most charitable word possible. In Nazi Germany, for instance, once a neurotic group captured the national state, universities were virtually powerless and betrayed all their old ideals. It was not the universities that stood out against Hitler, but those who were motivated by an intense Christian commitment, both the Jehovah's Witnesses and the Confessional Church. The weakness of the universities in this regard reflects what might be termed a "spiritual" defect in the super-culture itself. The spiritual foundation of the super-culture is of course the sub-culture of science, and while science produces and encourages many ethical values, especially the value of veracity, it does not in equal measure develop the virtue of courage. It is a sub-culture which is well adapted to orderly, well-established communities where human relations are not conducted primarily on the basis of threat. Consequently it is ill-adapted to face pathological conditions in the human community and it does not have within itself an adequate prophylaxis to meet these pathological conditions. Thus the helplessness of science in the face of pathological conditions in the national state and in the international community is unfortunately not surprising, for this is something which is built into the scientific sub-culture itself.

It may be indeed that part of the solution to this problem and the thing that may save science from the weaknesses of its own sub-culture

is the nature of the university community and the fact that science is
imbedded in it. The university community is broader than the scientific
community, simply because it is universal. It includes those aspects
of human life and behavior which lie outside the scientific sub-culture,
such as art, religion, literature, and so on, which belong more to the
folk-culture than they do to the super-culture. The university indeed
is the major interface between the folk-culture and the super-culture and
as such it should be the major mediator between the two. Therefore
the threat to the university as an institution which is posed by the development of a large "grants" economy in almost all the developed societies
is something which should be viewed with alarm and taken very seriously.
In the United States especially, the university as an institution is in
grave danger of losing its autonomy as a community, partly because
there is an active labor market in faculty members, so that their prime
loyalty is to their profession rather than to the institution at which they
happen to be teaching temporarily, and also because even in the vital
area of research the fact that the major sources of support now lie outside
the universities either in foundations or in government is tending to
destroy the university as a major decision-making entity in the intellectual
community. There was a time in the University of Michigan, for instance,
when the Rackham Fund, administered by the university community
itself, was a major source of support for research. Today it is not the
university which provides funds for research but the individual faculty
member who goes out and gets a grant from outside sources. It is hardly
surprising under these circumstances that the sense of community of the
university has been seriously weakened.

SOMETHING could be done about all this if anybody cared. The
pull of the labor market might be weakened if faculty were given more
real responsibility for university government. On the other hand, it is
highly doubtful whether they really want it. The centrifugal pull of
outside research money might also be counteracted if the government and
the foundations were more concerned to give research money directly
to the university to be administered by it, like the Rackham Fund. At
the moment, however, one sees little movement in this direction, and
one may expect to see a further weakening in the university as an academic
community which will render it all the more subject to being taken over
by the local folk-culture. It is hard, therefore, to be very optimistic
about the future of the university as a source of a new world order and
a new world loyalty.

Nevertheless, the case is not hopeless and one is always prepared to
be surprised. The very fact, as we noted earlier, that the logic of the
growth of knowledge forces universities into universality may make them
a likely place for the rise of a new culture which will combine the virtues
of the scientific sub-culture with the emotional and identity-producing
necessities of the folk-culture. This is likely to take place, however,

only if the universities accept more responsibility than they do now for the total learning process in society, extending through the school system, back into the family, and forward into the political and economic system. If the university would visualize itself as a focus in which the total learning process of the society becomes clarified and then enlivened, it might play a much greater role in the society of the future than it does now.   There would be dangers in such a move, dangers of corruption by power, dangers of too great conformity and of too great concentration of intellectual and spiritual power.   In the absence, however, of any other agency which today seems capable of performing the function of spiritual leadership towards the universal society—for both state and church are too much infected with the parochial, too little enlarged to the universal—it may be that the university will have to take on this role simply by default. If it can do so with a clear-sighted humility we may be in better shape to deal with the dangerous future than if it accepts the role blindly and reluctantly.

ACCOMPLISHMENTS AND PROSPECTS
OF THE PEACE RESEARCH MOVEMENT
(with the assistance of
Hanna and Alan Newcombe)

Arms Control and Disarmament,
1 (1968): 43-58

Accomplishments and Prospects of the Peace Research Movement

THE PEACE research movement is a name which might be given to the activity of a small group of scientists, composed for the most part of social scientists, who are concerned to apply the methods of science, especially of social science, which is where the problem lies, to the practical problem of diminishing the incidence of war and increasing the incidence of peace in the international system. The father of the peace research movement is unquestionably Theodore Lentz of St. Louis, Missouri, whose book, *Towards a Science of Peace* [1] in 1955 was the first clear statement of the problem. The grandfathers are undoubtedly Quincy Wright, associated for many years with the University of Chicago, and happily still with us, whose great work on *A Study of War* [2] did much to establish war and peace as significant and legitimate objects of scientific study, and Lewis F. Richardson, an English meteorologist who lived much of his life in Scotland, and spent the last 20 years of his life working on mathematical and statistical theories of war and peace. His two great works, *Arms and Insecurity* [3] and *Statistics of Deadly Quarrels* [4] circulated in microfilm for many years. Indeed, almost the distinguishing mark of the first generation of peace researchers is that they read Richardson in microfilm. They were, however published in 1960. Richardson brought the skills of the natural scientist to the problem, and the fact that he was not trained in the social sciences gives his work something of the characteristics of the highly gifted amateur. Nevertheless, his mathematical theory of arms races and his quantifications of history are something from which every peace researcher must start, and his work has left an indelible imprint on what has followed.

As is common in the intellectual life the fecundity of the fathers has been prodigious and has produced a large number of active workers in the generation of the sons. A recent bibliography of fairly current items [5] lists 112 different names, and while not all of these might think of themselves as peace researchers I can think of a number of names not on this particular list, so that we certainly have an "invisible college", in the language of De Solla Price, of between 100–200 workers, most of them social scientists in good standing, many of them men of considerable distinction in their own field, who visualize themselves as working in peace research.

Another symptom of a new intellectual movement is the development of journals and research institutes. The earliest journal in this field was unquestionably a mimeographed, later offset, publication called *The Bulletin of the Research Exchange on the Prevention of War* which by now must be a collector's item. The first issue was published by a little group, mostly of psychologists, which grew out of the Society for the Psychological Study of Social Issues about 1952, and called themselves the Research Exchange on the Prevention of War. This was the immediate ancestor of the *Journal of Conflict Resolution* which started publication at the University of Michigan in 1956. While the interests of the *Journal of Conflict Resolution* go beyond the international system to the study of conflict as whole, its sub-title, *A Quarterly for Research Related to War and Peace*, indicates the major focus of its interest. This has provided an important channel for publication and communication in the past twelve years. Three other journals have specialized in this field, *The Journal of Peace Research*, edited in Oslo, and *The Proceedings of the Peace Research Society (International)* edited by Walter Isard in Philadelphia, and the *International Peace Research Newsletter* edited by Elise Boulding in Ann Arbor, Michigan. Each of these four journals is now associated with an institution. The *Journal of Conflict Resolution* is edited from the Centre for Research on Conflict Resolution at the University of Michigan, in the development of which Mr. William Barth as Assistant Director has been a key figure, the *Journal of Peace Research* is put out by the Peace Research Institute in Oslo in which Dr. Johan Galtung has been the key figure, the *Peace Research Society (International)* is mainly the work of Dr. Walter Isard, and the *International Peace Research Newsletter* is now published by the International Peace Research Association, which was founded at Groningen in Holland in 1965 with Dr. Bert Röling as its secretary. Two journals of abstracts should be noted: *Peace Research Abstracts Journal*, published by the Canadian Peace Research Institute, Clarkson, Ontario, and *Current Thought on Peace and War*, edited by L. Larry Leonard, Wisconsin State University, Oshkosh, Wisconsin.

Surrounding this central "invisible college" is a large penumbra of activity and interest in the general field of the study of the international system, the study of national security and in the study of human behaviour in general. Peace and war, as usually understood, are phenomena associated primarily with the international system. There have been those, therefore, who have argued that there is really no field of peace research, that all it is is the study of the international system and the more we know about the international system and the better our arrangements for collecting and processing our information about it, the further are we likely to get with the practical problem of peace. There is something in this view; certainly as an object of scientific inquiry the international system is the same objective reality whether it is studied by peace researchers, by traditional international relations specialists or by research institutes associated with national foreign offices or departments of defense. The problem of reality testing in social systems, however, is very difficult, [6] especially in a system which is subject to rapid dynamic change, and the perception of that reality may be affected substantially by the preconceptions of the perceivers. On the whole, the difference between the peace research group and other investigators of the international system lies in certain value pre-suppositions which give rise to differences in time perspective. The peace research group puts a low value on the existing international system and is interested in changing it. It looks upon the international system not as a stationary object to be investigated, but as a system in space-time in process of rapid change. It is more interested in change than in equilibrium, more interested in how to change the system than in how to operate it successfully. There is a real difference between those research workers who take the existing international system as given and who operate mainly within its existing institutions and limits, and those who do not accept the international system as given but who are interested primarily in the dynamics of its transformation. Peace research workers are mainly in the latter group. While, then, the two groups have a great deal to learn from each other and in fact do learn from each other, there is a sufficient difference in emphasis to make the peace research group differentiate itself rather self-consciously from the others. If one may use an analogy from the physical sciences, what I would call for want of better word the "conventional" research workers in the field of the international system and national security are like the chemists of the 19th century who believed in the immutability of the elements and were concerned only with their properties and combinations. The peace research group is more like the investigator of radioactivity who perceives that the elements can be transmuted and were not simply givens of the physico–chemical universe. Similarly, the conventional international relations reseachers take the national state as given along with the present institutions of the international system. Peace research workers are more interested in transmutation and in the development of new kinds of national states and international systems which would prove to be less costly and less dangerous than the present ones. Those who accept the present international system as necessary and valid will tend to shut themselves off from possibilities of transformation. It is only those who do not accept the present international system as either necessary or valid who are capable of widening the agenda to include these transformations which we believe are necessary for the survival of the human race.

The peace research movement is barely 15 years old and encompasses perhaps not more than 200 people around the world. It is perhaps too soon to ask what it has accomplished. The answer to that question will have to be found in the future. Nevertheless, something can be said about what has been going on and we can guess at least as to some possible effects.

Dr. Hanna and Dr. Alan Newcombe, editors of Peace Research Abstracts Journal, in their excellent summary, *Peace Research around the World* [7] used the following classification:

I.   Fundamental Studies and Theories

A—International Systems   1. Historical-Descriptive
                                          2. Quantitative-Historical
                                          3. Simulation
                                          4. Theory
                                          5. Data Collection

B—Crisis Research	1.	Crisis Decisions
	2.	Tension Measurement
C—Conflict Studies	1.	History
	2.	Theory
	3.	Small Group Experiments
	4.	Causes of War
D—Attitudes	1.	Attitude Surveys and Scales
	2.	Images and Perceptions
	3.	Attitude Change
E—Research on the Future	1.	General
	2.	Disarmed but Revolutionary World
	3.	Transition to and Nature of Stabilized World
F—Integration Studies	1.	Political Integration
	2.	International Non-Govermental Organizations
	3.	Impact of Student Exchange
G—Economic Studies	1.	Conversion to a Peace Economy
	2.	Economic and Technical Assistance
H—International Law	1.	General
	2.	Definition of Aggression
	3.	Codification of Co-existence
I—Disarmament Studies	1.	The Armament-disarmament spectrum
	2.	Deterrence
	3.	Disarmament Inspection
	4.	UN Police Force

II. Action Research

A—Protest Actions	1.	Efficacy of protest
	2.	Study of participants
B—Non-Violence		

III. Conclusions

In a brief notice such as this we cannot even cover all the categories and the following is illustrative rather than definitive.

A.1. Historical-Descriptive

There is an enormous amount to be done by historians writing with the theory of the international system in mind. A good example of this is the work of Vern Bullough [8] on the co-existence of the Russian and Persian empires to its final breakdown. A Peace Research Section of the American Historical Association has been organized and much more along these lines may be expected in the future. A notable effort in this direction at the international level is the volume *La Paix* issued by the Jean Bodin Societé. [9]

A.2. Quantitative-Historical

These studies have aroused a good deal of excitement among peace researchers and were pioneered indeed by Lewis F. Richardson in his *Statistics of Deadly Quarrels.* [10] The work of R. J. Rummel and Raymond Tanter, [11] which is part of the Dimensionality of Nations project at Yale University, was stimulated to a considerable extent by the work of Karl Deutsch. Perhaps the most notable finding is the lack of correlation between domestic and foreign conflicts. This, however, is challenged by the work of Michael Haas. [12] Another major project in quantitative historical studies is that of J. David Singer at the University of Michigan. [13] This covers a longer period than the others (1815–1945) and concentrates particularly on alliances. A particularly interesting finding here is the marked shift in behavior of the international system between the 19th and 20th Centuries. Another project which covers a shorter period more intensively is that of William Gamson and Andre Modigliani. [14] Here again an important finding is that the international system behaves very differently at different times which the author defines as times of "confrontation" and "non-confrontation." Along somewhat similar lines is a study by Lloyd Jensen. [15] He correlated Soviet and United States willingness to compromise as measured by the number of concessions and retractions in negotiations with their confidence in their deterrent as reflected in military expenditures and in public opinion polls. The conclusion is that some lack of confidence in the deterrent provides an incentive to negotiation.

The United Nations is a focus of a good deal of research interest and indeed really deserves a category of its own. There have been two principal methods of study, one as represented, for instance, by the work of Chadwick Alger [16] and Robert H. Cory, Jr. [17] which stresses information collecting from the delegates by means of direct inquiry through questionnaire and interview. The other method is represented by the work of Hayward R. Alker, [18] Bruce Russett, [19] and Charles Wrigley, [20] which depends mainly on the statistical analysis of the actual records at the United Nations, such as, for instance, voting. An interesting problem on which research may have had some impact on policy outcomes is on the effects of voting procedures in the United Nations and the possible effect of weighted voting. [21] A Study made of this problem in the United States Department of State may have affected policy in this matter. [22]

A.3. The Use of Simulation in the Study of the International System

Harold Guetzkow at Northwestern is particularly associated with this method. [23] It is perhaps too early to appraise the research value of various forms of simulation, though their value as teaching devices especially in the arousing of interest is hardly open to question. Simulation does for the study of social systems something of what the experimental laboratory does for the other sciences, in the sense that it permits the investigation of systems which do not exist in nature and cannot be studied by simple observation. There is a great deal of unpublished work in this field. One should also perhaps include under the heading of simulation the study of experimental game situations. These, however, are noted later (cf. *C.3*).

A.4.   Theories of International Systems

There has been a great deal of interest and, one hopes, a substantial development in the field of the theory of the international system in recent years. Most of this is relevant to peace research though not necessarily specifically directed towards it. Thus, J. David Singer discussed "the level of analysis problem in international relations theory". [24] Inis L. Claude [25] and Morton A. Kaplan [26] have discussed the classification of international systems. John W. Burton [27] stresses the possibility of change in national images and the development of conventions of non-intervening behaviour. K. E. Boulding [28] has developed an elaborate theory of the international system and national viability based fundamentally on the economic theory of oligopoly. At this point the theory of the international system tends to shade over into conflict theory, which will be examined later.

A theoretical development which has barely reached the stage of publication is that of a "phase" theory of the international system as developed by K. E. Boulding. Various phases of the international system are distinguished such as stable war, unstable war, unstable peace and stable peace, somewhat parallel to phases in physical systems. A phase diagram is suggested in which the stability of the phases is related to specific characteristics of the international system, such as the extent of the threat system on the one hand or the extent of the integrative system on the other. Up to now the theory has not produced any empirical applications, but it is suggestive of ways to move in the future.

A.5.   Data Collection

One of the major problems of the international system has been the tendency of inadequate and indeed corrupt systems of data-collection and processing to produce images of the world in the minds of decision-makers which are quite unrealistic. [29] There is nothing in the international system, for instance, to correspond to the data collection and processing apparatus which results in the computation of the gross national product. Important pioneering work in this connection is being done by the Yale Political Data Program, especially in the international field, by Bruce Russett. [30]

B.1.   Crisis Research

The international system tends to have cycles of rising and falling tension not wholly unlike the business cycle. The peaks of this cycle are crises and a study of crises, while it might be classified under the general study of the international system, is perhaps of sufficient importance to deserve a separate category. Interesting work in this field has been done in the Stanford Studies in International Conflict and Integration at Stanford University under the general direction of Robert C. North. [31] This program began with an extremely careful analysis of the events which immediately led to the outbreak of the first World War, but it has also been applied to the 1962 Cuban crisis. [32]

B.2.   Tension Measurement

Proposals have been made from time to time for the compilation of indices of tension or hostility in the international system derived, for instance, from content analysis but up to now these proposals have not seemed to have borne any fruit.

C.1.   Conflict Studies; History of Conflict

There are studies here which might be classified under *A*.2 but which have a somewhat broader application. Raoul Narroll studies a cross-section of primitive societies and discovers that while deterrents did not deter, militarism did frequently lead to expansion. [33] He has since expanded these studies substantially in an unpublished volume, taking sample periods of recorded history as his basic data.

C.2   Conflict Theory

This is a large field which has perhaps best been summarized by Anatol Rapoport. [34] Lewis Richardson's pioneering work on the theory of arms races [35] has been continued and refined by Paul Smoker [36] in a series of brilliant papers. Game theory has an enormous literature of its own. In its pure form it has been rather disappointing in its applications, mainly because it is most powerful when applied to zero-sum games which nobody in his senses ever plays. In the form of what might be called, however, two-person interaction schemes, it has proved, as we shall see, extremely fruitful in empirical research. At one end also game theory has opened up into what might be called bargaining theory. This actually has a long history in economics. At the hands of writers like T. C. Schelling [37] it has opened up substantial new insights. Writers like Robert A. Levine [38] and Fred Ikle [39] developed what might be called a descriptive theory in international bargaining, which at least helps us to organize our thinking about the process.

C.3.   Small Group Experiments in Conflict

Conflict theory has opened up a large new field of small group experiments in recent years, most of which have a good deal of relevance for peace research. Anatol Rapoport is performing a classic series of experiments at the University of Michigan in various forms of two-person games, especially the prisoner's dilemma. [40] Morton Deutsch and Robert M. Krauss have performed a series of experiments of slightly broader scope, but with perhaps less theoretical orientation. [41] These experimental games do something for social systems a little bit like what the fruit fly did for genetics. They provide us with a simplified version of a system which has many of the essential properties of the more complex system. Thus, in the experimental games we get simplified but quite operationally defined concepts which correspond to general social responses such as trustworthiness, forgiveness, repentance and so on. In the simplified system relations may be perceived which are obscure in the more complex systems of real life, though because of the somewhat artificial character of the situations we should be somewhat chary of accepting the results too blindly. Thus, Rapoport's spectacular finding that women are much less co-operative than men may tell us as much if not more about sex differences and attitudes towards artificial situations as it does about attitudes to conflict. The dilemma of experimentation is that the more realistic the experiment the less control the experimenter usually has over it. Thus, Muzafer Sherif's famous Robbers' Cave experiment, [47] while it is realistic and seems to have strong practical applications may owe some of its results to local and specific peculiarities, which might not be replicated in other situations.

An example of a theoretical idea which seems almost self-evident and yet which seems suitable for small group research but has not yet produced much is Charles E. Osgood's notion of graduated reciprocated initiatives in tension reduction (GRIT). [43]

The general problem of the psychology of violence and aggression has continued to attract the attention of the experimental psychologists, notably Leonard Berkowitz [44] and Elton V. McNeil. [45] Otto Klineberg should also be mentioned in this connection. [46]

D.1   Attitude Studies

Public opinion studies are clearly relevant to the investigation of those images of the international system which bear upon the decision-making process. There are, of course, many publics, and the problem of whose attitudes and images are important and how the various publics react on each other is still largely unsolved. Jerome Laulicht has done interesting work in connection with this. [47] There have been a considerable number of studies of what might be called syndromes of attitude and belief, many of which go back to the famous study of the authoritarian personality by T. W. Adorno and others almost 20 years ago. [48] The work of Milton Rokeach [49] is particularly noteworthy in this connection. A great deal of work of this kind remains at the descriptive level and has lacked the theoretical framework to account for how people get the way they are.

D.2.   Images and Perceptions

A related field of inquiry might be called image research into the images which people of different nations have of themselves and of others. Urie Bronfenbrenner's work [50] on the "mirror images" of the United States and the Soviet Union, and Ole R. Holsti's study of Dulles' images [51] are examples of research of this kind. Again, not much attention has been paid to the learning process by which these images are created.

D.3.   Attitude Change

There is of course work going on of great importance in attitude change and in human learning. This is going on, however, mainly at the level of small group experiments in fairly simple artificial systems. This, no doubt, reflects the relative state of knowledge in regard to statics and dynamics. There is descriptive work in complex systems and dynamic and theoretical work in simple systems, but not much relationship between the two. Nevertheless, one hopes the connection may be made in the future.

In attitude change and human learning the work of Herbert Kelman [52] who distinguishes three processes of attitudes change, compliance, identification and internalization, is especially noteworthy. At a more general level the work of Leon Festinger [53] is of great potential importance for the study of change in the international system. These applications do not seem yet to have been made. The basic principle is that images change under the impact of "cognitive dissonance" or inconsistency among various parts of the image of the world. K. E. Boulding's work on *The Image* [54] is also relevant at this point. It is hard to over-emphasize the importance of research into the human learning process in any question involving the dynamics of society and while much of this is not directly related to peace research it forms an essential part of its background.

E.   Research on the Future

This topic is included because a great many people who are interested in peace research see it as part of a much larger intellectual enterprise which consists essentially in the effort to understand the total dynamics of the world social system with a view to assisting mankind in what is perceived as a great transition from the age of civilization (3000 B.C. to the present) to a new state of society which Boulding has described as "post-civilization." [55] In this view war is regarded as a characteristic of the age of civilization which will disappear in post-civilized society and peace research is mainly the study of that transition. There is indeed another "invisible college" which overlaps but extends beyond that of the peace researchers which might almost be called the futurologists. This, however, is a topic so large, involving as it does the whole relation of technology to values, the dynamics of different parts of the social system, and the relations between the international system and internal revolutionary movements and the whole problem of the "great transition" so we cannot do more than notice the connection and pass by to more limited topics

F.1.   Integration Studies—Political Integration

One of the important dimensions of the international system is its integrative structure and one method of measuring this is through measures of "trans-national participation" which have been studied by Robert C. Angell. [56] A particularly important aspect of this trans-national participation is the development of international non-governmental organizations, "Ingos." These have been studied by Paul Smoker. [57] There is a very strong dynamic of growth in this field, interrupted only by the two World Wars. A conclusion which seems to be of some importance here is that countries which tend to be isolated from the international communications network also tend to be trouble spots.

G. Economic Studies

The main focus of interest of peace researchers in economics studies has been in studies of the impact of the "war industry", that is, that part of the economy which is devoted to national defense, on the rest of the economic system. There have been quite a large number of studies now which have concentrated on the effects of disarmament on the economic systems of various countries. [58] The first major study in this area was that of Emile Benoit and K. E. Boulding. [59] There have been a considerable number of studies in particular countries. The U.S. Arms Control and Disarmament Agency [60] has done a study and so has the Council of Economic Advisers in the United States. [61] The conclusions of all this work are fairly standardized. Disarmament would release substantial economic resources for other things and there is no reason to suppose that given adequate fiscal and monetary policy that this transfer would involve much unemployment. The folk belief that only a large war industry keeps the developed economies from unemployment and depression is easily shown to be an illusion. On the other hand, the transition would require careful policy and a more liberal attitude towards increase in the national debt than now prevails in the United States. [62]

Wider studies of the impact of the war industry on the whole world economy have been programmed by Emile Benoit and have been opening up some neglected areas in the field of the general economic impact of the war industry. [63]

H. International Law

A great many important studies are being made in this field. The work of Arthur Larson at Duke University is particularly to be noted. The field, however, cannot be covered in a brief notice like this, and as it has a certain independence of its own it should be reserved for another occasion.

I. Disarmament Studies

A great deal of work has been going into the problem of the dynamic interactions of the defense organizations and the war industries of the various countries. There have been a large number of studies of systems of deterrence. Of these those organized by Thomas W. Milburn [64] under the Michelson project are of great interest. A historical study has been made by Bruce M. Russett [65] and another by Raoul Naroll. [66]

I.3. Disarmament Inspection

A great deal of effort and money has been put into research on problems of inspection Project Vela of the US Department of Defense, concerned with the detection of underground tests, has had an enormous impact on the science of seismology. This subject again is so large that it would really require an independent report and can only be mentioned here.

II. Action Research

There are strong similarities in the motivations which have given rise to the peace research movement, on the one hand, and the peace movement, as a movement of protest and political action on the other. Both tend to involve people with strong dissatisfactions with the present international system and with strong motivations to change it. It has been a fundamental principle that the peace research movement from the beginning is primarily a movement within the scientific community and that it represents therefore activity which is sharply differentiated from protest and political action. Nevertheless, the common motivation might be expected to lead not only to strong personal interactions between the two movements but also to an interest in applying the methods of peace research to the study of the peace movement itself. Unfortunately, what has been done in this respect is meagre, for the peace movement is small in numbers, poor in financial resources and intense in commitment to its own images. It is not surprising therefore that most of the funds for the support of peace research have come from outside the peace movement and that there is even a certain hostility towards peace research within the peace movement. The one exception to this rule seems to be Canada where the Canadian Peace Research Institute represented by Norman Alcock has attracted modest support from persons associated with the peace movement. [67] There have been some scattered studies of people who participate in peace action, for instance, by Paul Ekman, [68] Jerome Frank [69] and Elise Boulding [70] but there seems to be no major study in prospect either of the peace movement itself or of the effects of different kinds of peace action.

III. Conclusions

Any report on the peace research movement today is a bit like reporting on an embryo in the fifth month. It moves and it kicks but not very much more can be said about it. It represents a fraction of 1 per cent of the intellectual resources which are being devoted to war, war preparations and plans for destruction. It has established its legitimacy in the intellectual community if only by the quality of the people who are attracted to it. The fact that UNESCO now recognizes it officially through the International Peace Research Association is perhaps the equivalent of a marriage certificate. It has not yet established its legitimacy with the élites who run the established order in any country (except Sweden, where an official Peace Research Institute has been established).

Where it gets support from government grants and foundations it is largely because of the personal reputations and qualities of the people who are involved in it, not because of any desire on the part of these sources of funds to foster peace research. It certainly does not come out with an imposing set of conclusions for solving the world's problems. Nevertheless, it has had an impact. A subtle transformation can be noted (and incidentally should be studied) in the content of the conventional journals of international relations and in the language and publications of foreign offices and departments of defense. The establishment of the Arms Control and Disarmament Agency in the United States was a very important symbolic step towards respectability. The White House Conference on International Co-operation of 29 November–1 December 1965 represented a legitimation of this kind of activity which would not have been possible 10 years before. In spite of many setbacks and discouragements, therefore, there is reason to hope that this lively embryo may come to a new birth for mankind.

References

[1]   T. LENTZ, *Towards a Science of Peace, Turning Point in Human Destiny*. Bookman Associates, New York, (1955).
[2]   Q. WRIGHT, *A Study of War*, 2 vols. University of Chicago Press, Chicago, (1942).
[3]   L. F. RICHARDSON, *Arms and Insecurity: A Mathematical Study of the Causes and Origins of War*. Quadrangle Books, Chicago, (1960).
[4]   L. F. RICHARDSON, *Statistics of Deadly Quarrels*. Quadrangle Books Chicago, (1960).
[5]   H. and A. NEWCOMBE, *Peace Research Around the World*. Canadian Peace Research Institute, Clarkson, Ontario, (1966).
[6]   K. E. BOULDING, Reality Testing and Value Orientation in International Systems: The Role of Research. *International Social Science Journal.* **17**, 404–416, (1965).
[7]   [5], p. 13.
[8]   V. L. BULLOUGH, The Roman Empire vs. Persia; a Study of Successful Deterrence. *Journal of Conflict Resolution* **7**, 55–68, (1963).
[9]   LA PAIX. *Recuelis de la Societe Jean Bodin pour l'Histoire Comparative des Institutions*, XIV, XV. Editions de la Librairie Encyclopedique, Bruxelles (1961, 1962).
[10] [4].
[11] R. J. RUMMEL, Testing some Possible Predictors of Conflict Behaviour Within and Between Nations. *Proceedings of International Peace Research Conference* (Chicago, November, 1963) (1964).
      R. TANTER *Dimensions of Conflict Behaviour Within and Between Nations*, 1958–60 Northwestern University, Evanston, Illinois, (1964).
      R. TANTER, Dimensions of Conflict Behaviour Within and Between Nations. *Journal of Conflict Resolution* **10**, 41–64, (1966).
      R. J. RUMMEL, *The Dimensionality of Nations Project, in Comparing Nations*, R. MERRITT and S. ROKKAN (Eds.), Yale University Press, New Haven, (1966).
      R. J. RUMMEL, A Field Theory of Social Action with Application to Conflict Within Nations. *Yearbook of the Society for General Systems*, **10**, (1965).
[12] M. HAAS, Societal Approaches to the Study of War. *Journal of Peace Research*, **4**, 307–321, (1965).
[13] J. D. SINGER and M. SMALL, *Alliance Aggregation and the Onset of War* 1815–1945, in *Quantative International Politics: Insights and Evidence*. J. D. SINGER (Ed.). Free Press New York, (in press).
[14] W. GAMSON and A. MODIGLIANI, Tensions and Concessions: The Empirical Confirmation of Belief Systems About Soviet Behaviour. *Social Problems*, **11**, 34–48, (1963).
[15] L. JENSEN, Military Capabilities and Bargaining Behaviour. *Journal of Conflict Resolution*, **9**, 155–163, (1965).

[16] C. ALGER, Interaction in a Committe of the United Nations General Assembly, in *International Yearbook of Political Behaviour Research*, J. D. SINGER (Ed.), **7,** (1965).

C. ALGER, Intergovernmental Relations in Organizations and Their Significance for International Conflict, in *The Nature of Human Conflict*, E. B. McNEIL (Ed.), Prentice-Hall, N.J. (1965).

C. ALGER, Non-Resolution Consequences of the United Nations and Their Effect on International Conflict. *Journal of Conflict Resolution*, **5,** 128–145, (1961).

C. ALGER, *Personal Contact in International Organizations*, in *International Behaviour*, Herbert Kelman (Ed.) Holt, Rinehart & Winston, New York, (1965).

C. ALGER, United Nations Participation as a Learning Experience. *Public Opinion Quarterly*, **27,** 411–426, (1963).

[17] R. H. CORY Jr., Images of the U.S. Disarmament Negotiating System. *Journal of Arms Control*. 654–662, (Oct. 1963).

[18] H. R. ALKER, Dimensions of Conflict in the U.N. General Assembly. *American Political Science Review* (Sept. 1964).

[19] H. R. ALKER and B. RUSSETT, *World Politics in the General Assembly*. Yale University Press, New Haven, Conn. (1965).

[20] C. WRIGLEY, Paper at *Peace Research Society (International) Conference*, University of Pennsylvania, Philadelphia, Pa. (November 1965).

[21] C. S. MANNO, Selective Weighted Voting in the U.N. General Assembly, *International Organization* **20,** *Winter* 37–62, (1966).

S. F. MANNO, Majority Decisions and Minority Responses in the U.N. General Assembly, *Journal of Conflict Resolution*, **10,** 1–20, (1966).

[22] U.S. DEPARTMENT OF STATE. *Weighted Voting in the United Nations*. Mimeo summary, 6 pp., (November 2, 1963).

[23] H. GUETZKOW et al., *Simulation in International Relations: Developments in Research and Teaching*. Prentice-Hall, N.J. (1963).

H. GUETZKOW and L. JENSEN, Research Activities on Simulated International Processes. *Background*, **9,** 261–274, (1955).

[24] J. D. SINGER, The Level of Analysis Problem in International Relations. *World Politics* **14,** 77–92, (1961).

[25] I. L. CLAUDE, *Power and International Relations*. Random House, New York, (1962).

[26] M. A. KAPLAN, *System and Process in International Politics*. Wiley, New York, (1957).

[27] J. W. BURTON, *Peace Theory: Preconditions of Disarmament*. Alfred Knopf, New York, (1962).

J. W. BURTON, *International Relations Theory*. Cambridge University Press, New York, (1965).

[28] K. E. BOULDING, *Conflict and Defense*. Harper, New York, (1962).

[29] [6].

[30] B. RUSSETT et al., *World Handbook of Political and Social Indicators*. Yale University Press, New Haven, Conn., (1964).

[31] R. C. NORTH et al., *Progress Reports on the Stanford Studies in International Conflict and Integration*, (issued periodically since 1963).

[32] O. R. HOLSTI, R. A. BRODY and R. C. NORTH, Measuring Affect and Action in International Reaction Models: Empirical Materials From the 1962 Cuban Crisis. *Peace Research Society (International) Conference Papers*, **2,** 170–190, (1965).

[33] R. NAROLL, Does Military Deterrence Deter? *Trans-Action* **3,** 14–20, (1966).

[34] A. RAPOPORT, *Fights, Games, and Debates*. University of Michigan Press, Ann Arbor, Mich., (1960).

[35] [3].

[36] P. SMOKER, Fear in the Arms Race: A Mathematical Study, *Journal of Peace Research*, **1**, 55–64, (1964).

P. SMOKER, A Pilot Study of the Present Arms Race. *General Systems Yearbook*, **8**, 61–76, (1963).

P. SMOKER, Trade, Defence, and the Richardson Theory of Arms Races: A Seven Nation Study. *Journal of Peace Research*, **2**, 161–176, (1965).

P. SMOKER, The Arms Race As a Mathematical Model: A Contribution from Physics and Mathematics. Paper at *International Peace Research Conference*, Cracow, Poland (Summer 1965).

P. SMOKER, The Arms Race: A Wave Model. *General Systems Yearbook*, **10**, (1965).

[37] T. C. SCHELLING, *The Strategy of Conflict*. Harvard University Press, Cambridge, Mass., (1960).

[38] R. A. LEVINE, Arms Agreement: A Model of Stalemate. *Journal of Conflict Resolution*, **6**, 308–318, (1962).

[39] F. C. IKLÉ, *How Nations Negotiate*. Harper and Row, New York, (1964).

[40] A. RAPOPORT and A. M. CHAMMAH, *Prisoner's Dilemma, A Study in Conflict and Cooperation*. University of Michigan Press, Ann Arbor, Mich., (1965).

[41] M. DEUTSCH, Trust and Suspicion. *Journal of Conflict Resolution*, **2**, 265–279, (1958).

M. DEUTSCH, The Effect of Motivational Orientation Upon Trust and Suspicion. *Human Relations*, **13**, 123–140, (1960).

M. DEUTSCH and R. M. KRAUSS, The Effect of Threat Upon Inter-Personal Bargaining. *Journal of Abnormal and Social Psychology*, **61**, 181–189, (1960).

M. DEUTSCH and R. M. KRAUSS, Studies of Inter-Personal Bargaining. *Journal of Conflict Resolution*, **6**, 52–76, (1962).

[42] M. SHERIF, Creative Alternatives to a Deadly Showdown. *Trans-Action*. 3–7, (Jan. 1964).

[43] C. E. OSGOOD, *An Alternative to War or Surrender*. The University of Illinois Press, Urbana, Illinois, (1962). See also for empirical study, W. GAMSON and A. MODIGLIANI, *The Carrot and/or the Stick*. Working Document No. 10, Carnegie Project No. 4, Center for Research on Conflict Resolution, University of Michigan, Ann Arbor, Mich., (November 1964).

[44] L. BERKOWITZ, *Aggression: A Social Psychological Analysis*. McGraw Hill, New York, (1962).

[45] E. B. MCNEIL, Psychology and Aggression. *Journal of Conflict Resolution* **3**, 195–293, (1959).

E. B. MCNEIL, (Ed.) *The Nature of Human Conflict*. Prentice-Hall, Englewood Cliffs, N.J., (1965).

[46] O. KLINEBERG, *The Human Dimension in International Relations*. Holt, Rinehart & Winston, New York, (1964).

[47] J. LAULICHT, Canadian Foreign Policy Attitudes: Some Major Conclusions. *International Social Science Journal*, **17**, 3, (1965).

J. LAULICHT, Public Opinion and Foreign Policy Decisions, *Journal of Peace Research*, 147–160, (1965).

[48] T. W. ADORNO et al., *The Authoritarian Personality*. Harper, New York, (1950).

[49] M. ROKEACH, *The Open and Closed Mind: Investigations Into the Nature of Belief Systems and Personality Systems*. Basic Books, New York. (1960).

[50] U. BRONFENBRENNER, The Mirror Image in Soviet-American Relations: A Social Psychologist's Report. *Journal of Social Issues*, **17**, 45–56, (1961).

U. BRONFENBRENNER, *Allowing for Soviet Perceptions* in *International Conflict and Behavioural Science*, R. FISHER (Ed.) Basic Books New York, (1964).

[51] O. R. Holsti, The Belief System and National Images: A Case Study. *Journal of Conflict Resolution*, **6**, 244–252, (1962).

[52] H. C. Kelman, Compliance, Identification, and Internalization: Three Processes of Attitude Change. *Journal of Conflict Resolution*, **2**, 51–60, (1958).
H. C. Kelman, Processes of Opinion Change. *Public Opinion Quarterly*, **25**, 57–78, (1961).

[53] L. Festinger, *Conflict, Decision and Dissonance.* Stanford University Press, Berkeley, Calif., (1964).
L. Festinger, *Theory of Cognitive Dissonance.* Row, Peterson, Evanston, Ill., (1957).

[54] K. E. Boulding, *The Image: Knowledge in Life and Society.* University of Michigan Press, Ann Arbor, Mich., (1956).

[55] K. E. Boulding, *The Meaning of the Twentieth Century.* Harper and Row, New York. (1964).

[56] R. C. Angell, The Growth of Transnational Participation. Paper to *American Sociological Association* (August 1965).
R. C. Angell, An Analysis of Trends in International Organizations. *Peace Research Society (International) Papers*, **3**, (1965).

[57] P. Smoker, A Preliminary Empirical Study of an International Integrative Subsystem. *International Association (Journal of the Union of International Associations)* (November 1965).

[58] A. G. Newcombe and H. Newcombe (compilers), *The Economic Consequences of Disarmament. A Collection of Abstracts from the Files of Peace Research Abstracts.* Canadian Peace Research Institute, Clarkson, Ontario, (1964).

[59] K. E. Boulding and E. Benoit, *Disarmament and the Economy.* Harper & Row, New York (1963).

[60] U.S. Arms Control and Disarmament Agency. The Economic and Social Consequences of Disarmament. *ACDA Publ.*, **6**, July 1962. Reprinted in S. H. Mendlovitz (Ed.), *Legal and Political Problems of World Order.* World Law Fund, New York, (1962).

[61] G. Ackley (Chairman), Report of the Committee on the Economic Impact of Defense and Disarmament. U.S. Government Printing Office, Washington, D.C. (July, 1965).

[62] E. Benoit, The Propensity to Reduce the National Debt Out of Defense Savings. *American Economic Review*, **51**, 455–459, (1961).

[63] *International Peace Research Newsletter*, **3**, 16, (1965).
E. Benoit, (Ed.) *Disarmament and World Economic Dependence.* Columbia University Press, New York (1967).

[64] T. W. Milburn, The Concept of Deterrence: Some Logical and Psychological Considerations. *Journal of Social Issues*, **17**, 3–11, (1961).
T. W. Milburn, What Consittutes Effective Deterrence? *Journal of Conflict Resolution*, **3**, 138–145, (1959).

[65] B. M. Russett, The Calculus of Deterrence. *Journal of Conflict Resolution*, **7**, 97–109, (1963).

[66] [33].

[67] J. Laulicht and N. Z. Alcock, The Support of Peace Research. *Journal of Conflict Resolution*, **10**, 198–208, (1966).

[68] P. Ekman *et al.*, Divergent Reactions to the Threat of War. *Science* 88–94, (1963).

[69] J. Frank, Commitment to Peace Work: A Preliminary Study of Determinants and Sustainers of Behavior Change. *American Journal of Orthopsychiatry*, **35**, 106–119, (1965). Cf. brief report in *War/Peace Report*, 7–9, (April 1965).

[70] E. BOULDING, *Who Are These Women? A Progress Report on a Study of the Women Strike for Peace*, in *Behavioral Science and Human Survival*, M. Schwebel (Ed.), Science and Behavior Books, Palo Alto, Calif. (1965).

THE CITY AS AN ELEMENT
IN THE INTERNATIONAL SYSTEM

Daedalus, 97, 4 (Fall 1968): 1111-1123

The City as an Element in the International System

AN INTERNATIONAL system may be defined as a set of social organizations or organized groups of people whose relations are governed mainly by threat and the perception of threat. Defined this broadly, the international system goes back a long way in human experience, and the primitive international systems of the paleolithic era may seem to have little resemblance to the complex international system of today. Nevertheless, in social evolution something like an international system has nearly always been present and can be thought of as a segment of the total ecological system of mankind that is at least moderately recognizable and has something of an evolutionary pattern of its own.

In spite of the observation that even very primitive peoples have organized groups, the relations among which are governed by some kind of threat system, a case can be made for the proposition that the international system as we would recognize it today emerges only with the development of cities and civilization—civilization, of course, being what goes on in cities. The threat relations among paleolithic people seem to be sporadic and very casual. In any case, before the invention of agriculture man was too near the margin of subsistence in most places to have any surplus left over, either for more elaborate organization or for organized fighting.

The domestication of plants and animals seems to have led at first to a degree of relative affluence in which productive activity paid off better than predatory, and hence the threat system seems to have been fairly well muted. A great many neolithic villages seem to have been undefended.

As long as population was sparse in relation to agricultural land, this idyllic Garden of Eden could persist. The rise of cities may well have been associated with population pressure that made simple expansion of the old way of life impossible. The first cities seem to have been created by internal threat systems. In the early days, this appears to have been mainly a spiritual threat. A charismatic priesthood somehow persuades the farmer to hand over some of his surplus food, and with this food the priests, the artisans, and the builders of temples, houses, and walls are fed, but not much comes back to the farmer.

The simplest model both of the city-state and of the international system would suppose each city to have a small agricultural hinterland around it, from which the surplus of food flows into the city and which receives from the city primarily spiritual goods or threats. At this stage at any rate, the city would have little in the way of products to export. The spiritual threat of the priest is usually succeeded by the more material threat of the king who uses the food that he extracts from the farmers to feed soldiers who can extract the surplus that feeds them by material threat. An international system develops out of this because of the fundamental principle that threat capability and credibility diminish with distance from the origin of the threat, since threat capability has a cost of transport. Consequently at a certain distance from the king or the city, its threat capability and credibility decline to the point where they can no longer control behavior. At this point, there is an opportunity for another king or city. Once the second city is established there comes to be a boundary of equal strength between the two cities, and we have an international system.

A model as simple as this, of course, could never have described a real situation, even in the earliest times. The system is always more complex than we have indicated. Even in the neolithic era, for instance, there seems to have been extensive trade covering thousands of miles. The development of metallurgy meant a quite early development, at least of specialized villages that exported metals in return for food. The development of pottery, jewelry, weaving, and crafts producing transportable articles led to the development of organized trade; and trading cities, such as Tyre, had economic structures very different from the simple exploitative city and also played a very different role in the international system. The threat capability of a trading city, for instance, may be used not so much simply for the extraction of commodities from unwilling producers, as for the monopolization of trade opportunities, as in the case of Venice.

The next stage of development of the city and the international system is empire, which begins when one city conquers another without destroying it. A system of city-states is only stable if what I have called the "loss of strength gradient"—that is, the decline in threat capability and (or credibility)[1] per mile of distance traveled away from its origin—is very high. Thus, for the system of city-states to be stable, the threat capability of the city must be exhausted once it has covered an area that is capable of feeding the city from its food surplus. One city, then, cannot conquer another, for as it expands its threats beyond its own territory, it becomes too weak, and the other city becomes too strong.

The cost of transport of threat capability however, for instance in the shape of organized armies, soon fell below the critical limit that would permit the city-state to be stable. This happened first along the great river valleys simply because water transportation of anything, including threats, is very cheap. It is not surprising, therefore, that we get empires along the Nile, along the Tigris and the Euphrates, along the Indus, and along the Hoang-Ho. One of the puzzling questions of human history, incidentally, is why the pattern in America was so different, where the great river valleys like the Mississippi did not produce any early civilizations, but the wild mountains of Mexico and Peru did. The answer may be that a river had to flow through at least a semi-arid region in order to support an empire due to the extraordinary difficulties of transportation through forests. Certainly the desert plays something of the role of the sea in transportation. Just as the Roman Empire was the product of the Mediterranean and of sea transport, so the empires of the nomads of Central Asia were a product of relatively unobstructed land transportation in semi-arid regions. Forests grow faster than man, with primitive tools, can cut them down. He can only conquer the forested regions once the techniques of clearing have gone beyond a certain point. Even the arid lands cannot support an empire without something like a horse, which is probably why the incipient city-states of the Southwest Pueblos in the United States never developed into empires, having neither navigable rivers nor horses.

In the empire, there is a sharp distinction between the capital city and the provincial cities. The capital city is more purely exploitative, though the empire as a system usually involves the collection of surplus food by the provincial cities, some of which is retained and some of which is passed on to the capital city. There is probably more incentive, however, for the provincial cities to become producers of specialized manufactures and to begin to exchange these with food producers for food. Here the exchange system slowly develops and spreads as an alternative to the threat system. Finally, with the advent of the so-called Industrial Revolution and the rise of science-based technology, we begin to get virtually a-political cities like Birmingham (England) or Detroit, which grow up on a basis of pure production and exchange, usually outside the old political structures. These commercial and industrial cities play virtually no direct role in the international system though their indirect influence may be great in strengthening the power of the nation-state and the capital city to which they happen to be attached. Thus the rise of cities like Birmingham, Manchester, and Sheffield undoubtedly increased the power of Great Britain in the international system from the eighteenth century on. This increase in power, however, was largely accidental in the sense that it was not particularly planned by the central authorities and owed little to success or failure in war. What we had here was a quite independent dynamic of the exchange system that had a spillover effect on the international system.

The United States is an even more striking example of a country that has risen to power in the international system largely because of economic development through production and exchange. In the United States, the fact that the capital city of Washington was relatively insignificant over most of its history and even today is far from being the largest city symbolizes and illustrates the peculiar nature of this political organism. In the ideal type of national state, the capital city is the largest city in the country and dominates the life of the country, acting as a centralized focus for inputs of information and outputs of authority and, as the derivation of the word implies, as a "head" to the body of the rest of the country. One thinks of Paris, Rome, Madrid, Vienna, Warsaw, Copenhagen, Tokyo. The list could be extended. By contrast, Washington, Canberra, Ottawa, and, one should no doubt add, Brazilia play a different role in their respective countries. These might almost be called "economic" as opposed to "political" countries in which the major centers, such as New York, Montreal, Sydney, São Paulo are commercial and industrial cities rather than administrative and military centers. In this connection, it is interesting to note that even the state capitals of many American states are relatively minor cities like Lansing, Springfield, and Sacramento, and it is highly significant that the capital of West Germany is

Bonn. One feels that it is almost a pity that the capital of France did not remain permanently at Vichy!

Another important aspect of the city in the international system is its role in creating security against threats and violence. In classical civilization, human life was frequently more secure against violence in the city than it was in the country. Adam Smith observes, for instance, that "order and good government, and along with them the liberty and security of individuals, were, in this manner, established in cities at a time when the occupiers of land in the country were exposed to every sort of violence."[2] Even today, one sees the contrast between the landscape of France and England where the greater authority of the central power permitted men to live in open farmsteads in the country without undue fear of violence and the landscape of Germany where farmers still huddle together in villages and the countryside between villages is empty of habitation. In earlier times the city wall was a symbol of the security of the city's inhabitants. Like all forms of security, this tended to break down in the long run, and virtually all walled cities have been destroyed at some time or another. Nevertheless, in what children call the "olden days," the inhabitant of the city did enjoy at least a temporary security frequently superior to that of his rural brother. Without this, indeed as Adam Smith again points out, the accumulation that went on in the cities, the increasing division of labor, and the improvement of technology would probably have been impossible, for unless the fruits of accumulation are reasonably secure, people will not accumulate.

With the advent of aerial warfare and especially the nuclear weapon, the position of the city is radically changed. The city and the civilian who lives in it have now become hostages, and the civilian's chances of survival in a major war are much less than that of his rural brother or even that of a member of the Armed Forces. In the modern world, both the city and the civilian are expendable to the lust of the national state. This has created a complete reversal of the traditional pattern. Whereas in the earlier period the national state fostered the growth of nonpolitical cities by creating relatively large areas free from the threat of serious violence, today the national state is one of the greatest threats to its cities. Hiroshima and Nagasaki, after all, were commercial not political cities and were sacrificed to the senseless ambition of the national state. It would be very surprising if in the next "X" years Boston, Cleveland, Seattle, and so on are not similarly sacrificed on the altar of the present national system. The cities have become helpless pawns in an international system that is developing rapidly toward a major breakdown.

I have argued on another occasion that there are many reasons why the classical city, clearly bounded in space and organized from within by a strong sense of community, is incompatible with modern technology and is likely to survive only in special cases as a kind of anomaly.[3] The ecological structure of the classical city depended on a high resources cost, both of transportation and communication. The city was clustered and bounded; spatially it tended to have a ring structure centered around a market square, a cathedral, or some other civic center. Its population density was high, and there was usually a fairly sharp boundary that separated it from the countryside.

Both the economic and the political structures of the modern world are dominated by the reduction in cost of transport of people, commodities, information, and violence. Clustering of any kind is a result of cost of transport of something. If cost of transport was zero, we would expect activity of all kinds to be uniformly spread over space. The lowering of cost of transport, therefore, inevitably reduces clustering and increases dispersion. We see this very clearly in what is happening to the cities. The central cities are decaying and disintegrating. The level of amenity in them has fallen, the level of violence has risen. The central cities may decay completely, and an urban structure may emerge that looks something like chicken wire; a network of ribbon development enclosing areas of country and rural settlement. The automobile, the telephone, the television, and the missile with a nuclear warhead—all move the ecological system in the same direction.

The critical question under these circumstances is what happens to the structure of community. Before the twentieth century, community was structured geographically in fairly well-defined ways. In his political role especially, a citizen belonged to a well-defined local community, whether village, town, or city, toward which he felt some attachment and some obligations. Beyond this were regional political organizations, such as counties and states, and beyond these again the national state. A great deal can be learned about the prevailing image of community by simply asking large numbers of people "Where do you live?" or "Where do you come from?" The answer, of course, depends somewhat on the context. If one is abroad, for instance, one would tend to respond by giving the name of one's national state. In the United States, one would be unlikely to respond by giving the name of one's county. A great many people probably do not even know it, for this is not a salient community. One suspects there might be almost an even chance of giving the name of a state or the name of a city. Some people would say "I come from Dedham," some might say "I come from Massachusetts." A person from Syracuse might even say "I come from upstate New York," thereby dissociating himself from the appendage at the lower end of the Hudson. On the other hand, a man may say "I come from Boston" when he actually lives in Concord, or "I come from New York" when he really lives in Scarsdale.

There can be little doubt that the impact of the modern world is to diminish allegiance to the local community and especially to the central city. The increase in mobility assures this. In the days when a man lived all his life in the place where he was born and where his forefathers had lived for generations, there was a strong tie to the local community. In the modern world, hardly anybody lives where he was born and a man changes his location many times during his life. Under these circumstances the sense of allegiance to the local community as something special declines, and if the local political community is to be run successfully, it must rely less and less on allegiances and sentiment. It will have to rely on professionalization and the use of exchange in order to attract the kind of support necessary. Everybody recognizes that the great problem of the central city today is that the people who make the decisions about it do not live there and do not feel themselves to be part of its community. They may live in the suburbs or in another part of the world altogether. Hence the city as a decision-making unit is really disintegrating. From being a social organism, it has declined to being a chance aggregation without even the organizational structure that permits the decisions to be made that will affect the local community. One sees this, for instance, in the field of banking, finance, and corporate management where decisions may be made that profoundly affect the future of a particular community by people who have never even seen it. We see this even more dramatically in the international system where the decision of a man in the White House consigns the people of cities on the other side of the world to the flames. We have passed from the stage where the cities nurtured civilization to a world in which the city is simply a victim of forces far beyond its own control, a sacrificial lamb on the altar of corporate or national ambition. The great danger here is that the sense of local community will be wholly eroded by the sense of impotence on the part of local people and local decision-makers. This can create a situation in which the cities almost literally fall apart. The city is something that nobody loves, and what nobody loves will die.

It is not surprising, therefore, that in the modern world the city is in deep crisis. It is an aggregation of humanity that has lost its sense of community and cannot, therefore, provide a human identity. St. Paul was able to say with pride that he was a citizen of no mean city. Would the same be said by a resident of Harlem or of any of our central cities? The cities of today that are not mean, like Venice, Florence, Kyoto, and one might almost add Williamsburg, are the fossil relics of a departed age. There are a great many things in our own age and in our society in which we can take great pride—the pictures of Mars, the conquest of disease, the great universities, even let me say with some trepidation, the middle-class suburbs with pleasant lawns, solid comforts, and relaxed neighborliness. The city, however, is not on this list, perhaps because it is really a survival from a past age, and we have not yet made the adjustments that can transform it into something worthy of the rest of our accomplishments.

The crux of the problem is that we cannot have community unless we have an aggregate of people with some decision-making power. The impotence of the city, perhaps its very inappropriateness as a unit, is leading to its decay. Its impotence arises, as I have suggested earlier, because it is becoming a mere pawn in economic, political, and military decision-making. The outlying suburb is actually in better shape. It is easier for a relatively small unit to have some sense of community, and the suburb at least has a little more control over its own destiny. It is somewhat less likely to be destroyed in war. Its economic base tends to be diversified as its residents commute over a wide area; hence its fate is not in the hands of a single decision-maker. Its local government, its school board, and other community agencies often are able to gather a considerable amount of support and interest from the people they serve.

It is not wholly absurd to ask whether we should not abolish the city altogether as a political organization. Let us divide Chicago and Detroit into thirty suburbs, small enough so that they have some chance of achieving a sense of local community and local responsibility for things that can be done locally. Then, of course, we would need "functional federalism"—metropolitan water boards covering a wide area, air-pollution agencies, educational finance institutions that would equalize local opportunities without destroying local initiative, police forces of different levels of size and function, and so on. Political scientists have often lamented about the multitude of political agencies in the United States, but the case against this may easily have arisen out of a prissy desire for tidiness. In terms of productivity, a multiplicity of agencies may be precisely what the times require. We seem quite incapable of expanding the central cities out into their suburban environment. Perhaps we should try reversing the recipe and move the suburbs into the city, building up around them a network of functional agencies.

The problem of integrating the city into the world community is much more difficult than the problem of reorganizing it locally. Nevertheless, the future of the city as an institution probably depends more on the future of the international system than it does on any other aspect of social life. More than any other aspect of the sociosphere, the international system is destroying the city, either physically by bombing or more critically by eroding its problem-solving capacity through the withdrawal of both intellectual and physical resources into the international system itself. The brain drain into the international system and the war industry is one of the principal reasons why the city receives so little attention and why what attention it has received in such efforts as urban renewal and public housing has been largely disastrous. The impact of urban renewal and of throughways on a city is physically not unlike that of a small nuclear weapon, but with less damage to bodies and perhaps more damage to minds. Both urban renewal and nuclear destruction come from the national state. They are both thunderbolts hurled at the city from afar without regard to the tender ecological structure of its life and community. The cities by themselves, of course, cannot solve the problem of the world community, though one would think they might exercise a little bargaining power on it. The difficulty here is twofold. In the first place, the cities seem to have astonishingly little bargaining power in general. This is a puzzling phenomenon. One looks, for instance, in the United States at the extraordinary bargaining power of the agricultural interest, even at a time when it has shrunk to an almost insignificant proportion of the total electorate. By comparison with the apparent impotence of the cities, one sees the even more astonishing bargaining power of the military, who both starve and threaten the cities and eat high off the hog at a time when the cities have to be content with scraps. The second difficulty is that the international system is not really salient to the people who live in cities, even though it affects them so profoundly. The decision-makers in the international system are few, they are remote, and it all seems a long way from the experience of the ordinary citizen. Hence he is inclined to "leave this to father" even when the great White House father is dangerously incompetent in these matters. It is not the importance of a problem that determines how much attention will be paid to it, but its salience. Unfortunately, importance and salience are very loosely related, sometimes even negatively related.

All these difficulties resolve themselves into a single structural deficiency. There are virtually no channels in society or in the world at large by which the city as such can exercise bargaining power. One wonders what would happen if the cities were represented directly, as states, not only in the United States Senate, but in the United Nations. Could we envisage a new Hanseatic League of cities against the national state and the military establishments that are threatening to destroy them? All these suggestions, alas, sound like brainstorming and pipe dreams.

Nevertheless, what we face here is perhaps the most important single example of a much larger problem of political and social organization. The conflict in the world today—underlying the cold war at the international level, civil rights and the Black Power movement in the United States, and the inability of so many tropical countries to resolve their internal conflicts to the point where economic development becomes possible—is a conflict of two political concepts. The names "individualism" and "collectivism" are quite inadequate to describe these concepts, but these are probably the best words we have. On the one hand, there is the political ideal of the individual acting as an individual and independent person in a larger community, exchanging his capacities with other individuals in a social contract and in a market economy, expressing his political activity primarily by voting in elections on the one-man, one-vote basis. In political organization, this leads to what we might call "atomistic parliamentarism." In economic organization, it leads to capitalism and the free market. In religious organization, it leads to Protestantism and sectarianism; in family life, to the free choice of partners. It goes along with the life style of mobility and rootlessness, entrepreneurship, achieved rather than ascribed status, and so on. On the other side, we have the collective ideal stressing the notion that the identity of the individual is so bound up with the community with which he identifies that he can only become an individual as part of a community. His political activity here is exercised by activity influencing the decisions and the bargaining power of a series of concentric communities, rather than as an individual among other individuals. This leads toward a consensus-oriented society, totalitarianism, socialism, catholicism, monasticism, associationism, such things as trade unions and professional associations, collective rather than individual bargaining, and the corporate rather than the parliamentary state. Each of these philosophies has its own virtues and vices, and almost any political system is some sort of uneasy compromise between the two. Some lean toward one side, and some toward the other. At the present moment in history, the crisis of the cities has arisen because in *no* political structure is the city adequately represented. At the level of individualistic democracy, the city has lost its sovereignty and independence. It has become a pawn in the sense that its local autonomy has been destroyed. At the level of collective organization, the city is not organized as a bargaining unit. It does not bargain with the other agencies of society, such as the national state or the corporation, as effectively, shall we say, as the labor unions bargain with the employers. The city, therefore, gets the worst of both worlds. Its citizens as such are effective neither as political individuals nor as members of a bargaining collectivity.

Much of the same problem is seen in the Negro or other minority groups. The rise of the Black Power movement is in a sense a breakdown of individualistic democracy at this level. On the other hand, the Black Power solution is also likely to fail, because black power is not very great and the movement is likely to raise expectations that will probably be disastrously disappointed. One sees the same problem in the demands for "student power," which are simply not constructive, though occasionally they can be destructive, as in Latin America and Japan. Nevertheless, the student is not satisfied to be a mere individual and feels the need of identifying himself with a collectivity.

The synthesis and reconciliation in both structure and philosophy of the two political "modes," as they might be called, of individualism and collectivism perhaps represent the greatest single long-run problem of the human race at its present state of development. The city, or at least the urban collectivity, is one of the principal arenas in which this problem is or is not being worked out, as the case may be. Almost the only consideration that leads to any hopefulness about the future is that communication and aggregation foster the process of human learning. In the age of civilization, the concentration of people in cities unquestionably contributed to the slow growth of knowledge, simply because of the facilitation of communication that this concentration implied. Rural isolation leads to rural backwardness and cloddishness. The implications of the words "civilized," "civil," "urbane," and even "civilian," as over against "rustic" and "bucolic," suggest the values that have arisen from easy urban communication. The country may be the depository of traditional virtue, but new ideas come out of the wicked city. The city, therefore, historically has been the main source of change, both in the international system and in all aspects of the social system, as it has produced new ideas, new ideologies, new philosophies, and new technologies. The towns, as Adam Smith observes, improve the country. The decay of the city today does not represent a return to rural virtue or to rural ignorance. It is a symptom, if anything, of the urbanization of the whole world. The communications revolution has created, in effect, a world city, and this is why the local cities are in decay. It is to be hoped, therefore, that we can look forward to new knowledge, new ideas, and even a transformation of the international system that will give us security, arising out of the knowledge process of the world.

The essential key to this process may be the development of self-consciousness in the city dweller that he is a member of a city and indeed of the world city. One suspects that the unexploited bargaining power of the city is great simply because the city, disorganized as it is, is inevitably a focus or nodal point of the world network of communication. Airports are the synapses of the world communications network; so in a sense are the television stations and the newspapers of the city. So are its universities. It is a pretty fair generalization in the theory of location to say that the synapses, the gaps, or the switches in the communications and transportation network produce the city in the first place. This is why, for instance, so many cities have arisen at ports, at heads of navigation, and at points of trans-shipment. In a world in which the transportation of communication is beginning to overshadow the transportation of commodities, the city—because of its position in the communications network—has real power that is as yet unexploited, mainly because it is not self-conscious. If I can take a leaf out of the book of Karl Marx, and this is one occasion where the leaf may be better than the book, we may urge the rise of self-consciousness in the cities, a rise of their joint self-consciousness of the community as a world city representing the constructive and developmental forces of humanity as against the essentially backward-looking or destructive tendencies of the country and the military. Our motto, therefore, perhaps should be "Cities of the world unite, you have nothing to lose but your slums, your poverty, and your military expendability." On this note of modest long-run optimism, I had better conclude for fear that the pessimism of the short run catches up with us first.

REFERENCES

1. It is the credibility of the threat which really matters from the point of view of its ability to organize social systems. Credibility in very complex ways is related to capability. The relationship is closer in the case of material threat than in the case of spiritual threat where capability is hard to demonstrate, but where the threat often justifies itself: for example, the fear of Hell. Even in the case of material threat, credibility can remain long after capability has disappeared. Nevertheless, in the long run there must be a tendency for capability and credibility at least to run parallel.

2. Adam Smith, *The Wealth of Nations*, Book 3, Ch. 3.

3. Kenneth E. Boulding, "The Death of the City: A Frightened Look at Post-civilization," in *The Historian and the City*, eds. Oscar Handlin and John Burchard (Cambridge, 1963), pp. 133–45. Also in Kenneth E. Boulding Collected Papers Vol. II (Colorado Associated University Press, 1971), p. 265–279.

REVOLUTION AND DEVELOPMENT

In: *Changing Perspectives on Man,* Ben Rothblatt, ed.
Chicago: Univ. of Chicago Press,
1968, pp. 209-226

REVOLUTION AND DEVELOPMENT

L ET ME BEGIN by talking about development not only as a process in economic and social life, but as a process in the whole universe. What we call economic development is only one aspect of a larger developmental process in society, and this developmental process is just the tag end, from our point of view, of the whole evolutionary process in this part of the universe. Biological evolution and social development, indeed, are two aspects of an essentially continuous process. Both biological and social evolution can be usefully described by a mutation-selection model, even though in its usual form this is a rather empty theory with not much predictive power. The processes of social evolution are, of course, different and more elaborate than the processes of biological evolution. The similarities, however, are great enough to assure us that we are dealing with a single process in time.

In social evolution, as in biological evolution, we can distinguish between genotypes and phenotypes. On the whole, the genotype is what mutates and the phenotype is what is selected, although this distinction is often fairly rough. In social evolution the processes of reproduction are much more complex than they are in biology, because we have a lot more than two sexes. Even though, in a quite literal sense, an automobile plant is the womb of an automobile, automobiles are not produced by an orgasm, despite many appearances to the contrary. A distant observer from outer space might conclude from simple observation that automobiles were reproduced sexually. We know, however, that the process is a great deal more complicated; hence the possibility of messing up the genotype material is much larger in social evolution than it is in biological evolution.

The social genotypes are things like blueprints, plans, ideas, symbols, sacred histories, and all the things which organize production both of artifacts and of social organizations. Genotypes are things which have the power of organizing role structures, for evolution, on the whole, is evolution of roles. They are the acts, relations, and structures in society which are social organizers. Then the phenotypes consist of the organizations which they produce: families, universities, firms, churches, states; also commodities and artifacts, automobiles, libraries, microphones, clocks, and so on. All these things are species of the social system and they have a kind of ecology of their own, just as there is an ecological system in the field or the forest. In the larger ecological system of the world, indeed, the artifacts and commodities of man, considered as species, compete ecologically with natural species. The automobile, for instance, has competed very successfully with the horse. In these days man, his artifacts and his organizations have become dominant in the ecological system of the world. Pretty soon nothing will survive which is not in some sense domesticated.

The world ecological system consists not only of ecological equilibrium but also of ecological succession, and it is the latter which constitutes the evolutionary process. This process is not continuous, but exhibits "gear changes." It seems to go on at a certain pace for a long time and then suddenly there is an acceleration and a shift to a new rate of evolution. The development of life was one such gear change; the development of the vertebrate was certainly another one; and the development of man was a very fundamental change, because with the biological evolution of the human nervous system the possibility of social evolution opened up—that is, evolution within the human nervous system itself. This goes on at a very rapid pace. Within social evolution we also distinguish gear changes. The first was the shift from the Paleolithic into the Neolithic with the invention of agriculture and the domestication of crops and livestock. This produced a settled village, an increase in the length of human life, and an acceleration in the growth of human knowledge. The next gear change was the urban revolution, of some five thousand years ago, or perhaps eight thousand. Now we are going through what I have elsewhere called a third great transition, a new gear change in the evolutionary process as a result of the rise of science and social self-consciousness.

In explaining social evolution we have to look for the social genotypes—relationships between people and organizations which are capable of organizing roles and role structures. I distinguish three main categories of social genotypes, which I call the threat system, the exchange system, and the integrative system. More categories might be distinguished but, in our culture at least, everything has to be divided into three parts.

The threat system begins when somebody says to someone else, "You do something nice to me or I'll do something nasty to you." This is a fairly powerful organizer; it is the basis of the urban revolution and of civilization, which, I should hasten to add, I regard as a most disagreeable state of man, which is now in process of passing away.

The threat system is capable of producing a moderately elaborate society. It produced the classical civilizations, which depended on the prior existence of agriculture and the food surplus from the food producer, and on a threat system to take the food surplus away from the food producer and to feed the kings and the priests, the artisans and the soldiers, who constituted the cities. The threat system produced slavery and it produced war, but it has a limited horizon of development. The trouble with slavery, as Adam Smith pointed out, is that it does not produce much economic development because the slave owner has no incentive and the slave has no opportunity. The slave owner has it made anyway, and if the slave thinks of an invention the slave owner thinks he is trying to get out of work and slaps him down. It is not surprising therefore that the threat system goes so far and no further.

Exchange is a somewhat different kind of process. It begins fairly early, perhaps, as anthropologists have described, as "silent trade." The little booths of the merchants spring up under the shadow of the temple, which is a spiritual threat system, or the castle, which is a material threat system, and the network of exchange begins its almost continuous and irresistible growth. Exchange begins when someone says to someone else, "If you do something nice to me, I'll do something nice to you." This is, as economists have always pointed out, a positive game sum, in which everybody becomes better off. Furthermore, exchange encourages the division of labor, and this increases the productive powers of labor, which develops exchange still further, which develops the division of labor still further, and so we go on in an enormous cumulative process.

The threat system is a Sisyphean system. It is like pushing uphill a stone which is always breaking away and running down into destruction, the collapse of empire, wars, and revolutions. Once we get to exchange we push the stone over the top of the hill and we are chasing it. The world is working with us and development is constantly fostered by the famous "invisible hand." As a result the exchange system has a much higher horizon of development than the threat system—a horizon which we certainly have not reached yet.

It is possible, however, that the exchange system does have a developmental horizon, perhaps because we have run into difficulties about under-consumption and secular stagnation, perhaps because a pure exchange system does not develop the kind of integrative structure which will legitimate and support it. This was Schumpeter's great argument,[1] He argued that a market economy had to have sacred institutions which would legitimate it and that the rationality of the market tended to destroy these. It is pretty hard to love a bank much, yet without

[1] J. A. Schumpeter, *Capitalism, Socialism, and Democracy* (New York: Harper, 1942).

a network of affection and support the exchange system tends to delegitimize itself and hence to destroy itself. I think it was Schumpeter who said, "The only thing wrong with capitalism is that nobody loves it." This, however, is a pretty important defect.

My third category, the integrative system, is something of a ragbag without the unity of the other two, but we must have it because there are a number of social organizers which are neither threats nor exchange. The integrative system consists of a number of diverse social organizers, all of which, however, revolve around the establishment of things like community, status, legitimacy, love, loyalty, benevolence, and malevolence. An integrative system begins when somebody says to someone else, "You do something and I'll do something because of what you are and what I am and what we both are, because we are all in the same boat, or because we love each other, or hate each other, or because we are all Seventh-Day Adventists or all Americans or all human beings," though this last is rather implausible. Without the integrative system, neither the threat system nor the exchange system can really operate. If either of these is to have any kind of developmental power there has to be an integrative matrix within which they can be legitimated.

With an unlegitimated threat, for instance, you can be a bandit, and organize a temporary social system by saying, "Your money or your life." If you want to be a bandit twice, however, you have to be either a landlord or a tax-collector— that is, you have to legitimate the relationship in a whole network of acceptance, law, security, community, and so on. Community is perhaps the key word in the integrative system, for it is around this that all the other concepts revolve.

All actual social systems and all actual organizations involve all three of these genotypes. Nevertheless, it is not difficult to classify the social phenotypes according to which of the three genotypes predominates in them. Thus the threat system produces phenotypes in the shape of kings, armies, empires, and some kinds of temples and churches. Not all religions are based on threat, but early religions frequently were. The priest, for instance, says to the farmer, "You give me part of your crops or I won't do the rituals and the crops won't grow." Farmers, being nice, innocent types—at least they used to be— believe this and so they support the priest with part of their surplus crops. Armed forces are still more obviously a phenotype of the threat system, and these, of course, are still very much with us.

The exchange system dominates such phenotypes as firms, banks, corporations, insurance companies, and all those organizations which exist primarily in a market environment— which exist by the transformations involved in exchange and production. Some of these have become very large, like General Motors, which, while it does not rival the United States Department of Defense, is exceeded by only eleven countries in its gross product. The corporation does not use threats or love very much to survive. Nobody says, "Ask not what General Motors can do for you, ask only what you can do for General Motors," because we expect General Motors to do something for us. This is the meaning of exchange.

Exchange, however, as Adam Smith again pointed out, can function as a social organizer only if there is reasonable security of private property—that is, the threat system has to be controlled or organized to the point where property is reasonably secure in the possession of the owner. We cannot have exchange without property, because property is what is exchanged. It is only as the institution of property is legitimated in some way that exchange can develop and organize the division of labor. Property, of course, can be either private or public, and the concept is certainly not abolished by socialism. It is one of the paradoxes of the ideological struggle of our time that whatever success socialism has had has been because it has been able to legitimate property in the form of public property. The weakness of the market economy has often arisen from the difficulty it finds in legitimating the property concept.

What "security" means in this connection is that the people who make decisions should be able to enjoy their fruits and suffer their consequences. Otherwise exchange would not result in development, and would not result in a division of labor and the improvement of the productive powers. Given this security and legitimation, however, exchange can certainly work miracles, as we have seen recently in Germany and Japan, and indeed in the whole extraordinary development we have had for the last two-hundred years.

There are also phenotypes which are dominated by the integrative system: such things as the family and the church, and, even more strikingly, institutions like the Elks, the bridge club, or the little league, which have almost no function except developing integrative relationships.

Just as is true in the biological sphere, as we have seen earlier, organizations have mixtures of genes, which might almost be called social chromosomes—that is, threats, exchange, and love in different proportions. Even the most idealistic utopian community has a little bit of a threat system, at least in the form of potential expulsion; even an organization like an armed force has to rely on a certain amount of exchange, and a good deal of integrative activity, in terms of morale-building and so on. Exchange organizations likewise have to exist in a matrix of a threat system, insofar as law and order and security of property depend on this, and also in an integrative matrix. Even General Motors has to be loved a little. We may not need to be passionate about it, but it has to be accepted in some sense as legitimate before it can really operate in the long run.

The key to all these developmental processes, I argue, is the growth of knowledge properly interpreted. If we ask of the evolutionary process what it is that evolves, the answer has to be some form of information or improbability of structure, and this is the key to the whole process right from the primordial hydrogen atom. Matter and energy are subject to an inexorable law of conservation. Chemistry, for instance, is a moderately dismal science, because in the material world nothing is ever lost or gained in total. We have pure zero-sum games of redistribution of the elements. If one has more, somebody else has less. Matter as such, once the elements are set up, is obviously incapable of development, at least until the social system resumes the evolution of the elements from where it left off some four to six billion years ago. This is why materialism as a developmental philosophy has serious weaknesses.

The contemplation of energy is even more depressing. Thermodynamics is an even more dismal science than chemistry, and, as a matter of fact, much more dismal than economics. Thermodynamics says that nothing you do is any good in the long run. Available energy is not even conserved, but is spent. We are all spendthrifts, living on our capital of potential, of which we cannot even be parsimonious. Entropy goes on increasing all the time, and entropy is everybody's enemy.

The evolutionary process, as Schrödinger describes it,[2] is essentially the segregation of entropy. What this means is that even though we spend our capital of energy potential we build up what is left into more and more improbable forms. Evolution is the development of the improbable. Thermodynamics, of course, proclaims the ultimate conquest of the probable, that is, chaos, unless something funny happens to the universe at the end, as it probably does. Maybe Brahma does breathe the universe in and out every ten billion years.

Once the evolutionary process has produced structures with the improbable capacity for self-reproduction we are off on an evolutionary voyage, destination unknown.

There seem to be two processes at work in evolution, which correspond roughly to the genotype and the phenotype. The first, by which the genotype reproduces itself, might be called

[2] Erwin Schrödinger, *What Is Life?* (Cambridge: Cambridge University Press, 1951).

"printing." In this process a structure simply reproduces itself in the material world in the way a print shop operates. This is apparently the way the gene reproduces itself. It acts as a three-dimensional printing set which has the capacity of attracting its own pattern into it, producing a mirror image of itself in the material world, and the mirror image then reproduces the gene. The gene, therefore, can print itself on the material world indefinitely, provided it has the material environment around it. The same might be said of the *Chicago Tribune*, which is a kind of gene of Chicago, though fortunately not the only one.

The second process might be called organization, by which the genotype produces the phenotype. We see this also in society as well as in biological evolution. Thus Mr. Harper's idea and Mr. Rockefeller's fifty million dollars in a rather improbable sacred history produced the University of Chicago. The genotypes print themselves and then proceed to organize the phenotypes.

We see the processes reflected in the miracle of teaching itself. After a teacher finishes a successful class, the students know more and he knows more too. This is not at all like exchange in which if I give you something I have less of it. In teaching I give you something and I have more of it. It is a widow's cruse.

Knowledge, of course, is also lost by people forgetting it and by people getting old and dying. Death is an enormous brain drain and all human knowledge is lost every generation. This is why we have to have all sorts of educational institutions to reproduce it. The more easily it can be produced, however, the more easily it can be expanded.

What I am arguing, therefore, is that all developmental processes are fundamentally learning processes—processes by which more and more improbable structures come into being through these related operations of printing and organization. Economic development is just part of this larger process, though perhaps the most visible and the most measurable part. Political and moral and aesthetic development are observable processes but they are hard to identify and measure, and it is often hard even to tell which way is up. There is certainly development, for instance, from Shakespeare to the Beatles, but its direction is not wholly certain.

If we could get a measure of the entropy of structures we might have a pretty good measure of development. An entropy theory of value is by no means absurd, for value is improbability, and the more valuable anything is the less probable it is.

Whether economic development is really measurable or not, it has the great advantage that it has a measure in terms of something like per capita real income or per capita real gross national product. It is tempting, therefore, to take the rate of economic growth as a first approximation of the overall rate of development. A better measure might well be the increase of knowledge or the decrease of entropy, but this is hard to devise. We have some notion of the acceleration of the rate of growth of knowledge; in the Paleolithic it may have taken one hundred thousand years or more to double the stock of knowledge; in the Neolithic it may have doubled every five thousand years, and in civilized society, every thousand years. Today in many fields it is supposed to double every fifteen years, at least in quantity. Similarly, if we look at the per capita real income, this probably took one thousand years to double before 1600, but today in rather slow countries like the United States it doubles in thirty-seven years and in really developing countries like Japan it doubles every eight years. This seems to represent a real shift of gears.

No matter how we measure it, however, economic development is still a learning process. It is not merely a piling up of existing commodities, like agricultural surpluses. Development means changing structures, not piling up stock. It means producing new kinds of things and new kinds of people with new kinds of knowledge and skill. It involves a reorganization of society and a total learning process. We can even define capital as frozen knowledge—an improbable arrangement of the material world depending upon a prior improbable arrangement in the mental world. Thus, the microphone, and still more, the computer, is a fantastically improbable arrangement of matter which is here because somebody thought it up, and was able to think it up because of a long process of development of human knowledge going back thousands or perhaps tens of thousands of years. Man is now imposing his own knowledge on the material world.

The computer may easily represent another gear change. Computers have become almost quasi-biological organisms, without very much in the way of sex. They are, however, developing capacities for producing low-level knowledge. If this represents a really new element in the knowledge-building process it should also produce further acceleration in the rate of development.

The dominance of knowledge over material can be seen quite clearly if we observe how rapidly a society can recover from material destruction if the knowledge structure is unimpaired. Thus, in Japan and Germany where the physical capital was destroyed during the Second World War, it was restored in astonishingly short time because the human capital was practically unimpaired. In Indonesia, on the other hand, which had much less physical destruction, the absence of knowledge has produced a declining society.

Non-economic development also requires a learning process. It involves learning how to live at peace with each other. It involves learning how to make the fruits of virtue reasonably secure and the retributions of vice moderately certain. It involves learning to organize; for learning the skills of organization, perhaps, underlies all social development. The main obstacle even to economic development in countries where it is not happening is the inability to organize. Organization, however, is a skill; it is something that people have to learn. It is certainly not given genetically, but it is something that can be transmitted. Economic development also requires moral development. There has to be a minimum degree of trust. Exchange, for instance, is impossible without this minimum of trust. In a society in which nobody can be trusted unless he is a blood relation it is hard for economic development to go beyond the second cousins. In developed societies, such as the United States, abstract trust has got to the point where nobody checks on your baggage tickets at the airports and we can even have telephone credit cards. We have computerized billings which can be sabotaged in a minute by punching a few more holes in the card. In spite of the extraordinary vulnerability of complex societies to possible betrayals of trust, the odd thing is that we learn not to betray—that is, we learn not to indulge in prisoner's dilemmas and all these other little games that make everybody worse off.

An increase in the rate of development can be called "acceleration." Sometimes this takes place rather suddenly in a society, as it did, for instance, in Japan at the time of the Meiji Restoration or after the Second World War. Sometimes the acceleration may take a generation or more. We have mentioned earlier the acceleration that marked the end of the Paleolithic and the Neolithic periods. Even within the civilized period we can trace minor accelerations. In Europe, for instance, the fall of the Roman Empire seems to have produced one. The Roman Empire itself was technologically stagnant, and development in western Europe did not start up until Rome fell. It may be that one of the problems of China, and the reason why the great breakthrough into science did not take place there, is that it did not fall far enough.

The development of science, of course, is the great acceleration. It is a mutation of the learning process itself. It may, of course, turn out to be a flash in the pan, if it results in the human race destroying itself; on the other hand, it may be a mutation almost as important as the development of life itself. We are only beginning to see the full impact of it. Science did not **really** affect economic life very much until about 1860. The industrial revolution of the eighteenth century, about which so much fuss is made, was really the tag end of the folk technology of the Middle Ages. The steam engine was actually less complicated than the medieval clock and owed very little to science, though that little, for instance Boyle's law, may have been important. The real theory of the steam engine, which is thermodynamics, did not come until almost a hundred years after the steam engine itself; so obviously the steam engine owed nothing to it. After 1860, however, the story is different. The electrical industry would have been impossible without Faraday, Ohm, and Clerk-Maxwell. The nuclear industry likewise would have been impossible without Bohr and Einstein. Today it is quite likely that 75 per cent of the output of the economy is science based.

To come now, rather late in the day, to the second part of my title—a look at the role of revolution in the developmental process—revolution is a term which is used very loosely and sometimes means simply a large change in the system. It is sometimes used to mean what I have here called an "acceleration"; that is, a change in the rate of change. In the narrower and perhaps more exact sense of political revolution, it means some kind of overturn in the power structure by means of which an old elite is displaced by a new one, usually, though not necessarily, with a certain amount of violence and upheaval. Political revolutions sometimes, though not always, produce an acceleration. An acceleration tends to be produced if the incoming elite has a higher level of knowledge and organization relevant to development than the outgoing elite. If, before the revolution, those who have the will to develop do not have the power and those who have the power do not have the will, the society is likely to be fairly stagnant. In those circumstances a revolution which gives those who have the will the power is likely to produce an acceleration.

Revolutions, however, are costly. If they are violent they

produce a lot of émigrés, and one of the major products of revolution seems to be refugees. This represents a great waste of the talents of the society and an actual loss of the knowledge structure which it sometimes take a generation or two to recover. We might even classify revolutions into those that cost two generations, those that cost one, and those that cost none. The Russian Revolution was a two-generation revolution—that is, the country did not get back to the position of 1913 in terms of per capita income until the early 1950's. The French Revolution also was probably a two-generation revolution. The American Revolution seems to have been a one-generation revolution. It was costly in the sense that the refugees, that is, the Tories, were on the whole hard-working, respectable, and knowledgeable people, and American economic development did not really get off the ground until after 1815. The best examples of the costless or no-generations revolution would be the Glorious Revolution in England in 1688—though if we include Cromwell, that also was a two-generation revolution—and the somewhat equivalent Meiji Restoration in Japan in 1868. The Japanese experience is perhaps the best example of an acceleration without a revolution, which seems to me almost the ideal way of initiating development.

Under some circumstances, of course, acceleration may be impossible without a revolution, simply because the existing political structure of the society is so corrupt and ineffective. On the other hand, a country with a reserve bank of legitimacy in the shape, say, of an emperor, like the Japanese, is very lucky because it can achieve the transfer of power to a developmental elite with much less cost. Thus, I would always regard revolution as a cost, even if sometimes a necessary cost, and never as a gain in itself. A real obstacle to development is what might be called a revolutionary sentimentality, as one tends to get it on the Left, which idealizes the process of revolution itself. This can be a serious obstacle to development, as we see it, for instance, in Indonesia and in Cuba.

In the early days of the Cuban Revolution I was invited to give some lectures on development in Havana, an invitation which I, unlike many of my fellow economists, found it impossible to resist. It was during what might be called the New Deal phase of the revolution, before it turned to the extreme Left, and the people who invited me, I regret to say, mostly had to flee the country shortly afterward. I tried to point out on that occasion that while revolution was like an orgasm, if you wanted development you had to have a womb, because development was a learning process which required peace, quiet, and long uninterrupted growth. I am afraid this doctrine was not popular, because on the whole the mystique of revolution is a masculine mystiqe. I am inclined to think that what development requires is a feminine mystique, and that the masculine mystique is on the whole an enemy to it. The United States was fortunate in that its revolutionary leaders, with the possible exception of Jefferson, were not very revolutionary. Very often, however, the people who can lead a successful revolution, such as Sukarno and Castro, are not suited to lead the developmental process which should follow. If you have to have a revolution, there is a lot to be said for having a revolutionary leader who has the gift of dying young, and can be succeeded by a developmental leader who has very different qualities.

In conclusion, I would like to try to apply some of these considerations to one of the major problems of our own day, the so-called ideological struggle and the cold war, which revolves around the question of the relative merits of the capitalist free market development on the one hand and the socialist centrally planned development on the other. This is an argument which arouses such fierce emotions that it is hard to deal with it rationally. Nevertheless, I think we have to admit that there are many ways of developing, and the distinction between developing and stagnant societies cuts across the distinction between socialist and capitalist societies. We can perhaps distinguish four types of societies in the modern world following

these two classifications. There is first the successful market
society, like Japan, most of Western Europe, and the United
States. Japan has actually had the highest rate of development
known in human history, about 8 per cent per annum per capita
in the last twenty years. Many other capitalist societies, however, have been in the 5–6 per cent class, and even the relatively
stagnant ones, like Britain, have a slow development to some
extent by choice.

The next category might be called the successful socialist
societies, which include the Soviet Union and the Eastern
European countries. Their rate of development has been less
than the most successful capitalist societies, and rarely exceeds
6 per cent per annum; and this has been achieved also at a high
social cost in terms of inefficient investment, a distorted price
system, and a certain amount of political oppression.

The third category is that of the unsuccessful capitalist
societies, which would include most of the colonial and ex-
colonial countries, even those like many Latin-American societies which have been free from formal colonialism for a long
time but have retained a colonial structure.

Then at the bottom of the list we have the unsuccessful socialist countries, where there has been not merely stagnation but
retrogression, as we have seen in Indonesia, Burma, possibly
Ceylon, Syria, and Perón's Argentina. One is almost tempted
to call the Asian group, at any rate, the Laski countries, because
many of their leaders learned their economics from Harold
Laski in London in the 1920's. What they learned from him,
unfortunately, was how to destroy the invisible hand without
providing a visible hand—which merely leads to a capacity
for getting the worst of all possible worlds. These countries have
managed to destroy the developmental processes of the market
without substituting the developmental processes of a genuine
centrally planned economy. The case of China is ambiguous.
After a rather successful period in the 1950's, it has had a severe
setback as a result of its essentially sentimental revolutionism,

which has tried to create a perpetual revolution rather than getting on with the sober business of growth.

My general conclusion, therefore, is that while there is occasionally a case for revolution, there is practically no case for revolutionism as an ideology, and that as an ideal, revolutionism should always be regarded as a cost, not as a gain, provided that our real objective is development. One should always leave the possibility open, however, that the objective may not *be* developmental. The revolutionist is frequently motivated by malevolence; that is, there are certain people or certain classes that he hates and will damage even to his own cost. Malevolence means that you are willing to make somebody else worse off even if as a result you are worse off yourself. This is an unfamiliar concept to economists, who are astonishingly nice people, and who have the naïveté to believe that the world is ruled by selfish behavior. Selfishness, however, is a high moral virtue compared with malevolence and envy, and a great deal of human behavior unfortunately falls far below the selfish ideal. Only economists, surely, could have thought up the Pareto optimum, which implies that I will approve of a situation in which somebody else becomes better off even if I am no better off. This no doubt reflects the eighteenth-century character of economics and its descent from a moral philosopher, known as Adam Smith, who, while he was skeptical about undue altruism, did not approve of malevolence.

A great deal of revolutionism, however, is motivated by spite. The first collectivization in the Soviet Union, for instance, did enormous damage to their developmental process because of spite against the kulaks. By contrast, development is fostered by non-malevolent attitudes, and by what I have sometimes called the presbyterian virtues: honesty, punctuality, temperance, the keeping of promises, and a mild benevolence toward others. This is a moral climate which fosters development—not the moral climate of spite which is so characteristic of revolutionism. I think I am prepared to say, therefore, that even where revolution may be necessary as a prerequisite for development it is always a symptom of a low state of moral and political development. Where revolution succeeds it is because it is a teacher; it is, however, an expensive teacher, and the search for a better one is a highly rewarding enterprise.

RESEARCH FOR PEACE

Science Journal (England), 5A, 4
(Oct. 1969): 53-58

Research for peace

Most national policies today are designed to operate within a system of unstable peace. But the world seems to be quite close to the unstable-stable peace boundary. Massive inputs of information will be needed to make the phase change

A MAJOR PART of modern day science and technology is supported more or less directly from defence bugets. The international conflicts which still divide the world provide the driving force for this massive military investment in science. So far, very little effort has been made to understand the true nature of these conflicts; so little, indeed, that many scientists remain unaware of the achievements (or even the existence) of the peace research movement. This is hardly surprising; it has been barely 15 years since the movement got underway, and in view of the fact that it is a miniscule effort compared with what goes into the war industry, not too much can be expected. Nevertheless, a number of theoretical models of conflict situations have been devised, together with a body of data both at the descriptive and the theoretical levels. In this article I shall attempt to explain how this information can help towards an understanding of the nature

Kenneth E. Boulding is professor of economics at the University of Colorado. A Quaker who took his first degree at Oxford, Professor Boulding was for 18 years professor of economics at the University of Michigan. He has written widely on economic theory and the theory of conflict; his present work is concerned with the theory of the grants economy.

of war, and provide ways of avoiding it.

The origins of the peace research movement, like the origins of many significant movements, are somewhat obscure. They can, however, be traced back to two important sources. The first was the work of Quincy Wright of the University of Chicago, whose studies of the nature of war opened up a new field for historical research. The other was Lewis F. Richardson, a British meteorologist, who developed between 1920 and 1940 a remarkable mathematical theory of the international system, and opened up a whole field of what might be called 'politicometrics'. Although the work of Richardson existed in the form of microfilm, it was not published until 1960, which shows perhaps how far ahead of his time he was. By now there are perhaps 200 people who think of themselves as engaged in peace research—still a tiny number compared with those actively engaged in improving the weapons of war.

PEACE AND WAR are primarily properties of the international system, though domestic conflict and conflict between individuals may also be a legitimate subject for peace research. In considerable measure, then, peace research can be

regarded as a sub-section of international system research. Indeed it may be asked whether it is a really significant sub-section, for it is after all the international system which is the reality to be studied, whether by people who identify themselves as peace researchers or by people who do not. An analogy may perhaps clarify the point. Peace research is to international studies somewhat as research into weather control is to meteorology. Both international studies and meteorology are studying large complex systems with many different methodologies. While everybody talks about the weather, not many people try to do anything about it, except the people in weather control. Weather control is applied meteorology, just as peace research is applied international systems. There is, however, a certain difference in emphasis between the pure study and the applied. What may be called 'conventional' international studies tends to take the existing international system for granted and then seeks to find out how it works, perhaps in the hope of being able to operate it more successfully. Peace researchers, on the whole, are profoundly dissatisfied with the existing international system which they regard as impossibly costly and dangerous and are interested in un-

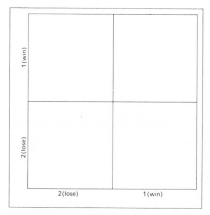
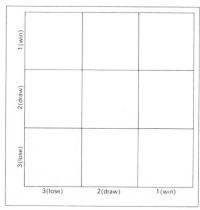

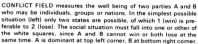

CONFLICT FIELD measures the well being of two parties A and B who may be individuals, groups or nations. In the simplest possible situation (left) only two states are possible, of which 1 (win) is preferable to 2 (lose). The social situation must fall into one or other of the white squares, since A and B cannot win or both lose at the same time. A is dominant at top left corner, B at bottom right corner.

The more complex status field (right) allows the possibility of equal status or a draw. Again, only the white parts of the diagram are possible. This diagram can be used as a crude description of different social systems: slavery, for instance, could be mapped into the top left-hand corner, with A as the ruling class and B as the ruled. Equality of status (usually a myth) maps into the 2-2 box of the diagram

derstanding it primarily because they are interested in changing it.

Any intellectual activity which claims to be a science must have a body of theory or models about the segment of the world which it is investigating, and must also have the ability to collect information which can be used to test the theoretical models, either descriptively or predictively. The theoretical models of peace research are derived from two principal sources—from conflict theory on the one hand and from the specialized theory of international systems on the other. Conflict is characteristic of nearly every social system and sub-system. It is found in the family, in religion, in academic life, in the firm, in industrial relations, as well as in international relations. Although the patterns of conflict differ substantially from one field to another, there are also profound similarities. Conflict theory is concerned with building models which at the most general level capture these similarities and at the same time are capable of expansion to include the differences.

CONFLICT in a social system may be defined as a situation in which there are at least two identifiable parties (which may be either individuals, groups or organizations) such that a change or 'move' in the social system makes one party better off, either in their own estimations or as measured by some more objective

criteria. A 'conflict field' may be defined as the set of figures which measure the welfare of the parties involved.

The simplest conflict field might be called the 'status field', as shown on this page. Here there are two parties, A and B, each of which can have one of two states, labelled 1 and 2, of which 1 is preferable to 2. In a game, for instance, 1 might be 'win' and 2 might be 'lose'. Obviously, only the unshaded parts of the field are possible. In the top left-hand square A is dominant; in the bottom right-hand square B is dominant; and the general social field must be capable of being mapped into one or other of these squares. This can be extended to include a 'draw' or equality of status, as in the second illustration.

The effect of status conflict is to establish a status order which will be accepted by all parties. If the parties are equally matched, the cost of establishing this order may be very high. The 'pecking order' and related phenomena in animals are good examples of status conflict. There are frequently genetic mechanisms for reducing the cost of this conflict, for if it is too high the species will not survive. In social systems, likewise, there have developed a larger number of mechanisms for reducing the cost of status conflict. Sometimes a class structure is established through a threat system, the most extreme form of which is slavery. In

this case, for instance, the system would fall into the upper left hand box in the second diagram, with A as the ruling class and B as the ruled. Another solution is that of equality, which may be partly myth and partly reality, in which case the system falls into the 2-2 box.

As status becomes more and more finely divided, it passes over into economic conflict, which might almost be defined as a situation in which the status or welfare of each party is independent of the welfare of the other. This is illustrated in the diagrams on page 349, where the vertical dimension measures the welfare of A and the horizontal dimension the welfare of B. Assuming for the moment infinitely divisible units, welfare may be measured in terms of some objective index—or as per capita real income —or it may theoretically be measured by the subjective judgment of either A or B. Various restrictions can be imposed on this field. The most severe restriction, which restores it almost to status conflict, is what is known as a constant-sum game. Suppose that the social system fitted the line AB then any increase in A's welfare—by, say, a dollar—would inevitably result in an opposite decline in B's welfare. An even more extreme limitation would be imposed if the line which represented the only possible points on the field passed through the zero point, as A'OB'. This would represent a zero-sum game in which a

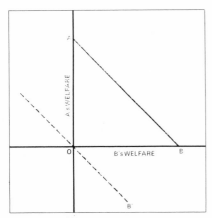

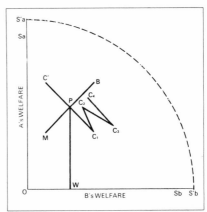

CONSTANT-SUM GAME is shown (left) in a diagram which plots the welfare of A vertically and that of B horizontally. The freedom of choice can be reduced by lines such as AB, where improvement in the welfare of A reduces the welfare of B. Passing through zero, line A'B' is an even tougher restriction. Economic conflict is shown in a more general case in the diagram on the right. Starting at the point

P four moves are possible: P to B is a benign move; P to M is malign; P to C' is a conflict move which helps A but harms B; and P to C is a conflict move which helps B but hinders A. The zig-zag line from P to C_4 shows that it is possible to get benefits for both parties from a series of conflict moves. $S_a S_b$ is a 'possibility boundary' which limits the extent of benign movement; energy is required to reach $S'_a S'_b$

positive welfare for either party would involve an equal negative welfare for the other.

The kind of limitations involved in constant- or zero-sum games are so severe that they are rarely if ever found in practice. A social system involving a conflict of this kind will be so unprofitable to both parties that it will soon be abandoned or modified. The more general case of economic conflict is shown in the next diagram (above right). Suppose we start from a position of the system which is represented by the point P, where B's welfare is OW and A's welfare is WP. Four types of 'moves' in the system can then be distinguished. A benign move, such as from P to B, is one which makes both parties better off. A malign move, such as from P to M, makes both parties worse off. A conflict move from P to C, makes A better off and B worse off, and a conflict move from P to C_1 makes B better off and A worse off.

Suppose there is now a succession of conflict moves, which is quite likely to be the case in social systems. For instance, B makes a decision which moves ,the system from P to C_1; A then retaliates, moving to C_2; B retaliates in turn to C_3, A to C_4 and so on. In this case, in spite of the fact that each move is a conflict move, the overall result is benign because at ⌐ both parties are better off than they are at P. On the other hand, it would be quite easy to move in the

opposite direction—for instance, from C_4 to C_3 to C_2 to C_1 to P, in which case the conflict would be malign. One of the great problems of social organizations is how to discourage malign conflict and to encourage benign conflict.

The difference between the two is clear from the diagram. If the dollar is used as a convenient abstract unit of measurement, the rate of conflict can be defined as the number of dollars gained by the gainer for each dollar lost by the loser (the slope of the line PC_1). Whether conflict is benign or malign depends in a rather complicated way both on the rate of conflict in successive moves and on the magnitude of the moves. Generally, however, the conflict is more likely to be benign if the rate of conflict is low. For two successive moves of equal length, the overall effect will be benign if the product of the two rates of conflict is less than unity; it will be malign if it is greater than unity; and neutral if it is equal to unity. The question of what determines the rate of conflict is also very important and is still a very difficult one, the theory of which has not yet been fully worked out. Perhaps all that can be said at present is that the stronger the sense of community among the parties the more likely it is that the rate of conflict will be low and that successive conflict moves will be benign.

Benign movement, however, may not go on for ever. In any field of this kind,

there is likely to be a 'possibility boundary' (such as the line S_aS_b) which is defined by the total resources of the system. Benign processes if continued long enough will end up on this boundary, after which the only moves possible are conflict moves or malign moves. The simplest case is where the boundary describes a constant sum, in which case we reduce to lines such as AB in the previous diagrams. It is quite possible in reality, however, that the boundary will be non-linear. Even here an important proposition emerges: that when the system is at the boundary its resources may either be put into conflict—in moving back and forth along the boundary—or they may be diverted to development—that is, pushing the boundary 'out' to a position such as $S'_aS'_b$. Generally speaking, the more resources devoted to conflict itself, the less can be spared for development and the less likely, therefore, it is that the general dynamics of the system will be benign. Development is usually preceded by some sort of resolution of status conflict, either by the acceptance of unequal status through some ideology, or by the development of more equal status through say democratic institutions.

TO CARRY FURTHER the consideration of the type of movement in the social system which is mapped into the conflict field, a further concept needs to be developed—that of a strategy or decision field. Here it is supposed that a move in the social system can be represented as a change in the strategy or decision of either party. Decisions or strategies are usually multidimensional, a strategy necessarily so, for it is a decision about a whole series or set of other decisions. Nevertheless, for the moment suppose strategy can be represented along a linear scale, as in the diagram shown below. Here B's strategy is measured horizontally and A's strategy vertically, so that every point on the field represents a combination of strategies and can. be mapped into a point in the field of the preceding diagram. The concept of the strategy field is fundamental both in the theory of games and in the theory of viability. In the theory of viability it is supposed that each of the parties has a 'survival boundary' beyond which it cannot survive. Thus, in this diagram the coloured region represents A's survival area and the grey part is B's survival area. The intersecting region is the area of mutual survival, and in the white area of the field neither A nor B can survive. In this diagram it is assumed that A can always move vertically while B can always move horizontally. Even though there is an area of mutual survival, each party can of course move to a position where the other party cannot survive. This is what I have called 'conditional viability'. Each party can exist only at the mercy of the other. A and B might be two firms, the strategy of each being the price

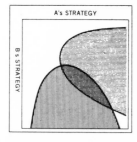

A's STRATEGY

B's STRATEGY

STRATEGY FIELD assumes that any move in a social system can be represented as a change in the strategy or decision of either party, measured on linear scale. In the diagram A's strategy is measured vertically and B's horizontally. The coloured region is the area within which A can survive and the grey region shows B's survival area; where the two overlap both A and B can survive. Since A can move vertically and B horizontally, both are capable of moving to a position where the other cannot survive; this is known as 'conditional viability'

of goods produced; alternatively A and B might be two nations, the strategy being the size of the war industry or the threat system. In a situation such as this, the question of the dynamics of the moves becomes of supreme importance. Who moves first; though he who moves first, if he is not able to move far enough, may not always win and may indeed be eliminated—like a hunter who wounds a tiger.

An interesting variety of cases can be developed. One of great significance for the international system is that the probability of unconditional viability diminishes with every decline in the cost of making effective threats. Thus, as the cost of delivering nuclear weapons declines, it becomes increasingly easy for one nation to put another into a position in which it cannot survive. Another proposition is that for every given system of logistics of threat capability there is some minimum size of the unconditionally viable political unit. The advent of the missile and the nuclear weapon has virtually destroyed all unconditional viability. A system of conditional viability, however, is a very different and much less comfortable system from one of unconditional viability and the world has not yet adapted to it.

GAME THEORY on the whole deals with discrete strategy fields in which strategy is not a continuous variable but a number of discrete decisions. The strategy field is then represented by a game matrix as in the diagram on page 351 (left). Here it is supposed that A and B have only two strategies, which for vividness are labelled 'good' or 'bad'. Each of the four boxes of the matrix then represents a possible combination of strategies. The moves of the game then depend on the payoffs—that is, the relative welfare of the two parties in each of the four boxes. What is significant here is the direction in which the payoffs are higher, which can be represented by arrows—vertical arrows for A and horizontal arrows for B. As they are drawn in this diagram, it suggests that if B is good then it pays A to be bad. If A is good it pays B to be bad. But if either of them is bad, it pays the other of them to be bad. The equilibrium position of the game matrix is that towards which the arrows converge.

This diagram is an illustration of what may be called 'perverse dynamics'. These are situations in which the dynamics of the system produce malign conflict moves, making everybody worse off. A very famous special case of this type of situation is the 'prisoner's dilemma', so called because of the original illustration which was used to describe it, in which A and B are two prisoners; in each case

'good' means not informing on the other and 'bad' means informing on the other. Both are better off if neither informs; but if one does not inform it pays the other to inform, and when one has informed it pays the remaining one to inform, so both end up in the 'bad-bad' box.

Another example of a perverse dynamic process would be an armaments race in which 'good' represents disarmament and 'bad' represents arms. If both countries are disarmed, they are both better off, but if one is armed, it pays the other to arm, and so they both end up being armed. This is one of the few conflict models which have been worked out extensively, both theoretically and empirically, especially through the work of Anatol Rapoport. Models like the prisoner's dilemma have been compared to the 'fruit flies' of experimental genetics. They are simple enough to permit experimental verification, yet complex enough to include a great many of the features of real world systems. Rapaport's experimental results are of great interest. They suggest that after an initial period of what might be called 'naive trust', players tend to deteriorate into the bad-bad box as naive trust is betrayed. After a while, however, there develops a more sophisticated trust based on a learning process which involves the development of 'long-sightedness'—that is, the realization that temporary gains will invariably result in ultimate loss. This may lead to the kind of movement represented by the dotted arrow in the diagram, which involves at least tacit co-operation between the parties. The implications for this for peace in the international system are profound. It means that in the absence of superordinate organization (world government) the development of stable peace depends on the long learning by which the sophisticated type of trust is developed.

Another very interesting example of perverse dynamics which is closely related to the theory of strategy space is the arms race theory of Lewis F. Richardson. Richardson relates the rate of change of the size of the war industry of one country to its perception of the rate of change of the war industry of another, which gives a set of simultaneous differential equations which can be solved. I have developed a simpler version which can perhaps be more easily generalized, in which it is supposed that the actual size of the war industry of each country is a function of the size of the war industry in all others. This gives n unknowns and n equations which, if they are well behaved, can be solved.

The interesting question here is under what circumstances there is an equilibrium in such a system. The conclusions are rather depressing. An equilibrium is

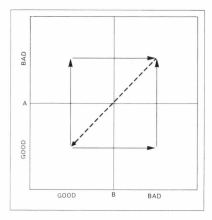

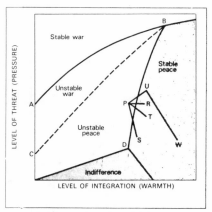

PRISONER'S DILEMMA is an example of the kind of game that can be described by a game matrix. Here A and B have only two strategies—'good' and 'bad'. It is also assumed that if A is good it favours B to be bad, and that if B is good it favours A to be bad; this is shown by the direction of the arrows. If, for instance, A and B are prisoners and A is being good by not informing on B, it pays B to inform on A. Once B has informed, it pays A to inform as well. So both end up in the 'bad-bad' box. The coloured line is speculative: it assumes that both A and B eventually realize that temporary gains end in ultimate loss and co-operate to move to the 'good-good' box

PHASE DIAGRAM is a deliberate analogy with the freezing of water, in which pressure is replaced by level of threat and temperature by level of integration between countries. The model suggests that the international system may fall into a variety of different phases—stable war, unstable war, unstable peace, stable peace or indifference. Parts of the international system have already made the transition from unstable peace to stable peace (Scandinavia), while other parts are still stuck in stable war (the Middle East). Indifference arises when two countries are so widely separated that interaction between them is negligible. Most of world is in unstable peace

only possible if the 'reactivity coefficient' (the amount by which one nation increases its war industry for each dollar increase by a potential enemy) is less than one, and the more nations there are the smaller this coefficient has to be for equilibrium to be possible. This means that the system has to be less reactive than we would ordinarily expect for any equilibrium to be possible. This theory also suggests that long-sightedness is the only road towards disarmament (again in the absence of any superordinate authority) but such long-sightedness may develop as the result of a social learning process. All this suggests that one key to development of peace is the conscious understanding of what determines possible failures of the international system.

ANOTHER FRAMEWORK which is particularly valuable in peace research is the model of the international system as a phase system. This is illustrated in the diagram on this page (right). The actual boundaries are merely intended to be suggestive of the concepts and are not based on empirical evidence. Here two major dimensions of the international system are plotted—the level of threat measured vertically and the level of

integration measured horizontally. (A deliberate analogy is implied with the phase system of water and ice, with threat representing pressure and integration representing temperature.) The level of the threat can be measured in general by the size of the war industry, either in absolute or in relative terms. The percentage of the total product of the system which is devoted to military budgets might, for instance, be a measure of this. This is a very crude index and would have to be modified in practice by some considerations of disposition and logistics. The level of integration might be measured by a composite index involving amount of trade, amount of communication, perhaps a content analysis of verbal messages suggesting the level of malevolence, and so on.

The figure then identifies five phases of the international system. Where the threat level is very high and the integrative level is low we get stable war, a situation in which the only communication between the parties is by some violence. At a somewhat lower level of threat or a higher level of integration this passes into unstable war, in which war is interrupted by periods of peace, but during which war is regarded as the norm;

the Middle East today would be a good example of this phase. At still lower levels of threat and higher levels of integration, we get unstable peace, which has been characteristic of most of the international system for the past 200 years; this is a condition in which peace if regarded as the norm (even the US Air Force advertises "Peace is our profession"). At very low levels of threat or integration there may be a phase of indifference between two countries that are so far apart that they do not really impinge on each other. Then at high levels of integration, we may get stable peace, which is a situation in which the countries are in contact, but in which the probability of war between them is so small that it is below the threshold where it affects behaviour. In the past 100 years or so islands of stable peace have been developing in a world system of unstable peace, the principal islands' being North America and Scandinavia. One of the problems of peace research is to develop the conditions under which these islands of stable peace could expand.

The actual position of these phase boundaries is of course very difficult to ascertain, especially as they may be changing under various conditions of general dynamic stress, for social systems do not exhibit the delightful stability in parameters which physical systems usually observe. The importance of the position of these phase boundaries, and especially of their slope, is that they determine where efforts towards peace are going to be most effective. Suppose, for instance, that the system is at position P in unstable peace. We can move to stable peace, assuming that the phase boundary has a positive slope, either by increasing the level of integration of the system by moving from P to R, or by diminishing the level of threat—that is, by disarmament—moving from P to S, or by some combination of the two, say, from P to T which may be even easier. The most effective division of effort between working on the level of integration and on the level of threat depends on the nature of these phase boundaries, and is by no means apparent at first sight.

The situation is further complicated by the fact that there are certainly constraints on the possible dynamics of the system. It can be argued, for instance, that over time there is tendency for an upward drift in both the level of threat and the level of integration, so that the actual movement may be even something like P to U. Once it is generally perceived, however,' that the system is in stable peace there may be sharp reductions in the level of threat and as the level of threat diminishes the level of integration may also be correlated with this positively, so there may be a movement, say, from U to W. Another way of approaching the same problem would be to examine the probability of war, as measured, for instance, by the number of months of war out of a ten year period, for various states of the international system. We could then plot lines of equal probability of war (P_w) on the figure with the line AB representing $P_w = 1$, BD representing $P_w = 0$, and CB perhaps $P_w = 0.5$. R. Naroll's work on deterrence suggests that this approach might be possible, even with quite crude quantifications of the historical record.

THE DEVELOPMENT of more sophisticated images of the international system on actual policies can hardly be overestimated. We have seen this in economics, where the development of national income statistics and a few simple macro-economic models have revolutionized economic policy, at least in the Western countries. The ambition of the peace research movement is to create a similar intellectual revolution in the field of the international systems which should lead to profound changes in national defence policies, leading to the abandonment of the now untenable system of unilateral national defence and the de-

velopment of a genuinely balanced policy for stable peace. At the moment the international system is profoundly unbalanced on the side of threats, which is precisely why we have unstable peace or even unstable war in places. The idea that it is possible to have national policies for stable peace is something which is barely on the horizon. Most national policies now are directed towards the operation of the system of unstable peace. Nevertheless, I suspect that the bulk of the international system is actually very close to the phase boundary between unstable peace and stable peace and that a growth in general sophistication about the nature of the international system may well push us over the boundary in large segments of the systems. Getting over a phase boundary in physical or social systems always presents certain difficulties. In physical systems it usually requires large inputs or outputs of energy; in social systems it requires large inputs of information. These inputs are not infinite, however, and we have at least some chance of providing them.

We must not underestimate the difficulties in the way of peace research. The problem of reality testing in the international system is extremely difficult, more so perhaps than in any other area of the social system and much more than in most physical systems. This is in part because the system is almost by nature highly probabilistic. The mere fact that it tends to be dominated by a small number of decision makers means that the random element is the international system is very large. There is little doubt, for instance, that if Hitler had died in infancy, the history of the first half of the twentieth century would have been different. Decisions in the international system are made by men of ordinary intelligence, elevated, often by chance, to positions of great power and operating with an information system which is almost designed for corruption. It is not surprising that the system operates so badly and is so costly.

In a highly probabilistic system, theoretical models are extremely hard to test, as meteorologists know all too well. If we predict a future event with a probability of 50 per cent, we cannot be proved wrong, and reality testing is nothing more nor less than the detection of error in prediction. Furthermore, the international system is characterized by secrecy, by deception and by sudden shifts in its parameters—as Richardson showed so elegantly in his discussion on war moods. It is therefore less accessible than most systems to the scientific method. Nevertheless, it is not wholly random and wherever there is order there is a possibility that it can be perceived.

In the present crisis of the planet the probability that the whole evolutionary

experiment in this part of the universe might come to an end is not zero, even though it may well be a very small positive number. Conscious effort directed towards reducing this probability could hardly fail to produce some payoffs. No further justification of peace research would seem to be necessary.

STABILITY IN INTERNATIONAL SYSTEMS: THE ROLE OF DISARMAMENT AND DEVELOPMENT

In: *International Security Systems: Concepts and Models of World Order,* Richard B. Gray, ed. Itasca, Ill.: F. E. Peacock Publishers, 1969, pp. 193-210

STABILITY IN INTERNATIONAL SYSTEMS: THE ROLE OF DISARMAMENT AND DEVELOPMENT

The international system is a fairly well defined section or sub-set of the total world social system that I have described elsewhere as the sociosphere, which is the sphere of all human beings, their communications, inputs and outputs, and organizations. The international system consists of the nation-states, particularly in their relations with each other. There are activities and aspects of nation-states which are concerned with purely domestic problems and which do not participate directly in the international system, though the distinction between, for instance, domestic policy and foreign policy becomes harder to draw all the time, simply because of the great interrelatedness of all aspects of the social system. Thus, American agricultural policy, which looked on the face of it to be a purely domestic matter, has become through its effects one of the major elements of the international system, simply because we have used the food surpluses which resulted from our agricultural policy as instruments of national influence in the world arena. As the old World War II slogan had it, "food will win the war and write the peace," which, insofar as it was true, makes food very much a matter of international, rather than domestic policy.

Besides the nation-states, we should also include the international organizations such as the United Nations and its various agencies, also the non-governmental agencies of which there are now about

1700 or more, in fields such as religion, philanthropy, science, commerce and so on, and we perhaps should even include the international corporations which at times negotiate with governments almost as if they were sovereign states, and indeed represent concentrations of economic power which exceed those of most sovereign states. There are only 11 countries, for instance, with a gross national product exceeding that of General Motors.

The international system is governed principally by threats, and to a smaller extent by exchange and by integrative relationships of community, affection and respect. The threat system is represented by the world war industry which is about 140 billion dollars a year, which is roughly equal to the total income of the poorest half of the human race. The exchange elements of the international system consist of two very different activities. First, there are the activities of diplomacy which are concerned mainly with the exchange of intangibles, such as position, although they may deal with such things as territories, indemnities and so on. Then in the second place we have international trade, though it is a question how much of this should be included in the international system proper, as a great deal of it is really exchange among individuals and is simply part of the world economy rather than of the international system. In the socialist countries where international trade is monopolized by the state it can be regarded much more logically as part of the international system. Even in market societies, insofar as it is regulated by tariffs, quotas and international agreements, it is at least highly relevant to the international system. The integrative aspects of the international system consist of such things as traditional enmities, friendships, and alliances, and communities of nations such as the French community or the British Commonwealth which are held together by common sentiment, perhaps a common culture, rather than by any specific threat or even by exchange. There is, in addition, the weak but growing sense of world community as reflected in the international institutions and intangible but nevertheless real phenomenon, world public opinion.

An economist is tempted to look at the international system in terms of cost-benefit analysis. The main problem here is that, whereas the costs are tangible and easy to assess, the benefits are intangible and very hard to evaluate. The costs not only consist of the world war industry and the cost of diplomatic establishments, foreign offices, state departments, and so on, something over 150 billion dollars altogether, but should also include the insurance premiums which would theoretically be paid to cover the chance of damage in future wars both to life and to property. Our assessment of these will be highly subjective. It could well, however, be the same order of magnitude as the actual economic costs of the war industry, though in most actual wars it has usually cost the destroyer more to destroy something than the value of the thing destroyed. If we put 20 billion as the lower limit of potential war damage insurance, and perhaps 100 billion as the upper limit, this gives us a total annual cost of the international system of something like 200 billion dollars a year plus or minus, shall we say, 30 to 50 billion.

If this huge cost is to be justified in terms of benefit, an enormous value must be placed on the non-economic benefits of nationality, identity, patriotism and so on which keep the human race divided. These are real benefits, they could be estimated perhaps by asking what an individual would sacrifice in order not to have to change his culture. Thus the benefits of the international system are in proportion to the inability of individuals to adjust to different cultures. People in traditional cultures can hardly imagine themselves in any other type of society. They would rather die, literally, than be anything but what they are. As we move towards developed cultures the cost of culture change becomes less; migration becomes frequent; change of nationality becomes frequent and the benefits of the international system therefore diminish as people find it easier to adjust to culture change. It is quite reasonable to suppose that with increased education and mobility around the world the benefits of the international system will decline sharply and as its costs are tending to increase all the time at some point round about this period of human history the increasing costs are likely to intersect the falling benefits and the international system, in its present form, at any rate, will no longer be worth keeping up. Whether this point of time is in the past or in the future is very much a matter of opinion and will depend on our private assessment of the costs and benefits of the system.

Both the cost and the benefits of the international system are very much affected by its stability. This word really covers two different though related concepts. The first is stability in the sense of the capacity of the international system to maintain over time an existing distribution of territories and power. This might be called stability of the "map" or the existing structure of the international system. The second concept is stability in the sense of the capacity of the system for maintaining a stable peace even perhaps in the midst of territorial and power changes. Thus the international system might be quite unstable in the first sense with constantly shifting boundaries and power orders, but it might be able to accomplish these changes without breaking down into war, in which case it would have stable peace. This is unlikely but not inconceivable.

In the period of human history which is now coming to a close, which might be called the age of civilization, the international system has been very unstable in both meanings of the term. It has been characterized through most of its history by the almost continuous rise and fall of nations and empires, boundaries are continually shifted over the face of the earth, and relative power positions have seldom been maintained for very long. There have been certain periods of relative stability, such as the last 400 years of the Roman Empire in the west, and the corresponding Han period in China, but even these represent somewhat shifting islands of stability in a highly unstable total structure, and these stable periods also represent a fairly small proportion of the total time span. The average life expectancy of a nation or empire is certainly not more than a few hundred years. Similarly, over most of the age of civilization the international system rarely exhibits a stable peace.

Like all other systems, the international system exhibits phases, though these are not as sharply defined as, shall we say, are the phases of ice, liquid and steam in the case of water. It may exhibit stable war, as it did in the Indian subcontinent for many centuries, or in medieval Europe before the Truce of God or between Christianity and Islam over long periods. It may exhibit unstable war in which war is occasionally interrupted by periods of peace, but in which war is regarded as a normal state. This may pass almost imperceptibly into unstable peace in which peace is regarded as a norm and war as an interruption, and this may pass into stable peace in which the probability of war is so low as to be negligible. In the long pull, one can perceive a progression in these phases with, for instance, unstable peace gradually replacing unstable war, and with wider and wider areas of stable peace within states or even between them. It is the principal argument of this paper that there are good reasons to suppose that we are now approaching a critical phase boundary in the international system, in which we have a good chance of moving from unstable peace to stable peace over considerable parts of the world, though not perhaps in the near future over the total system. Certainly for the last 300 years the international system has been characterized by unstable peace. Peace has been regarded as a norm and war as an interruption, even though the actual periods of time spent in both states may have been about equal. Within this total system of unstable peace we have seen developing islands of stable peace, even within the international system itself, as well as inside the particular national states where stable peace has been maintained for long periods.

In the last 200 years we have seen developing a phenomenon which was very rare before then, that is, stable peace between nations in parts of the international system without much in the way of supranational organization. We see this for instance in North America, we see it in Scandinavia, we see it between the U.S. and the British complex, we see it perhaps within the Socialist camp, and there are even signs of this developing throughout all western Europe and between the U.S. and the Soviet Union. If this happens it will represent a subtle but very significant shift in the nature of the total international system from a system in which unstable peace is the norm with islands of stable peace to one where stable peace is the norm with islands of unstable peace in, say, Asia and Africa. From this it could be a relatively short step, as human history goes, to a world system of stable peace, though this may easily take a hundred years or more. Thus the world wars of the twentieth century may perhaps be seen in retrospect as the last agonies of an expiring system in spite of their size and destructiveness. Systems indeed, both in biological and social evolution, often achieve their greatest and most spectacular examples at the moment preceding their dissolution.

In order to justify this proposition that we are on the phase boundary between stable and unstable peace in the international system, a proposition which would seem outrageous to most people raised in conventional education to regard the age of civilization as a permanent state of affairs, we must point to two further propositions. The first is that the instability both of the international structure and of peace itself is essentially a characteristic of the age of civilization, that is, the phase of the total social system which is characterized by agriculture, food surplus from the food producer and an organized threat system or political power which is able to take the food surplus away from the food producer and with it to feed kings, priests, and their servants, artisans, and armies. War is endemic in a system of this kind for a number of reasons. The first is that the existence of what I have called "a loss of strength gradient" implies that the threat system of a particular center of power loses its credibility as one moves away from the center. This is a fundamental principle, incidentally, of all territoriality, even among animals. This means that a new center of power can establish itself at a certain critical distance from an old center, this distance depending on the loss of strength gradient itself, that is, on how much threat diminishes as we go away from the threatener. Once two such centers of power have been established, however, there comes to be what I have called a boundary of indifference between them at which their powers are approximately equal and the position of this boundary will be unstable, depending on the rise or fall in the relative power of the two parties. In a threat system, however, threats are only effective in producing change as long as they are credible, and their credibility tends to depreciate as time goes on. Credibility then has to be reestablished by carrying out a threat and this is usually done at some point at which existing boundaries have become obsolete. A challenge is made, and if it is not resisted the whole threat credibility of the challenged party will be destroyed. A challenge therefore makes it highly probable that both parties will have to carry out their threats towards each other.

Thus unstable peace is highly characteristic of a system of deterrence, that is, a system in which threats are not carried out in the short run because of counter threats ("If you do something nasty to me I will do something nasty to you."). Deterrence, however, in spite of the doctrine of the American Air Force, is inherently unstable simply because of the fact that threats cannot be credible if there is no chance of their being carried out. If, however, the chance of their being carried out is positive, if we wait long enough they will be carried out. Thus a system of nuclear deterrence inevitably implies a positive probability of nuclear war. Whether this probability is 5% per annum or 1% or 0.1% we do not really know. My own personal estimate is that it is somewhere between 1% and 5%. This may not seem very much in any one year but if we accumulate it for 100 years the chance of a nuclear war breaking out in this period is very great. In the long run, therefore, deterrence always breaks down and we must reckon the chance of enormous nuclear destruction as one of the real costs of the present international system.

It is easy to see why in the age of civilization war was endemic and unstable peace even verging towards unstable war a normal state of affairs. Few people, least of all historians, would be likely to dispute this proposition. What may be more disputed is the proposition that the age of civilization is now coming to an end and that we are going through a great transition into a new stage of man which I used to call post-civilization until I found that this frightened people, and which I now call "the developed society," the developed society being what the process of development carries us towards. That we are now going through a profound and quite unprecedented process of development can hardly be denied. The last hundred years especially have seen spectacular changes in man's capability. Just where this process is taking us and what the developed society looks like at the end of it is more open to question. I frankly do not know what this society looks like in detail because it is quite impossible to predict even material invention, never mind social invention, and it is highly probable that we will have a great deal of both before the process of development which we are passing through even begins to decelerate. It is becoming clear, however, that many of the characteristics of the total social system which gave rise to unstable peace in the age of civilization are now passing away and I have a good deal of confidence that the developed society, whatever it looks like, will be characterized by stable peace, whatever its other ecstasies or horrors. My conclusion is drawn from the observation mentioned earlier that the costs of the system of unstable peace are rising rapidly whereas its benefits are falling sharply, and that there is every prospect that both these processes will continue into the future.

The reason is that both these processes rest on a deeper underlying process which is the continuous and rapid rise in human knowledge and skill as a result of the development of science and the scientific subculture. This has an enormous impact in the first place on the economy and on the ability of man to produce goods and services. The real impact of science on the economy only begins about 1860 with the development of chemical industries, later the electrical industry, still later the nuclear and biological industries, which could not have existed without a previous base in the pure sciences. The so-called industrial revolution of the eighteenth century, incidentally, was prescientific, although science was rising in the middle of it; in the eighteenth century and even early nineteenth century it was technology that assisted the growth of science rather than the other way around. The steam-engine produced thermodynamics, but it was the physics of electricity that produced the electrical industry.

In societies that have been able to take advantage of this enormous development, which include most of the countries of the temperate zone right around the world, there has been an enormous increase in per capita output and income. This has not been derived from the exploitation of others but has been derived from the increase in internal productivity as a result of the application of scientific knowledge. Agriculture is one of the most spectacular examples of this process. Even a hundred years ago one farmer could hardly feed more than two families, and the United States, for instance, had more than 50% of its population in agriculture even as late as the late nineteenth century. Today, in developed societies, one farmer can easily feed twenty, and a good farmer one hundred families, and not only has the productivity of labor increased but the productivity of land has likewise increased, though not as spectacularly. The old economic reasons for war and conquest have therefore largely disappeared. In the modern world, if a country wants to get rich, it should stay home and mind its own business well. From the nineteenth century on—and perhaps even earlier—being a great power has been a cost rather than a revenue as the history of Great Britain and France and even more that of Portugal and Spain testify. Empire, in 1967, is how the colonies exploit the mother country. It is human resources which are dominant in the developmental process, not natural resources, and if human resources, and especially high-level human resources are wasted in war and imperial ambition they will not be available for domestic development. The economic lag of both Britain and France, for instance, from 1860 on is clearly due to this phenomenon. Countries like Sweden and the United States which from that time on put very little into the international system or into the military developed at a much more rapid rate than those countries which expended their blood and treasure on the establishment and maintenance of empire. As I have also said elsewhere, in the modern world we can get $10 out of nature for every $1 we can squeeze out of man.

The second phenomenon of development which has transformed the international system is the impact of science-based technology on weapons, and particularly on the range of the deadly missile. This is one of the major factors determining the loss of strength gradient in a military threat system and it has exhibited an almost constant increase from David's sling, to the medieval crossbow, to firearms, and now to the guided missile with a nuclear warhead. If we think of an army itself as a kind of human missile, its capacity to operate away from home also depends on the technology of transportation which has likewise been improving rapidly. For any given level of military technology there is some optimum or at least minimum size of the viable political unit which employs these methods. The city-state and the feudal baron were defensible against bows and arrows and spears, for walls and castles could keep them out. With the invention of gunpowder neither could survive in the military sense, although they may survive as social fossils like Monaco or San Marino, through sheer inertia and lag. The guided missile with the nuclear warhead has really done for the national state, even the largest national state, what gunpowder did for the feudal baron. It has destroyed its military viability and if the institution itself is to survive it will have to be profoundly transformed. Thus, after the invention of gunpowder, the feudal baron had to transform himself into a gentleman with an undefended manor house instead of a castle. Similarly, the survival of the national state in the modern world depends on its ability to organize disarmament, for in a world of armed deterrence it will surely be destroyed, simply because its cost of upkeep is so high and its returns in terms of human welfare are so low. In the next hundred years certainly the national state will only be able to retain its legitimacy by abandoning its threat capability. The same thing, we may notice, happened to the institution of the monarchy between the 17th and 19th centuries. The only monarchs who survived the loss of the viability of their threat system were the monarchs that transformed themselves into symbols of legitimacy as in Britain, the Netherlands and Scandinavia. The monarchs that tried to hang on to their power tended to lose not only their power but their heads.

It is fairly easy to see where we have to go. How to get there is the problem. It is the dynamics of the transition that bedevils us and there are reasons for both optimism and pessimism about it, pessimism certainly in the short run, optimism perhaps in the long run, if we can last that long.

It is easy to list a good many reasons for pessimism. The first is the fact that the image of the world and of the international system which most people have in their minds and especially the image which is held by those people in middle life who are the actual decision-makers of the international system, is based primarily on their knowledge and experience of the age of civilization. To people with this image of the world, which is largely engendered by all systems of formal education, the idea that stable peace can be achieved is so shocking that it seems either utopian or even downright immoral. Even the Bible says, after all, that there will be wars and rumors of wars, and the history books certainly confirm this. There is not therefore much clear realization of the extraordinary transition through which the world is passing and most of the decision-makers of the international system are still behaving as if we were still living in the nineteenth century. One can add to this a further note of pessimism in that most people in positions of power today are in their fifties or sixties and this generation was so deeply traumatized by the experiences of the 1920s and the 1930s in their youth that they are virtually incapable of any realistic appraisal of the international system. Thus in the United States what I have called the "Munich trauma" dominates the thinking of those who are responsible for the international system and makes most of them live in a world which has passed away.

Another obstacle to the development of stable peace is almost peculiar to the United States; it is the widespread folk belief that only a large military establishment nourished continually by the threat of war can preserve full employment. We still have a strong memory that it was Hitler that got us out of the great depression, and there is enough truth in this to make it seem plausible. This factor undoubtedly accounts for the hawkishness of the labor movement and the lukewarmness of the average American about disarmament. There is widespread agreement among economists that this image is quite unfounded. Indeed, anyone who believes seriously that the American economy cannot function effectively in the absence of a large war industry should be a Communist, for this would clearly represent a massive failure of the whole American system. In fact, however, the allegation is quite untrue as oddly enough the Communists themselves have recognized. The economic problems of adjustment to disarmament, while they are perfectly real, are by no means insuperable, and it is fairly easy to run this problem through the various models of the American economy and to see what would have to be done in detail in order to make this adjustment. Far from the war industry being a support to the American economy it is a millstone around its neck. It results in an internal brain drain into the space-military complex of very large dimensions which is seriously crippling the future development of

basic and civilian industries. If furthermore we contrast the structure of the American economy, say in 1929, and today, we find that
the 10% of the gross national product which was represented by the
military, which was only 1% in 1929, comes almost wholly out of
personal consumption so that as consumers we are actually almost
15% worse off than we would be if there were no war industry.

A third source of pessimism is the technical difficulty involved in
negotiating an agreed process of mutual disarmament which leaves
the relative power structure sufficiently unchanged to retain confidence in the process itself. This is partly a matter of the dynamics of
the total system and partly a matter of skills in negotiation and
international agreement. The problem of the general equilibrium of
an international system based on military threat can be illustrated by
the following simple model, which derives essentially from Lewis
Richardson.

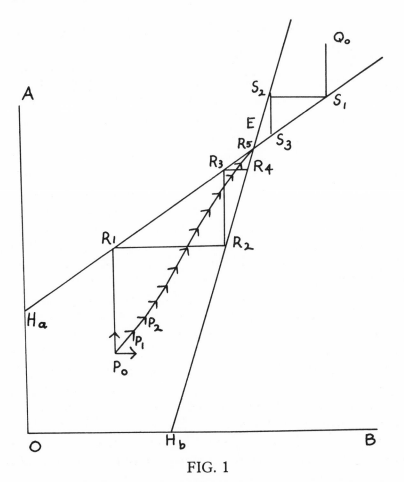

FIG. 1

Let us assume a bipolar system with only two powers, A and B, and suppose that we can express the size of the military system of each by a single magnitude, as measured shall we say in dollar terms. We will suppose also that each perceives the military system of the other to be what it "is," that is, that each country or the decision-makers thereof has an identical image of the total system. We can then postulate partial equilibrium functions represented by the two curves in Figure 1. Here we measure the size of A's military establishment or threat system along OA and B's along OB. The line H_aE is A's particular equilibrium curve showing the equilibrium size of A's military establishment, at which A will feel comfortable, for each size of B's establishment. H_bE is the corresponding curve for B. If these curves intersect as at E this will be an equilibrium position for the system as a whole. In the case of the diagram it is a stable equilibrium and the system will move towards it eventually from any point in the field. Suppose for instance that we were at a position such as P_0, both A and B will feel threatened and wish to increase their forces in the direction of the arrows as shown, the resultant movement will carry us to P_1, then to P_2, and so on until we reach equilibrium at E. This is the essential dynamics of an arms race. If we suppose as an extreme case that each country moves alternately to its position of partial equilibrium the system will move along the line $P_0R_1R_2R_3R_4R_5$ etc. again ending at E. If now we start with an initial position such as Q_0 above the position of equilibrium we will have a "disarmament race" following a path such as $Q_0S_1S_2S_3$ etc. In the international system disarmament races are rare, although they are not unknown, mainly because whatever equilibrium there is is usually approached from below. In many cases, furthermore, there is no equilibrium at all. The lines H_aE, H_bE do not intersect and the system explodes until it reaches some kind of a boundary in war, which is likely to result in a radical change of the system, perhaps with the disappearance of one of the parties.

If now we want to achieve a disarmament, that is, movement of the position of equilibrium E towards the origin at O we must be able to manipulate the parameters of the system, that is, the position of the partial equilibrium curve H_aE and H_bE. If these curves are linear they can be expressed in terms of two parameters. The first might be called the initial hostility or initial militarism of the parties as represented by the intercept on the corresponding axis, such as OH_a for A or OH_b for B. This is the size of the armed force which each party would have even in the absence of any armed force of the other party. The other parameter is the slope of the lines which represents the reactivity of the two countries, that is, how much each will increase its armed force for each unit increase of the armed force of the other. In order to have any position of equilibrium at all, the reactivities must be less than one, that is, an increase in the dollar of one armed force must produce an increase of less than a dollar in the other. Insofar as the reactivity of unity might be regarded as normal ("a dollar of ours for a dollar of theirs"), the chances for stability even in a bilateral system would not seem to be very high unless the countries are abnormally unreactive.

The problem of disarmament in the absence of agreement on overarching international order or world government is how to reduce both the initial hostilities and the reactivities of the countries concerned. There are several possible avenues towards this end. One is the deliberate cultivation of friendly relations through cultural exchange, reassuring speeches and so on. This will tend to lower both initial hostilities and reactivity, as an increase in the armed force of one will be perceived as less of a threat by the other and is hence less likely to result in corresponding increase. Another possibility to which surprisingly little thought has been given has been the development of a differentiation between threat, counter threat and defensiveness in terms of both capability and credibility. Thus if A feels himself to be threatened by B he may have three options or a mixture of all three. He may increase his own threat to B. This is simple deterrence, and as suggested above it is always unstable in the long run. This means simply that A increases his capability of doing damage to B unconditionally and as presumably B is aware of this, then A's increased threat is credible. There is a loose connection in fact between capability and credibility, partly because of the sheer difficulties of the information system in this regard of knowing what capability people actually have and in the second place there is a psychological problem of whether people have the will to use capability. A rough distinction can nevertheless be made between a decision to increase unconditional threat and a decision to increase conditional threat, that is, counter threat. Counter threat would be a capability of A to do damage to B only in the event of B doing damage to A. The technology of counter threat, however, is very little developed, mainly because it is much easier to develop systems of unconditional threat and also because where the system is not regarded as a totality and where decision-makers operate solely from the point of view of short-run national interest, unconditional threat is usually preferred, as giving apparently greater power. The third possibility is defensiveness, which means A reducing the capability of B to inflict damage upon him. In military technology the distinction among these three types of decision is very fuzzy and the term "defense" is usually extended to mean all three. From the point of view of the stability of the international system, however, there is much to be said for a policy which concentrates on the second and third of these possibilities and excludes the first altogether. This will unquestionably have the result of diminishing the reactivity of the nations and would bring down the equilibrium of the system towards disarmament.[1]

Agreement on disarmament is likely to be difficult to arrive at, and unstable even when achieved, unless it goes hand in hand with a shift in the equilibrium of the threat system towards lower levels. Such agreement, however, may in itself be a method of achieving a change in the equilibrium, simply because the very existence of armaments increases hostility and reactivity. Hence, if the system could ever get down to zero, there is a good chance it would stay there, and there are many historical examples of the stability of total disarmament. Personal disarmament is one such example, which was achieved not so much by agreement as by unilateral behavior. Canadian-American relations are a good example of stable disarmament achieved by agreement. On the other hand, there have also been examples where agreed disarmaments have not been stable, like the Washington Naval Agreement of 1922. We always have to look at disarmament as a constituent of a total system, and whether it will be successful or not depends very largely on the nature of the system in which it is imbedded.

Another problem of achieving disarmament might be described in terms of the "frictions" of the system. A system might, for instance, be at Q_0 in Figure 1 but would not move towards disarmament simply because of inertia, habit and social frictions. The pressures for movement and decision in society have to be of a certain

---

[1] For fuller explanation of this model see K. E. Boulding, *Conflict and Defense* (New York: Harper and Row, Publishers, 1962), and "The Parameters of Politics," *University of Illinois Bulletin*, LXIII, 139 (July 15, 1966), 3-21, and in this volume, Chapter 18.

magnitude before they can overcome the resistances. These resistances are likely to be larger the longer the system has been in
existence in its present phase so that everybody is habituated to it;
they are likely to be larger also if the change involves a good deal of
uncertainty. In an uncertain world we tend to cling to the familiar,
and the present international system, difficult and dangerous as it is,
at least carries the illusion that it is familiar, although in fact it is
not. Frequently it requires a new generation to overcome these
inertias. The new broom not only sweeps clean, it sweeps, whereas
the old broom all too often stays in the corner.

It is hard not to be somewhat pessimistic as one looks at the
obstacles towards the establishment of stable peace and the appalling
penalties of failing to establish it. Nevertheless, the outlook, especially the long-run outlook, is by no means wholly dark, and while a
prophet indulges in cheerfulness at his peril, it would be unfair to
conclude this brief summary without at least a glance at the more
favorable omens. Something which is favorable even in the short or
medium run is the fact that there seems to be a fairly small
probability in the next 25 or even 50 years of major reversals in the
power order of the principal actors in the international system.
Perhaps the most important long-run cause of instability in the
structure of the international system is differences in the relative rate
of economic growth on the part of different countries and political
constellations. The last 200 years have seen constant and rapid
change in the relative position of nations, in terms, for instance, of
such measures as their gross national product, simply because there
have been long-run differences in the rates of economic development. Statistics of these matters do not go back much earlier than
the mid-nineteenth century and reliable statistics not much before
1929, but one might hazard a guess that in terms of gross national
product in, shall we say, 1700, China would be at the top, France
perhaps second, England third, perhaps Russia fourth, Spain fifth,
though all this is mere conjecture. What is certain is that the U.S.,
Germany and Italy were nowhere simply because they did not exist
as actors in the international system. In the course of 250 years we
have seen the U.S. rise from insignificance to far and away the top
position; Germany outstripped France in the 19th century once it
had been unified, Britain probably outstripped France in the 18th
century and early 19th century, China stagnated or even declined,

Russia increased from the end of the 19th century so that today the
order reads approximately as follows, with gross national product in
billions of dollars as of 1957:

U.S.	443
U.S.S.R.	122
United Kingdom	61
West Germany	50
Peoples Republic of China	46
France	42
Canada	33
India	29
Japan	28
Italy	25
Brazil	18
Poland	13
Australia	13
Indonesia	11
Belgium	11
Sweden	10

This particular order is unlikely to change significantly certainly
for 25 years. The Soviet Union is certainly not going to overtake the
U.S. in this period. The relative position of the United Kingdom
may decline and indeed has already done so, for West Germany has
now overtaken it but this is probably not enough to upset the
equilibrium in Europe. The Peoples Republic of China may move
to third place, although if it continues its present upheavals it may
not. Japan is likely to move up rapidly but this again will probably
not upset the equilibrium of the international system. The gross
national product, of course, is a very imperfect measure of power in
the international system, although it is better than nothing and the
order of gross national product is certainly a rough measure of
national power. The present pattern therefore of the U.S. as the
greatest power with three times the gross national product of the
Soviet Union in the second place and the Soviet Union again with
two or three times the gross national product of whatever power
occupies the third place is a pattern that is likely to persist certainly
for one generation or perhaps even for two, short, of course, of
nuclear war itself, or of unforeseen catastrophes. The one thing
which might upset this picture is confederation, especially a confederation of Europe, which unitedly now has a gross national product

of about the same order of magnitude as the U.S. and twice that of the Soviet Union. This, however, does not seem to be very probable. It is quite reasonable, therefore, to suppose that the two World Wars of the twentieth century were the result of a period of very remarkable instability in the structure of the international system marked in the first place by the meteoric rise of the U.S. in the world, and in the second place by the rise of Germany in Europe.

Whenever there is what may be called an "overtake point" at which one country overtakes another in its wealth or power, the existing international order is likely to be challenged, and the danger of war rises severely. The danger is particularly acute when one country surpasses another in a particular region and yet another country surpasses all others in the world as a whole. Thus we may perhaps interpret the Napoleonic wars as reflecting the rise of the power of France relative to other continental states throughout the eighteenth century and the rise of the power of England relative to France in the world as a whole. The world wars of the twentieth century might be similarly interpreted in regard to the rise of Germany in Europe and the U.S. in the world. One does not, of course, have to be a determinist in these matters, but we can regard an overtake period as increasing the probability of war. Whether war actually breaks out depends to some extent on fortuitous factors such as the rise of a charismatic individual, such as Napoleon or Hitler. There have been cases, indeed, where we have had overtake periods without war, of which perhaps the best example is the relations of the United States with Great Britain. Anybody looking at the world in 1815 might have argued with a good deal of confidence that there would have to be a great war between Britain and the U.S. in order to decide who would be top dog. In fact this did not happen and by a series of almost accidental lucky events such as the Rush-Bagot agreement of 1817 and the gradual settlement of the Canadian frontier stable peace was slowly established and the British accepted an inferior power position with astonishing realism and good grace. What it was, however, that made the British realistic and the Germans unrealistic I do not pretend to know. What does give one a little confidence in the future, however, is the reflection that the 150 or 200 years through which we have just passed have been a period in which the strains of the international system have been gigantic and it is not surprising therefore that it has been so often convulsed by war. The period that lies ahead looks like much quieter water from the point of view of the strains, though of course one can always be surprised by unexpected combinations and new constellations of power. In another 100 years, of course, the situation may look very different. There may be a United Latin America to challenge the United States. China may have emerged from its difficulties and again may challenge the United States. Certainly it may challenge the Soviet Union. The spectacular economic rise of Japan may pose difficulties if its present irenic and rational mood does not last. Nevertheless a prediction of calmer waters ahead than behind seems not unreasonable at this time and this is perhaps one of the major sources of hope for the human race, that we may have a period of reduced strain in which we can build up the organizations which can cope with strain when it reappears.

A final source for long-run optimism is that man is after all a learning animal, capable indeed of very rapid rates of learning. The problem of establishing stable peace is essentially a problem in human learning: the learning of realistic images of the world and the learning of values which make for survival rather than for destruction. Learning, even in perception, moves towards the payoffs. Our image of the world is what it is mainly because it pays us to see it this way. The payoffs to stable peace are so enormous that it is hard to believe that there is not a very long steady trend towards learning how to do it. The way is littered with the debris of old avalanches from the mountains of the past and there is a very real probability that we will not succeed in finding it. Nevertheless the chance of success is not zero, and it may be a higher number than many of us now think. To the task of raising that number—and hoping for luck or providence to keep the black ball in the bag until it can be eliminated—I commend us all, for there is surely no greater task which confronts the human race at this particular moment of its history.

THE BALANCE OF PEACE

In: *Papers,* Peace Research Society
(International), Vol. XIII,
1970, pp. 59-65

THE BALANCE OF PEACE

The thesis of this paper is that a national policy for stable peace is possible, that we do not have such a policy now, and that the main engine of such a policy is the development of the proper balance or proportion between three different kinds of power—threat power, exchange power and integrative power.

The international system, like all systems, can exhibit a number of phases. It is only a slight oversimplification to suppose that between two nations we can always identify whether a state of war or a state of peace exists between them. In the relations of any two nations then we can distinguish four phases: 1) stable war, in which peace is virtually nonexistent; 2) unstable war, in which war is interrupted by periods of peace; 3) unstable peace, in which peace is interrupted by periods of war; and 4) stable peace, in which war is virtually nonexistent. Different parts of the system may exhibit all four of these phases at different times. Thus, we have something like stable war in Vietnam. We have something like unstable war in the Middle East, where at least some of the parties think of war as the "norm" and peace as an interlude. Most of the international system today is in unstable peace. We have, however, developed islands of stable peace in North America and Scandinavia where the probability of war between the countries concerned is so low as to be insignificant. Development in the international system may almost be defined as the process by which we pass from stable war to stable peace. This is a long precarious learning process with many setbacks. In the past, like economic development, it has happened largely by accident, without explicit policy. Today, just as we have policies for economic development, it should now be possible to have policies for developmental processes toward stable peace. These we do not have largely because of the absence of any image that these processes are possible. Virtually all nations today in the field of unstable peace are aware that this is a highly dangerous, and indeed an untenable, system in the nuclear age, yet they have no clear policy for getting out of it.

Part of the failure of the imagination here originates in a failure to realize that there are at least three kinds of power, and that the phase of the international system, whether it is, for instance, in unstable peace or stable peace, depends very much on the proportions of resources devoted to the use of these three kinds of power.

The first kind of power, and the most obvious one, is threat power. This represents the capability for producing "bads," that is, negative goods for some other party, "the enemy." Military organizations in these days are primarily devoted to the production of threat capability. There is another use for military organization, which is conquest, which is very close to theft, that is, the removals of goods from one ownership to another without consent of the owner, but in the modern world this is rare and most military organization is concerned with creating threat credibility in the hope of affecting the behavior of others through threat. Threat power has been important historically in organizing social systems, but has had a limited horizon of development. In the modern world it tends to collapse into deterrence, that is, a threat-counterthreat system which is very costly to both sides, largely ineffective in achieving any positive ends, and also dangerously unstable. The idea that deterrence can be stable is a total illusion, for if deterrence were stable it would cease to deter, that is, there must be a positive probability of threats being carried out or they will cease to be credible and will cease to affect behavior. A system of deterrence, therefore, is a system under indeterminant sentence of death. We do not know when deterrence will break down, but we are sure that it must break down sometime.

The second kind of power, exchange power, arises because of man's capacity for producing things which other people want and to exchange these for things that he wants. This of course is economics. Exchange is a very powerful social organizer. Whereas the threat system has a low horizon of development, that is, it goes so far and then becomes trapped in its own increasing costs, the exchange system has a very wide horizon of development which we have still not reached. In the international system exchange power may be used in part as a substitute for threat. Tribute, for instance, may be cheaper than defense under certain circumstances, and in the world this is increasingly likely to be the case, with the rise in the cost of defense and a possibly falling cost of tribute.

The third type of power, integrative power, is harder to recognize. It is so invisible, indeed, I have had to invent a name for it. In the long-run, however, it may turn out to be the most important kind of power in the social system. This is the kind of power, for instance, which a child has over his parents, and which will induce them to sacrifice for their child. It is the kind of power which arises because of people's concepts of community and identity. A person or a group acquires integrative power because of their position in some generally accepted structure of community, whether this is a family, a church, a nation, or a world. Up to now, integrative power in the international community has been very weak. This type of power, however, is something which is bound to develop as the sense of the community of mankind grows, especially under the impact of the space age. The concept of earth as we see it from space as a beautiful little spaceship, clothed in the everchanging mantle of the atmosphere, with a crowded crew and limited resources is bound to have an enormous impact on man's image of his world and of himself, and this in turn will have a profound impact on the international system.

What phase the international system will be in depends very much on the proportion of resources devoted to these three kinds of power. In stable war, everything is devoted to the threat system, there is no exchange system, no trade, and no sense of community. In unstable war, as we have it in the Middle East, the intervals of peace develop because of the necessity for developing exchange power, even as an adjunct to a threat system. We cannot produce "bads" unless we can produce "goods." In this phase, however, the sense of community is negative and there is high active malevolence between societies, so there is no integrative power at all. The movement into unstable peace takes place almost imperceptibly through the growth of exchange and perhaps certain growth of a sense of community. Exchange pays off so much better than threat that the exchange system tends to grow at the expense of the threat system. As it grows and as the sense of community grows, we begin to perceive war as an interruption or breakdown of the normal system, which is peace. This system has characterized a large part of the world for at least the last two or three hundred years. Stable peace is separated from unstable peace by a "phase boundary" which is not easy to cross. As the sense of community grows, however, nations begin to take as a feature of their own national interest the preservation of other nations, that is, we begin to get the first beginnings of benevolence in the international system. When this rises to a certain point, the threat system becomes virtually obsolete and plans for invasion gather dust in the files of war offices.

Up to now the international system has exhibited a dynamic which has been largely independent of conscious policy. The transition from one phase to another has been achieved either by a long slow cumulative learning process by which men have learned what kind of actions pay off and what kind do not and partly by sheer accident and the occasional accumulation of random processes. Thus, the achievement of stable peace in North America, for instance, was partly the result of a succession of rather lucky accidents—the Rush-Bagot Agreement of 1817, the settlement of the Canadian border in 1839, the fact that the British did not intervene in the American Civil War and so on. Each of these may have had a fairly low probability, but the dice somehow fell on the right numbers and stable peace was achieved.

If now we are to have a conscious policy for stable peace on the part of any nation, its decisions in regard to the international system must have the following properties: in the first place, any decision involves a range of alternatives and it must be possible to rank these alternatives in the order of their value in achieving stable peace. For this to be possible there must be an image in the mind of the decision-maker of a model of the international system in which movement in the direction of stable peace can be defined. That is to say, from any given position in the system, the decision-maker must define a movement towards stable peace as "up" and he must know which way is "up" and which out of a range of possible decisions has the highest value in terms, shall we say, of its probability of moving the system in the upward direction. These are no easy conditions to fulfill, and it is not surprising that up to now no nation has had a very successful conscious policy for stable peace, even though the desire for peace is professed by nearly everybody.

One of the great problems here is the absence of useful models of the international system and the absence of measurement by which the models can be given substance. We may point to the analogy here with unemployment policy, which

up to the last generation was remarkably unsuccessful and in the present generation has been much more successful simply because of the development of a relatively
simple theoretical model plus the development of a measurement system which
could clothe the model with real numbers. The difficulties of measurement, and
indeed of information collection, are much greater in the international system
than they are in the economic system. Nevertheless, it would be the height of
folly to assume that the peak of human achievement in this regard had already
been reached.

A complete model of the system involving the three variables outlined above
would be extremely complicated, but Figure 1 illustrates the nature of the problem.
Any point within the triangle XYZ represents a certain division of the system
between the three elements. If X represents 100 per cent Exchange, Y, 100 per cent
Integration, and Z, 100 per cent Threat, then a point such as P represents PT per cent
Threat, PI per cent Integration, and PE per cent Exchange, where PI is drawn
parallel to XY and the other lines accordingly. We can divide this triangle into
areas corresponding to our four phases. I have suggested the phase boundaries
CC', between Stable and Unstable War, BB', between Unstable War and Unstable
Peace, and AA', between Unstable Peace and Stable Peace. As we we move towards 100 per cent Threat at Z, we are more likely to get stable war; as we move
towards 100 per cent Integration, Y, we are more likely to get stable peace. Exchange may be rather neutral in this regard, but in the diagram we have suggested
that it is more inclined to stable peace than stable war. The actual phase boun-

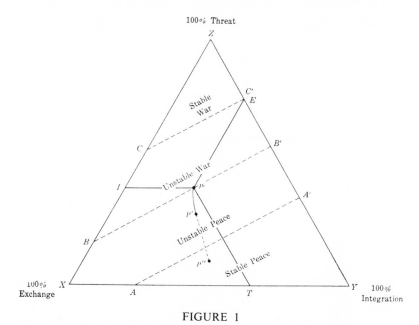

FIGURE 1

daries, of course, remain very much a matter of conjecture.

The critical question now, of course, is the dynamics of the system. Suppose we are at the point P; which way will it move? This depends partly on the internal dynamic of each system. There is some tendency for an internal dynamic of each separate system towards expansion and the overall result, of course, depends on which system predominates. If the threat system has reached something of an equilibrium, there may be a tendency for exchange and integration to increase absolutely, in which case threats will diminish proportionately and we may move, for instance, from P to P'. It is not at all absurd to visualize a long-run dymamic of the system in which the exchange and integration elements gain at the expense of threat, and eventually the system crosses the phase boundary into stable peace, shall we say, at P', with only a small amount of threat and relatively large amounts of exchange and integration.

The question of policy now becomes whether conscious intervention can affect the dynamics of a system of this kind. Unfortunately, such dynamic systems are extemely complicated and may not be at all well behaved mathematically, that is, they may exhibit sharp discontinuities and all sorts of odd mathematical properties. If the phase boundaries turned out to be roughly parallel to the line XY, we could simplify the system substantially by reducing it to two variables by amalgamating the exchange and the integrative aspects of it under a single factor, which we might call the X factor. We can then represent the state of the system by a point on a simple Cartesian field, as in Figure 2. Here we measure the threat factor, T, vertically and the X factor horizontally, X representing some kind of amalgamation of what might be called the "non-threat factors." We can then suppose that the rate of change of each factor per unit of time is a function of the quantities of the factors at that point. We can then suppose a series of contours, such as T_1T_2, such that all the points on each of the contours represent a combination of T and X for which the rate of change of T, dT is a constant. If we suppose that line T_1T_2 is the contour $dT = 0$, then for all points above and to the right

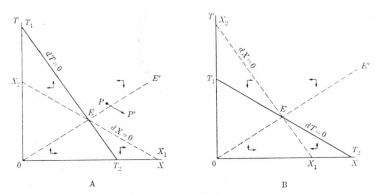

FIGURE 2

of this we may suppose dT is negative, that is, the total resources devoted to threat will decline, and, for all points below and to the left of it, dT will be positive, and the threat system will increase. Similarly, the dotted line, X_1X_2, is the contour $dX = 0$, out of the family of contours representing a constant dX. dX then will be negative above and to the right of the line X_1X_2 and positive below and to the left of this line.

If now we look at the total dynamics of this system we see that in Figure 2A the point E where lines T_1T_2 and X_1X_2 intersect is a point of unstable equilibrium. In the area bounded by X_1ET_2, both T and X will increase and there will be a movement towards the line X_1ET_2. Similarly, above and to the right of the line T_1EX_2, both X and T will diminish and there will be a movement towards the line T_1EX_2. Within the triangle T_1EX_2, however, X will increase and T will diminish, and if this goes on long enough the system will move to the point X_1. Similarly, in the area X_1ET_2, T will increase and X will diminish, and the system will move towards T_1. What this means is that there is some boundary line, such as OEE', which represents an unstable equilibrium in which the system will move towards E, but that from any point below and to the right of this line, the system will move to all integration at X_1. At any point above and to the left of this line, the system will move to all threats at T_1. That this kind of dynamic is not altogether fanciful is reflected in the fact that some segments of the international system have in fact moved into stable peace, which would be the case at X, and some have moved into stable war, which would be the case at T_1. If now the parameters of the system are rather different, as in Figure 2B, where the curves have the same meaning as in Figure 2A but are placed somewhat differently, we see here that there is a stable equilibrium at the point of intersection E which might very well lie in the phase of unstable peace, depending, of course, on exactly where the phase boundaries are. The stability of the phase of unstable peace in a large part of the international system for a considerable time is evidence also of the possible realism of this model.[1]

What these non-threat elements will be will differ, of course, from country to country. They may involve, for instance, support of international institutions, international law, the acceptance of treaty obligations, the acceptance of international conventions and so on. It may mean an increase in cultural exchange,

---

[1] The assumption on which the functions of Figure 2 have been drawn is that dT and dX are related to T and X by the following equations:

$$dT = t - aT - bX \tag{1}$$
$$dX = x - cT - dX \tag{2}$$

The assumption here is that the rate of increase of the threat system will be smaller the larger are both the threat element and the integrative element, and the same assumption is made for the rate of increase in the integrative element. This seems not intrinsically unreasonable. On the other hand, possible reversal of the sign of these parameters cannot be excluded. There is no need, of course, to assume that the functions are linear, though if they diverge very much from linearity peculiar mathematical situations may arise. If we suppose, incidentally, that dT is also a function of dX, and dX of dT, that is, that the rate of change of one element depends on the rate of change of the other, which again is not wholly implausible, enormous mathematical complications open up and the system becomes very peculiar, indeed, with possibilities of real breakdown. We cannot stop at this point, however, to explore these complications.

in all those elements of the international system which have only been developing really in the last hundred years, but which do constitute non-threat elements in the system. It may mean greater support of efforts for disarmament on the other side. One of the important conclusions of this type of analysis, indeed, is that the movement towards stable peace is most likely to be successful when it involves a combination of reduction in the threat element and increase in the non-threat element rather than through any one of these alone.

The conclusion of all this argument is that national policies for stable peace are possible, but in the present state of knowledge are not easy, but that the search for these policies, and especially for an information and theoretical system which can support them, is one of the highest priorities of the human race and one of the greatest tasks of peace research.

CAN THERE BE A NATIONAL POLICY FOR STABLE PEACE?

AAUW Journal, 63, 4 (May 1970): 172-174

Can There Be a National Policy for Stable Peace?

□ Almost every political leader affirms frequently his attachment to peace. Today few people believe war is more than a very high and disagreeable cost of the present international system. Nevertheless, war industry now costs the world about $200 billion a year. Even though most of the world is at peace, war is always being waged somewhere on the globe. No one can have any confidence that peace is stable. This contrast between the professed objectives of statesmen and their achievements is very striking. One suspects this is because there is no clear view as to how stable peace might be achieved. Or even what it is. Our statesmen want peace in very much the same sense that they want a fine day for a picnic. It is a good thing if it comes along, although nobody believes one can really have a policy about it.

The first step toward a policy for stable peace is an understanding of what it is and the belief that it is possible. *Stable peace is possible because it already exists.* For at least a hundred years, perhaps longer, the international system, while it has been characterized by unstable peace breaking down occasionally into war, has had imbedded within it islands of stability. North America since about 1870 is an example. So is Scandinavia, since 1815. Today all of Western Europe may be close to stable peace, though not quite over the line. Stable peace is a well defined condition of international relations between two or more countries in which the threat of armed intervention becomes a negligible factor in the relationship, and in which the armed forces of the various countries cease to have active plans for the invasion of the others.

These islands of stable peace have been achieved largely by accident, by good luck rather than by good management. In the case of North America, especially regarding relations between the United States and Canada and the British complex, the "doves" won over the "hawks" on three or four occasions. The Rush-Bagot agreement of 1817 achieved a partial and incomplete disarmament of the Great Lakes frontier. The United States did not get 54-40 and did not fight. The British did not intervene in the American Civil War. And after decades of a succession of what might almost be regarded as lucky accidents of this kind, the disarmed frontier became a habit. This may be attributed in part to a realistic adjustment by the British complex to the rising power of the United States and to the fact that the United States was so busy with westward expansion that the absorption of Canada did not seem worth the trouble. Whatever the underlying factors, and no doubt they are complex, the fact remains that a long historical process took place which eventually resulted in stable peace.

A similar process seems to have taken place in Scandinavia, culminating in a peaceful separation of Norway and Sweden in 1904. This may stand out eventually as one of the most important events of the 20th century, representing a type of maturity in international relations which ought to be the model for the future and which was indeed a partial model for the peaceful liquidation of the great colonial empires in the last 20 years.

Islands of Peace

Almost the only source of optimism for the future of the human race is that a learning process does go on in history and occasionally we learn the right things. The world may now be close to a very fundamental change in the international system, a change which has not been consciously planned. Until now we have had an international system of unstable peace

with islands of stable peace. As these islands grow larger, we may soon find that we have a reversal of the pattern: a world with islands of unstable peace in a general framework of stable peace. There now is a good chance we might achieve stable peace on the North American and Scandinavian pattern around the whole belt of the Temperate Zone including North America, all of Europe, the Soviet Union and Japan, as well as many outlying areas in the Southern Hemisphere. We may still have islands of unstable peace in Asia and Africa and even Latin America for some time to come, but if these can be contained, so that wars, when they occur, are local, it may turn out that the two world wars of the 20th century will be seen as death-struggles of an old system, unique events which are never likely to be repeated.

A number of factors have brought about the potentiality for this change. The most important, perhaps, is the sheer rise of science-based technology. This has had two impacts. First, it has enormously diminished the value of threats as a way of getting rich. Before the rise of science, imperialism allowed some people to become wealthy by exploiting others. But after the rise of science, the exploitation of man became obsolete simply because the exploitation of nature pays off so much better. The second impact of science-based technology has been caused by the development of the nuclear weapon and the missile with a world wide range. This has outmoded unilateral national military defense and is forcing us into a system of multilateral defense in which everybody, in effect, defends everybody else.

Frontiers Taken Off Agenda

The processes by which stable peace have been achieved in the past are not well understood; nevertheless, they clearly involve learning new kinds of international behavior by trial and response as well as processes involving formal agreements and treaties. The first requirement of stable peace is an understanding on the part of countries concerned that frontiers are to be taken off the agenda except for mutually agreeable adjustments. The main purpose of threats and armed forces in the past has been to achieve frontier adjustments. If this is no longer regarded as legitimate, the major reason for armaments and for war disappears.

I am not sure any country has had a conscious policy of maintaining stable peace with its neighbors, although perhaps Sweden comes as close to this as any. Sweden has not, it should be

noted, disarmed; a fairly high proportion of its total product is still in the war industry. It does not, however, seem to plan to use its armaments except in case of actual invasion. This would suggest another condition which would make stable peace much easier: a general agreement that all armed forces will be kept at home on the soil of the country which they are supposed to defend.

The probability of stable peace has been increased considerably by the fact that as a result of the two world wars, most frontiers, especially in the Temperate Zone, now correspond roughly with cultural frontiers and most nations in that zone are fairly homogeneous culturally. Almost the only major place in Europe where national frontiers and cultural frontiers do not coincide is in the Tyrol, where the Italian Tyrol is still very largely Austrian in culture. A boundary adjustment there would remove one of the last remaining obstacles to a general settlement of international boundaries in Europe. In Africa, on the other hand, most boundaries are quite arbitrary. Many of them are a result of ill-formed and amateurish decisions like those made in Berlin in 1878, and do not correspond at all to cultural boundaries. This is a potential source of serious conflict if machinery is not soon devised to handle it. In Asia there are countries like Thailand where the national boundary at many points does not correspond to cultural boundaries. The boundary between China and the Soviet Union presents serious problems. In Eastern Europe also there are some problems of this kind such as Hungarians in Rumania, Albanians in Yugoslavia and Macedonians scattered between three countries. These problems for some reason do not seem so serious in the socialist camp.

What Can One Country Do?

A very important question is how far a unilateral policy directed toward achieving stable peace is possible. There are obvious limits to what one country can do, for in effect every major country has a veto power in the matter of peace. Nevertheless, a single country can do a great deal toward setting in motion a general process in the international system which will increase the probability of stable peace. In the last 15 years, Khrushchev's doctrine of peaceful co-existence was envisaged as a unilateral attempt in the direction of stable peace. It did not fulfill all the conditions, expecially in regard to non-intervention. It has produced, however, a favorable reaction on the part of the United States and other countries, and resulted in a substantial easing of international tension between the Soviet Union and the West, though not in Asia. The United States has tended to be passive in this matter as it has been passing through a highly militaristic phase of its history, as a result perhaps of its experiences of disarmament and disillusionment after both world wars.

Phasing is one of the greatest problems. If a peaceful phase in one country coincides with a militant phase in another, the militancy in the second seems more likely to produce militancy in the first than the peacefulness in the second. If, however, two peaceful phases coincide, the chance of a dynamic leading to stable peace is much better. Perhaps it was fortunate that Khrushchev and Eisenhower were contemporaneous.

The real key to the movement toward stable peace at the moment lies in Europe rather than in Asia. All that is really required is a mutual agreement to take boundaries off the agenda for at least 25 years. During this time we may hope growth of the world community, and especially of the European community, may proceed to the point where disputes can be settled judicially rather than by violence. The crucial problem, of course, is that of Germany. For the sake of the peace of Europe, the Germans must renounce all claims on present Polish territories and they must agree to postpone the problem of reunification for at least a generation. This would not preclude cooperation of the two Germanys, for instance, for mutual diplomatic services, economic agreements and transportation. In any event, a formal union of the two Germanys at this time seems to be out of the question since neither, one suspects, really wishes to give up its identity. On the other hand, the sentimental forces for union might be satisfied by the kind of joint operations and agreements which could open up in the next few years. Just as the Berlin Wall in a sense made the whole problem of Berlin easier because it defined it sharply, so an agreement to stabilize existing boundaries would make it much easier to manage the conflict between the two Germanys. If each could be given security, each might bargain toward unity.

Another condition for a settlement in Europe is some sort of agreement or understanding between NATO and the Warsaw Pact countries. If the German conflict can be managed successfully, there seems no insuperable reason why a wider agreement cannot be achieved, again on the basis of respecting existing frontiers and an understanding of mutual security. The most difficult problems may actually come from within the Soviet Union which, along with Portugal, is the last remaining colonial empire and in which the pressures for independence for the Baltic countries and even the central Asian countries will become stronger in the next generation, simply because of the logic of comparison—if Poland can be an independent socialist country within the United Nations, why cannot Lithuania which has at least a history as ancient and a culture as distinct? In the next 25 or 50 years, we may need machinery to help these countries obtain independence without fundamentally threatening the Russians themselves. Russia would actually gain from the break-up of the Soviet Union just as the British and the French have gained from the break-up of their old empires.

Also in the Interest of Peace

The symbol of the achievement of stable peace is disarmament. The very fact both the United States and the Soviet Union have asserted that general and complete disarmament is their long-run policy is evidence that stable peace is at least regarded as the long-term ideal even if there is no clear understanding of the dynamic process by which we can get there. The formation of the United States Arms Control and Disarmament Agency was an important step forward even though the agency itself has been rather weak. It represents a pressure group within the government toward thinking about disarmament. A great deal more work needs to be done, however, on the technical problems which are involved in the social dynamics of disarmament: that is, the process within the social system by which disarmament actually comes about. There is no reason why the United States, together with whatever countries it could enlist, could not present the UN with a substantial sum of money to establish a UN arms control and disarmament agency for serious technical work on this problem.

The United States could also do a great deal in a more self-conscious way toward long-run improvement of the international climate through such things as cultural exchange and a greatly increased use of the international agencies on both world and regional levels for joint undertakings of many kinds. Up to now these kinds of activities have been considered peripheral operations in the international system. In the future they should be regarded as central for it is on a deliberate policy toward increasing the "warmth" of the international system that the best chance of a movement toward stable peace really rests.   □

THE PHILOSOPHY OF PEACE RESEARCH

In: *Proceedings of the International Peace
Research Association Third Conference,* Vol. 1.
Assen, Netherlands: Royal VanGorcum,
1970, pp. 5-19

THE PHILOSOPHY OF PEACE RESEARCH

Peace research is a subset of a larger set of human activity, research in general, which takes place in a great number of fields. The product of all research is some change in the noosphere, as de Chardin calls it, that is, the total sphere of knowledge and information structures as it spreads, however tenuously, around the globe. The first product is a change in the image of the world in the mind of the researcher, and this is transmitted to others through various means of communication, the written word, the spoken word, and so on. Research, of course, is not the only means of changing the noosphere. Literature, oratory, laws, the mass media, rhetoric, violence, and personal experience of man or nature change images of the world which are present in human minds or even in human artifacts. What distinguishes research from these other activities is that it is conducted by a group of people who think of themselves in some sense as scientists, that is, as members of the scientific subculture, and who therefore place high value on instrumentation, careful records, quantification where possible, and the testing of testable theories.

Research tends to be divided into pure research, which arises primarily from the curiosity of the researcher and the dynamics of the knowledge structure itself, and applied research, which tends to produce knowledge which is useful in the solution of practical problems or to apply existing knowledge to the solution of practical problems.

Peace researchers are a small subset of the total research community. There are probably not more than a few hundred people over the world who visualize themselves in this role. It is on the whole applied research, although it differs from much applied research in that, like pure research, it arises primarily out of the interests of the researchers. The outside world is not yet convinced enough of the usefulness of peace research to promote it and finance it, with one or two exceptions, such as the Swedish government, which supports the Stockholm International Peace Research Institute and the United States government, which supports the United States Arms

Control and Disarmament Agency. A few private foundations and individuals support it, but on the whole the major activity comes out of the concern of the peace researchers themselves. It might almost be described therefore as pure research with a strong applied interest. A great deal of it arises out of the curiosity of the researcher, but the curiosity is not idle, it is bound up with a strong conviction on the part of most peace researchers that war is highly undesirable and that an international system which constantly produces war is in need of radical change. It is the hope of most peace researchers, therefore, that it will result in changes in the noosphere, particularly of the image of the conflict processes and international systems which will lead to increasing the possibility of peace and diminishing the probability of war.

All research can be ranged on something of a continuum between "hard" research on the one hand and "soft" research on the other. The certainty of knowledge tends to increase as it moves toward the hard end of the spectrum, but its significance often tends to increase as we move towards the soft end. This may not always be the case, but there are strong tendencies in this direction. There is a danger that hard research can degenerate into a narrow experimentalism in small and artificial systems, and so gain very accurate knowledge about things that are in themselves trivial. At the other end soft research wanders off into grandiose philosophising which may deal with important questions but deals with them in a way that does not lead to any very certain knowledge.

Between these two extremes, however, we can identify some legitimate differences in research emphasis. Hard research is characterized by three major elements.

1. Information is collected by a sampling process with known error out of a known universe, so we can say with considerable accuracy whether what is true of the sample is also true of the universe.

2. Theoretical models are developed which are in principle testable, that is, disprovable by appeal to information collected from the real world. Ideally these models should produce clear predictions or expectations which then can be clearly verified or not verified by the information mentioned above. As a science develops, instrumentation, that is, devices for improving the discriminatory power of the information collecting system, becomes of increasing importance. Both the predictions and the observation or verifications tend to become more refined.

3. The third essential process is the revision of models or theories in the light of the fulfillment or disappointment of the expectations which they have produced. Such revision will only take place if we cannot revise the process of inference by which the expectations were derived from the theories, or if we cannot deny the perception of fulfillment or disappointment. This is why the use of mathematics and quantification of information has been of such importance in science, for this makes it much easier to fulfill the above conditions. By this whole process it is hoped that knowledge will increase through the successive elimination of error. This is not, I suspect, a necessary process. The elimination of one error may lead to a revision of a model into even greater error, but it is at least a reasonable expectation that the continual and successive elimination of error eventually leads the models towards the truth.

Many systems which are of great importance to mankind are so complex that they are not susceptible to rigorous investigation through hard research and it is not surprising, therefore, that the quest for significance and relevance leads into a looser or softer type of research activity than the above rigorous demands would necessitate. Corresponding to the above three conditions for hard research, we have three conditions for soft research.

1. Where fully sampled and instrumented information is not possible, the researcher endeavours to collect information in as objective and unbiased way as he can, trying to eliminate his personal biases and using his judgment as to what seems to be the best kind of sample.

2. Models or theories may be developed which are useful in interpreting the world around us, but which are not fully testable. Even in the physical sciences, we find many examples of the soft research of this kind, for instance, in meteorology. Wherever, indeed, the theoretical models produce predictions with a degree of probability less than one hundred per cent, exact testing is impossible, for we are never sure whether the prediction has been fulfilled. If a meteorologist, for instance, predicts a fifty per cent chance of rain tomorrow, there is no way in which he can be proved wrong. Similarly, if a peace researcher estimates that a certain international situation contains a twenty per cent probability of war, it is hard to prove him wrong too. Probabilistic systems, indeed, can only be tested by large numbers of observations which can give an empirical probability and in social systems, especially in the international system, this is usually not possible.

3. Models are revised in the light of cumulative information collected

according to the principle above. Without revision, I think we could say we do not have research, though this does not mean that all models are revised every time they are questioned. The revision process which goes on in soft research is perhaps less likely to lead to unmistakably true images of the world than those in hard research. Nevertheless, as long as progress towards the truth is made, research is justified no matter how soft, provided, of course, that we do not overestimate how much progress is in fact made.

A question of great importance which is causing a great deal of difficulty among peace researchers is that of the limits or the boundaries of peace research. It is obviously foolish to try to draw an exact line between what is peace research and what is not, for some things the relevance of which is not immediately apparent may turn out to be highly relevant indeed in the long run. Furthermore, knowledge is one, a single inter-related "body," and any boundaries that we draw are bound to be somewhat arbitrary. Nevertheless, there is a real problem with limited resources as to what are the limits of a field of discourse within which there is most likely to be fruitful interaction, for we obviously cannot interact with everybody. There is also a problem in an applied field such as this as to where lie the priorities, that is, what problems should we concentrate on in the immediate future – what is urgent and what is not. There is a serious division among peace researchers on this problem at the moment, which might even threaten the communication system of the entire peace research movement, and so the question of boundaries is by no means without practical importance.

One can distinguish three clusters of views on this subject. We first have what might be called the narrow view, which is perhaps particularly characteristic of researchers in the United States. This is the view that the problem of peace and war can be separated to a considerable extent from the other problems of the social system simply because the international system within which the problems of peace and war mainly occur is itself a distinct system with properties of its own and a certain degree of independence of others, such as religious or economic systems. In this view, therefore, peace research is mainly directed towards the international system, towards understanding it better, developing better theoretical models of it, and improving its information systems, studying its institutions, all with the ultimate view of modifying it in directions which will increase the probability of peace and diminish the probability of war. The ultimate ideal is indeed stable peace in which the probability of war is virtually zero. In this narrow sense than the main object of the peace research movement is to understand the dynamics of the international system with a view to understanding what kinds of policies, decisions, and strategies, can move it in the direction of stable peace and away from the direction of war.

This view rests perhaps also on the feeling that war itself is the most urgent problem which faces the human race today and that unless we solve this one we will not be able to solve any of the others. On this view, then, the peace research movement tends to concentrate on the conflict resolution process in the international system. From this it spreads out laterally on one side to conflict resolution processes in general, simply because all conflict processes have a great deal in common and what we can learn from conflict in one field often throws light on the nature of conflict in another. It is not surprising, therefore, to find peace researchers even of the "narrow school" taking great interest in resolution of industrial conflict situations and so on, but the primary focus always is what can these less destructive conflicts teach us about the appallingly destructive conflicts which occur within the international system.

On the other side, peace researchers of this type move out into the international system and study it in general. In this they may often cooperate with those students of the international system who are not primarily interested in changing it in the direction of peace. A good deal of the applied research in the international system, indeed, such as done by the Rand Corporation or the Hudson Institute in the United States or the Institute for Strategic Studies in England, is directed towards how to operate international conflict from the point of view of one of the parties, rather than from the point of view of how to resolve it peacefully. It is a little unfair to call these researchers "war" researchers because they are interested in peace as a value, but only when it is not inconsistent with the national interest as they conceive it. Given the understanding, however, that war researchers are neither monsters nor necessarily hostile to peace, we may perhaps be permitted to use the name. Both war researchers and peace researchers, however, are largely studying the same thing, which is the international system, and it is not surprising, therefore, that in spite of the sharp divergence of their value systems or their objectives, the work which they do is often very similar and they find it useful to communicate with each other. We will explore some of the dilemmas which this creates later in the paper.

The second school of peace researchers might be called the "broad school," whose most distinguished representative is Johan Galtung of Norway. This rejects the view that peace research should be mainly confined to the study of the international system itself, spurning this as merely "negative peace" and advocating the study of "positive peace", by which sometimes seems to be meant rectification of any condition anywhere which might be defined as injustice, oppression, discrimination, anything, in fact, which gives rise to what might be called legitimate conflict. The study of positive peace presumably involves the study of how these conflicts can be resolved in the least costly and least violent manner. Many of these conflicts, however, impinge only peripherally on the international system and are not major causes for international war. Consequently, to those of the narrow school, the broad school seems to be taking too much under its hat and diluting peace research by an attempt to study virtually all social problems. One suspects indeed that positive peace cannot be achieved until the whole world is a utopia which will take a long time, whereas negative peace, in the sense of Galtung, is something which is not wholly off the human agenda. It is understandable, therefore, that the narrow school gets impatient with the broad school for wanting to bring everything into peace research whether it is relevant or not, whereas the broad school gets impatient with the narrow school for being insensitive to the social problems which it has felt are perhaps equally urgent as the problems of war and peace. There is perhaps a real difference here in the sense of priorities which cannot easily be resolved. The point perhaps at which these two schools come together, however, is the point at which the larger social problems of poverty, underdevelopment, stagnation, discrimination, race and class and so on, impinge on the international system itself and hence increase or decrease the probability of international war.

The third school might be called the radical school. It consists mostly of young people who have grown up since the Second World War, especially in England and in Scandinavia. They tend to wear beards and have a fancy for what might be called academic guerilla theater. They are not inhibited by the customs of personal courtesy which tended to characterize the older generation and they have moral feelings which are so strong that morals are regarded as a substitute for manners. They tend to think of themselves as Marxists or neo-Marxists and they tend to regard both the narrow and the broad schools as having sold out to the enemy, which is American imperialism and corporate capitalism. They seem singularly insensitive to the virtues of political freedom or to the possible defects in totalitarian societies. They regard the older generation of peace researchers as obsessed by the cold war and by the necessity for resolving conflicts, as they regard this conflict essentially as no longer crucial and the thing that interests them is how to increase conflict which is "objective" but of which people are not aware. They tend to see the developmental process in terms of a revolutionary dialectic, and they have a surprisingly static view of the economic process. In their research they tend to look for an economic or class basis for conflict and are disappointed when they cannot find any. They tend to regard symbolic and integrative systems as somehow unreal and examples of "false consciousness." Apparently the only objective conflicts are those in which some people get more economic goods and some get less.

I have tried to be objective according to the canons of soft research in these descriptions. However, I cannot avoid the conviction that radical peace research is a drastic retrogression back towards a frame of reference which to my mind was discredited at least a generation ago. Nevertheless, I would strongly be against any attempt to expel the radicals from the peace research movement, simply because the only function of organization in the research field is to enable us to learn from one another and I think all three of the schools have something to learn from each other. There has been a tendency, I think, in the narrow school to assume a little too easily that conflicts are dominated by perverse dynamic processes which make everybody worse off. Hence they, or I should say we, as I have no hesitation in proclaiming my personal adherence to the narrow school, have tended to underestimate the significance of those situations in which conflict moves are not only inevitable but in which it matters which way they go, that is, whether A is better off when B is worse off, or whether B is better off and A is worse off. There is a certain tendency for the narrow school to treat the whole problem of peace and war as if it were a problem in the Paretian optimum, that is, how do we prevent people moving to situations in which everybody is worse off. This seems to me a highly legitimate concern which I defend strongly and I would defend the proposition also that this must be at the core of peace research. Nevertheless, even when Paretian optima are arrived at, there may still be real conflicts which are of importance. This is something which cannot be neglected.

From the broad school, also, the narrow school can learn that a study of the international system which is too isolated from the other systems of the world is likely to overlook certain important inputs into the international system from others. I think we have something to learn from the radicals too that there is a real danger that peace researchers are in some danger of cooperating too enthusiastically with the powers that be in the hope of changing their decisions and that occasionally a negative, obstreperous, and even discourteous denial of legitimacy may be what a situation needs.

There are psychoanalytic overtones in this whole business of course. Part of the loutishness of the radicals is an expression of a kind of oedipus complex against the father figures of the older generation. The young are always a bit loutish, though why this generation of radicals should have elevated loutishness to a high moral virtue is something which I confess puzzles me profoundly, especially as it is likely to interfere considerably with the achievement of their objectives. There is something here akin to the conflict of cultures in developing societies. The life experience of the older generation and of the younger generation in this day has been so fantastically different that it is not surprising there is a generation gap of unusual magnitude. I see even the loutishness, indeed, as an attempt on the part of the young to cut off communication with the old because of the need of reorganizing and giving meaning to their own life experience which communications from the older generation can only upset. It does seem to be a great pity, however, that they are trying to reorganize their own experience through a body of Marxist doctrine which strikes one of my generation, at any rate, as a hopelessly inadequate to carry the enormous complexities of our own day.

Even though the answers which the radicals give may be wholly unacceptable, the questions which they ask cannot be silenced. Two questions in particular must be faced by the peace research community, and indeed by all research communities, in the coming generation. The first of these is the relation of research to ideology; the second is the relation of research to power, especially political power.

I would define an ideology, or to use a more old-fashioned word, a "faith," as a coherent system of ideas, a kind of Gestalt in the noosphere which has its survival value not so much because of its testability or correspondence with some real world outside, but because of its coherence, and because of its role in the organization of cultures which themselves have survival value. Almost every culture, indeed, is built around an ideology of some sort. Without this, the patterns of trust and easy communication which are necessary to form a community are hard to develop. If someone is perceived as "one of us," our defenses are down, we speak freely, we understand what we say to one another, and the very facilitation of communication tends to create a sense of community. This is true even where the thing which identifies the other person as "one of us" bears only a minor relation to the total life of the community. One sees this, for instance, in the extraordinarily powerful subcultures and intense community life which develops around a religious faith such as Mormonism or Seventh Day Adventism, where the actual content of the faith may have only but a tenuous relationship to the culture which it creates. It is the sharing of the faith rather than its specific content which creates community. The same thing is true in perhaps a lesser degree of socialist societies, where, however, the form of culture which is developed perhaps has a closer relationship to the faith which inspires it.

The difference between the epistemological processes which lead to the survival of ideologies and those which lead to the survival of scientific theories and concepts lies in the conditions of survival themselves. Ideologies will survive if the communities around which they are organized survive, and communities survive for many reasons which have nothing to do with the ideology which provides, as it were, their excuse for coming into being. Hence, ideologies may survive for reasons which are quite unconnected with their truth, though an ideology which is outrageously untrue is likely to lessen the survival value of the community which organizes around it. The very fact, however, that the life of the community may not be closely related to the ideology itself suggests that the survival of ideologies is at least only very loosely related to their truth.

In the scientific community, by contrast, the survival of systems of theories and ideas does not depend on the survival value of the community which is built around them, but on the direct capacity of the systems for being tested. This indeed is precisely the reason why the development of the scientific subculture has given rise to such an enormous explosion in knowledge. The ideology of science is an ideology of testing and revisionism. This ideology creates a scientific subculture, but the survival of the subculture is not related to any specific scientific ideas, only to the method. Hence, the content of science changes with great rapidity whereas the content of other ideologies does not. This very fact, however, leads to a certain tension between science and ideology in so far as the content of scientific models diverges from that of the ideological framework. We have seen this process at work in all the great world faiths, whether Christianity, Judaism, Islam, Buddhism, or Marxism. These tensions may be partly resolved by compartmentalization and it can also be met by modifying the ideology. The reverse attempt on the part of ideological systems to modify science has usually been disastrous, but the scientific images of the world themselves change so rapidly that acute conflicts are sometimes resolved simply by waiting for changes in the scientific image.

A conflict which should also be noted appears between ideologies, as, for instance, between Christianity and Nationalism. There is no easy formula for resolving these conflicts. In so far as ideology is a creator of identity, it has to be respected, even where it is not believed. Otherwise, communication becomes impossible between people of different ideologies. Even something that seems as benign as peace research, therefore, may easily be perceived to be threatening, especially if it creates images of the world which are at variance with the ideological identities of the people who practice it.

A closely related question, much too large to be treated in this paper, is that of the relation of knowledge to power, and particularly the relation of the kind of knowledge which peace research may produce to the distribution and exercise of political, economic or other kinds of power. There is no question that change in the noosphere also changes the power structure. Knowledge may, for instance, produce new weapons and if some party has a monopoly of knowledge of this kind, it clearly influences his power position in the threat system. The nuclear weapon is a good case in point, but it must be recognized that the growth of knowledge underlies all developments in weaponry and even the purest of knowledge may turn out to have applications in this field which will change the power structure.

Similarly, knowledge has a very profound effect on productivity. The great rise in productivity which has taken place in the last two hundred years, indeed, is very largely a result of the applications of what often started out as pure science to processes of commodity production. If this kind of knowledge, again, is distributed unequally it will affect the distribution of economic power. Countries which have participated in and have been open to the knowledge revolution of science have enjoyed an increase in their economic power. Countries which do not participate so fully in this movement will suffer a relative decrease in economic power. Even the fact, therefore, that scientific knowledge is at least theoretically open to all and is in the public domain does not mean that it cannot result in redistributions of power.

A third form of power which is not perhaps so widely recognized as the other two, but may even be more important in the long run, is what I have called integrative power. This is the kind of power which arises because a person occupies a niche in the integrative system, that is, because he has widely recognized status or legitimacy on one side, or even at the other extreme, because he is an object of pity and compassion. A man who loses the respect of others is likely to find his integrative power diminished. The loss of legitimacy of any person or any institution can lead to the destruction of whatever threat power or economic power that they may previously have had, simply because neither threats, nor exchange, nor property can organize society if it is not legitimated. My own view is that the dynamics of legitimacy tend to dominate all other dynamic processes in society, and yet the processes by which legitimacy is gained or lost are very little understood.

Peace research in so far as it results in an increase in knowledge is likely to operate mainly through integrative power rather than through either threat power or productivity and exchange power. This is not to deny the possibility of an impact of peace research even in weapon systems. The analysis of these systems, for instance, which is a very legitimate task of peace research, may reveal that one thing which leads to instability and escalation in them is the inability to distinguish between weapons which are defensive in the sense that they reduce the perceived threat of another to their owner and weapons which are offensive in the sense that they threaten the potential enemy but do not reduce his threat to the first party. The whole argument as between first strike and second strike capability of nuclear weapons relates to this problem. If all weapons could only be activated by the first strike of another, then obviously no weapons would ever be activated. Peace research, therefore, may well suggest that certain weapon systems are more likely to lead to war than others. Nevertheless, we would not expect this impact of peace research to be very large. Similarly we would not expect peace research to have much effect on relative productivities or on economic power, although even here if we produce knowledge about conflict resolution in industrial relations, this may well increase the economic power of those who take advantage of this knowledge. One of the greatest obstacles to economic development in many countries is the incapacity of the society for resolving internal conflict, so that economic development might well be in part a by-product of peace research.

One would expect the major impact of peace research to be on the distribution of integrative power, in so far as the kind of knowledge that it produces is likely to affect the distribution of status, respect, and legitimacy. Thus, genuine knowledge of the essential parameters of the international system could, one hopes, lead to a legitimation and increased status for those policies and their advocates which would move the system towards stable peace, and would decrease the status and legitimacy of the "hawks," whose policies of unilateral national defense increase the probability of war. We must face the fact, however, that the impact of knowledge of any kind on the distribution of power in society is very complex and extremely hard to predict and there is no guarantee that even peace research will necessarily redistribute power towards everybody that we approve of and away from everybody that we disapprove of. This, however, is a risk that we must be prepared to take.

A question which is especially on the minds of the radicals is whether the fact that peace research may be financed by the representatives of those already in positions of power will divert it in directions which will reinforce the existing power structure and prevent what may be envisioned as desirable redistributions. This is a question that is extremely difficult to answer because of the complexity of the impact of knowledge on power distributions, but it is a question that continually needs to be asked. No researcher of any kind can afford to be indifferent to the effects of his research on the distribution of power, and even if the question should have no answer in our present state of knowledge, as is all too likely to be the case, this is no excuse for not continually asking it.

A more immediate problem which is exercising the peace research community at the moment is that of the roles, functions, and responsibilities of the peace research organizations, especially the International Peace Research Association, which is the official body under whose auspices this particular paper is given, and the Peace Research Society (International), which might almost be described as a "private enterprise organization," as it has been founded and operated very successfully virtually by a single individual, Dr.Walter Isard, of the University of Pennsylvania in Philadelphia.

There are two functions of associations of this kind about which there is not likely to be much disagreement. The first is the development and encouragement of an "invisible college," as de Sola Price calls it, of people whose work is meaningful to each other and who need to be in communication. The great function of conferences is for people in the same field to meet one another, to become personally acquainted so that they can exchange ideas and memoranda and so give each other mutual criticism and encouragement. Both criticism and encouragement are important. Criticism by others is an important element in the detection of error and is welcomed by every true scientist. On the other hand, criticism which is designed to insult or to destroy the identity of another person is inimical to learning and should be regarded with extreme disfavor.

A second function of these associations should be to exercise constant pressure for the improvement of information collection and processing in the international system and in conflict systems generally. One of the great problems of research in the international system is the strong element of secrecy which it contains. This introduces an element of corruption into the whole information collection and processing operation, which means that the decisionmakers in the system are all making decisions about an essentially imaginary world. This is one of the reasons at least why the system is so intolerably expensive and dangerous. Almost any movement towards "hardness" in the collection and processing of information about the international system would be beneficial. The peace research societies could very well take this as one of their major concerns.

A third possible, though highly controversial, function of the professional associations is that of "giving advice to the souvereign," either by acting in a consultative capacity for the international system decision-makers or by offering unsolicited advice. This is a delicate and difficult function and indeed has already caused serious difficulties in the Peace Research Society (International). This body called a conference in June 1968 in Cambridge, Massachusetts with the specific intention of bringing knowledge which might be available in the peace research community to bear on the solution of the conflict in Vietnam. The Proceedings of this conference have been published as The Papers, Volume X, of the Peace Research Society (International) and have been the occasion of a good deal of unfavorable comment, especially in Europe. It has been argued that the conference was one-sided and only represented the American position and that, in particular, there were papers by recognized "hawks," whose interest was not in an acceptable resolution of the conflict but in an American victory. My own view, frankly, is that the conference was well-intentioned and that it did, in fact, produce one or two suggestions which might be valuable in the search for a genuine solution.

While the rage of the radicals seems to be quite out of proportion to the issues involved, the issues themselves are important. One could almost parody the two opposing positions. On one extreme, the pacifistic position would argue that the function of peace research is simply to diminish the amount of resources spent in conflict, the results of the conflict being relatively indifferent. It does not really matter who wins; the important thing is to diminish the resources devoted to the conflict itself. At the other extreme we have the radical position which is in effect to decide who in the conflict is right and to put all our resources into seeing that the right side wins. In this particular case, of course, the radicals identify with the NLF in Vietnam and, indeed, in terms of peace research, it seems hard to differentiate their position from that of the American militarist who wants to win no matter how much it costs.

It is perhaps fortunate at the moment that we do have two societies in the field, for the Peace Research Society (International), being as it were "private," can afford to have internal quarrels and arguments which might disable or even destroy the more official International Peace Research Association. It does seem wise in the light of this experience that the International Peace Research Association should refrain at this stage in its development from any attempt to apply peace research to a particular situation or even to give any good advice. A great deal more work needs to be done indeed on the nature of not only the international system but social systems in general before the peace research community can be more than extremely tentative about giving advice to the decision-maker.

It may be indeed that the development of what might be called "peace engineering" will have to be done concurrent with, but independent of, peace research as a pure science, just as engineering in all fields has developed independently of pure science but in close relationship to it. An institute of peace engineering is by no means absurd, even at the present juncture and may be entirely practical in ten years, but it should probably be kept separate from the peace research associations.

The very conflicts within the peace research movement are a sign of its vitality. They represent also, in microcosm, many of the major conflicts which divide the outside world. The conflict of the generations is as old as

Cain, Abel, no doubt, having been the victim of a displaced oedipus complex. The conflict between the revolutionists and the evolutionists is perhaps more modern but certainly goes back to the beginning of civilization. It may become a crucial test of the peace research movement to see whether its own principles of conflict resolution can be applied to itself. If it fails here there is not much hope of its giving good advice to the world. The basic philosophy of peace research, however, is that there is something important to know, something that we still do not know that hurts us, in the whole matter of conflict, threats and war. If there is still something to know, then even if our own generation fails to discover it because of our internal conflicts, the great continent of our ignorance still stands there awaiting a new Columbus who will eventually discover it.

TOWARDS A TWENTY-FIRST CENTURY POLITICS

Colorado Quarterly, XX, 3 (Winter 1972): 309-319

Towards a twenty-first century politics

Any attempt to peer into the future must be regarded with the gravest suspicion. The record of prediction indeed is so dismal, even in respectable fields like demography, that some future Pure Food and Information Office may compel futurologists to stamp on all their predictions "Believing in this prediction may be harmful to the health." Nevertheless, the urge to predict is ineradicable, simply because of the basic dilemma of the human condition, which is that all knowledge is about the past and all decisions are about the future.

All prediction is derived from observing regular patterns in the past. The failures of prediction may come either from failure to perceive the true regularity of the past, which is something that we can hope to correct, or from changes in the patterns themselves, about which we can do very little. The most successful predictions are those which involve control, that is, the setting up of artificial systems, the regularities of which are known because we have created them. Thus, we can predict the temperature inside a thermostatically controlled room with a great deal of confidence, though the temperature outside is subject to great errors of prediction.

The political system is part of the general social system. Hence, a look into the future of politics would have to look at the general patterns of change of the whole social system, for all parts of it are interconnected.

Several kinds of patterns can be detected. One consists of mechanical "Newtonian" patterns, such as we find in population projections, projections of economic growth, and so on. The record of predictions by mechanical projection in social systems is surprisingly poor, mainly because of unforeseen changes in the parameters, or "constants," of the system, such as fertility or mortality rates in the case of population projections, or the marginal propensity to consume in the case of economic projections. However, we do know that all people that are alive today will be either one year older or dead this time next year. Thus, if mortality is assumed to be fairly constant, distortions in the age distribution may be expected to appear in thirty years' time, in age groups thirty years older than where they are now. Thus, the bulge in the American birth rate, from about 1947 to 1961, is showing up as a bulge in enrollments in ages ten to twenty-four in schools and colleges now and will appear as a high proportion of people between the ages of forty and fifty-four in 2001. A similar principle applies to all capital goods. Short of some catastrophe, most of the houses that are here today will be around in twenty years. There is a great principle of persistence and monotony that tomorrow is going to be very much like today. Were it not for this indeed the world would really fall apart.

All "trends" are mechanical predictions, and are likely to be falsified. We may improve them by taking account of secondary or third differentials, that is, rates of change of rates of change, or even rates of change of rates of change of rates of change. We may perceive that some process is slowing down or speeding up, or even that the rate at which it is slowing down is increasing.

A lot of superficial evidence suggests that the enormous change in the condition of man which followed the development of science and its application to technology now is slowing down very rapidly. I have argued that the great period of change was my grandfather's life, say, from 1860 to 1920. As I look back on my own childhood in the 1920s, the world was not strikingly different as far as ordinary daily life was concerned. We had electric lights, automobiles, the beginning of the radio, movies, and the telephone. The technical changes of my lifetime, apart from television and perhaps antibiotics, have not very much affected daily life. Such things as nuclear energy, radar, lasars, and space travel have not as yet made much impact on the life of the ordinary man. By contrast, one thinks of my grandfather in 1920 looking back at his childhood in a remote English village in 1860, without automobiles, without telephones, without electricity, without movies, without radio, virtually without any of the things that we think of as the "modern world," except perhaps for a railroad train twenty miles away. His childhood could not have been all that different from his grandfather's, and his grandfather's, right back to Queen Elizabeth and further.

I have seen much less change than my grandfather, and my

children may see much less change than I. Predictions of this sort, on the other hand, are peculiarly likely to be falsified. Any particular growth process is likely to exhibit eventually diminishing rates of growth, that is, it will follow the familiar S curve. It can always be interrupted, however, by a new impetus, that is, by the development of new growth and potential. This has happened innumerable times in human history and there is certainly nothing to indicate that it will not happen again. We might, for instance, have something dramatic coming out of molecular biology with wholly new forms of life. We might get a real breakthrough in the understanding of human learning, which would cause dramatic social changes. Even at the physical level, we might break through into some kind of gravity shield, which would revolutionize the energy picture. We might find sources of energy within the subatomic particles. We might even find something wholly new and unsuspected. The probability of all these things, however, seems at the moment moderately low, and the expectation of declining rates of growth, both of knowledge and of productivity, is not at all unreasonable. The United States, indeed, is already witnessing a noticeable decline in the rate of increase of labor productivity, especially since 1967. This may, of course, be a very temporary phenomenon, or it may be the shadow of what I have been calling ZPPG, that is, zero population and productivity growth, even perhaps within present lifetimes.

Another source of knowledge about the future might be called the "maturation principle." We see this in a simple form in biological growth. We always expect a kitten to grow up into a cat, never into a rhinoceros. Similarly, the enormous growth process which has been taking place in the human race, in terms of its physical expansion and increase in per capita incomes and in terms ultimately of its knowledge stock, is also something that is likely to have "maturity." The maturity of the "stationary state" casts its shadow across the present, just as the shadow of the adult that he is to be falls across the life of the growing child and pushes him into all sorts of activities, like education, which otherwise he might not want.

The shadow of coming maturity is just now touching our present society in our worries about pollution, exhaustion of resources, the impact of population growth, and the uneasy feeling that headlong development might lead to disaster. Over the twenty-first century, however, the shadow of maturity will fall very darkly. Long before the end of the twenty-first century it will become clear that the "linear economy" that we have now, that runs from mines and fossil fuel sources to dumps, cannot go on indefinitely. A major effort will have to be made towards a "spaceship technology," which will probably involve reliance on solar energy for power and on the recycling of materials, together with zero population growth.

As we look forward towards the future of politics, we must recognize that here we are dealing with the most erratic and unpredictable segment of society, mainly because the key to political dynamics lies in what I have called the integrative system in society, that is, the complex of relationships involving such matters as status, identity, and community, with relationships such as legitimacy, trust, loyalty, benevolence, and, of course, their opposites. These processes are frequently subject to sharp discontinuities.

Politics participates also in two other major types of processes in social life, *dialectical* and *developmental*. Dialectical processes involve the conflict of opposing systems, in which one may win and the other may lose, the issue often being determined by quite random elements. Developmental or evolutionary processes proceed through social mutation and selection. Mutation is a highly unpredictable process. It involves the creation of evolutionary potential, what I have elsewhere called a "revelation," the sort of thing we have in the early Christian church and with the first followers of Mohammed, or in Marx in the first International, and also in the beginnings of science as a social movement in the seventeenth century. We get the same phenomenon on a smaller scale in inventions, both of commodities or techniques, machines or social inventions, like the postage stamp or the deductable-at-source income tax. Mutations are almost inherently unpredictable, for if they could be predicted, we would in many cases already have them. The selective processes are again far from being regular and predictable. Who predicted the failure of the Edsel? Or the collapse of the British liberal party? Or the demise of capitalism in Cuba? Or the success of the Beatles?

Even in systems as complex as this, however, there are certain cues and clues. What we are really considering is a process in what might be called "macro learning," or the whole process of change in the "noosphere," as de Chardin calls it, that is, in the total cognitive and emotive content of the three billion or so human nervous systems. Two processes are at work here—the constant replacement of decedent old minds by decaying younger ones and the constant learning process that goes on in particular minds. Where different generations have different learning experiences, this may be highly significant for the future. Today, for instance, the generation which is in powerful positions was for the most part deeply traumatized by the First World War, the Great Depression, and the Second World War. By the year 2000, this generation will have passed from the scene and a generation with a different set of traumas will be in control.

One of the most puzzling problems in social dynamics is that of the spread and decline of ideologies, legitimacies, loyalties, and so on. Institutions which seem impregnable collapse overnight simply because there is an epidemic spread of loss of belief in them. The collapse of the European empires in the twentieth century is a good case in point. In 1910 the legitimacy of the British and French empires seemed unassailable. By 1930 hardly anybody believed in them anymore, and by 1950 they were well on their way to liquidation. One thing that certainly helps to destroy legitimacy is dramatic disappointments or betrayals. The First World War certainly helped to destroy the legitimacy of the previous international order, simply because its human costs were so excessive.

As one looks at the integrative structure, one can see a number of contradictory trends, which again makes prediction very difficult. This might be called the "iceberg principle." We never know when the erosion of the invisible part of the iceberg has gone far enough to turn it over. We have seen in the twentieth century a remarkable decay in the legitimacy of war as an institution. War songs are an index of this. The First World War produced a large number of stirring pro-war songs. The Second World War produced practically none, whereas the Vietnam War has produced nothing but anti-war songs. On the other hand, we now stand in a curious limbo, in which neither war nor peace is legitimate, and the agonized and confused reaction of the American public to the Calley trial is an indicator of this general confusion. What we see here is in part again the shadow of coming maturity. In the spaceship earth, obviously, war is an absurdly extravagant luxury which cannot be tolerated. The planet is simply too precarious for playing such childish games.

We see the same kind of ambiguity in regard to economic institutions. Both socialism and corporate capitalism are showing signs of a crisis of legitimacy. The legitimacy of socialism is being seriously undermined simply by experience. The fact that we have now had experience with centrally planned socialist societies for fifty years has revealed they are neither very much better nor very much worse than capitalist societies. They exhibit many of the defects of corporate capitalism—diseconomies of scale, inflexible hierarchies, distortions of the reward system, and they certainly have no better record than the capitalist countries when it comes to the question of pollution. The pressures of a Plan are just as hard on the environment as the pressures of the market. Furthermore, socialist societies have revealed themselves to be singularly defenseless against personal tyranny, as under Stalin, against the corruption of the arts and even the sciences, and the wildest criticisms of Madison Avenue surely pale beside the massive conformist horror of Mao's Little Red Book. Abolishing private property does not lead into a society where everybody does things for love; rather it leads into a society dominated by terror at its worst and propaganda at its best.

On the other side of the line, corporate capitalism also is facing some severe crises. It has been unable to solve the problem of keeping full employment without inflation, and has chosen inflation. Social democracy, in part, at any rate, has been a fraud. It has redistributed income to the rich in the name of redistributing it to the poor. The problems of pollution and exhaustion are of mounting significance, even though one should not underestimate some very real successes, for instance, in managing air and water pollution and in soil conservation.

The two hundred billion dollars of the world war industry continues to be not only an appalling economic burden on the world but also represents a positive probability of almost irretrievable disaster in nuclear war. It is not surprising, therefore, that considerable numbers of people, especially young people, on both sides of the Iron Curtain are seriously questioning the legitimacy of the system under which they live. On the other hand, the "greening" generation is very green indeed. It has produced no adequate analysis of the present world situation. Where it fancies itself as radical, it falls back on hopelessly obsolete nineteenth-century ideas, and its lifestyle and ideal seem to be essentially that of a minor landlord, producing what might unkindly be called a "twiddle class," twiddling its dirty-green thumbs while the "squares" keep the world going.

No existing political ideology seems to me, therefore, to be relevant to the twenty-first century. My crystal ball is no better than anybody else's, and I do not know what kind of new symbolic formulation will provide the "revelation" out of which the evolutionary potential of the twenty-first century must grow. I can, however, suggest some of the real problems which any twenty-first century ideology will have to solve.

The first such problem is that of the reward structure in society. All human activity tends to move towards the higher rewards and away from the higher penalties. Monetary rewards, of course, are only part of the picture, as economists have always recognized. The total reward structure is of crucial importance, however, in deciding in what direction human activity will go. If virtue is penalized and vice is rewarded, virtue will languish and vice will prosper. If people can produce negative commodities, whether pollution or deception, immorality or crime, without having to pay negative prices, these negative commodities will be produced in too large quantity. If people are not rewarded for producing positive commodities, these will not be produced in sufficient quantity. The problem is particularly acute in the case of public goods and public bads, which require political action, which in turn requires a sense of community, if the "freeloader principle" is not to exercise its baleful influence.

A public good may be defined as one which I could enjoy, even if I did not pay for it, as long as other people will provide it. The diminution of public "bads," like air pollution, is a very similar category. If I can get away with not paying my taxes while everybody else does, I will be able to enjoy the products of the public goods financed by these taxes and will not have to sacrifice for them. I will then be a "freeloader." If it pays everybody to be a freeloader, however, everybody *will* be a freeloader, the public goods will not be provided at all, and everybody will be worse off than they otherwise would have been. This really implies a non-existence theorem about anarchism. There has to be some form of "government," that is, legitimated coercion, if public goods are to be provided. The legitimation arises because everybody is willing to be coerced as long as everybody else is.

Reward structures are not everything, however. We also have to struggle with the problem of identity structures. It is not enough to be rewarded for doing—we must also be rewarded for being, even if these rewards are largely internal. Increasingly, as traditional societies in which identity is not much of a problem, simply because there is no choice, are replaced by modern societies in which individuals have a choice of identity, the problem of making a wise choice becomes more and more acute. The decay of parental and all adult authority opens to young people a choice of becoming drug addicts, slaves to lust, and work-shy slobs, as well as the choice of selecting an identity which will lead into an adult maturity. Neither the family identity, the national identity, the religious identity, nor the occupational identity are as powerful and satisfactory as they used to be. Yet there seems very little to take their place except the pathological identity. The search for the truly human identity which is appropriate to the spaceship earth is one of the great tasks of the next hundred years and the political ideology which can solve this problem may well be the one that will win out.

A third problem is that of the proper allocation of intellectual resources. Almost any crisis is a symptom of misallocations of intellectual resources in the past. We have been putting our minds on unreal or insoluble problems instead of on the real, soluble ones. Our inability to mobilize intellectual resources for the real problems of the human race may be the most disastrous legacy which the twentieth century will give to the twenty-first. We have been frittering away our resources in weaponry and space, and even in organ transplants and sophisticated medicine. We should have been devoting ourselves to studying conflict, identity, and human learning. Our massive ignorance about the learning and reality-testing process may well be the ultimate limitation on our ability to solve any of our problems. It is clear that we are in great need of social inventions which will enable us to achieve disarmament and stable peace, the reduction of crime and social disorganization, the increase in the productivity and incomes of the potentially productive poor, and the

development of an adequate "grants economy" for the inherently unproductive. We need to be able to deal with racial, cultural, and
sexual heterogeneity. We need to find a way of satisfying the demands of social justice at a bearable cost.

These are grave challenges. None of them, however, seem to be
beyond the human capacity. If in the twentieth century we have
been going through both the pains and the joys of adolescence, with
its rapid physical growth and emotional disturbances, as well as rapid
learning, we may perhaps look at the twenty-first century as a magic
number symbolizing man's majority and his achievement of maturity.
The fact above all which makes me an optimist is the knowledge
that we are a very long way from having exhausted the biological
capacity of the human nervous system. There is always a chance, of
course, that the good may die young, but man is not even that good.
He has at least a reasonable chance of blundering through his
troubled adolescence into a more serene maturity. In the hope of
increasing that chance, however slightly, the occasion seems to call
for the modest manifesto which follows:

A Manifesto for the Twenty-first Century

The twenty-first century symbolizes the maturity of mankind, in
which we may indeed receive the key that will open the door to the
universe. It is in the twenty-first century that man must make the
first great strides towards establishing a spaceship earth, with a world
society based on permanent sources of energy, such as the sun, and
on the recycling of materials, a society freed from the burden of
destitution and violence, in which different cultures can flourish
without fear and the enormous richness of the human potential can
progressively be realized. Unless mankind can make this precarious
and dangerous transition, it is by no means impossible that the whole
evolutionary experiment in this part of the universe will come to an
end.

The existing political, social, economic, and religious institutions
of the world have evolved in an era in which the problems of the
transition to the spaceship earth were not present, and it is not surprising, therefore, that they are inadequate to this task. It is a task
they were not created to perform. While many elements in the existing structures and institutions of society can be adapted to play a part

in the great transition to come, there will also be a great need for social invention, for new institutions, new modes of learning, new ways of thinking, and new ways of life. Half a million years of accelerating human expansion are now coming to an end. This very fact creates a grave psychological crisis for the human race, to which however it will have to adapt if it is to survive. The twentieth century is the age of preparation. It demands intense activity in understanding and preparing for the transition to come.

We cannot now predict the specific nature of the inventions, either physical or social, which will be necessary in order to achieve this great transition, for if we could specify them we would have them now. Nevertheless, we can prepare for them by throwing off the dead weight of obsolete ideas, by constantly testing our beliefs against the messages that return to us from the world around us, and by rejecting purely subjective solutions, either in ideology or in drugs, and by pressing forward to catch a vision of the world that has to be, constantly trying to formulate the real problems to which we must find answers. This is no time to run after the perpetual motion of self-contained intellectual systems or for trying to square political circles in devoting ourselves to the solution of insoluble problems.

The most crucial, and yet the most difficult, tasks that lie ahead may well be in the field of political invention. It is clear that no existing political ideologies or institutions, either of the right or of the left, are at all adequate to deal with the enormous political tasks of the great transition, for they all belong to the era of human expansion, and are quite inadequate to deal with the politics of the spaceship earth. While we cannot now specify the institutions of spaceship politics, we can at least begin to see some of its characteristics in the tasks which it must fulfill.

First, it must be cybernetic. There must be an apparatus to perceive and indicate the divergence between any present position of the system and some boundary of destruction and system death, and there must be an apparatus also once this divergence is perceived to turn a system that is moving towards this boundary away from it. This involves an information apparatus for perceiving states of the social system far beyond our present capability, and the improvement of this capability therefore stands out as a most urgent task of the social sciences. The creation of an engine to act on these perceptions goes beyond the social sciences and must be the creation of political leadership.

In the second place, the political organization must provide a satisfactory reward structure. The rewarding of virtue and the punishment of vice, and the ability to detect one from the other, are essential to the operation of a dynamically satisfactory system, and without this its cybernetic character cannot be achieved.

In the third place, there must be defenses within the total system against the perverse dynamics by which things go from bad to worse —such things as addiction, pollution, arms races, and perverse dialectical processes; and the task of constructing institutions which can perform this function is one of the greatest challenges to the social inventiveness of the human race. So far we have performed it very badly.

In the fourth place, there must be a social matrix within which satisfactory personal identities can be developed. Identity failure is the greatest source of human pollution. We need a massive search for the sources of identity failure and for the building of institutions which can defend us against it. Human beings are created by the interaction of their own internal growth processes with the large and continual inputs which come to them from their social and natural environment. The only ultimate object of social, economic, and political institutions is the production of high quality human beings. All other goals are partial and intermediary compared to this, and this indeed will be the primary task in the spaceship earth.

The dangers and difficulties of the present time are very great. Nevertheless, the only unforgivable sin is despair, for that will justify itself. Man is very far from having exhausted the potential of his extraordinary nervous system. The troubles of the twentieth century are not unlike those of adolescence—rapid growth beyond the ability of organizations to manage, uncontrollable emotion, and a desperate search for identity. Out of adolescence, however, comes maturity in which rapid physical growth with all its attendant difficulties comes to an end, but in which growth continues in knowledge, in spirit, in community, and in love; it is to this that we look forward as a human race. This goal, once seen with our eyes, will draw our faltering feet towards it.

BIBLIOGRAPHY

BIBLIOGRAPHY OF PUBLISHED WORKS
Through 1973
Compiled by Vivian L. Wilson

Key : CP — Reprinted in *Kenneth E. Boulding Collected Papers* I-V
BE — Reprinted in *Beyond Economics*
RI — Further reprint information available from the author

1932

ARTICLES

The Place of the "Displacement Cost" Concept in Economic Theory. *Economic Journal*, 42, 165 (Mar. 1932): 137-141. CP I, pp. 1-7.
The Possibilities of Socialism in Britain. *Plan* (Exeter College, Oxford), 1, 4 (May 1932): 25-27.

1934

ARTICLE

The Application of the Pure Theory of Population Change to the Theory of Capital. *Quarterly Journal of Economics*, 48 (Aug. 1934): 645-666. CP I, pp. 9-32.

1935

ARTICLES

A Note on the Consumption Function. *Review of Economic Studies*, 2, 2 (Feb. 1935): 99-103. CP I, pp. 33-39.
The Theory of a Single Investment. *Quarterly Journal of Economics*, 49, 3 (May 1935): 475-494. CP I, pp. 41-62.

1936

ARTICLES

Professor Knight's Capital Theory: A Note in Reply. *Quarterly Journal of Economics,* 50, 3 (May 1936): 524-531.
Time and Investment. *Economica,* NS 3, 10 (May 1936): 196-220. CP I, pp. 63-89. Reply. *Economica.* NS 3, 12 (Nov. 1936): 440-442.

1937

BOOK REVIEW

Review of E. C. van Dorp, A Simple Theory of Capital, Wages, and Profit or Loss. *Economic Journal* 47, 187 (Sept. 1937): 522-524.

1938

ARTICLES and PAMPHLET

An Experiment in Friendship. *American Friend,* 26, 26 (Dec. 22, 1938): 541-542.
In Defense of the Supernatural. *Friends Intelligencer,* 95, 41 (Oct. 8, 1938): 677-678.
Making Education Religious. *American Friend,* 26, 20 (Sept. 29, 1938): 408-409.
Paths of Glory: A New Way With War. (pamphlet) Glasgow: University Press, for the John Horniman Trust, 1938. 32 pp.
Worship and Fellowship. *Friends Intelligencer,* 95, 35 (Aug. 27, 1938): 579-580.

BOOK REVIEW

Review of W. L. Valk, Production, Pricing, and Unemployment in the Static State. *Economic Journal,* 48, 189 (Mar. 1938): 92-93.

1939

ARTICLES

Equilibrium and Wealth: A Word of Encouragement to Economists. *Canadian Journal of Economics and Political Science,* 5, 1 (Feb. 1939): 1-18. CP I, pp. 91-110.

In Praise of Maladjustment. *Friends Intelligencer,* 96, 32 (Aug. 12, 1939): 519-520.
A Pacifist View of History. *Fellowship,* 5, 3 (Mar. 1939): 10-11.

BOOK REVIEW

Quantitative Economics. Review of John R. Hicks, Value and Capital, An Inquiry into Some Fundamental Principles of Economic Theory; and Henry Schultz, The Theory of Measurement of Demand. *Canadian Journal of Economics and Political Science,* 5, 4 (Nov. 1939): 521-528.

1940

ARTICLES

In Praise of Selfishness. *Friends Intelligencer,* 97, 9 (Mar. 2, 1940): 131-132.
The Pacifism of All Sensible Men. *Friends Intelligencer,* 97, 50 (Dec. 14, 1940): 801.
A Service of National Importance. *American Friend,* 28, 25 (Dec. 5, 1940): 521-522.
Some Reflections on Stewardship. *American Friend,* NS 28, 22 (Oct. 24, 1940): 452-454.

1941

ARTICLE

The Economics of Reconstruction. *American Friend,* 29, 9 (Apr. 24, 1941):177-178.

BOOK

Economic Analysis. New York: Harper & Brothers, 1941. xviii + 809 pp. See also: 1948, 1955, 1966.

1942

ARTICLES and PAMPHLETS

The Abolition of Membership. *American Friend,* 30, 17 (Aug. 13, 1942): 350-351.
A Deepening Loyalty. *Friend,* 115, 26 (June 25, 1942): 467-468.

In Praise of Danger. *Friend*(London), 100, 2 (Jan. 9, 1942): 9-10.

New Nations for Old. (Pendle Hill Pamphlet No. 17) Wallingford, Pa: Pendle Hill, 1942. 40 pp.

The Practice of the Love of God. (William Penn Lecture; pamphlet) Philadelphia: Religious Society of Friends, 1942. 31 pp.

Taxation in War Time: Some Implications for Friends. *American Friend*, 30, 8 (Apr. 9, 1942): 152-167.

The Theory of the Firm in the Last Ten Years. *American Economic Review*, 32, 4 (Dec. 1942): 791-802. CP I, pp. 111-124.

What Is Loyalty? (reflections on "A Statement of Loyalty Issued by Members of the Society of Friends," Mar. 28, 1918) *Friends Intelligencer*, 99, 27 (July 4, 1942): 425-426.

1943

ARTICLE

The Problem of the Country Meeting. *Friends Intelligencer*, 100, 46 (Nov. 13, 1943): 748-749.

1944

ARTICLES

Desirable Changes in the National Economy After the War. (presentation at the American Farm Economic Association meeting, St. Louis, Sept. 1943) *Journal of Farm Economics*, 26, 1 (Feb. 1944): 95-100. CP I, pp. 125-132.

The Incidence of a Profits Tax. *American Economic Review*, 34, 3 (Sept. 1944): 567-572. CP I, pp. 145-152.

Is It the System or Is It You? *Highroad*(Nov. 1944): 14-17.

A Liquidity Preference Theory of Market Prices. *Economica*, NS 11, 42 (May 1944): 55-63. CP I, pp. 133-143. RI.

Nationalism, Millennialism and the Quaker Witness. *American Friend*, 32, 20 (Oct. 5, 1944): 397-398.

Personal and Political Peacemaking: Application of the Friends Peace Testimony. *American Friend*, 32, 17 (Aug. 24, 1944): 347-348.

BOOK REVIEW

Review of Robert A. Brady, Business as a System of Power. *Journal of Land & Public Utility Economics* (Feb. 1944): 85.

VERSE

The Nayler Sonnets. *Inward Light,* 19 (Spring 1944): 4-13. Also published as: There Is A Spirit (The Nayler Sonnets). New York: Fellowship Press, 1945. 26pp.

1945

ARTICLES

The Concept of Economic Surplus. *American Economic Review,* 35, 5 (Dec. 1945): 851-869. Errata. *American Economic Review,* 36, 3 (June 1946): 393. CP I, pp. 191-211.

The Consumption Concept in Economic Theory. *American Economic Review* (Papers and Proceedings of the 57th American Economic Association annual meeting, Washington, D.C., Feb. 1945), 35, 2 (May 1945): 1-14. CP I, pp. 153-168.

The Home as a House of Worship. *Inward Light,* 27 (Nov. 1945): 6-8.

In Defense of Monopoly. *Quarterly Journal of Economics,* 59, 4 (Aug. 1945): 524-542. CP I, pp. 169-189. Reply. *Quarterly Journal of Economics,* 60, 4 (Aug. 1946): 619-621.

The Prayer of Magic and the Prayer of Love. *Friends Intelligencer,* 102, 15 (Apr. 4, 1945): 235-236.

Times and Seasons. *Friends Intelligencer,* 102, 6 (Feb. 10, 1945): 88.

Where Is the Labor Movement Moving? *Kiwanis Magazine,* 30, 2 (Feb. 1945): 11, 31-32.

BOOKS

The Economics of Peace. New York: Prentice-Hall, 1945. ix + 277 pp. Translations: French, German, Japanese, Spanish. Reissued: Freeport, New York: Books for Libraries Press, 1972. 260 pp.

There Is a Spirit (The Nayler Sonnets). See: Verse, 1944.

1946

ARTICLE

In Defense of Monopoly: Reply. See: Articles, 1945.

BOOK REVIEWS

Reply to Hayek. Review of Herman Finer, Road To Reaction. *Nation,* 162, 1 (Jan. 5, 1946): 22-23.

Standard American Protestantism. Review of Norman E. Nygaard, *America Prays.*
American Friend, 34, 23 (Nov. 14, 1946): 455.

1947

ARTICLES

Economic Analysis and Agricultural Policy. (presentation at the Canadian Political
Science Association meeting, Quebec, May 1947) *Canadian Journal of
Economics and Political Science*, 13, 3 (Aug. 1947): 436-446. CP I, pp. 219-
231.

The Inward Light. *Canadian Friend*, 44, 2 (July 1947): 5-6.

A Note on the Theory of the Black Market. *Canadian Journal of Economics and
Political Science*, 13, 1 (Feb. 1947): 115-118. CP I, pp. 213-218. RI.

BOOK REVIEW

Review of Melvin G. DeChazeau *et al.*, Jobs and Markets: How to Prevent Inflation and Depression in the Transition (Committee for Economic Development Research Study). *Review of Economic Statistics*, 29, 1 (Feb. 1947): 52-54.

1948

ARTICLES

Comment on Mr. Burk's Note. (The Net National Product Concept) *American
Economic Review*, 38, 5 (Dec. 1948): 899.

Does Large Scale Enterprise Lower Costs? Discussion. (with others) *American
Economic Review* (Papers and Proceedings of the 60th American Economic
Association annual meeting, Chicago, Dec. 1947), 38, 2 (May 1948): 165-
171.

Price Control in a Subsequent Deflation. *Review of Economics and Statistics*, 30, 1
(Feb. 1948): 15-17.

World Economic Contacts and National Policies. In: *The World Community*,
Quincy Wright, ed. (papers prepared for the 23rd Harris Foundation Institute,
Highland Park, Ill., Mar. 1947). Chicago: University of Chicago Press, 1948,
pp. 95-100; discussion, pp. 101-144.

BOOK

Economic Analysis. Revised edition. New York: Harper & Brothers, 1948. xxvi
+ 884 pp.

BOOK REVIEWS

Samuelson's Foundations: The Role of Mathematics in Economics. Review article
of Paul Samuelson, Foundations of Economic Analysis. *Journal of Political
Economy*, 56, 3 (June 1948): 187-199. CP I, pp. 233-247.
Professor Tarshis and the State of Economics. Review article of Lorie Tarshis, The
Elements of Economics. *American Economic Review*, 38, 1 (Mar. 1948): 92-
102.
Review of D. McCord Wright, The Economics of Disturbance. *Review of
Economics and Statistics*, 30, 1 (Feb. 1948): 74.

1949

ARTICLES

Collective Bargaining and Fiscal Policy. *Industrial Relations Research Association
Proceedings*, 2 (Dec. 1949): 52-68. CP I, pp. 275-291. RI.
The Economic Consequences of Some Recent Antitrust Decisions: Discussion.
(with others) *American Economic Review* (Papers and Proceedings of the 61st
American Economic Association annual meeting, Cleveland, Dec. 1948), 39,
3 (May 1949): 320-321.
Is Economics Necessary? (presentation in the Sciences of Society Symposium at the
Centennial Celebration of the AAAS, Washington, D.C., Sept. 1948) *Scientific
Monthly*, 68, 4 (Apr. 1949): 235-240. BE, pp. 1-13. CP I, pp. 249-261. RI.
The Theory and Measurement of Price Expectations: Discussion. (with others)
American Economic Review (Papers and Proceedings of the 61st American
Economic Association annual meeting, Cleveland, Dec. 1948), 39, 3 (May
1949): 167-168.

BOOK REVIEW

Review of Sumner H. Slichter, The American Economy: Its Problems and
Prospects. *Annals of the American Academy of Political and Social Science*,
261 (Jan. 1949): 201-202.

1950

ARTICLES and PAMPHLET

The Background and Structure of a Macro-Economic Theory of Distribution. In:
Economic Theory in Review, C. Lawrence Christenson, ed. (Social Science
Series No. 8). Bloomington: Indiana University Publications, 1950, pp. 66-81.
Income or Welfare? *Review of Economic Studies*, 17 (2), 43 (1949-50): 77-86. CP
I, pp. 263-274.
The Models for a Macro-Economic Theory of Distribution. In: *Economic Theory
in Review*, C. Lawrence Christenson, ed. (Social Science Series No. 8).
Bloomington: Indiana University Publications, 1950, pp. 82-95.

Protestantism's Lost Economic Gospel. *Christian Century*, 67, 33 (Aug. 16, 1950): 970-972.
Religious Perspectives of College Teaching in Economics. (pamphlet) New Haven, Conn.: Edward W. Hazen Foundation, 1950. 24 pp. BE, pp. 177-197. RI.

BOOK

A Reconstruction of Economics. New York: John Wiley & Sons, 1950. xii + 311 pp. Translation: Portuguese. Paperback edition: New York: Science Editions, 1962.

BOOK REVIEW

Humane Economics. Review of Wilhelm Röpke, The Social Crisis of Our Time. *Christian Century*, 67, 44 (Nov. 1, 1950): 1295.

1951

ARTICLES

Asset Identities in Economic Models. In: *Studies in Income and Wealth*, Vol. 14 (papers from the Conference on Income and Wealth, Apr. 1950). New York: National Bureau of Economic Research, 1951, pp. 229-247; comments, pp. 247-256; reply, pp. 256-258. CP I, pp. 293-311.
Can We Control Inflation in a Garrison State? *Social Action*, 17, 3 (Mar. 15, 1951): 3-24. CP III, pp. 1-24.
Comments. (on Professor Dr. Wolfgang F. Stolper, "The Economics of Peace") *Weltwirtschaftliches Archiv* (Keil, Germany), 66, 1 (1951): 146-147.
Defense and Opulence: The Ethics of International Economics. *American Economic Review* (Papers and Proceedings of the 63rd American Economic Association annual meeting, Chicago, Dec. 1950), 41, 2 (May 1951): 210-220. CP I, pp. 313-325.
Wages as a Share in the National Income. In: *The Impact of the Union: Eight Economic Theorists Evaluate the Labor Union Movement*, D. McCord Wright, ed. (edited report of the Institute on the Structure of the Labor Market, American University, May 1950). New York: Harcourt Brace, 1951, pp. 123-148; discussion, pp. 149-167. CP I, pp. 327-354.
What About Christian Economics? *American Friend*, 39, 23 (Nov. 8, 1951): 361.

BOOK REVIEWS

M. Allais' Theory of Interest. Review article of Maurice Allais, Économie et Intérêt. *Journal of Political Economy*, 59, 1 (Feb. 1951): 69-73.

Review of R. H. Coase, British Broadcasting. *Journal of Higher Education*, 22 (Feb. 1951): 110.

Democracy and the Economic Challenge. Review of the 1950-51 William W. Cook Lectures on American Institutions. *Michigan Alumnus Quarterly Review*, 57, 18 (May 26, 1951): 185-191.

Review of I. M. D. Little, A Critique of Welfare Economics. *Economica*, 18, 70 (May 1951): 207-209.

Review of George Kingsley Zipf, Human Behavior and the Principle of Least Effort. *American Economic Review*, 41, 3 (June 1951): 449-450.

1952

ARTICLES

A Conceptual Framework for Social Science. *Papers of the Michigan Academy of Science, Arts, and Letters*, 37, (1952): 275-282. BE, pp. 55-63. CP IV, pp. 1-10.

Economics as a Social Science. In: *The Social Sciences at Mid-Century: Essays in Honor of Guy Stanton Ford.* Minneapolis: University of Minnesota Press, for the Social Science Research Center of the Graduate School, 1952, pp. 70-83. CP III, pp. 25-40.

The Great Revolution. (summary of Baltimore Yearly Meeting lecture, Mar. 1952) *Friends Intelligencer*, 109, 17 (Apr. 26, 1952): 231-232.

Implications for General Economics of More Realistic Theories of the Firm. *American Economic Review* (Papers and Proceedings of the 64th American Economic Association annual meeting, Boston, Dec. 1951), 42, 2 (May 1952): 35-44. CP I, pp. 355-366.

Religious Foundations of Economic Progress, *Harvard Business Review*, 30, 3 (May-June 1952): 33-44. BE, pp. 196-211. CP III, pp. 41-51. RI.

Welfare Economics. In: *A Survey of Contemporary Economics*, Vol. II, B. Haley, ed. Homewood, Ill.: Richard D. Irwin, for the American Economic Association, 1952, pp. 1-34; comment, pp. 34-38. CP I, pp. 367-402.

BOOK

Readings in Price Theory, Vol. VI. (edited with George J. Stigler) Homewood, Ill.: Richard D. Irwin, for the American Economic Association, 1952. x + 568 pp.

BOOK REVIEWS and DISCUSSION

Discussion of papers by Daniel H. Brill, ''Social Accounting and Economic Analysis;'' Ruth P. Mack, ''Contrasts in Patterns of Flows of Commodities and Funds;'' and Karl Brunner and Harry Markowitz, ''Stocks and Flows in Monetary Analysis.'' *Econometrica*, 20, 3 (July 1952): 497-498.

Memorial Anthology. Review of Arthur F. Burns, ed., Wesley Clair Mitchell, The Economic Scientist. *Scientific Monthly,* 75, 2 (1952): 129-130.

Review of National Bureau of Economic Research, Studies in Income and Wealth, Vol. 13 (Conference on Income and Wealth).*Econometrica,* 20, 1 (Jan. 1952): 107-108.

Shirtsleeve Economics. Review of William A. Paton, Shirtsleeve Economics. *Michigan Alumnus Quarterly Review* (Summer 1952): 360.

Review of Norbert Wiener, The Human Use of Human Beings: Cybernetics and Society. *Econometrica,* 20, 4 (Oct. 1952): 702.

VERSE

The Busted Thermostat. *Michigan Business Review,* 4, 6 (Nov. 1952): 25-26.

1953

ARTICLES

The Contribution of Economics to the Understanding of the Firm—I Marginal Analysis. In: *Contemporary Economic Problems* (Lectures from the Economics-in-Action Program). Cleveland, Ohio: Case Institute of Technology, 1953, pp. 15-27.

The Contribution of Economics to the Understanding of the Firm—II The Theory of Organization and Communications. In: *Contemporary Economic Problems* (Lectures from the Economics-in-Action Program). Cleveland, Ohio: Case Institute of Technology, 1953, pp. 28-40.

Economic Issues in International Conflict. (lecture at Vanderbilt University, Dec. 1951) *Kyklos,* 6, 2 (1953): 97-115. CP V, pp. 1–22.

Economic Progress as a Goal in Economic Life. In: *Goals of Economic Life,* Dudley Ward, ed. New York: Harper & Brothers, 1953, pp. 52-83. CP III, pp. 53-86.

The Fruits of Progress and the Dynamics of Distribution. *American Economic Review* (Papers and Proceedings of the 65th American Economic Association annual meeting, Chicago, Dec. 1952), 43, 2 (May 1953): 473-483. CP I, pp. 403-415.

The Quaker Approach in Economic Life. In: *The Quaker Approach,* John Kavanaugh, ed. New York: G. P. Putnam's Sons, 1953, pp. 43-58.

The Skills of the Economist. In: *Contemporary Economic Problems* (Lectures from the Economics-in-Action Program). Cleveland, Ohio: Case Institute of Technology, 1953, pp. 3-14.

Toward a General Theory of Growth. (paper presented at the Canadian Political Science Association meeting, London, June 1953) *Canadian Journal of Economics and Political Science,* 19, 3 (Aug. 1953): 326-340. BE, pp. 62-82. CP III, pp. 87-103. RI.

BOOK

The Organizational Revolution: A Study in the Ethics of Economic Organization.
New York: Harper & Brothers, 1953. xxxiv + 286 pp. Translation: Japanese.
Paperback edition: Quadrangle Books, 1968. xxxvi + 235 pp.

BOOK REVIEWS

Projection, Prediction, and Precariousness. Review article (with others) of Gerald
Colm, The American Economy in 1960. (National Planning Association Staff
Report). *Review of Economics and Statistics*, 35, 4 (Nov. 1953): 257-260.
Correction and Apology. *Review of Economics and Statistics*, 36, 1 (Feb.
1954): 100.
Economic Theory and Measurement. Review of The Cowles Commission,
Economic Theory and Measurement: Twenty Year Research Report, 1932-
1952. *Kyklos*, 6, 2 (1953): 149-152.
Review of V. A. Demant, Religion and the Decline of Capitalism. *Journal of
Religious Thought*, 10, 2 (Spring-Summer 1953): 180-181.
Review of Benjamin Higgins, What Do Economists Know? *Journal of Business*,
26, 2 (Apr. 1953): 139.
A Note on the Theory of Investment of the Firm. Review of Friedrich and Vera
Lutz, The Theory of Investment of the Firm. *Kyklos*, 6, 1 (1953): 77-81.

1954

ARTICLES

Comment. (Sales and Output Taxes) *American Economic Review*, 44, 1 (Mar.
1954): 129.
An Economist's View of the Manpower Concept. In: *Proceedings of a Conference
on the Utilization of Scientific and Professional Manpower* (National Manpower
Council Conference, Arden House, Columbia University, Oct. 1953). New
York: Columbia University Press, 1954, pp. 11-26; discussion, pp. 26-33.
BE, pp. 12-27. CP I, pp. 417-432.
The Principle of Personal Responsibility. *Review of Social Economy*, 12, 1 (Mar.
1954): 1-8. BE, pp. 210-218. CP IV, pp. 11-20.
The Skills of the Economist (in Portuguese): I. A arte do economista; II. As
aplicacões da economia aos problemas de emprêsa: a analise marginal; III. As
aplicacões da economia ao estudo do comportamento humano: a teoria do
comportamento econômico; IV. A aplicacão da ciência econômica aos
problemas de govêrno; V. Contribuicões da ciência econômica às outras
ciências; VI. A ciência econômica e o futuro da humanidade. *Revista Brasilerra
de Economia*, 189 (Mar. 1954).
Twenty-Five Theses on Peace and Trade. *Friend*, 127 (Mar. 4, 1954): 290-292.
CP V, pp. 23–27. RI.

BOOK REVIEWS

Projection, Prediction, and Precariousness: Correction and Apology. See: Book Reviews, 1953.

Review of Milton Friedman, Essays in Positive Economics. *Political Science Quarterly*, 69, 1 (Mar. 1954): 132-133.

The Concept of Property in Modern Christian Thought. Review of Frank Grace, The Concept of Property in Modern Christian Thought. *Michigan Alumnus Quarterly Review* (May 1954): 272-273.

Review of Kenneth D. Roose, The Economics of Recession and Revival. *Annals of the American Academy of Political and Social Science*, 296 (Nov. 1954): 178.

1955

ARTICLES

An Application of Population Analysis to the Automobile Population of the United States. *Kyklos*, 8, 2 (1955): 109-122. CP I, pp. 433-450.

Contributions of Economics to the Theory of Conflict. *Bulletin of the Research Exchange on the Prevention of War*, 3, 5 (May 1955): 51-59. CP V, pp. 29–39.

In Defense of Statics. *Quarterly Journal of Economics*, 69, 4 (Nov. 1955): 485-502. CP I, pp. 465-484. RI.

The Malthusian Model as a General System. *Social and Economic Studies*, 4, 3 (Sept. 1955): 195-205. CP I, pp. 451-463. RI.

Notes on the Information Concept. *Exploration* (Toronto), 6 (1955): 103-112. CP IV, pp. 21-32.

Parity, Charity, and Clarity: Ten Theses on Agricultural Policy. *Michigan Daily*, Oct. 16, 1955, p. 3. CP III, pp. 121-125.

Possible Conflicts Between Economic Stability and Economic Progress. *Farm Policy Forum*, 8, 1 (1955): 30-36.

BOOK

Economic Analysis. 3rd edition. New York: Harper & Brothers, 1955. xx + 905 pp. Translations: Burmese, Japanese, Portuguese, Turkish.

BOOK REVIEWS

Review of T. Haavelmo, A Study in the Theory of Economic Evolution: Contributions to Economic Analysis, III. *Kyklos*, 8, 1 (1955): 91-92.

Review of Albert Lauterbach, Man, Motives, and Money: Psychological Frontiers of Economics. *Social Order*, 5, 3 (1955): 135-136.

French Keynes. Review of Pierre Mendes-France and Gabriel Ardant, Economics and Action (UNESCO Publication). *Christian Century*, 72, 36 (Sept. 7, 1955): 1024.

Review of Clarence B. Randall, Economics and Public Policy; and A Foreign Economic Policy for the United States. *Christian Century*, 72, 22 (June 1, 1955): 657-658.

VERSE

The Conservationist's Lament; The Technologist's Reply. *Population Bulletin* (Aug. 1955): 70. Also in: *Man's Role in Changing the Face of the Earth*, William L. Thomas, Jr., ed. (international symposium, Princeton, N.J., June 1955). Chicago: University of Chicago Press, for the Wenner-Gren Foundation for Anthropological Research and the National Science Foundation, 1956, p. 1087. RI.

1956

ARTICLES

Changes in Physical Phenomena: Discussion. (with others) In: *Man's Role in Changing the Face of the Earth*, William L. Thomas, Jr., ed. (international symposium, Princeton, N.J., June 1955). Chicago: University of Chicago Press, for the Wenner-Gren Foundation for Anthropological Research and the National Science Foundation, 1956, pp. 917-929.

Commentary. (Perspectives on Prosperity) *Social Action*, 22, 8 (Apr. 1956): 15-16.

Economics and the Behavioral Sciences: A Desert Frontier? *Diogenes*, 15 (Fall 1956): 1-14. CP III, pp. 105-120.

Economics: The Taming of Mammon. In: *Frontiers of Knowledge in the Study of Man*, Lynn White, Jr., ed. New York: Harper & Brothers, 1956, pp. 132-149. BE, pp. 26-42.

General Systems Theory: The Skeleton of Science. *Management Science*, 2, 3 (Apr. 1956): 197-208. BE, pp. 81-97. CP IV, pp. 33-46. RI.

Industrial Revolution and Urban Dominance: Discussion. (with others) In: *Man's Role in Changing the Face of the Earth*, William L. Thomas, Jr., ed. (international symposium, Princeton, N.J., June 1955). Chicago: University of Chicago Press, for the Wenner-Gren Foundation for Anthropological Research and the National Science Foundation, 1956, pp. 434-448.

Limits of the Earth: Discussion. (with others) In: *Man's Role in Changing the Face of the Earth*, William L. Thomas, Jr., ed. (international symposium, Princeton, N.J., June 1955). Chicago: University of Chicago Press, for the Wenner-Gren Foundation for Anthropological Research and the National Science Foundation, 1956, pp. 1071-1087.

Some Contributions of Economics to the General Theory of Value. *Philosophy of Science*, 23, 1 (Jan. 1956): 1-14. CP II, pp. 1-16.

Statement Before the Subcommittee of the Senate Committee on Foreign Relations, U.S. Congress (on behalf of the Friends Committee on National Legislation). In:

Control and Reductions of Armaments (Hearing of the Committee). Washington, D.C.: U.S. Government Printing Office, 1956, Part 8, pp. 418-437.

Structure and Stability: The Economics of the Next Adjustment. In: *Policies to Combat Depression* (Conference of the Universities-National Bureau Committee for Economic Research). Princeton, N.J.: Princeton University Press, for the National Bureau of Economic Research, 1956, pp. 59-76. CP II, pp. 17-34.

BOOK

The Image: Knowledge in Life and Society. Ann Arbor: University of Michigan Press, 1956. 175 pp. Translations: German, Japanese. Paperback edition: Ann Arbor: University of Michigan Press, 1961. 184 pp.

BOOK REVIEWS

Review of J. T. Bonner, Cells and Societies. *American Anthropologist*, 58, 1 (Feb. 1956): 216.

Review of Neil W. Chamberlain, A General Theory of Economic Process. *Social Order*, 6, 3 (Mar. 1956): 128-130.

Ecumenical Social Thought. Review of Edward Duff, The Social Thought of the World Council of Churches. *Social Order*, 6, 8 (Oct. 1956): 392-397.

Review of C. Addison Hickman and Manford H. Kuhn, Individuals, Groups, and Economic Behavior. *Southern Economic Journal*, 23, 2 (Oct. 1956): 188-190.

Review of L. M. Lachmann, Capital and Its Structure. *American Economic Review*, 46, 5 (Dec. 1956): 988-989.

Warning to Nineveh. Review of Gunnar Myrdal, An International Economy: Problems and Prospects. *Christian Century*, 73, 37 (Sept. 12, 1956): 1053-1054.

1957

ARTICLES

Does the Absence of Monopoly Power in Agriculture Influence the Stability and Level of Farm Income? In: *Policy for Commercial Agriculture: Its Relation to Economic Growth and Stability* (papers submitted by panelists appearing before the Subcommittee on Agricultural Policy of the Joint Economic Committee, U.S. Congress). Washington, D.C.: U.S. Government Printing Office, 1957, pp. 42-50. CP II, pp. 111-121. RI.

Economic Theory: The Reconstruction Reconstructed. In: *Segments of the Economy — 1956: A Symposium* (Economics-in-Action Program, Case Institute of Technology, Summer 1957). Cleveland, Ohio: Howard Allen, 1957, pp. 8-55. CP II, pp. 35-85.

A Look at the Corporation. In: *The Lamp* (75th Anniversary of Jersey Standard). New York: Standard Oil Company (N.J.), 1957, pp. 6-7.

A New Look at Institutionalism. *American Economic Review* (Papers and Proceedings of the 69th American Economic Association annual meeting, Cleveland, Dec. 1956), 47, 2 (May 1957): 1-12. CP II, pp. 87-100.

Organization and Conflict. *Journal of Conflict Resolution*, 1, 2 (June 1957): 122-134. RI.

Some Contributions of Economics to Theology and Religion. *Religious Education*, 52, 6 (Nov.-Dec. 1957): 446-450. BE, pp. 217-226. CP IV, pp. 47-53.

Some Reflections on Inflation and Economic Development. In: *Contribuções à Análise do Desinvolvimento Econômico* (Festschrift in honor of Eugenio Gudin). Rio de Janeiro: Instituto Brasileiro de Economia da Fundacão Getúlio Vargas, 1957, pp. 61-67. CP II, pp. 101-109.

BOOK REVIEWS

Review of Joe S. Bain, Barriers to New Competition: Their Character and Consequences in Manufacturing Industries. *Administrative Science Quarterly*, 2, 1 (June 1957): 116-118.

Review of John Maurice Clark, Economic Institutions and Human Welfare. *American Economic Review*, 47, 5 (Dec. 1957): 1004-1005.

Review of Lester de Koster, All Ye That Labor; An Essay on Christianity, Communism and the Problem of Evil. *Reformed Journal* (July-Aug. 1957): 20.

The Parsonian Approach to Economics. Review of Talcott Parsons and Neil J. Smelser, Economy and Society: A Study in the Integration of Economic and Social Theory. *Kyklos*, 10, 3 (1957): 317-319.

1958

ARTICLES

The Current State of Economics. *Challenge*, 6, 10 (Aug.-Sept. 1958): 18-24.

Democracy and Organization. *Challenge*, 6, 6 (Mar. 1958): 13-17. CP V, p. 41.

Evidences for an Administrative Science: A Review of the Administrative Science Quarterly, Volumes 1 and 2. *Administrative Science Quarterly*, 3, 1 (June 1958): 1-22. RI.

The Jungle of Hugeness: The Second Age of the Brontosaurus. *Saturday Review*, 41, 9 (Mar. 1, 1958): 11-13. CP II, pp. 123-131. RI.

"The Organization Man"—Fact or Fancy? In: *The Emerging Environment of Industrial Relations*. East Lansing: Michigan State University, 1958, pp. 66-69.

Religion and the Social Sciences. In: *Religion and the State University*, Erich A. Walter, ed. Ann Arbor: University of Michigan Press, 1958, pp. 136-155. CP IV, pp. 55-76.

Secular Images of Man in the Social Sciences. *Religious Education*, 53, 2 (Mar.-Apr. 1958): 91-96. CP IV, pp. 77-84. RI.

The Sputnik Within. *Liberation*, 2, 10 (Jan. 1958): 13-14.

Statement Before the Subcommittee on Agricultural Policy of the Joint Economic Committee, U.S. Congress. In: Policy for Commercial Agriculture: Its Relation to Economic Growth and Stability (Hearings of the Committee). Washington, D.C.: U.S. Government Printing Office, 1958, pp. 16-18.

Three Concepts of Disarmament. *American Friend* (Special issue on Disarmament), NS 46, 4 (Feb. 20, 1958): 53-54.

Universal, Policed Disarmament as the Only Stable System of National Defense. In: *Problems of United States Economic Development.* New York: Committee for Economic Development, Jan. 1958, pp. 361-367.

BOOKS

Principles of Economic Policy. Englewood Cliffs, N.J.: Prentice-Hall, 1958. vi + 440 pp. Translations: Portuguese, Spanish.

The Skills of the Economist. Cleveland, Ohio: Howard Allen, 1958. vi + 193 pp. Editions: British, Canadian. Translation: Japanese.

BOOK REVIEWS

Review article of Thomas C. Cochran, The American Business System: A Historical Perspective, 1900-1955. (with John Kenneth Galbraith) *Business History Review*, 32, 1 (Spring 1958): 116-121.

Review of Instituto Brasileiro de Economia da Fundacão Getúlio Vargas, Contribuicões a Análise do Desinvolvimento Econômico (Festschrift in honor of Eugenio Gudin). *American Economic Review*, 48, 3 (June 1958): 462-463.

Theoretical Systems and Political Realities. Review of Morton A. Kaplan, System and Process in International Politics. *Journal of Conflict Resolution*, 2, 4 (Dec. 1958): 329-334.

Review of Erik Lundberg, Business Cycles and Economic Policy. *Annals of the American Academy of Political and Social Science*, 318 (July 1958): 179.

The Myth of the Ruling Class. Review of James H. Meisel, The Myth of the Ruling Class: Gaetano Mosca and the ''Elite.'' *Michigan Alumnus Quarterly Review*, 65, 10 (Dec. 6, 1958): 88-89.

Groaning Table. Review of Wilbur Schramm, Responsibility in Mass Communication. *Christian Century*, 75, 9 (Feb. 26, 1958): 252.

VERSE

The Brandywine River Anthology. (written for a seminar for educators sponsored by the Du Pont Company, Wilmington, Del., Mar. 1958) *Michigan Business Review*, 10, 2 (Mar. 1958): 7-9.

T. R. *Library of Congress Journal of Current Acquisitions* (15th Anniversary issue including "The Theodore Roosevelt Centennial Exhibit"), 15, 3 (May 1958): 100.

1959

ARTICLES

Foreword. In: *Population: The First Essay*, by T. R. Malthus. Ann Arbor, Mich.: Ann Arbor Paperbacks, 1959, pp. v-xii. CP II, pp. 133-142.

The Knowledge of Value and the Value of Knowledge. In: *Ethics and the Social Sciences*, Leo R. Ward, ed. (lectures at Notre Dame, Fall 1957). Notre Dame, Ind.: Notre Dame University Press, 1959, pp. 25-42. CP IV, pp. 85-104.

National Images and International Systems. (paper presented at the American Psychological Association meeting, Washington, D.C., Aug. 1958) *Journal of Conflict Resolution*, 3, 2 (June 1959): 120-131. CP V, pp. 49-62. RI.

Organizing Growth. *Challenge*, 8, 3 (Dec. 1959): 31-36. CP IV, pp. 105-112.

Symbols for Capitalism. *Harvard Business Review*, 37, 1 (Jan.-Feb. 1959): 41-48. CP II, pp. 143-152. RI.

BOOK REVIEWS

Review of Bernard Biet, Theories Contemporaines du Profit. *Econometrica*, 27, 2 (Apr. 1959): 321.

Review of Arthur H. Cole, Business Enterprise in Its Social Setting. *Administrative Science Quarterly*, 4, 3 (Dec. 1959): 361-362.

Review of John Kenneth Galbraith, The Affluent Society. *Review of Economics and Statistics*, 41, 1 (Feb. 1959): 81.

The Mighty Dollar. Review of F. Ernest Johnson and J. Emory Ackerman, The Church as Employer, Money Raiser and Investor. *Christian Century*, 76, 47 (Nov. 25, 1959): 1376-1377.

Review of John B. Rae, American Automobile Manufacturers: The First Forty Years. *Technology and Culture*, 1, 1 (Winter 1959): 104-105.

1960

ARTICLES

Capital and Interest. *Encyclopedia Britannica*, Vol. 4 (1960): 799-801. CP II, pp. 309-322. RI.

The Costs of Independence: Notes on the Caribbean. *Challenge*, 9, 3 (Dec. 1960): 14-18.

Decision-Making in the Modern World. In: *An Outline of Man's Knowledge of the Modern World*, Lyman Bryson, ed. New York: McGraw-Hill, 1960, pp. 410-442.

The Domestic Implications of Arms Control. *Daedalus* (Special issue on Arms Control), 89, 4 (Fall 1960): 846-859. CP V, pp. 63–78. RI.

The Present Position of the Theory of the Firm. In: *Linear Programming and the Theory of the Firm*, K. E. Boulding and W. Allen Spivey, eds. New York: Macmillan, 1960, pp. 1-17. CP II, pp. 153-171.

Scientific Nomenclature. *Science*, 131, 3404 (Mar. 18, 1960): 874, 876; *Science*, 131, 3412 (May 20, 1960): 1556-1567.

Standards for Our Economic System: Discussion. (with others) *American Economic Review* (Papers and Proceedings of the 72nd American Economic Association annual meeting, Washington, D.C., Dec. 1959), 50, 2 (May 1960): 23-24.

A Theory of Small Society. *Caribbean Quarterly* (Jamaica), 6, 4 (1960): 258-269. CP IV, pp. 113-126.

Violence and Revolution: Some Reflections on Cuba. *Liberation*, 5, 2 (Apr. 1960): 5-8.

BOOK

Linear Programming and the Theory of the Firm (edited with W. Allen Spivey). New York: Macmillan, 1960. x + 227 pp. Translation: French.

BOOK REVIEWS

Philosophy, Behavioral Science, and the Nature of Man. Review article of Hannah Arendt, The Human Condition; and Christian Bay, The Structure of Freedom. *World Politics*, 12, 2 (Jan. 1960): 272-279.

Review of Edward S. Mason, ed., The Corporation in Modern Society. *Business History Review*, 34, 4 (Winter 1960): 499-501.

Review of Reinhold Niebuhr, The Structure of Nations and Empires. *Review of Religious Research*, 1, 3 (Winter 1960): 122-124.

Review of Overton H. Taylor, The Classical Liberalism, Marxism, and the Twentieth Century. *American Economic Review*, 50, 1 (Mar. 1960): 168-169.

Review of Willard L. Thorp and Richard E. Quandt, The New Inflation. *Journal of the American Statistical Association*, 55, 291 (Sept. 1960): 616-617.

Review of Geoffrey Vickers, The Undirected Society: Essays on the Human Implications of Industrialisation in Canada. *Journal of Political Economy*, 68, 4 (Aug. 1960): 419-420.

1961

ARTICLES and PAMPHLET

Contemporary Economic Research. In: *Trends in Social Science*, Donald P. Ray, ed. (presentations at the special symposium held by the Section on Social and Economic Sciences, AAAS, Washington, D.C., 1958). New York: Philosophical Library, 1961, pp. 9-26.

The Dynamics of Disarmament. *Intercollegian.* 78, 8 (May 1961): 10-14.

Economic Resources and World Peace. In: *The Challenge of the '60s* (Lecture-Seminary Series 1960-61). Palo Alto, Calif.: Palo Alto Unified School District, 1961, pp. 27-35.

Our Attitude Toward Revolution. *Think,* 27, 7 (July-Aug. 1961): 27-29.

Perspective on the Economics of Peace. (pamphlet) Part I of Economic Factors Bearing upon the Maintenance of Peace (Report to the Committee on Research for Peace). New York: Institute for International Order, 1961. 38 pp.

Political Implications of General Systems Research. (presidential address to the Society for General Systems Research, AAAS, Indianapolis, Dec. 1958) *General Systems Yearbook,* Vol. VI (1961): 1-7. CP IV, pp. 127-135.

The Public Image of American Economic Institutions. In: *American Perspectives: The National Self-Image in the Twentieth Century,* Robert E. Spiller and Eric Larrabee, eds. Cambridge, Mass.: Harvard University Press, 1961, pp. 117-133. CP III, pp. 127-145.

A Pure Theory of Conflict Applied to Organizations. In: *Conflict Management in Organizations* (Report of a seminar conducted by the Foundation in cooperation with the Center for Research on Conflict Resolution, University of Michigan, Oct. 1961). Ann Arbor, Mich.: Foundation for Research on Human Behavior, 1961, pp. 43-51. CP V, pp. 79-89. RI.

Qu'est-ce que le progrès économique? (What is Economic Progress?; in French) *Cahiers de l'Institut de Science Économique Appliquée* (Paris), 110 (Feb. 1961): 147-155. CP II, pp. 173-180.

Reflections on Poverty. In: *The Social Welfare Forum, 1961* (Proceedings of the 88th Annual Forum, Minneapolis, May 1961). New York: Columbia University Press, for the National Conference on Social Welfare, 1961, pp. 45-58. CP II, pp. 181-196.

Social Dynamics in West Indian Society. *Social and Economic Studies,* 10, 1 (Mar. 1961): 25-34.

Some Difficulties in the Concept of Economic Input. In: *Output, Input, and Productivity Measurement* (Studies in Income and Wealth, Vol. 25; National Bureau of Economic Research conference, Carnegie Endowment International Center, New York, Oct. 1958). Princeton, N.J.: Princeton University Press, 1961, pp. 331-345. CP II, pp. 197-208.

Study of the Soviet Economy: Its Place in American Education. (discussion with others) In: *Study of the Soviet Economy,* Nicholas Spulber, ed. (Russian and East European Series, Vol. 25). Bloomington: Indiana University Publications, 1961, pp. 104-128.

The U.S. and Revolution. In: *The U.S. and Revolution: An Occasional Paper on the Free Society.* Santa Barbara, Calif.: Center for the Study of Democratic

Institutions, 1961, pp. 4-7. CP V, pp. 91–96. RI.

Where Do We Go From Here, If Anywhere? In: *Proceedings of the Fourteenth National Conference on the Administration of Research* (held at the University of Michigan, Sept. 1960). University Park: Pennsylvania State University Press, 1961, pp. 66-72. CP II, pp. 209-217.

BOOK REVIEWS

French Window. Review of Raymond Aron, Introduction to the Philosophy of History. *Christian Century*, 78, 33 (Aug. 16, 1961): 981.

Review of Jean Fourastié, The Causes of Wealth, translated by Theodore Caplow. *Technology and Culture*, 2, 3 (Summer 1961): 262-264.

Trying to Square the Circle. Review of Charles J. Hitch and Roland McKean, The Economics of Defense in the Nuclear Age. *Bulletin of the Atomic Scientists*, 17, 3 (Mar. 1961): 115-116.

Nothing Rash. Review of P. B. Medawar, The Future of Man: Predictions of a Biologist. *Christian Century*, 78, 20 (May 17, 1961): 623.

Review of Gunnar Myrdal, Beyond the Welfare State: Economic Planning and Its International Implications. *Administrative Science Quarterly*, 6, 1 (June 1961): 107-109.

Review of Talcott Parsons, Structure and Process in Modern Societies. *Psychiatry*, 24, 3 (Aug. 1961): 278-279.

The Nightmare of Rationality. Review of Thomas C. Schelling, The Strategy of Conflict. *Contemporary Psychology*, 8, 2 (June 1961): 426-427.

Review of Dan Wilson, An Opening Way (Pendle Hill Pamphlet No. 113). *Quaker Life*, 2, 7 (July 1961): 189.

VERSE

A Shelter For All.(Preamble to a Statement issued by the Friends National Conference on World Order, Richmond, Ind., Oct. 1961) *Friends Journal*, 7, 23 (Dec. 1, 1961): 489.

1962

ARTICLES

Better R-E-D Than Dead. *New Republic* (Special issue on Time for a Keynes: An Inquiry into What New Economic Thinking Is Required for the U.S. in the Sixties), 147, 16 (Oct. 20, 1962): 15-16.

Can We Afford a Warless World? *Saturday Review*, 45, 40 (Oct. 6, 1962): 17-20. RI.

Economics and Accounting: The Uncongenial Twins. In: *Studies in Accounting Theory*, W. T. Baxter and Sidney Davidson, eds. London: Sweet and Maxwell, 1962, pp. 44-55. CP II, pp. 219-232. RI.

The Ethical Perspective. In: *Christians Face Issues of High Moment In Our Changing Economy* (papers for the National Study Conference on the Church and Economic Life, Pittsburgh, Nov. 1962). New York: National Council of Churches, 1962, pp. 35-44. CP IV, pp. 137-148. RI.

Ethics and Business: An Economist's View. (presentation at a seminar, Pennsylvania State University, Mar. 1962) In: *Ethics and Business.* University Park: Pennsylvania State University College of Business Administration, Sept. 1962, pp. 1-14. BE, pp. 225-238. RI.

An Interdisciplinary Honors Course in General Systems. *Superior Student* (Boulder, Colo.), 4, 7 (Jan.-Feb. 1962): 31.

Is Peace Researchable? *Continuous Learning* (Toronto), 1, 2 (Mar.-Apr. 1962): 63-69. CP V, pp. 97–105. RI.

Knowledge as a Commodity. (presentation at a special session co-sponsored by the American Economic Association, AAAS meetings, Denver, 1961) In: *Series Studies in Social and Economic Sciences* (Symposia Studies No. 11). Washington, D.C.: National Institute of Social and Behavioral Science, June 1962, pp. 1-6. BE, pp. 139-150.

Notes on a Theory of Philanthropy. In: *Philanthropy and Public Policy*, F. G. Dickinson, ed. (NBER Conference on Philanthropy, Merrill Center for Economics, Long Island, N.Y., June 1961). New York: National Bureau of Economic Research, 1962, pp. 57-71. CP II, pp. 233-249.

The Peace Research Movement. *Council for Correspondence Newsletter* (1962): 25-32. RI.

The Prevention of World War III. *Virginia Quarterly Review*, 38, 1 (Winter 1962): 1-12. CP V, pp. 107–119. RI.

A Pure Theory of Death: Dilemmas of Defense Policy in a World of Conditional Viability. In: *Behavioral Science and Civil Defense,* George W. Baker and Leonard S. Cottrell, Jr., eds. (presentations at the conference on Behavioral Science and Civil Defense, Washington, D.C., May 1961; National Academy of Sciences-National Research Council Publication No. 997). Washington, D.C.: National Academy of Sciences, 1962, pp. 53-69. BE, pp. 112-130.

The Relations of Economic, Political and Social Systems. *Social and Economic Studies* (Special issue on the Conference on Political Sociology in the British Caribbean, Jamaica, Dec. 1961), 11, 4 (Dec. 1962): 351-362. BE, pp. 96-111. CP IV, pp. 149-162.

The Role of the Price Structure in Economic Development. (with Pritam Singh) *American Economic Review* (Papers and Proceedings of the 74th American Economic Association annual meeting, New York, Dec. 1961), 52, 2 (May 1962): 28-38. CP II, pp. 251-263.

Social Justice in Social Dynamics. In: *Social Justice,* Richard B. Brandt, ed. (based on lectures presented under the auspices of the William J. Cooper Foundation, Swarthmore College, Spring 1961). New York: Prentice-Hall, 1962, pp. 73-92. BE, pp. 239-257. CP IV, pp. 163-184.

Some Questions on the Measurement and Evaluation of Organization. In: *Ethics and Bigness: Scientific, Academic, Religious, Political, and Military,* Harlan Cleveland and Harold D. Lasswell, eds. (papers prepared for the 16th meeting of the Conference on Science, Philosophy and Religion in Their Relation to the

Democratic Way of Life, held at the Jewish Theological Seminary of America, New York, Aug. 1960). New York: Harper & Brothers, 1962, pp. 385-395. BE, pp. 129-140. CP III, pp. 147-159.

The University, Society and Arms Control. *Journal of Conflict Resolution,* 7, 3 (Sept. 1963): 458-463; *Journal of Arms Control* (joint volume; Proceedings of the International Arms Control Symposium, Ann Arbor, Mich., Dec. 1962), 1, 4 (Oct. 1963): 552-557.

War as an Economic Institution. In: *The Causes of War* (Final Report of the 3rd Annual Seminar on International Affairs, Nov. 1961). Montreal: Sir George Williams University, 1962, pp. 38-48.

Where Are We Going, If Anywhere? A Look at Post-Civilization. *Human Organization* (Special issue on Major Issues in Modern Society), 21, 2 (Summer 1962): 162-167. RI.

BOOK

Conflict and Defense: A General Theory. New York: Harper & Brothers, 1962. ix + 343 pp. Translation: Japanese. Paperback edition: New York: Harper & Brothers, 1963. ix + 349 pp.

BOOK REVIEWS

Review of John Maurice Clark, Competition as a Dynamic Process. *Annals of the American Academy of Political and Social Science,* 343 (Sept. 1962): 181-182.

Political Non-Science. Review of Marshall E. Dimock, The New American Political Economy; and C. E. Ayres, Toward a Reasonable Society. *Science,* 136, 3515 (May 11, 1962): 509-510.

An Economist's View. Review of George Caspar Homans, Social Behavior: Its Elementary Forms. *American Journal of Sociology,* 67, 4 (Jan. 1962): 458-461.

Pacifists, Too, Must Think. Review article of Herman Kahn, Thinking About the Unthinkable. *Fellowship,* 28, 14 (Sept. 1, 1962): 27-30.

Review of Gardiner C. Means, Pricing Power and the Public Interest: A Study Based on Steel. *Administrative Science Quarterly,* 7, 2 (Sept. 1962): 266-268.

Review of Fred L. Polak, The Image of the Future, Vols. I and II, translated from the Dutch by Elise Boulding. *Journal of Political Economy,* 70, 2 (Apr. 1962): 192-193.

Review of Kurt Samuelsson, Religion and Economic Action, translated from the Swedish by E. Geoffrey French. *Journal of Political Economy,* 70, 4 (Aug. 1962): 423-424.

Review of Allen M. Sievers, Revolution, Evolution and the Economic Order. *Journal of Finance,* 17, 4 (Dec. 1962): 705-706.

VERSE

Some Reflections. In: *The Church in a World That Won't Hold Still* (Report of the 4th National Study Conference on the Church and Economic Life, Pittsburgh, Nov. 1962). New York: National Council of Churches, 1962, p. 48.

1963

ARTICLES

Agricultural Organization and Policies: A Personal Evaluation. In: *Farm Goals in Conflict: Farm Family Income, Freedom, Security* (presentations at the Second Conference on Goals and Values in Agriculture sponsored by the Center for Agricultural and Economic Development, Feb. 1963). Ames: Iowa State University Press, 1963, pp. 156-166. CP III, pp. 161-173.

The Death of the City: A Frightened Look at Post-Civilization. In: *The Historian and the City,* Oscar Handlin and John Burchard, eds. (papers presented at the Conference on the City and History, Harvard Summer School, Cambridge, July 1961).Cambridge, Mass.: M.I.T. Press, 1963, pp. 133-145. CP II, pp. 265-279.

The Future Corporation and Public Attitudes. In: *The Corporation and Its Publics; Essays on the Corporate Image,* John W. Riley, Jr., ed. (Papers prepared for the Foundation for Research on Human Behavior Symposium, Gould House, Ardsley-on-Hudson, N.Y., Spring 1961) New York: John Wiley & Sons, 1963, pp. 159-175. CP III, pp. 175-193.

The Misallocation of Intellectual Resources. *Proceedings of the American Philosophical Society,* 107, 2 (Apr. 1963): 117-120. BE, pp. 149-157. CP III, pp. 195-200.

Pacem in Terris and the World Community. (with others; comments on the Pope's Encyclical) *Continuum,* 1, 2 (Summer 1963): 214-217.

Preface. (with Emile Benoit) In: *Disarmament and the Economy,* Emile Benoit and Kenneth Boulding, eds. New York: Harper & Row, 1963, pp. vii-x.

The Role of Law in the Learning of Peace. *Proceedings of the American Society of International Law* (1963): 92-103. CP V, pp. 121–134.

The Society of Abundance. In: *The Church in a Society of Abundance,* Arthur E. Walmsley, ed. New York: Seabury Press, 1963, pp. 9-27. CP IV, pp. 185-205.

Towards a Pure Theory of Threat Systems. *American Economic Review* (Papers and Proceedings of the 75th American Economic Association annual meeting, Pittsburgh, Dec. 1962), 53, 2 (May 1963): 424-434. CP V, p. 135. RI.

The Uses of Price Theory. In: *Models of Markets,* Alfred R. Oxenfeldt, ed. (papers presented at the Conference on Appraisals of the Market Models of Price Theory, Arden House, Harriman, N.Y., Apr. 1962, and a later conference) New York: Columbia University Press, 1963, pp. 146-162. CP II, pp. 281-299.

The World War Industry as an Economic Problem. In: *Disarmament and the Economy,* Emile Benoit and Kenneth Boulding, eds. New York: Harper & Row, 1963, pp. 3-27.

BOOK

Disarmament and the Economy. (edited with Emile Benoit; final report of the Program of Research on Economic Adjustments to Disarmament, READ, sponsored by the Center for Research on Conflict Resolution, University of Michigan). New York: Harper & Row, 1963. 310 pp.

BOOK REVIEWS

Two Recent Studies of Modern Society. Review of Sebastian de Grazia, Of Time, Work, and Leisure; and Hugh Dalziel Duncan, Communication and Social Order. *Scientific American*, 208, 1 (Jan. 1963): 157-160.

Review of Milton Friedman, Capitalism and Freedom. *Journal of Business*, 36, 1 (Jan. 1963): 120-121.

The Knowledge Industry. Review of Fritz Machlup, The Production and Distribution of Knowledge in the United States. *Challenge*, 11, 8 (May 1963): 36-38.

Review of Victor Perlo, Militarism and Industry — Arms Profiteering in the Missile Age. *American Economic Review*, 53, 4 (Sept. 1963): 809-810.

Review of Joan Robinson, Economic Philosophy. *American Sociological Review*, 28, 4 (Aug. 1963): 657-658.

Review of W. Lloyd Warner, The Corporation in the Emergent American Society. *American Journal of Sociology*, 68, 6 (May 1963): 702.

Review of Quincy Wright, William M. Evan, and Morton Deutsch, eds., Preventing World War III: Some Proposals. *Annals of the American Academy of Political and Social Science*, 348 (July 1963): 225-226.

VERSE

Arden House Poetry. In: *Models of Markets*, Alfred R. Oxenfeldt, ed. (presentations at the Conference on Appraisal of the Market Models of Price Theory, Arden House, Harriman, N.Y., Apr. 1962, and a later conference). New York: Columbia University Press, 1963, pp. 369-371.

1964

ARTICLES and PAMPHLET

The Dimensions of Economic Freedom. In: *The Nation's Economic Objectives*, Edgar O. Edwards, ed. (lectures presented during Rice University's 50th Anniversary, Spring 1963). Chicago: University of Chicago Press, 1964, pp. 107-122. BE, pp. 256-274. CP III, pp. 201-218. RI.

The Economist and the Engineer: Economic Dynamics of Water Resource Development. In: *Economics and Public Policy in Water Resource Development*, Stephen C. Smith and Emery N. Castle, eds. (papers presented to the

Committee on the Economics of Water Resources Development of the Western Agricultural Economics Research Council). Ames: Iowa State University Press, 1964, pp. 82-92. CP III, pp. 219-231.

The Evolutionary Potential of Quakerism. (Pendle Hill Pamphlet No. 136) Wallingford, Pa.: Pendle Hill, 1964. 31 pp.

General Systems as a Point of View. In: *Views on General Systems Theory,* Mihajlo D. Mesarovic, ed. (Proceedings of the Second Systems Symposium, Case Institute of Technology, Cleveland, Apr. 1963). New York: John Wiley & Sons, 1964, pp. 25-38. CP IV, pp. 207-222.

Knowledge as an Economic Variable. (paper presented at the Japanese Association of Theoretical Economics meeting, Tokyo, Fall 1963) *Economic Studies Quarterly* (Tokyo), 14, 3 (June 1964): 1-6. CP II, pp. 301-308.

Market: Economic Theory. *Encyclopedia Britannica,* Vol. 14 (1964): 913-914.

The Need for a Study on the Psychology of Disarmament. *Our Generation Against Nuclear War* (Supplement on Peace Research), *3, 2* (Oct. 1964): 39-41.

Needs and Opportunities in Peace Research and Peace Education. *Our Generation Against Nuclear War* (Supplement on Peace Research), 3, 2 (Oct. 1964): 22-25. CP V, pp. 149–154.

The Place of the Image in the Dynamics of Society. (based on an address before the Public Relations Institute, Cornell University, Aug. 1961) In: *Explorations in Social Change,* George K. Zollschan and Walter Hirsch, eds. Boston: Houghton-Mifflin and London: Routledge and Kegan Paul, 1964, pp. 5-16. CP IV, pp. 223-236.

The Possibilities of Peace Research in Australia. *Australian Outlook* (Melbourne), 18, 2 (Aug. 1964): 165-169.

Realism and Sentimentalism in the Student Movement. *ICU* (International Christian University, Tokyo), 11 (1963/64): 74-75.

Toward a Theory of Peace. In: *International Conflict and Behavioral Science — The Craigville Papers,* Roger Fisher, ed. (papers prepared for the American Academy of Arts and Sciences Institute on Behavioral Science Research Toward Peace, Craigville, Mass., Aug. 1962). New York: Basic Books, 1964, pp. 70-87.

Two Principles of Conflict. In: *Power and Conflict in Organizations,* Robert L. Kahn and Elise Boulding, eds. (based on two seminars conducted by the Foundation for Research on Human Behavior, 1960 and 1961). New York: Basic Books, for the Foundation for Research on Human Behavior, Ann Arbor, Mich., 1964, pp. 75-76.

Why Did Gandhi Fail? In: *Gandhi — His Relevance for Our Times,* G. Ramachandran and T. K. Mahadevan, eds. Bombay: Bharatiya Vidya Bhavan, for the Gandhi Peace Foundation, 1964, pp. 129-134. CP V, pp. 155–162. RI.

BOOK

The Meaning of the Twentieth Century: The Great Transition. New York: Harper & Row, 1964. xvi + 199 pp. Edition: British. Translations: Italian, Japanese, Portuguese, Spanish. Paperback edition: New York: Harper Colophon Books, 1965. 208 pp.

BOOK REVIEWS

Review of David Braybrooke and Charles E. Lindblom, A Strategy of Decision: Policy Evaluation as a Social Process. *American Sociological Review,* 29, 6 (Dec. 1964): 930-931.

Review of Richard M. Cyert and James G. March, A Behavioral Theory of the Firm. *American Sociological Review,* 29, 4 (Aug. 1964): 592-593.

The Content of International Studies in College: A Review. Review article of Ernst B. Haas and Allen S. Whiting, Dynamics of International Relations; Charles A. McClelland, College Teaching of International Relations; Hans J. Morgenthau, Politics Among Nations; A. F. K. Organski, World Politics; Norman Padelford and George A. Lincoln, The Dynamics of International Politics; James Rosenau, ed., International Politics and Foreign Policy: A Reader in Research and Theory; Charles P. Schleicher, International Relations; and John G. Stoessinger, The Might of Nations. *Journal of Conflict Resolution,* 8, 1 (Mar. 1964): 65-71.

Review of Alfred Kuhn, The Study of Society: A Unified Approach. *Accounting Review,* 39, 2 (Apr. 1964): 530-531.

Review of La Paix, Recueils de la Societe Jean Bodin, pour L'Histoire Comparative. Editions de la Librarie Encyclopedique. *Comparative Studies in Society and History,* 6, 2 (Jan. 1964): 217-219.

Word Meanings in Economics. Review of Fritz Machlup, Essays on Economic Semantics, Merton H. Miller, Walter D. Fackler, and Tom E. Davis, eds. *Monthly Labor Review,* 87, 5 (May 1964): 577.

Statistical Image. Review of Angus Maddison, Economic Growth in the West: Comparative Experience in Europe and North America. *Science,* 146, 3648 (Nov. 27, 1964): 1151-1152.

Ice Enveloped in Fire. Review of Anatol Rapoport, Strategy and Conscience. *Peace News* (London), 1480 (Nov. 6, 1964): 8.

1965

ARTICLES

America's Great Delusion. *Labor Today,* 4, 3 (June-July 1965): 21, 23.

The Changing Framework of American Capitalism. *Challenge,* 14, 2 (Nov.-Dec. 1965): 39-42. CP III, pp. 251-256.

The Communication of Legitimacy. *Channels* (Western Michigan University) (Spring 1965): 24-28. CP IV, pp. 237-243.

The Concept of World Interest. In: *Economics and the Idea of Mankind,* Bert F. Hoselitz, ed. (under the auspices of the Council for the Study of Mankind). New York: Columbia University Press, 1965, pp. 41-62. RI.

The Difficult Art of Doing Good. (lecture in the 1964 Summer Lecture Series, University of Colorado) *Colorado Quarterly,* 13, 3 (Winter 1965): 197-211. CP IV, pp. 245-261.

The Dilemma of Power and Legitimacy. In: *Power and Responsibility, Proceedings of the Institute of World Affairs* (held in Pasadena, Calif., Dec. 1964), Vol. XL. Los Angeles: University of Southern California, 1965, pp. 183-188.

Economic Libertarianism. In: *Conference on Savings and Residential Financing, 1965 Proceedings.* Chicago: U.S. Savings and Loan League, Sept. 1965, pp. 30-42; discussion, pp. 42-57. BE, pp. 41-54. CP II, pp. 345-358.

Economics. In: *System Engineering Handbook,* Robert E. Machol, ed. New York: McGraw-Hill, 1965, pp. 35-1 to 35-8.

The Economics of Human Conflict. In: *The Nature of Human Conflict,* Elton B. McNeil, ed. Englewood Cliffs, N.J.: Prentice-Hall, 1965, pp. 172-191. CP II, pp. 323-344.

The Future of the Social Sciences. *Science Journal* (London), 1, 7 (Sept. 1965): 3.

Great Society, or Grandiose? *Washington Post,* Dec. 5, 1965, p. E3. RI.

How Scientists Study ''Getting Along.'' In: *Our Working World: Neighbors at Work, Teacher's Resource Unit.* Chicago: Science Research Associates, 1965.

Insight and Knowledge in the Development of Stable Peace. In: *No Time But This Present, Studies Preparatory to the Fourth World Conference of Friends 1967.* Birmingham, Eng.: Friends World Committee for Consultation, 1965, pp. 210-219.

Looking Ahead to the Year 2000. *Fellowship,* 31, 5 (May 1965): 26-29.

The Menace of Methuselah: Possible Consequences of Increased Life Expectancy. (address before the Washington Academy of Sciences, Mar. 1965) *Journal of the Washington Academy of Sciences,* 55, 7 (Oct. 1965): 171-179. CP IV, pp. 263-273.

Population and Poverty. *Correspondent,* 35 (Autumn 1965): 38-40. CP II, pp. 359-363. RI.

Reality Testing and Value Orientation in International Systems: The Role of Research. (paper presented at the 6th International Studies Association annual meeting, Colorado Springs, Colo., Apr. 1965) *International Social Science Journal,* 17, 3 (Apr. 1965): 404-416; French translation: 432-445. RI.

Reflections on Protest. *Bulletin of the Atomic Scientists,* 21, 8 (Oct. 1965): 18-20. CP V, pp. 173–178. RI.

Research and Development for the Emergent Nations. In: *Economics of Research and Development,* Richard A. Tybout, ed. (OSU Conference on Economics of Research and Development, Oct. 1962). Columbus: Ohio State University Press, for the Mershon Center for Education in National Security, 1965, pp. 422-437; comments, 438-447. CP III, pp. 233-250.

Social Sciences. In: *The Great Ideas Today,* R.M. Hutchins and M. J. Adler, eds. Chicago: Encyclopedia Britannica, 1965, pp. 254-285. CP IV, pp. 275-306.

Statement Before the Subcommittee on Fiscal Policy of the Joint Economic Committee, U.S. Congress. In: *Fiscal Policy Issues of the Coming Decade* (materials submitted to the committee). Washington, D.C.: U.S. Government Printing Office, 1965, pp. 17-18.

War as a Public Health Problem: Conflict Management as a Key to Survival. In: *Behavioral Science and Human Survival,* Milton Schwebel, ed. (based on presentations at the American Orthopsychiatric Association annual meeting, Washington, D.C., Mar. 1963). Palo Alto, Calif.: Science and Behavioral Books, 1965, pp. 103-110. CP V, pp. 163–172.

War as an Investment: The Strange Case of Japan. (with Alan H. Gleason) *Peace Research Society (International) Papers* (Chicago Conference, 1964), Vol. III (1965): 1-17. CP III, pp. 257-275. RI.

BOOK REVIEWS

Review of David T. Bazelon, The Paper Economy. *Administrative Science Quarterly*, 9, 4 (Mar. 1965): 450-451.

Review of Karl De Schweinitz, Jr., Industrialization and Democracy: Economic Necessities and Political Possibilities. *American Economic Review*, 15, 1 (Mar. 1965): 181-182.

Is Economics Obsolescent? Review of Adolph Lowe, On Economic Knowledge: Toward a Science of Political Economics. *Scientific American*, 212, 5 (May 1965): 139-143.

The Medium and the Message. Review of Marshall McLuhan, The Gutenberg Galaxy: The Making of Typographic Man; and Understanding Media, The Extensions of Man. *Canadian Journal of Economics and Political Science*, 31, 2 (May 1965): 268-273. CP IV, pp. 307-314.

Scabbard or Sword? Review of Walter Millis, An End To Arms (Center for the Study of Democratic Institutions Book); and Thomas S. Power with Albert A. Arnhym, Design for Survival. *Book Week*, May 2, 1965, pp. 15, 17.

1966

ARTICLES and PAMPHLET

Arms Limitation and Integrative Activity as Elements in the Establishment of Stable Peace. *Peace Research Society (International) Papers* (Vienna Conference, 1966), Vol. VI (1966): 1-10.

The Concept of Need for Health Services. (one of a series of papers on Health Services Research sponsored by the HSR Study Section of the U.S. Public Health Services) *Milbank Memorial Fund Quarterly*, Part 2, 44, 4 (Oct. 1966): 202-225. CP III, pp. 277-298.

Conflict Management as a Learning Process. In: *Ciba Foundation Symposium on Conflict in Society*, Anthony de Reuck and Julie Knight, eds. (symposium at the Ciba Foundation, London, June 1965).London: J. & A. Churchill, 1966, pp. 236-248; discussion, pp. 249-258. CP V, pp. 179–193.

Economics and Ecology. In: *Future Environments in North America*, F. Fraser Darling and John P. Milton, eds. (conference of the Conservation Foundation, Airlie House, Warrenton, Va., Apr. 1965). Garden City, N.Y.: Natural History Press, 1966, pp. 225-234. CP III, pp. 299-310.

The Economics of Knowledge and the Knowledge of Economics. (Richard T. Ely Lecture) *American Economic Review* (Papers and Proceedings of the 78th American Economic Association annual meeting, New York, Dec. 1965), 56, 2 (May 1966): 1-13. CP II, pp. 365-379. RI.

The Economics of the Coming Spaceship Earth. In: *Environmental Quality in a Growing Economy, Essays from the Sixth RFF Forum*, Henry Jarrett, ed. Baltimore, Md.: Johns Hopkins Press, for Resources for the Future, 1966, pp. 3-14. BE, pp. 273-287. CP II, pp. 381-394. RI.

The Ethics of Rational Decision. (presentation at the 27th Operation Research Society of America national meeting, Boston, May 1965) *Management Science*, 12, 6 (Feb. 1966): B-161 to B-169. CP IV, pp. 315-325. RI.

Expecting the Unexpected: The Uncertain Future of Knowledge and Technology. In: *Prospective Changes in Society by 1980, Including Some Implications for Education*, Edgar L. Morphet and Charles O. Ryan, eds. (papers prepared for the First Area Conference, Denver, June 1966). Denver, Colo.: Designing Education for the Future, July 1966, pp. 199-215. BE, pp. 156-175. CP IV, pp. 327-343. RI.

Impressions of the World Conference on Church and Society. (held at the World Council of Churches Ecumenical Center, Geneva, Switz.) *Quaker Life*, 7, 9 (Sept. 1966): 287-289.

Is Scarcity Dead? *Public Interest*, 5 (Fall 1966): 36-44. CP III, pp. 311-321. RI.

The Knowledge Boom. *Challenge*, 14, 6 (July-Aug. 1966): 5-7.

Notes on the Politics of Peace. *Bulletin of the Atomic Scientists*, 22, 7 (Sept. 1966): 30-32.

The Parameters of Politics. (Edmund J. James Lecture on Government, Apr. 1966) Urbana: *University of Illinois Bulletin*, 63, 139 (July 15, 1966): 1-21. CP V, pp. 195–215.

The Peculiar Economics of Water. *Chemistry*, 39, 9 (Sept. 1966): 20-21.

The Political Consequences of the Social Sciences. (First Annual Political Awards Dinner Lecture, Dec. 1965; pamphlet) Kalamazoo: Michigan Center for Education in Politics, Western Michigan University, 1966. 13 pp.

A Profile of the American Economy. *America Illustrated* (in Russian), 10, 120 (1966): 10-13; *America Illustrated* (in Polish), 10, 93 (1966): 8-11. RI.

Quakerism in the World of the Future. (summary of Carey Memorial Lecture, Baltimore Yearly Meeting, Summer 1965) *Friends Journal* 12, 2 (Jan. 15, 1966): 29-31.

The Role of the Museum in the Propagation of Developed Images. *Technology and Culture*, 7, 1 (Winter 1966): 64-66.

Towards the Development of a Security Community in Europe. *Proceedings of the Sixteenth Pugwash Conference on Science and World Affairs, Sopot, Poland*, Vol. V (Sept. 1966): 122-130.

Verifiability of Economic Images. In: *The Structure of Economic Science: Essays on Methodology*, Sherman Krupp, ed. Englewood Cliffs, N.J.: Prentice-Hall, 1966, pp. 129-141. CP III, pp. 323-337.

The Wisdom of Man and the Wisdom of God. In: *Human Values on the Spaceship Earth.* New York: Council Press, for the Commission on Church and Economic Life of the National Council of Churches, 1966, pp. 1-33.

BOOKS

Economic Analysis. 4th edition; two volumes. New York: Harper & Row, 1966.
Vol. I: Microanalysis. xxiv + 720 pp. Vol. II: Macroanalysis. xviii + 280 pp.
Translations: Japanese, Spanish.

The Impact of the Social Sciences. New Brunswick, N.J.: Rutgers University
Press, 1966. vi + 117 pp. Edition: Indian. Translations: Arabic, French,
Japanese.

BOOK REVIEWS

Review of Kalman J. Cohen and Richard M. Cyert, Theory of the Firm: Resource
Allocation in a Market Economy. *Econometrica,* 34, 4 (Oct. 1966): 902-903.

Review of James S. Coleman, Introduction to Mathematical Sociology. *American
Sociological Review,* 31, 1 (Feb. 1966): 131-132.

Review of Fred Charles Ikle, How Nations Negotiate. *American Journal of
Sociology,* 71, 5 (Mar. 1966): 601-602.

Review of Oskar Lange, Wholes and Parts: A General Theory of System Behavior,
translated from the Polish by Eugenius Lepa. *Econometrica,* 34, 2 (Apr. 1966):
510.

Space, Technology, and Society: From Puff-Puff to Whoosh. Review of Bruce
Mazlish, ed., The Railroad and the Space Program: An Exploration in
Historical Analogy. *Science,* 151, 3713 (Feb. 25, 1966): 979.

Review of Robert K. Merton, On the Shoulders of Giants; A Shandean Postscript.
American Sociological Review, 31, 1 (Feb. 1966): 104-105.

Knowledge v. Wisdom in the Relation Between Scientists and the Government.
Review of Don K. Price, The Scientific Estate. *Scientific American,* 214, 4
(Apr. 1966): 131-134.

Review of Anatol Rapoport and Albert Chammah, Prisoner's Dilemma: A Study
in Conflict and Cooperation. *Michigan Daily,* Feb. 2, 1966, p. 4. Also:
Michigan Quarterly Review, 6, 2 (Spring 1967): 142-144.

A "Space Ship" That May Explode. Review of Barbara Ward, Space Ship Earth.
Fellowship, 32, 9 (Sept. 1966): 29.

Review of E. G. West, Education and the State: A Study in Political Economy.
University of Chicago Law Review, 33, 3 (Spring 1966): 615-618.

VERSE

The Feather River Anthology. *Industrial Water Engineering,* 3, 12 (Dec. 1966):
32-33. RI.

Summary. (of The Range of Human Conflict: A Symposium; American
Psychiatric Association meeting, May 1965) *Bulletin of the Menninger Clinic,*
30, 5 (Sept. 1966): 313-314.

1967

ARTICLES and PAMPHLET

The Basis of Value Judgments in Economics. In: *Human Values and Economic Policy: A Symposium*, Sidney Hook, ed. (Proceedings of the 8th Annual New York University Institute of Philosophy, Washington Square, New York, May 1966). New York: New York University Press, 1967, pp. 55-72. CP II, pp. 395-414.

The Boundaries of Social Policy. *Social Work*, 12, 1 (Jan. 1967): 3-11. CP IV, pp. 345-355. RI.

Dare We Take the Social Sciences Seriously? (vice-presidential address, Section K, AAAS, Washington, D.C., Dec. 1966) *American Behavioral Scientist*, 10, 10 (June 1967): 12-16. CP IV, pp. 357-363. RI.

Dialogue on Peace Research. (with Milton Mayer; Pendle Hill Pamphlet No. 153) Wallingford, Pa.: Pendle Hill, 1967. 30 pp.

Divided Views on Tax Increase. (letter to the editor) *New York Times*, Oct. 15, 1967, Sec. 4, p. 11.

An Economist Looks at the Future of Sociology. *et al.*, 1, 2 (Winter 1967): 1-6. CP IV, pp. 365-372.

Evolution and Revolution in the Developmental Process. In: *Social Change and Economic Growth* (presentations at the annual meeting of Directors of Development Training and Research Institutes, Bergen, Norway, July 1966). Paris: Development Centre of the Organization for Economic Co-operation and Development, 1967, pp. 19-29. CP V, pp. 217–229.

Human Resources Development as a Learning Process. (paper presented at the Human Resources Development Conference, Iowa State University, Oct. 1966) *Farm Policy Forum*, 19, 2 (1966-1967): 27-35. CP III, pp. 339-349. RI.

The Impact of the Draft on the Legitimacy of the National State. In: *The Draft, A Handbook of Facts and Alternatives*, Sol Tax, ed. (Proceedings of the University of Chicago Conference on the Draft, Dec. 1966). Chicago: University of Chicago Press, 1967, pp. 191-196. CP V, pp. 231–236. RI.

Is There a General Theory of Conflict? In: *Industrial Conflict and Race Conflict: Parallels Between the 1930's and the 1960's.* (Proceedings of the 1967 Annual Spring Meeting, Detroit, May 1967). Madison, Wisc.: Industrial Relations Research Association, 1967, pp. 4-12.

The Learning and Reality-Testing Process in the International System. *Journal of International Affairs*, 21, 1 (1967): 1-15. BE, pp. 286-302. CP V, p. 237.

The Learning Process in the Dynamics of Total Societies. In: *The Study of Total Societies*, Samuel Z. Klausner, ed. Garden City, N.Y.: Doubleday Anchor Books, 1967, pp. 98-113. CP IV, pp. 373-390.

The Legitimacy of Economics. (address presented at the 42nd Western Economic Association annual conference, Boulder, Colo., Aug. 1967) *Western Economic Journal*, 5, 4 (Sept. 1967): 299-307. CP II, pp. 415-425. RI.

The Price System and the Price of the Great Society. In: *The Future of Economic Policy*, Myron H. Ross, ed. (lectures at Western Michigan University, Winter 1966; Michigan Business Papers, No. 44). Ann Arbor: University of

Michigan Bureau of Business Research, Graduate School of Business Administration, 1967, pp. 57-73.

The Prospects of Economic Abundance. In: *The Control of Environment: A Discussion at the Nobel Conference*, John D. Roslansky, ed. (held at Gustavus Adolphus College, Jan. 1966). Amsterdam: North-Holland Publishing Company, 1967, pp. 39-57. CP II, pp. 427-445.

The Role of the War Industry in International Conflict. *Journal of Social Issues* (Special issue on Conflict and Community in the International System), 23, 1 (Jan. 1967): 47-61. CP V, pp. 255–271. RI.

The Scarcity of Saints. *Gandhi Marg 42*, 11, 2 (Apr. 1967): 162-163.

Technology and the Integrative System. In: *Today's Changing Society, A Challenge to Individual Identity*, Clarence C. Walton, ed. (Report of an Arden House conference, Columbia University, Nov. 1966). New York: Institute of Life Insurance, 1967, pp. 57-73. CP IV, pp. 391-409. RI.

The "Two Cultures." In: *Technology in Western Civilization*, Vol. II, Melvin Kranzberg and Carroll W. Pursell, Jr., eds. New York: Oxford University Press, 1967, pp. 686-695. CP IV, pp. 411-422.

The University and Tomorrow's Civilization: Its Role in the Development of a World Community. (paper presented at the Higher Education in Tomorrow's World Conference, University of Michigan, Apr. 1967) *Journal of Higher Education*, 38, 9 (Dec. 1967): 477-483. CP V, pp. 281–289. RI.

BOOK REVIEWS

Keeping Book on Social Realities. Review of Raymond A. Bauer, ed., Social Indicators. *Science*, 155, 3762 (Feb. 3, 1967): 550-551.

Milking the Sacred Cow. Review of John Kenneth Galbraith, The New Industrial State. *Book Week*, July 18, 1967, pp. 2, 12.

The Scientific-Military-Industrial Complex. Review of John Kenneth Galbraith, The New Industrial State; and H. L. Nieburg, In the Name of Science. *Virginia Quarterly Review*, 43, 4 (Autumn 1967): 672-679. CP III, pp. 351-360.

Charted Journey Through Theories of Deterrence. Review of Philip Green, Deadly Logic: The Theory of Nuclear Deterrence. *Dissent*, 14, 4 (July-Aug. 1967): 496-498.

Review of Carl G. Gustavson, The Institutional Drive. *Technology and Culture*, 8, 4 (Oct. 1967): 534-535.

Review of Louis J. Halle, The Society of Man. *American Political Science Review*, 61, 3 (Sept. 1967): 843-844.

Fortune Telling. Review of Robert L. Heilbroner, The Limits of American Capitalism. *New York Review of Books*, 7, 12 (Jan. 12, 1967): 29-31.

Neoliberal Economics. Review of John Jewkes, Public and Private Enterprise (Lindsay Memorial Lectures given at the University of Keele, 1964). *Science*, 155, 3766 (Mar. 3, 1967): 1095.

Review of Lester B. Lave, Technological Change: Its Conception and Measurement. *American Journal of Sociology*, 72, 5 (Mar. 1967): 563.

Am I a Man or a Mouse—Or Both? Review of Konrad Lorenz,On Aggression;and Robert Ardrey, The Territorial Imperative: A Personal Inquiry into the Animal Origins of Property and Nations. *War/Peace Report*, 7, 3 (Mar. 1967): 14-17. CP V, pp. **273–280**. RI.

Man Versus Machine. Review of Ben B. Seligman, Most Notorious Victory: Man in an Age of Automation. *New York Times Book Review*, Jan. 1, 1967, p. 25.

Review of G. L. S. Shackle, A Scheme of Economic Theory. *Journal of Business*, 40, 1 (Jan. 1967): 102.

Review of Robert Solo, Economic Organizations and Social Systems. *Science*, 157, 3793 (Sept. 8, 1967): 1158-1159.

VERSE

The Old Agricultural Lag. In: *No Easy Harvest: The Dilemma of Agriculture in Underdeveloped Countries*, by Max Millikan and David Hapgood (based on the Conference on Productivity and Innovation in Agriculture in Underdeveloped Countries, Endicott House, Dedham, Mass., Summer 1964). Boston: Little, Brown and Company, for M.I.T.'s Center for International Studies, 1967, p. xii.

1968

ARTICLES, MONOGRAPH, and PAMPHLETS

Accomplishments and Prospects of the Peace Research Movement. (with Hanna and Alan Newcombe) *Arms Control and Disarmament*, 1, 1 (1968): 43-58. CP V, pp. **291–308**.

America's Economy: The Qualified Uproarious Success. In: *America Now*, John G. Kirk, ed. New York: Atheneum, for Metromedia, 1968, pp. 143-161. CP III, pp. 361-381.

Business and Economic Systems. In: *Positive Feedback*, John H. Milsum, ed. (based on papers presented at a Society for General Systems symposium, AAAS, Montreal, Dec. 1964). Toronto: Pergamon Press, 1968,pp. 101-117. CP III, pp. 429-447.

The City as an Element in the International System. *Daedalus* (Special issue on the Conscience of the City), 97, 4 (Fall 1968): 1111-1123. CP V, p. 309. RI.

Demand and Supply. In: *International Encyclopedia of the Social Sciences*, Vol.4. New York: Crowell Collier and Macmillan, 1968, pp. 96-104.

The Dynamics of Society. *Bell Telephone Magazine*, 47, 3 (May/June 1968): 4-7. CP IV, pp. 423-428.

The Economics and Financing of Technology in Education: Some Observations. In: *Planning for Effective Utilization of Technology in Education*, Edgar L. Morphet and David L. Jesser, eds. (Reports prepared for the National Conference, Denver, May 1961). Denver, Colo: Designing Education for the Future, 1968, pp. 367-372.

Education for the Spaceship Earth. *Social Education* (Special issue on International Education for the Twenty-First Century), 32, 7 (Nov. 1968): 648-652. RI.

The Effects of Military Expenditure Upon the Economic Growth of Japan. (edited with Norman Sun; monograph) Tokyo: International Christian University, for the Disarmament Research Team Project, June 1968.

Ethical Dilemmas in Religion and Nationalism. (1968 Felix Adler Lecture; pamphlet) New York: Ethical Culture Publications, 1968. 12 pp. RI.

Friends and Social Change. (pamphlet) Philadelphia: Friends General Conference of the Religious Society of Friends, 1968. 4 pp.

Grants Versus Exchange in the Support of Education. In: *Federal Programs for the Development of Human Resources*, Vol. 1 (A Compendium of Papers Submitted to the Subcommittee on Economic Progress of the Joint Economic Committee, U.S. Congress). Washington, D.C.: U.S. Government Printing Office, 1968, pp. 232-238. CP III, pp. 383-391.

Greatness as a Pathology of the National Image. In: *U.S. Foreign Policy: Responsibilities of a Superpower in International Politics* (Proceedings of the 1968 World Affairs Conference of North Western Illinois, Dixon-Sterling, Mar. 1968). Champaign: University of Illinois Extension in International Affairs, Sept. 1968, pp. 35-42.

A Historical Note from the President. *American Economic Review*, 58, 5 (Dec. 1968): 1509-1510.

Is Ugliness the Price of Prosperity? In: *Seminar on Environmental Arts and Sciences: Summary of Proceedings* (held in Aspen, Colo., Aug. 1968). Boulder, Colo.: Thorne Ecological Foundation, 1968.

The Legitimation of the Market. (C. Woody Thompson Memorial Lecture, Midwest Economics Association annual meeting, Chicago, Apr. 1967) *Nebraska Journal of Economics and Business*, 7, 1 (Spring 1968): 3-14. CP III, pp. 393-406.

Machines, Men and Religion. *Friends Journal*, 14, 24 (Dec. 15, 1968): 643-644.

Man's Choice: Creative Development or Revolution. In: *The United States in a Revolutionary World—Occasional Papers*, Robert H. Simmons, ed. (papers presented at a conference held at California State College, Los Angeles, Apr. 1968). Pasadena, Calif.: American Friends Service Committee, 1968, pp. 1-7.

The Many Failures of Success. *Saturday Review*, 51, 47 (Nov. 23, 1968): 29-31. RI.

The "National" Importance of Human Capital. In: *The Brain Drain*, Walter Adams, ed. (papers presented at an international conference, Lausanne, Switz., Aug. 1967). New York: Macmillan, 1968, pp. 109-119. CP II, pp. 461-473. RI.

A Peace Movement in Search of a Party. *War/Peace Report*, 8, 1 (Jan. 1968): 12-13.

Preface to a Special Issue. *Journal of Conflict Resolution* (Special review issue), 12, 4 (Dec. 1968): 409-411.

Reflection of the Election—An Interview with Kenneth Boulding. *Town and Country Review* (Boulder, Colo.), Nov. 14, 1968, pp. 4, 6.

Requirements for a Social Systems Analysis of the Dynamics of the World War Industry. *Peace Research Society (International) Papers* (Cambridge Conference, 1967), Vol. IX (1968): 1-8. RI.

Revolution and Development. In: *Changing Perspectives on Man,* Ben Rothblatt, ed. (1966 Monday Lectures Series). Chicago: University of Chicago Press, 1968, pp. 207-226. CP V, pp. 325–344.

The Role of Economics in the Establishment of Stable Peace. *Economisch-Statistische Berichten* (Rotterdam, Neth.) (Special issue in honor of the 65th birthday of Prof. Dr. J. Tinbergen), 53e, 2639 (Apr. 10, 1968): 332-334. CP III, pp. 407-411.

The Specialist With a Universal Mind. (guest editorial; paper presented to the Society for General Systems Research session, AAAS, New York, Dec. 1967) *Management Science,* 14, 12 (Aug. 1968): B-647 to B-653. RI.

Statement. (on Learning, Teaching, Education, and Development) In: *1968 Coloradan,* Vol. 70. Boulder: Associated Students of the University of Colorado, 1968, p. 166.

Town and Country Interviews Dr. Kenneth Boulding. *Town and Country Review* (Boulder, Colo.), Apr. 11, 1968, pp. 1, 11, 13-14; Apr. 18, 1968, pp. 8, 11-12.

The University as an Economic and Social Unit. In: *Colleges & Universities as Agents of Social Change,* W. John Minter and Ian M. Thompson, eds. (papers presented at the 10th Annual College Self-Study Institute, Boulder, Nov. 1968). Boulder, Colo.: Western Interstate Commission for Higher Education, 1968, pp. 75-87; discussion, pp. 89-128. CP III, pp. 413-427.

Values, Technology, and Divine Legitimation. In: *Science, Philosophy, Religion,* Lt. Gerald P. McCarthy, ed. (Proceedings of the 4th Annual Symposium, Sept. 1967). Kirtland Air Force Base, N.M.: Air Force Weapons Laboratory, 1968, pp. 4-16. RI.

What Can We Know and Teach About Social Systems? (paper presented at the Conference on Social Science in the Schools: A Search for Rationale, Purdue University, Feb. 1967) *Social Science Education Consortium Newsletter* (Boulder, Colo.), 5 (June 1968): 1-5. CP IV, pp. 429-435. RI.

BOOK

Beyond Economics: Essays on Society, Religion, and Ethics. Ann Arbor: University of Michigan Press, 1968. x + 302 pp. Translation: Japanese. Paperback edition: Ann Arbor Paperbacks, 1970. (Nominated for a National Book Award, 1970)

BOOK REVIEWS

Review of Général d'Armée André Beaufre, Deterrence and Strategy, translated from the French by Major-General R. H. Barry; and Arthur H. Dean, Test Ban and Disarmament: The Path of Negotiation. *Political Science Quarterly,* 83, 1 (Mar. 1968): 109-111.

Review of C. E. Black, The Dynamics of Modernization: A Study in Comparative History. *History and Theory,* 7, 1 (1968): 83-90.

Review of David Easton, A Systems Analysis of Political Life. *Behavioral Science,* 13, 2 (Mar. 1968): 147-149.

Observations Unlimited. Review of Eliot Janeway, The Economics of Crisis: War, Politics, and the Dollar. *New York Times Book Review,* 73, 3 (Jan. 21, 1968): 24.

"Prognostics": A Guide to Present Action. Review of Herman Kahn and Anthony J. Wiener, The Year 2000: A Framework for Speculation on the Next Thirty-Three Years. *Saturday Review,* 51, 6 (Feb. 10, 1968): 36-37.

In the Money. Review of Ferdinand Lundberg, The Rich and the Super-Rich; and Ben B. Seligman, Permanent Poverty: An American Syndrome. *New York Review of Books,* 11, 4 (Sept. 12, 1968): 40-42.

Asia: Soft States and Hard Facts. Review of Gunnar Myrdal, Asian Drama: An Inquiry into the Poverty Nations. *New Republic,* 158, 18 (May 4, 1968): 25-28.

Review of Report from Iron Mountain on the Possibility and Desirability of Peace. *Trans-action,* 5, 3 (Jan./Feb. 1968): 16. RI.

Review of Gordon Tullock, The Organization of Inquiry. *Journal of Economic Issues,* 2, 2 (June 1968): 259-261.

1969

ARTICLES and PAMPHLETS

David Fand's "Keynesian Monetary Theories, Stabilization Policy, and the Recent Inflation," A Comment. *Journal of Money, Credit and Banking,* 1, 3 (Aug. 1969): 588-589.

Die Zukunft als Möglichkeit und Design (The Future as Chance and Design; in German; paper presented to the 6th General Assembly and Congress of the International Council of Societies for Industrial Design, London, Sept. 1969) *Bauwelt 50* (Berlin), 60 (Dec. 15, 1969): 1807-1811. CP (in English) IV, pp. 525-534.

Economic Education: The Stepchild Too is Father of the Man. *Journal of Economic Education,* 1, 1 (Fall 1969): 7-11, CP III, pp. 449-455.

Economics as a Moral Science. (presidential address) *American Economic Review* (Papers and Proceedings of the 81st American Economic Association annual meeting, Chicago, Dec. 1968), 59, 1 (Mar. 1969): 1-12. CP II, pp. 447-460. RI.

Education and the Economic Process. In: *The Alternative of Radicalism: Radical and Conservative Possibilities for Teaching the Teachers of America's Young Children,* Thomas R. Holland and Catherine M. Lee, eds. (Proceedings of the 5th National Conference, Jan. 1969). New Orleans: Tri-University Project in Elementary Education for the U.S. Office of Education, Jan. 1969, pp. 72-82. RI.

Failures and Successes of Economics. *Think,* 35, 3 (May/June 1969): 2-6. RI.

The Fifth Meaning of Love—Notes on Christian Ethics and Social Policy. (paper presented at the Lutheran World Federation Consultation on Christian Ethics and True Humanity, Frankfurt, Germany, Aug. 1968) *Lutheran World*, 16, 3 (July 1969): 219-229. CP IV, pp. 437-449. RI.

The Formation of Values as a Process in Human Learning. In: *Transportation and Community Values* (Report of a conference held at Airlie House, Warrenton, Va., Mar. 1969). Washington, D.C.: Highway Research Board, National Academy of Sciences, 1969, pp. 31-38; discussion, pp. 39-45. CP III, pp. 457-466.

The Grants Economy. (presidential address, Michigan Economics Association, Grand Valley State College, Mar. 1968) *Michigan Academician*, 1, 1 and 2 (Winter 1969): 3-11. CP II, pp. 475-485.

Heretic Among Economists. (interview) *Business Week*, 2053 (Jan. 4, 1969): 80-82.

The Interplay of Technology and Values: The Emerging Superculture. In: *Values and the Future: The Impact of Technological Change on American Values*, Kurt Baier and Nicholas Rescher, eds. New York: Free Press, 1969, pp. 336-350. CP IV, pp. 451-467.

A Memorandum on the Facilitation of Behavioral Thinking: Four Modest Proposals for Highly Advanced Study. (with Richard Christie) *Subterranean Sociology Newsletter* (University of Michigan), 4, 1 (Oct. 1969): 5-8.

Modern Man and Ancient Testimonies. *Quaker Religious Thought*, 11, 1 (Summer 1969): 3-14.

The Need for a University of the Building Industry. (presentation to the ACSA Western Region meeting, Boulder, Colo., Nov. 1968) *American Institute of Architects Journal*, 51, 5 (May 1969): 79-81.

Preventing Schismogenesis. (comment on Richard Flacks, "Protest or Conform: Some Social Psychological Perspectives on Legitimacy") *Journal of Applied Behavioral Science*, 5, 2 (Apr./May/June 1969): 151-153. RI.

Public Choice and the Grants Economy: The Intersecting Set. *Public Choice*, 7 (Fall 1969): 1-2.

Research for Peace. *Science Journal* (London), 5A, 4 (Oct. 1969): 53-58. CP V, pp. 345-352.

The Role of Exemplars in the Learning of Community. *World Studies Education Service Bulletin* (London), 10 (Jan. 1969): 15-16.

The Role of Legitimacy in the Dynamics of Society. (Graduate School Lecture Series, 1967; pamphlet) University Park: Pennsylvania State University Center for Research, College of Business Administration, 1969. 13 pp. CP IV, pp. 509-523.

The Role of the Church in the Making of Community and Identity. (Ethan Allen Cross Memorial Lecture Series; pamphlet) Greeley, Colo.: First Congregational Church, 1969, 8 pp.

Some Unsolved Problems in Economic Education. In: *Five Levels of Incompetence: Report of the 1969 Grove Park Institute*, Thomas Vogt, ed. Washington, D.C.: Consortium of Professional Associations for Study of Special Teacher Improvement Programs (CONPASS), 1971, pp. 37-50.

Stability in International Systems: The Role of Disarmament and Development. In: *International Security Systems: Concepts and Models of World Order*, Richard B. Gray, ed. (based on the Department of Government Lecture Series, Florida State University, 1966-67). Itasca, Ill.: F. E. Peacock, 1969, pp. 193-210. CP V, pp. 353-372.

Statement Before the Subcommittee on Economy in Government of the Joint Economic Committee, U.S. Congress. In: *The Military Budget and National Economic Priorities* (Hearings of the Committee). Washington, D.C.: U.S. Government Printing Office, 1969, Part I, pp. 137-141. CP II, pp. 487-493.

The Task of the Teacher in the Social Sciences. In: *The Quest for Relevance: Effective College Teaching; Vol. III, The Social Sciences.* Washington, D.C.: American Council on Education, for the American Association for Higher Education, Mar. 1969, pp. 3-24. CP IV, pp. 469-490. RI.

Technology and the Changing Social Order. In: *The Urban-Industrial Frontier: Essays on Social Trends and Institutional Goals in Modern Communities,* David Popenoe, ed. (based on the Urban Frontier: 1966-86 Lecture Series, Rutgers University, 1966-67). New Brunswick, N.J.: Rutgers University Press, 1969, pp. 126-140. CP IV, pp. 491-507.

The Threat System. In: *The Cost of Conflict,* John A. Copps, ed. (Department of Economics Lectures, Western Michigan University, Winter Semester 1968; Michigan Business Papers No. 51). Ann Arbor: University of Michigan Bureau of Business Research, 1969, pp. 3-17.

What Don't We Know That Hurts Us? In: *Selected Readings in Economic Education,* Roman F. Warmke and Gerald Draayer, eds. (based on papers presented at the Experienced Teacher Fellowship Program, 1967-1968, and a related conference). Athens: Ohio University College of Business Administration, for the Ohio Council on Economic Education, 1969, pp. 3-17.

BOOK REVIEWS

Economics Imperialism. Review of David Braybrooke and Charles E. Lindblom, A Strategy of Decision; Mancur Olson, Jr., The Logic of Collective Action; and Bruce M. Russett, ed., Economic Theories of International Politics. *Behavioral Science,* 14, 6 (Nov. 1969): 496-500.

A Forecast by Scientists. Review of Nigel Calder, ed., Unless Peace Comes: A Scientific Forecast of New Weapons. *Virginia Quarterly Review,* 45, 1 (Winter 1969): 139-140.

Review of Morton Fried, Marvin Harris and Robert Murphy, eds., War: The Anthropology of Armed Conflict and Aggression. *Comparative Studies in Society and History,* 11, 1 (Jan. 1969): 109-111.

Dialogue with a Marxist. Review of David Horowitz, Empire and Revolution: A Radical Interpretation of Contemporary History. *Book World* (Chicago Tribune), 3, 31 (Aug. 3, 1969): 6.

Tragic Nonsense. Review of Herbert Marcuse, An Essay on Liberation. *New Republic,* 160, 13 (Mar. 29, 1969): 28, 30.

Case Study in Non-Decision. Review of Congressman Richard D. McCarthy, The Ultimate Folly: War by Pestilence, Asphyxiation and Defoliation. *New Republic,* 161, 22 (Nov. 29, 1969): 24-25.

Review of J. E. Meade, The Growing Economy. *Journal of Economic Literature,* 7, 4 (Dec. 1969): 1161-1162.

One of the Great Men. Review of Arthur E. Morgan, Observations. *Religious Humanism,* 3, 2 (Spring 1969): 92.

Growth and Grace: Incompatible? Review of D. B. Robertson, Should Churches Be Taxed?; Alfred Balk, The Religion Business; Nino Lo Bello, The Vatican Empire; and Arthur Herzog, The Church Trap. *Saturday Review*, 52, 6 (Feb. 8, 1969): 27-28.

Review of Kenneth Schneider, Destiny of Change: How Relevant is Man in the Age of Development? *Administrative Science Quarterly*, 14, 2 (June 1969): 318.

Large Projects and Larger Questions. Review of Philip Sporn, Technology, Engineering, and Economics; and Sheldon Novick, The Careless Atom. *Science*, 165, 3892 (Aug. 1, 1969): 483-484.

VERSE

The Ditchley Bank Anthology. *Michigan Business Review*, 21, 2 (Mar. 1969): 17-19. Also: *Journal of Money, Credit and Banking* (Conference of university professors of the American Bankers Association, Ditchley Park, Oxfordshire, Eng., Sept. 1968), 1, 3 (Aug. 1969): 354, 462, 507, 555, 624, 681.

X Cantos. *Michigan Quarterly Review*, 8, 1 (Winter 1969): 29-31. RI.

1970

ARTICLES and PAMPHLET

The Balance of Peace. *Peace Research Society (International) Papers* (Copenhagen Conference, 1969), Vol. XIII (1970): 59-65. CP V, pp. 373–381.

Can There Be a National Policy for Stable Peace? *AAUW Journal* (Special issue on Peace), 63, 4 (May 1970): 172-174. CP V, pp. 383–387.

Can We Curb Inflation Without Recession? If So, How? *Denver Post*, Feb. 15, 1970, p. 1.

The Challenge of the Great Transition. (in Japanese) Mainichi Newspapers (Tokyo), Mar. 3, 1970, p. 9.

The Crisis of the Universities. *Colorado Quarterly*, 19, 2 (Autumn 1970): 120-129.

The Deadly Industry: War and the International System. (introduction) In: *Peace and the War Industry*, Kenneth E. Boulding, ed. Chicago: Aldine, 1970, pp. 1-12. RI.

Factors Affecting the Future Demand for Education. In: *Economic Factors Affecting the Financing of Education*, Vol. 2, Roe L. Johns *et al.*, eds. Gainesville, Fla.: National Educational Finance Project, 1970, pp. 1-27. CP III, pp. 503-531. RI.

The Family Segment of the National Economy. (address at the American Home Economics Association annual meeting, Cleveland, June 1970) *Journal of Home Economics*, 62, 7 (Sept. 1970): 447-454.

Fragmentation, Isolation, Conflict. (address before the 1966 AAHE National Conference) In: *Twenty-Five Years: 1945-1970*, G. Kerry Smith, ed. San Francisco: Jossey-Bass, for the American Association for Higher Education, 1970, pp. 254-267.

Fun and Games with the Gross National Product—The Role of Misleading Indicators in Social Policy. In: *The Environmental Crisis: Man's Struggle to Live with Himself,* Harold W. Helfrich, Jr., ed. (lectures in the 1968-1969 Symposium in Environmental Crises, Yale University School of Forestry). New Haven: Yale University Press, 1970, pp. 157-170. CP III, pp. 467-482.

Fundamental Considerations. In: *Perspectives on Campus Tensions,* David C. Nichols, ed. Washington, D.C.: American Council on Education, 1970, pp. 3-17.

Gaps Between Developed and Developing Nations. In: *Toward Century 21: Technology, Society, and Human Values,* C. S. Wallia, ed. (based on the Human Values in a Technological Society Lectures, Stanford University, 1968). New York: Basic Books, 1970, pp. 125-134.

The Impact of the Defense Industry on the Structure of the American Economy. In: *Adjustments of the U.S. Economy to Reductions in Military Spending,* Bernard Udis, ed. (Report prepared for the United States Arms Control and Disarmament Agency, ACDA/E 156), Dec. 1970, pp. 399-433. Also in: *The Economic Consequences of Reduced Military Spending,* Bernard Udis, ed. Lexington, Mass.: D. C. Heath, 1973, pp. 225-252.

Is Economics Culture-Bound? *American Economic Review* (Papers and Proceedings of the 82nd American Economic Association annual meeting, New York, Dec. 1969), 60, 2 (May 1970): 406-411. CP II, pp. 495-502.

The Knowledge Explosion. In: *To Nurture Humaneness: Commitment for the '70's,* Mary-Margaret Scobey and Grace Graham, eds. Washington, D.C.: Association for Supervision and Curriculum Development, National Education Association, 1970, pp. 86-92.

A Look at National Priorities. *Current History,* 59, 348 (Aug. 1970): 65-72, 111. RI.

A New Ethos for a New Era. In: *Canada and the United States in the World of the Seventies,* R. H. Wagenberg, ed. (Proceedings of the 9th Annual Seminar on Canadian-American Relations, Nov. 1967). Windsor, Ontario: University of Windsor Press, 1970, pp. 91-98.

No Second Chance for Man. *Progressive* (Special issue on the Crisis of Survival), 34, 4 (Apr. 1970): 40-43. RI.

The Philosophy of Peace Research. In: *Proceedings of the International Peace Research Association Third General Conference 1969* (Karlovy Vary, Czech., Sept. 1969), Vol. 1, *Philosophy of Peace Research.* Assen, Netherlands: Van Gorcum, 1970, pp. 5-19. CP V, pp. 389–405.

The Real World of the Seventies and Beyond. In: *Training a Ministry in the Seventies for a World of the Seventies and Beyond: 1969 Conference* (held in Denver, Oct.-Nov. 1969). New York: Association for Clinical Pastoral Education, 1970, pp. 10-22.

The Role of the Undergraduate College in Social Change. *Perspectives* (Proceedings of the Association for General and Liberal Studies annual meeting, Colgate University, Oct.-Nov. 1969), 1, 3 (Feb. 1970): 17-20.

The Scientific Revelation. (presentation at the Conference on Science and the Morality of Intellect, University of Chicago, Feb. 1970) *Bulletin of the Atomic Scientists,* 26, 7 (Sept. 1970): 13-18. RI.

Social Systems Analysis and the Study of International Conflict. In: *Problems of Modern Strategy* (papers presented at the 10th Annual Conference, St. Catherine's College, Oxford, Sept. 1968; Studies in International Security: 14). London: Chatto and Windus, for The Institute for Strategic Studies, 1970, pp. 77-91.

Some Hesitant Reflections on the Political Future. In: *1970 Coloradan,* Vol. 72. Boulder: Associated Students of the University of Colorado, 1970, pp. 204-205.

Statement Before the Select Subcommittee on Education of the House Committee on Education and Labor, U.S. Congress. In: *Environmental Quality Education Act of 1970* (Hearings of the Committee). Washington, D.C.: U.S. Government Printing Office, 1970, pp. 597-605. RI.

The War Industry and the American Economy. (Third Annual William Carlyle Furnas Memorial Lecture, 1969; pamphlet) De Kalb: Northern Illinois University Department of Economics, 1970. 18 pp. CP III, pp. 483-501.

What Is the GNP Worth? (summary of lecture presented at the University of Pennsylvania, Philadelphia, Apr. 1970) In: *Earth Day—The Beginning: A Guide for Survival,* National Staff of Environmental Action, eds. New York: Arno Press, Bantam Books, 1970, pp. 143-144.

BOOKS

Economics as a Science. New York: McGraw-Hill, 1970. vii + 161 pp. Edition: Indian. Translations: Korean, Swedish.

Peace and the War Industry. (edited, and with an introduction; TRANSaction Book 11) Chicago: Aldine, 1970. ix + 159 pp. See also: Books, 1973.

A Primer on Social Dynamics: History as Dialectics and Development. New York: Free Press, 1970. ix + 153 pp. Translations: Dutch, Japanese.

The Prospering of Truth. (Swarthmore Lecture, London Yearly Meeting, 1970) London: Friends Home Service Committee, 1970. 51 pp.

BOOK REVIEWS

Evolution & Taxes. Review of Peter F. Drucker, The Age of Discontinuity: Guidelines to Our Changing Society; and Herbert Stein, The Fiscal Revolution in America. *TRANSaction,* 7, 6 (Apr. 1970): 81-82.

Review of William R. Ewald, Jr., ed., Environment and Policy: The Next Fifty Years; and Environment and Change: The Next Fifty Years (Commissioned on behalf of the American Institute of Planners' Fiftieth Year Consultation). *American Journal of Sociology,* 75, 5 (Mar. 1970): 878-880.

Review of John Hicks, A Theory of Economic History. *American Journal of Agricultural Economics,* 52, 4 (Nov. 1970): 619-620.

Review of Norman Uphoff and Warren F. Ilchman, eds., The Political Economy of Change: Theoretical and Empirical Contributions. *American Political Science Review,* 64, 2 (June 1970): 603-604.

Review of Nathan Leites and Charles Wolf, Jr., Rebellion and Authority: An Analytic Essay on Insurgent Conflicts (A RAND Corporation Research Study). *Annals of the American Academy of Political and Social Science,* 392 (Nov. 1970): 184-185.

Time as a Commodity. Review of Staffan B. Linder, The Harried Leisure Class. *New Republic,* 162, 8 (Feb. 21, 1970): 27-28.

Tantalizing Questions. Review of Margaret Mead, Culture and Commitment: A Study of the Generation Gap. *Virginia Quarterly Review,* 46, 2 (Spring 1970): 339-341.

Tools on a Grand Scale. Review of Emmanuel G. Mesthene, Technological Change: Its Impact on Man and Society (Harvard Studies in Technology and Society). *Science,* 168, 3938 (June 19, 1970): 1442.

When Cost Push Comes to Shove. Review of Arthur M. Okun, The Political Economy of Prosperity. *TRANSaction,* 7, 11 (Sept. 1970): 64-68.

1971

ARTICLES and MONOGRAPH

After Samuelson, Who Needs Adam Smith? (paper presented at the 83rd American Economic Association annual meeting, Detroit, Dec. 1970) *History of Political Economy,* 3, 2 (Fall 1971): 225-237. CP III, pp. 553-567.

The American Economy After Vietnam. (presentation at a symposium of the Maxwell Graduate School of Citizenship and Public Affairs, Syracuse University, Feb. 1970) In: *After Vietnam: The Future of American Foreign Policy,* Robert W. Gregg and Charles Kegley, Jr., eds. Garden City, N.Y.: Doubleday Anchor Books, 1971, pp. 307-323.

Discussion. (of Allen V. Kneese's "Environmental Pollution: Economics and Policy") *American Economic Review* (Papers and Proceedings of the 83rd American Economic Association annual meeting, Detroit, Dec. 1970), 61, 2 (May 1971): 167-169.

The Dodo Didn't Make It: Survival and Betterment. (presentation at the 3rd Symposium on Science and Society, University of Chicago, Nov. 1970) *Bulletin of the Atomic Scientists,* 27, 5 (May 1971): 19-22.

Environment and Economics. In: *Environment: Resources, Pollution & Society,* William W. Murdoch, ed. Stamford, Conn.: Sinauer Associates, 1971, pp. 359-367. CP III, pp. 569-579.

An Epitaph: The Center for Research on Conflict Resolution, 1959-1971. *Journal of Conflict Resolution,* 15, 3 (Sept. 1971): 279-280.

Knowledge as a Road to Peace. (keynote address of the COPRED Peace Workshop, Feb. 1971) *Bulletin of the Peace Studies Institute* (Manchester College, Ind.) (Aug. 1971): 1-4.

The Legitimacy of Central Banks. In: *Reappraisal of the Federal Reserve Discount Mechanism,* Vol. 2. Washington, D.C.: Board of Governors of the Federal Reserve System, Dec. 1971, pp. 1-13.

Letter on "Happiness." (in Japanese) *Sankei Shimbun Newspaper* (Tokyo), Jan. 1, 1971, p. 27.

The Meaning of Human Betterment. (Gerald L. Phillippe Memorial Lecture, University of Nebraska-Lincoln, Mar. 1971) *Nebraska Journal of Economics and Business*, 10, 2 (Spring 1971): 3-12. CP IV, pp. 601-612. RI.

The Misallocation of Intellectual Resources in Economics. In: *The Use and Abuse of Social Science*, Irving L. Horowitz, ed. (based on papers presented at a conference on Social Science and National Policy, Rutgers University, Nov. 1969). New York: E. P. Dutton, for TRANSaction Books, 1971, pp. 34-51. CP III, pp. 533-552.

The Need for Reform of National Income Statistics. In: *Proceedings of the Social Statistics Section, 1970* (ASA annual meeting, Detroit, Dec. 1970). Washington, D.C.: American Statistical Association, 1971, pp. 94-97. CP III, pp. 581-586.

People Eyeing 21st Century as Age When Mankind Matures. *Japan Times* (Tokyo), Jan. 1, 1971, p. 6.

The Pursuit of Happiness and the Value of the Human Being. (in Japanese) *Nihon Keizei Shimbun* (Japan Economic Journal; Tokyo), Jan. 1, 1971, Supplement 2, p. 39.

Toward a Modest Society: The End of Growth and Grandeur. In: *Economic Perspectives of Boulding and Samuelson* (Davidson Lectures—1970-71). Durham: Whittemore School of Business and Economics, University of New Hampshire, 1971, pp. 7-20; reply, pp. 21-22.

Toward the Year 2000. (presentation at the National Council for the Social Studies annual meeting, Houston, Nov. 1969; SSEC Monograph Series, Publication No. 132) Boulder, Colo.: Social Science Education Consortium, 1971. 14 pp.

Unprofitable Empire, Britain in India 1880-1967: A Critique of the Hobson-Lenin Thesis on Imperialism. (with Tapan Mukerjee) *Peace Research Society (International) Papers* (Rome Conference, 1970), Vol. XVI (1971): 1-21.

What Do Economic Indicators Indicate?: Quality and Quantity in the GNP. In: *The Economics of Pollution* (1971 Charles C. Moskowitz Lectures). New York: New York University Press, 1971, pp. 31-80.

Where Does Development Lead? *Les Carnets de l'enfance* (Assignment Children; Paris, UNICEF), 13 (Jan.-Mar. 1971): 48-57; summaries in French, Spanish and German, pp. 58-62.

A World-Famous "Economist-Philosopher" Gives His Views on Religion, Radicalism, the Hippies and More. (interview) *Seikyo Times* (Tokyo), 113 (Jan. 1971): 31-32, 37-38.

BOOKS

Kenneth E. Boulding Collected Papers, Vol. I: Economics (1932-1955), Fred R. Glahe, ed. Boulder: Colorado Associated University Press, 1971. xi + 492 pp.

Kenneth E. Boulding Collected Papers, Vol. II: Economics (1956-1970), Fred R. Glahe, ed. Boulder: Colorado Associated University Press, 1971. viii + 510 pp.

BOOK REVIEWS

Living With Violence. Review of Hannah Arendt, On Violence; and E. V. Walter, Terror and Resistance: A Study of Political Violence. *War/Peace Report*, 11, 6 (June July 1971): 17-18.

Review of Gottfried Dietze, Youth, University, and Democracy; Algo D. Henderson, The Innovative Spirit; and Lewis B. Mayhew, Arrogance on Campus. *AAUP Bulletin*, 57, 2 (June 1971): 296-297.

Review of E. J. Hobsbawm, Industry and Empire: An Economic History of Britain Since 1750. *History and Theory*, 10, 1 (1971): 147-149.

Review of John R. Platt, Perception and Change: Projections for Survival. *Michigan Quarterly Review*, 10, 4 (Fall 1971): 295-297.

Economists at a Family Picnic. Review of Joan Robinson, Economic Heresies: Some Old-Fashioned Questions in Economic Theory. *Business Week*, 2177 (May 22, 1971): 12.

The Intellectual Framework of Bad Political Advice. Review of W. W. Rostow, Politics and the Stages of Growth. *Virginia Quarterly Review*, 47, 4 (Autumn 1971): 602-607.

1972

ARTICLES and PAMPHLET

Economics and General Systems. In: *The Relevance of General Systems Theory: Papers Presented to Ludwig von Bertalanffy on His Seventieth Birthday*, Ervin Laszlo, ed. New York: George Braziller, 1972, pp. 77-92. RI.

Economics as a Not Very Biological Science. In: *Challenging Biological Problems: Directions Toward Their Solution*, John A. Behnke, ed. (25th Anniversary volume). New York: Oxford University Press, for the American Institute of Biological Sciences, 1972, pp. 357-375.

Future Directions. (with Martin Pfaff) In: *Redistribution to the Rich and the Poor: The Grants Economics of Income Distribution*, Kenneth Boulding and Martin Pfaff, eds. (Grants Economics Series). Belmont, Calif.: Wadsworth, 1972, pp. 387-390.

The Future of Personal Responsibility. *American Behavioral Scientist* (Special issue on Changing Attitudes Toward Personal Responsibility; presentations at the Insurance Company of North America Conference, Philadelphia, May 1971), 15, 3 (Jan./Feb. 1972): 329-359. CP IV, pp. 535-567.

Grants Economics: A Simple Introduction. (with Martin Pfaff and Janos Horvath) *American Economist*, 16, 1 (Spring 1972): 19-28.

The Grants Economy and the Development Gap. (with Martin Pfaff) In: *The Gap Between Rich and Poor Nations*, Gustav Ranis, ed. (Proceedings of the International Economic Association Conference, Bled, Yugoslavia, 1970). London: Macmillan Press, 1972, pp. 143-170.

The Household as Achilles' Heel. (premier lecture of the Colston E. Warne lecture series, American Council on Consumer Interests annual conference, Dallas, Apr. 1972) *Journal of Consumer Affairs*, 6, 2 (Winter 1972): 110-119.

Human Betterment and the Quality of Life. In: *Human Behavior in Economic Affairs: Essays in Honor of George Katona,* Burkhard Strumpel, James N. Morgan and Ernest Zahn, eds. Amsterdam: Elsevier Scientific, 1972, pp. 455-470.

Introduction. In: *Economic Imperialism: A Book of Readings,* Kenneth Boulding and Tapan Mukerjee, eds. Ann Arbor: University of Michigan Press, 1972, pp. ix-xviii.

Introduction. In: *Analysis of the Problem of War,* by Clyde Eagleton (Garland Edition). New York: Garland, 1972, pp. 5-7.

Japan Should Produce ''Things'' With Value Rather Than a ''Strong Yen.'' (interview in Japanese) *Nikkei Business* (Tokyo), Dec. 25, 1972, pp. 63-65.

Kenneth Boulding: The Arrival of Spaceship Earth. (interview) In: *Philosophers of the Earth: Conversations with Ecologists,* by Anne Chisholm. New York: E. P. Dutton, 1972, pp. 25-38.

The Liberal Arts Amid a Culture in Crisis. *Liberal Education* (Proceedings of the 58th Association of American Colleges annual meeting, Washington, D.C. Jan. 1972), 58, 1 (Mar. 1972): 5-17.

Man as a Commodity. In: *Human Resources and Economic Welfare: Essays in Honor of Eli Ginzberg,* Ivar Berg, ed. New York: Columbia University Press, 1972, pp. 35-49. CP III, pp. 587-603.

New Goals for Society? In: *Energy, Economic Growth, and the Environment,* Sam H. Schurr, ed. (papers presented at an RFF Forum, Washington, D.C., Apr. 1971). Baltimore: Johns Hopkins University Press, for Resources for the Future, 1972, pp. 139-151. CP IV, pp. 585-599.

The Role of the Social Sciences in the Control of Technology. (paper presented at the AAAS meeting, Boston, Dec. 1969) In: *Technology and Man's Future,* Albert H. Teich, ed. New York: St. Martin's Press, 1972, pp. 263-274.

The Schooling Industry as a Possibly Pathological Section of the American Economy. (paper presented at the American Educational Research Association annual meeting, New York, Feb. 1971) *Review of Educational Research,* 42, 1 (Apr. 1972): 129-143. CP IV, pp. 569-584.

The Three Faces of Power. In: *50 Years of War Resistance: What Now?* London: War Resisters' International, 1972, pp. 18-21.

Toward a Theory for the Study of Community. In: *Issues in Community Organization,* Lawrence Witmer, ed. (papers prepared for the University of Chicago Conference on Community Organization, Spring 1968). Chicago: Center for the Scientific Study of Religion, 1972, pp. 23-31.

Toward the Development of a Cultural Economics. *Social Science Quarterly* (Special issue including a symposium on the Idea of Culture in the Social Sciences), 53, 2 (Sept. 1972): 267-284. RI.

Towards a Pure Theory of Foundations. (paper prepared for the Kettering Foundation Conference on Foundations, Dayton, Nov. 1970; pamphlet) Danbury, Conn.: Non-Profit Report, 1972, 22 pp. (included with *Non-Profit REPORT,* 5, 3, Mar. 1972).

Towards a Twenty-First Century Politics. (40th Lecture on Research and Creative Work, University of Colorado, Apr. 1971) *Colorado Quarterly,* 20, 3 (Winter 1972): 309-319. CP V, pp. 407–419. RI.

The Weapon as an Element in the Social System. (presentation at the colloquium on Multipolar Strategy, Institute of International Studies, University of California, Berkeley, Mar. 1970) In: *The Future of the International Strategic System*, Richard Rosecrance, ed. San Francisco: Chandler, 1972, pp. 81-92.

BOOKS

The Appraisal of Change. (lectures given for the Japan Broadcast Company, October 1970; in Japanese) Tokyo: Nippon Hoso Shuppan Kyokai (Japan Broadcast Publishing Company), 1972. 176 pp.

Economic Imperialism: A Book of Readings. (edited with Tapan Mukerjee) Ann Arbor: University of Michigan Press, 1972. xviii + 338 pp.

Redistribution to the Rich and the Poor: The Grants Economics of Income Distribution. (edited with Martin Pfaff; Grants Economics Series) Belmont, Calif.: Wadsworth, 1972. 390 pp.

BOOK REVIEWS

Review of Martin Bronfenbrenner, Income Distribution Theory. *Journal of Economic Issues*, 6, 2 and 3 (Sept. 1972): 123-128.

The Wolf of Rome. Review of Jay W. Forrester, World Dynamics. *Business and Society Review*, 2 (Summer 1972): 106-109.

Search for Time's Arrow. Review of Nicholas Georgescu-Roegen, The Entropy Law and the Economic Process. *Science*, 175, 4026 (Mar. 10, 1972): 1099-1100.

The Gospel of St. Malthus. Review of Garrett Hardin, Exploring New Ethics for Survival: The Voyage of the Spaceship Beagle. *New Republic*, 167, 9 (Sept. 9, 1972): 22-25.

A Devil Theory of Economic History. Review of Michael Hudson, Super Imperialism: The Economic Strategy of American Empire. *Book World* (Washington Post), 7, 53 (Dec. 31, 1972): 7, 13.

Review of Fred Charles Ikle, Every War Must End. *Political Science Quarterly*, 87, 4 (Dec. 1972): 705-707.

Yes, The Wolf is Real. Review of Donella and Dennis Meadows *et al.*, The Limits to Growth. *New Republic*, 166, 18 (Apr. 29, 1972): 27-28.

Review of Bruce Russett, What Price Vigilance? The Burdens of National Defense. *American Political Science Review*, 66, 1 (Mar. 1972): 217.

VERSE

A Ballad of Ecological Awareness. In: *The Careless Technology: Ecology and International Development*, M. Taghi Farvar and John P. Milton, eds. (Record of the Conference on the Ecological Aspects of International Development, Airlie House, Warrenton, Va., Dec. 1968). Garden City, N.Y.: Natural

History Press, for the Conservation Foundation and the Center for the Biology of Natural Systems, Washington University, 1972, pp. 3, 157, 371, 669, 793, 955.

New Goals for Society? In: *Energy, Economic Growth, and the Environment,* Sam H. Schurr, ed. (papers presented at an RFF forum, Washington, D.C., Apr. 1971). Baltimore: Johns Hopkins University Press, for Resources for the Future, 1972, p. 139. CP IV p. 587. RI.

1973

ARTICLES and MONOGRAPH

Aristocrats Have Always Been Sons of Bitches. (interview) *Psychology Today,* 6, 8 (Jan. 1973): 60-64, 67-68, 70, 86-87. RI.

ASGE—In Retrospect and Prospect. *Association for the Study of the Grants Economy Newsletter,* 5 (Dec. 5, 1973): 2-3.

Can There Be a Growth Policy? In: *Man and His Environment: The Vail Experience* (Summary of the 3rd Vail Symposium, Aug. 1973). Vail, Colo.: The Printery, for the Town of Vail, 1973, p. 19.

The Challenge of Change. (Lecture 10 in "America and the Future of Man" Course By Newspaper) Distributed by Copley News Service for the Regents of the University of California in all major newspapers in the U.S., Dec. 6, 1973. RI.

Communication of the Integrative Network. In: *Communication: Ethical and Moral Issues,* Lee Thayer, ed. (based on a colloquia series at the Center for Advanced Study of Communication, University of Iowa, 1969-70). New York: Gordon and Breach, 1973, pp. 201-213.

Economic Theory of Natural Liberty. In: *Dictionary of the History of Ideas,* Vol. II, Philip P. Wiener, ed.-in-chief. New York: Charles Scribner's Sons, 1973, pp. 61-71.

The Economics of Ecology. In: *Final Conference Report for the National Conference on Managing the Environment* (held in Washington, D.C., May 1973). Washington, D.C.: Office of Research and Development, U.S. Environmental Protection Agency, 1973, pp. 11-13 to 11-17.

The Economics of Energy. *Annals of the American Academy of Political and Social Science* (Special issue on the Energy Crisis: Reality or Myth), 410 (Nov. 1973): 120-126.

Equality and Conflict. *Annals of the American Academy of Political and Social Science* (Special issue on Income Inequality), 409 (Sept. 1973): 1-8.

Foreword. In: *Image and Environment: Cognitive Mapping and Spatial Behavior,* Roger M. Downs and David Stea, eds. Chicago: Aldine, 1973, pp. vii-ix.

Foreword. In: *The People: Growth and Survival,* by Gerhard Hirschfeld. Chicago: Aldine, for the Council for the Study of Mankind, 1973, pp. xiii-xvi.

Foreword. In: *The Image of the Future,* by Fred Polak, translated from the Dutch and abridged by Elise Boulding. San Francisco and Amsterdam: Jossey Bass/Elsevier, 1973, pp. v-vi.

General Systems as an Integrating Force in the Social Sciences. In: University
    Through Diversity: A Festschrift for Ludwig von Bertalanffy, Vol. II, William
    Gray and Nicholas D. Rizzo, eds. New York: Gordon & Breach, 1973, pp.
    951-967.
Intersects: The Peculiar Organizations. In: *Challenge to Leadership: Managing in
    a Changing World* (A Conference Board Study). New York: Free Press, for the
    Conference Board, 1973, pp. 179-201.
Introduction. In: *Poverty and Progress: An Ecological Perspective on Economic
    Development,* by Richard G. Wilkinson. New York: Praeger, 1973, pp. xiii-xx.
Looking Ahead. Interview: Kenneth E. Boulding. In: *Economics '73-'74: Text.*
    Guilford, Conn.: Dushkin, 1973, pp. 10-11.
Love, Fear and the Economist. (interview) *Challenge,* 16, 3 (July-Aug. 1973): 32-
    39.
Organization Theory as a Bridge Between Socialist and Capitalist Societies. *Journal
    of Management Studies,* 10, 1 (Feb. 1973): 1-7.
Role Prejudice as an Economic Problem. (Part I of "Combatting Role Prejudice and
    Sex Discrimination: Findings of the American Economic Association Com-
    mittee on the Status of Women in the Economics Profession) *American
    Economic Review,* 63, 5 (Dec. 1973): 1049-1053.
The Shadow of the Stationary State. *Daedalus* (Special issue on The No-Growth
    Society), 102, 4 (Fall 1973): 89-101.
Social Dynamics. In: *Summer School in Peace Research: Grindstone Island 1973*
    (Report on the 4th Annual Summer School, June-July 1973). Dundas, Ont.:
    Canadian Peace Research Institute, Nov. 1973, p. 26.
Social Risk, Political Uncertainty, and the Legitimacy of Private Profit. (paper
    presented at the Public Utility Conference, East Lansing, Feb. 1971) In: *Risk
    and Regulated Firms,* R. Hayden Howard, ed. East Lansing: Michigan State
    University Graduate School of Business Administration, 1973, pp. 82-93.
System Analysis and Its Use in the Classroom. (with Alfred Kuhn and Lawrence
    Senesh; SSEC Monograph Series, Publication No. 157) Boulder, Colo.: Social
    Science Education Consortium, 1973. 58 pp.
A Theory of Prediction Applied to the Future of Economic Growth. In: *In-
    ternational Symposium "New Problems of Advanced Societies"* (held in
    Tokyo, Nov. 1972). Tokyo: Japan Economic Research Institute, 1973, pp. 53-
    61.

BOOKS

Kenneth E. Boulding Collected Papers, Vol. III: Political Economy, Larry D.
    Singell, ed. Boulder: Colorado Associated University Press, 1973. ix + 614 pp.
The Economy of Love and Fear: A Preface to Grants Economics. (Grants
    Economics Series) Belmont, Calif.: Wadsworth, 1973. 116 pp.
Peace and the War Industry. 2nd edition. (edited, and with a revised introduction;
    Transaction/Society Book Series—11) New Brunswick, N.J.: Transaction
    Books, 1973. 213 pp.
Transfers in an Urbanized Economy. (edited with Martin and Anita Pfaff; Grants
    Economics Series) Belmont, Calif.: Wadsworth, 1973. 376 pp.

BOOK REVIEWS

Multiply and Replenish: Alternative Perspectives on Population. Review of Howard M. Bahr, Bruce A. Chadwick, and Darwin L. Thomas, eds., Population Resources and the Future Non-Malthusian Perspectives. *Dialogue: A Journal of Mormon Thought*, 8, 3/4 (1973): 159-163.

Global Economics: A Failure So Far. Review of Jagdish N. Bhagwati, ed., Economics and World Order: From the 1970's to the 1990's. *War/Peace Report*, 12, 5 (July/Aug. 1973): 30-31.

Review of William Breit and Roger L. Ransom, The Academic Scribblers: American Economists in Collision. *Journal of Political Economy*, 81, 4 (July/Aug. 1973): 1041-1042.

Review of Lester R. Brown, World Without Borders. *International Development Review*, 15, 2 (1973): 30.

Zoom, Gloom, Doom and Room. Review of H. S. D. Cole *et al.*, eds., Models of Doom: A Critique of the Limits to Growth; Ralph E. Lapp, The Logarithmic Century: Charting Future Shock; and John Maddox, The Doomsday Syndrome. *New Republic*, 169, 6 (Aug. 11, 1973): 25-27.

Review of Edgar S. Dunn, Jr., Economic and Social Development: A Process of Social Learning. *Urban Studies* (Glasgow), 10, 1 (Feb. 1973): 105-106.

Big Families Do Pay. Review of Bernard James, The Death of Progress; Mahmood Mamdani, The Myth of Population Control: Family, Caste, and Class in an Indian Village; and Herbert N. Woodward, The Human Dilemma. *New Republic*, 168, 9 (Mar. 3, 1973): 22-23.

Review of Richard A. Peterson, The Industrial Order and Social Policy. *Administrative Science Quarterly*, 18, 4 (Dec. 1973): 555-556.

Review of John Rawls, A Theory of Justice. *Journal of Economic Issues*, 7, 4 (Dec. 1973): 667-673.

Review of G. L. S. Shackle, Epistemics & Economics: A Critique of Economic Doctrines. *Journal of Economic Literature*, 11, 4 (Dec. 1973): 1373-1374.

VERSE

COPRED, A Prophecy. (written at the Consortium on Peace Research, Education and Development Advisory Council meeting, Windsor, Ontario, Apr. 1973) *Peace and Change*, 1, 2 (Spring 1973): 60.

Reflections. In: *Final Conference Report for the National Conference on Managing the Environment* (held in Washington, D.C., May 1973). Washington, D.C.: Office of Research and Development, U.S. Environmental Protection Agency, 1973, p. iii.

Publications by Professor Boulding in 1974 and subsequent years will be listed in future bibliographies. — V.L.W.

ARTICLES, MONOGRAPHS, AND PAMPHLETS BY TITLE

The Abolition of Membership, 1942
Accomplishments and Prospects of the Peace Research Movement (with Hanna and Alan Newcombe), 1968
After Samuelson, Who Needs Adam Smith? 1971
Agricultural Organizations and Policies: A Personal Evaluation, 1963
The American Economy After Vietnam, 1971
America's Economy: The Qualified Uproarious Success, 1968
America's Great Delusion, 1965
An Application of Population Analysis to the Automobile Population of the United States, 1955
The Application of the Pure Theory of Population Change to the Theory of Capital, 1934
Aristocrats Have Always Been Sons of Bitches (interview), 1973
Arms Limitation and Integrative Activity as Elements in the Establishment of Stable Peace, 1966
ASGE—In Retrospect and Prospect, 1973
Asset Identities in Economic Models, 1951

The Background and Structure of a Macro-Economic Theory of Distribution, 1950
The Balance of Peace, 1970
The Basis of Value Judgments in Economics, 1967
Better R-E-D Than Dead, 1962
The Boundaries of Social Policy, 1967
Business and Economic Systems, 1968

Can There Be a Growth Policy? 1973
Can There Be a National Policy for Stable Peace? 1970
Can We Afford a Warless World? 1962
Can We Control Inflation in a Garrison State? 1951
Can We Curb Inflation Without Recession? If So, How? 1970
Capital and Interest, 1960
The Challenge of Change, 1973
The Challenge of the Great Transition (in Japanese), 1970
Changes in Physical Phenomena: Discussion (with others), 1956
The Changing Framework of American Capitalism, 1965
The City as an Element in the International System, 1968
Collective Bargaining and Fiscal Policy, 1949
Comment (Sales and Output Taxes), 1954
Comment on Mr. Burk's Note (The Net National Product Concept), 1948
Commentary (Perspectives on Prosperity), 1956
Comments (on Professor Dr. Wolfgang F. Stolper "The Economics of Peace"), 1951
The Communication of Legitimacy, 1965
Communication of the Integrative Network, 1973
The Concept of Economic Surplus, 1945

The Concept of Need for Health Services, 1966
The Concept of World Interest, 1965
A Conceptual Framework for Social Science, 1952
Conflict Management as a Learning Process, 1966
The Consumption Concept in Economic Theory, 1945
Contemporary Economic Research, 1961
The Contribution of Economics to the Understanding of the Firm—I Marginal
    Analysis, 1953
The Contribution of Economics to the Understanding of the Firm—II The Theory
    of Organization and Communications, 1953
Contributions of Economics to the Theory of Conflict, 1955
The Costs of Independence: Notes on the Caribbean, 1960
The Crisis of the Universities, 1970
The Current State of Economics, 1958

Dare We Take the Social Sciences Seriously? 1967
David Fand's "Keynesian Monetary Theories, Stabilization Policy, and the Recent
    Inflation," A Comment, 1969
The Deadly Industry: War and the International System, 1970
The Death of the City: A Frightened Look at Post-Civilization, 1963
Decision-Making in the Modern World, 1960
A Deepening Loyalty, 1942
Defense and Opulence: The Ethics of International Economics, 1951
Demand and Supply, 1968
Democracy and Organization, 1958
Desirable Changes in the National Economy After the War, 1944
Dialogue on Peace Research (with Milton Mayer), 1967
Die Zukunft als Möglichkeit und Design (The Future as Chance and Design; in
    German), 1969
The Difficult Art of Doing Good, 1965
The Dilemma of Power and Legitimacy, 1965
The Dimensions of Economic Freedom, 1964
Discussion (of Allen V. Kneese's "Environmental Pollution: Economics and
    Policy"), 1971
Divided Views on Tax Increase, 1967
The Dodo Didn't Make It: Survival and Betterment, 1971
Does Large Scale Enterprise Lower Costs? Discussion (with others), 1948
Does the Absence of Monopoly Power in Agriculture Influence the Stability and
    Level of Farm Income? 1957
The Domestic Implications of Arms Control, 1960
The Dynamics of Disarmament, 1961
The Dynamics of Society, 1968

Economic Analysis and Agricultural Policy, 1947
The Economic Consequences of Some Recent Antitrust Decisions: Discussion
    (with others), 1949
Economic Education: The Stepchild Too is Father of the Man, 1969
Economic Issues in International Conflict, 1953
Economic Libertarianism, 1965

Foreword (in Image and Environment: Cognitive Mapping and Spatial Behavior, Roger M. Downs and David Stea, eds.), 1973
Foreword (in The People: Growth and Survival, by Gerhard Hirschfeld), 1973
Foreword (in Population: The First Essay, by T. R. Malthus), 1959
Foreword (in The Image of the Future, by Fred Polak), 1973
The Formation of Values as a Process in Human Learning, 1969
Fragmentation, Isolation, Conflict, 1970
Friends and Social Change, 1968
The Fruits of Progress and the Dynamics of Distribution, 1953
Fun and Games with the Gross National Product—The Role of Misleading Indicators in Social Policy, 1970
Fundamental Considerations, 1970
The Future as Chance and Design (in German), 1969; (in English), 1974
The Future Corporation and Public Attitudes, 1963
Future Directions (with Martin Pfaff), 1972
The Future of Personal Responsibility, 1972
The Future of the Social Sciences, 1965

Gaps Between Developed and Developing Nations, 1970
General Systems as a Point of View, 1964
General Systems as an Integrating Force in the Social Sciences, 1973
General Systems Theory: The Skeleton of Science, 1956
Grants Economics: A Simple Introduction (with Martin Pfaff and Janos Horvath), 1972
The Grants Economy, 1969
The Grants Economy and the Development Gap (with Martin Pfaff), 1972
Grants Versus Exchange in the Support of Education, 1968
The Great Revolution, 1952
Great Society, or Grandiose? 1965
Greatness as a Pathology of the National Image, 1968

Heretic Among Economists (interview), 1969
A Historical Note from the President, 1968
The Home as a House of Worship, 1945
The Household as Achilles' Heel, 1972
How Scientists Study "Getting Along," 1965
Human Betterment and the Quality of Life, 1972
Human Resources Development as a Learning Process, 1967

The Impact of the Defense Industry on the Structure of the American Economy, 1970
The Impact of the Draft on the Legitimacy of the National State, 1967
Implications for General Economics of More Realistic Theories of the Firm, 1952
Impressions of the World Conference on Church and Society, 1966
In Defense of Monopoly, 1945
In Defense of Monopoly: Reply, 1946
In Defense of Statics, 1955
In Defense of the Supernatural, 1938
In Praise of Danger, 1942
In Praise of Maladjustment, 1939

In Praise of Selfishness, 1940
The Incidence of a Profits Tax, 1944
Income or Welfare? 1950
Industrial Revolution and Urban Dominance: Discussion (with others), 1956
Insight and Knowledge in the Development of Stable Peace, 1965
An Interdisciplinary Honors Course in General Systems, 1962
The Interplay of Technology and Values: The Emerging Superculture, 1969
Intersects: The Peculiar Organizations, 1973
Introduction (in Economic Imperialism: A Book of Readings, Kenneth Boulding
    and Tapan Mukerjee, eds.), 1972
Introduction (in Analysis of the Problem of War, by Clyde Eagleton), 1972
Introduction (in Poverty and Progress: An Ecological Perspective on Economic
    Development, by Richard G. Wilkinson), 1973
The Inward Light, 1947
Is Economics Culture-Bound? 1970
Is Economics Necessary? 1949
Is It the System or Is It You? 1944
Is Peace Researchable? 1962
Is Scarcity Dead? 1966
Is There a General Theory of Conflict? 1967
Is Ugliness the Price of Prosperity? 1968

Japan Should Produce "Things" With Value Rather Than a "Strong Yen"
    (interview in Japanese), 1972
The Jungle of Hugeness: The Second Age of the Brontosaurus, 1958

Kenneth Boulding: The Arrival of Spaceship Earth (interview), 1972
Knowledge as a Commodity, 1962
Knowledge as a Road to Peace, 1971
Knowledge as an Economic Variable, 1964
The Knowledge Boom, 1966
The Knowledge Explosion, 1970
The Knowledge of Value and the Value of Knowledge, 1959

The Learning and Reality-Testing Process in the International System, 1967
The Learning Process in the Dynamics of Total Societies, 1967
The Legitimacy of Central Banks, 1971
The Legitimacy of Economics, 1967
The Legitimation of the Market, 1968
Letter on "Happiness" (in Japanese), 1971
The Liberal Arts Amid a Culture in Crisis, 1972
Limits of the Earth: Discussion (with others), 1956
A Liquidity Preference Theory of Market Prices, 1944
A Look at National Priorities, 1970
A Look at the Corporation, 1957
Looking Ahead. Interview: Kenneth E. Boulding, 1973
Looking Ahead to the Year 2000, 1965
Love, Fear and the Economist (interview), 1973

Machines, Men and Religion, 1968
Making Education Religious, 1938

The Malthusian Model as a General System, 1955
Man as a Commodity, 1972
Man's Choice: Creative Development or Revolution, 1968
The Many Failures of Success, 1968
Market: Economic Theory, 1964
The Meaning of Human Betterment, 1971
A Memorandum on the Facilitation of Behavioral Thinking: Four Modest
    Proposals for Highly Advanced Study (with Richard Christie), 1969
The Menace of Methuselah: Possible Consequences of Increased Life Expectancy,
    1965
The Misallocation of Intellectual Resources, 1963
The Misallocation of Intellectual Resources in Economics, 1971
The Models for a Macro-Economic Theory of Distribution, 1950
Modern Man and Ancient Testimonies, 1969

National Images and International Systems, 1959
The "National" Importance of Human Capital, 1968
Nationalism, Millennialism and the Quaker Witness, 1944
The Need for a Study on the Psychology of Disarmament, 1964
The Need for a University of the Building Industry, 1969
The Need for Reform of National Income Statistics, 1971
Needs and Opportunities in Peace Research and Peace Education, 1964
A New Ethos for a New Era, 1970
New Goals for Society? 1972
A New Look at Institutionalism, 1957
New Nations for Old, 1942
No Second Chance for Man, 1970
A Note on the Consumption Function, 1935
A Note on the Theory of the Black Market, 1947
Notes on a Theory of Philanthropy, 1962
Notes on the Information Concept, 1955
Notes on the Politics of Peace, 1966

Organization and Conflict, 1957
"The Organization Man"—Fact or Fancy? 1958
Organization Theory as a Bridge Between Socialist and Capitalist Societies, 1973
Organizing Growth, 1959
Our Attitude Toward Revolution, 1961

Pacem in Terris and the World Community (with others), 1963
The Pacifism of All Sensible Men, 1940
A Pacifist View of History, 1939
The Parameters of Politics, 1966
Parity, Charity, and Clarity: Ten Theses on Agricultural Policy, 1955
Paths of Glory: A New Way With War, 1938
A Peace Movement in Search of a Party, 1968
The Peace Research Movement, 1962
The Peculiar Economics of Water, 1966
People Eyeing 21st Century as Age When Mankind Matures, 1971
Personal and Political Peacemaking, 1944

Perspective on the Economics of Peace, 1961
The Philosophy of Peace Research, 1970
The Place of the ''Displacement Cost'' Concept in Economic Theory, 1932
The Place of the Image in the Dynamics of Society, 1964
The Political Consequences of the Social Sciences, 1966
Political Implications of General Systems Research, 1961
Population and Poverty, 1965
Possible Conflicts Between Economic Stability and Economic Progress, 1955
The Possibilities of Peace Research in Australia, 1964
The Possibilities of Socialism in Britain, 1932
The Practice of the Love of God, 1942
The Prayer of Magic and the Prayer of Love, 1945
Preface (with Emile Benoit; in Disarmament and the Economy, Emile Benoit and
    Kenneth Boulding, eds.), 1963
Preface to a Special Issue, 1968
The Present Position of the Theory of the Firm, 1960
Preventing Schismogenesis, 1969
The Prevention of World War III, 1962
Price Control in a Subsequent Deflation, 1948
The Price System and the Price of the Great Society, 1967
The Principle of Personal Responsibility, 1954
The Problem of the Country Meeting, 1943
Professor Knight's Capital Theory: A Note in Reply, 1936
A Profile of the American Economy, 1966
The Prospects of Economic Abundance, 1967
Protestantism's Lost Economic Gospel, 1950
Public Choice and the Grants Economy: The Intersecting Set, 1969
The Public Image of American Economic Institutions, 1961
A Pure Theory of Conflict Applied to Organizations, 1961
A Pure Theory of Death: Dilemmas of Defense Policy in a World of Conditional
    Viability, 1962
The Pursuit of Happiness and the Value of the Human Being (in Japanese), 1971

The Quaker Approach in Economic Life, 1953
Quakerism in the World of the Future, 1966
Qu'est-ce que le progrès économique? (What is Economic Progress?; in French),
    1961

The Real World of the Seventies and Beyond, 1970
Realism and Sentimentalism in the Student Movement, 1964
Reality Testing and Value Orientation in International Systems: The Role of
    Research, 1965
Reflection of the Election—An Interview with Kenneth Boulding, 1968
Reflections on Poverty, 1961
Reflections on Protest, 1965
The Relations of Economic, Political and Social Systems, 1962
Religion and the Social Sciences, 1958
Religious Foundations of Economic Progress, 1952
Religious Perspectives of College Teaching in Economics, 1950

Report on Travels in the Labor Movement, 1944

Requirements for a Social Systems Analysis of the Dynamics of the World War Industry, 1968

Research and Development for the Emergent Nations, 1965

Research for Peace, 1969

Revolution and Development, 1968

The Role of Economics in the Establishment of Stable Peace, 1968

The Role of Exemplars in the Learning of Community, 1969

The Role of Law in the Learning of Peace, 1963

The Role of Legitimacy in the Dynamics of Society, 1969

The Role of the Church in the Making of Community and Identity, 1969

The Role of the Museum in the Propagation of Developed Images, 1966

The Role of the Price Structure in Economic Development (with Pritam Singh), 1962

The Role of the Social Sciences in the Control of Technology, 1972

The Role of the Undergraduate College in Social Change, 1970

The Role of the War Industry in International Conflict, 1967

Role Prejudice as an Economic Problem, 1973

The Scarcity of Saints, 1967

The Schooling Industry as a Possibly Pathological Section of the American Economy, 1972

Scientific Nomenclature, 1960

The Scientific Revelation, 1970

Secular Images of Man in the Social Sciences, 1958

A Service of National Importance, 1940

The Shadow of the Stationary State, 1973

The Skills of the Economist, 1953, and in Portuguese, 1954

Social Dynamics, 1973

Social Dynamics in West Indian Society, 1961

Social Justice in Social Dynamics, 1962

Social Risk, Political Uncertainty, and the Legitimacy of Private Profit, 1973

Social Sciences, 1965

Social Systems Analysis and the Study of International Conflict, 1970

The Society of Abundance, 1963

Some Contributions of Economics to the General Theory of Value, 1956

Some Contributions of Economics to Theology and Religion, 1957

Some Difficulties in the Concept of Economic Input, 1961

Some Hesitant Reflections on the Political Future, 1970

Some Questions on the Measurement and Evaluation of Organization, 1962

Some Reflections on Inflation and Economic Development, 1957

Some Reflections on Stewardship, 1940

Some Unsolved Problems in Economic Education, 1969

The Specialist With a Universal Mind, 1968

The Sputnik Within, 1958

Stability in International Systems: The Role of Disarmament and Development, 1969

Standards for Our Economic System: Discussion (with others), 1960

Statement (on Learning, Teaching, Education, and Development), 1968
Statement Before the Select Subcommittee on Education of the House Committee on Education and Labor, U.S. Congress, 1970
Statement Before the Subcommittee of the Senate Committee on Foreign Relations, U.S. Congress, 1956
Statement Before the Subcommittee on Agricultural Policy of the Joint Economic Committee, U.S. Congress, 1958
Statement Before the Subcommittee on Economy in Government of the Joint Economic Committee, U.S. Congress, 1969
Statement Before the Subcommittee on Fiscal Policy of the Joint Economic Committee, U.S. Congress, 1965
Structure and Stability: The Economics of the Next Adjustment, 1956
Study of the Soviet Economy: Its Place in American Education (discussion with others), 1961
Symbols for Capitalism, 1959
System Analysis and Its Use in the Classroom (with Alfred Kuhn and Lawrence Senesh), 1973

The Task of the Teacher in the Social Sciences, 1969
Taxation in War Time: Some Implications for Friends, 1942
Technology and the Changing Social Order, 1969
Technology and the Integrative System, 1967
The Theory and Measurement of Price Expectations: Discussion (with others), 1949
The Theory of a Single Investment, 1935
A Theory of Prediction Applied to the Future of Economic Growth, 1973
A Theory of Small Society, 1960
The Theory of the Firm in the Last Ten Years, 1942
The Threat System, 1969
Three Concepts of Disarmament, 1958
The Three Faces of Power, 1972
Time and Investment, 1936
Time and Investment: Reply, 1936
Times and Seasons, 1945
Toward a General Theory of Growth, 1953
Toward a Modest Society: The End of Growth and Grandeur, 1971
Toward a Theory for the Study of Community, 1972
Toward a Theory of Peace, 1964
Toward the Development of a Cultural Economics, 1972
Toward the Year 2000, 1971
Towards a Pure Theory of Foundations, 1972
Towards a Pure Theory of Threat Systems, 1963
Towards a Twenty-First Century Politics, 1972
Towards the Development of a Security Community in Europe, 1966
Town and Country Interviews Dr. Kenneth Boulding, 1968
Twenty-Five Theses on Peace and Trade, 1954
The "Two Cultures," 1967
Two Principles of Conflict, 1964

The U.S. and Revolution, 1961

Universal, Policed Disarmament as the Only Stable System of National Defense, 1958

The University and Tomorrow's Civilization: Its Role in the Development of a World Community, 1967

The University as an Economic and Social Unit, 1968

The University, Society, and Arms Control, 1962

Unprofitable Empire, Britain in India 1880-1967: A Critique of the Hobson-Lenin Thesis on Imperialism (with Tapan Mukerjee), 1971

The Uses of Price Theory, 1963

Values, Technology, and Divine Legitimation, 1968

Verifiability of Economic Images, 1966

Violence and Revolution: Some Reflections on Cuba, 1960

Wages as a Share in the National Income, 1951

War as a Public Health Problem: Conflict Management as a Key to Survival, 1965

War as an Economic Institution, 1962

War as an Investment: The Strange Case of Japan (with Alan H. Gleason), 1965

The War Industry and the American Economy, 1970

The Weapon as an Element in the Social System, 1972

Welfare Economics, 1952

What About Christian Economics? 1951

What Can We Know and Teach About Social Systems? 1968

What Do Economic Indicators Indicate? Quality and Quantity in the GNP, 1971

What Don't We Know That Hurts Us? 1969

What is Economic Progress? (in French), 1961

What is Loyalty? 1942

What Is the GNP Worth? 1970

What Lies Ahead? 1940

Where Are We Going, If Anywhere? A Look at Post-Civilization, 1962

Where Do We Go From Here, If Anywhere? 1961

Where Does Development Lead? 1971

Where Is the Labor Movement Moving? 1945

Why Did Gandhi Fail? 1964

The Wisdom of Man and the Wisdom of God, 1966

World Economic Contacts and National Policies, 1948

A World-Famous "Economist-Philosopher" Gives his Views on Religion, Radicalism, the Hippies and More (interview), 1971

The World War Industry as an Economic Problem, 1963

Worship and Fellowship, 1938

BOOKS BY TITLE

The Appraisal of Change (in Japanese), 1972
Beyond Economics: Essays on Society, Religion, and Ethics, 1968
Conflict and Defense: A General Theory, 1962
Disarmament and the Economy (edited with Emile Benoit), 1963
Economic Analysis, 1941; revised ed., 1948; 3rd ed., 1955; 4th ed., 1966
Economic Imperialism: A Book of Readings (edited with Tapan Mukerjee), 1972
Economics as a Science, 1970
The Economics of Peace, 1945
The Economy of Love and Fear: A Preface to Grants Economics, 1973
The Image: Knowledge in Life and Society, 1956
The Impact of the Social Sciences, 1966
Kenneth E. Boulding Collected Papers: Vol. I: Economics (1932-1955), Fred R.
    Glahe, ed., 1971; Vol. II: Economics (1956-1970), Fred R. Glahe, ed., 1971;
    Vol. III: Political Economy, Larry D. Singell, ed., 1973; Vol. IV: Toward a
    General Social Science, Larry D. Singell, ed., 1974; Vol. V: International
    Systems: Peace, Conflict Resolution and Politics, Larry D. Singell, ed., 1975
Linear Programming and the Theory of the Firm (edited with W. Allen Spivey),
    1960
The Meaning of the Twentieth Century: The Great Transition, 1964
The Organizational Revolution: A Study in the Ethics of Economic Organization,
    1953
Peace and the War Industry (edited, and with an introduction), 1970; 2nd ed.,
    1973
A Primer on Social Dynamics: History as Dialectics and Development, 1970
Principles of Economic Policy, 1958
The Prospering of Truth, 1970
Readings in Price Theory, Vol. VI (edited with George J. Stigler), 1952
A Reconstruction of Economics, 1950
Redistribution to the Rich and the Poor: The Grants Economics of Income
    Distribution (edited with Martin Pfaff), 1972
The Skills of the Economist, 1958
There Is a Spirit (The Nayler Sonnets), 1945
Transfers in an Urbanized Economy (edited with Martin and Anita Pfaff), 1973

BOOK REVIEWS BY AUTHOR

Ackerman. See: Johnson, 1959
Allais, Économie et Intérêt, 1951
Ardant. See: Mendes-France, 1955
Ardrey, The Territorial Imperative, 1967
Arendt, The Human Condition, 1960
_____, On Violence, 1971
Arnhym. See: Power, 1965
Aron, Introduction to the Philosophy of History, 1961
Ayres, Toward a Reasonable Society, 1962

Bahr *et al.*, eds., Population Resources and the Future Non-Malthusian Perspectives, 1973

Bain, Barriers to New Competition, 1957

Balk, The Religion Business, 1969

Bauer, ed., Social Indicators, 1967

Bay, The Structure of Freedom, 1960

Bazelon, The Paper Economy, 1965

Beaufre, Deterrence and Strategy, 1968

Bhagwati, ed., Economics and World Order, 1973

Biet, Theories Contemporaines du Profit, 1959

Black, The Dynamics of Modernization, 1968

Bonner, Cells and Societies, 1956

Brady, Business as a System of Power, 1944

Braybrooke and Lindblom, A Strategy of Decision, 1964 and 1969

Breit and Ransom, The Academic Scribblers, 1973

Brill, "Social Accounting and Economic Analysis," 1952

Bronfenbrenner, Income Distribution Theory, 1972

Brown, World Without Borders, 1973

Brunner and Markowitz, "Stocks and Flows in Monetary Analysis," 1952

Burns, ed., Wesley Clair Mitchell, The Economic Scientist, 1952

Calder, ed., Unless Peace Comes, 1969

Chadwick. See: Bahr *et al.*, 1973

Chamberlain, A General Theory of Economic Process, 1956

Chammah. See: Rapoport, 1966

Clark, Competition as a Dynamic Process, 1962

———, Economic Institutions and Human Welfare, 1957

Coase, British Broadcasting, 1951

Cochran, The American Business System (with John Kenneth Galbraith), 1958

Cohen and Cyert, Theory of the Firm, 1966

Cole, A., Business Enterprise in Its Social Setting, 1959

Cole, H. *et al.*, eds., Models of Doom, 1973

Coleman, Introduction to Mathematical Sociology, 1966

Colm, The American Economy in 1960 (with others), 1953; correction and apology, 1954

Cowles Commission, Economic Theory and Measurement, 1953

Cyert. See: Cohen, 1966

———and March, A Behavioral Theory of the Firm, 1964

Davis. See: Miller *et al.*, 1964

DeChazeau *et al.*, Jobs and Markets, 1947

de Grazia, Of Time, Work, and Leisure, 1963

de Koster, All Ye That Labor, 1957

De Schweinitz, Jr., Industrialization and Democracy, 1965

Dean, Test Ban and Disarmament, 1968

Demant, Religion and the Decline of Capitalism, 1953

Deutsch. See: Wright *et al.*, 1963

Dietze, Youth, University, and Democracy, 1971
Dimock, The New American Political Economy, 1962
Drucker, The Age of Discontinuity, 1970
Duff, The Social Thought of the World Council of Churches, 1956
Duncan, Communication and Social Order, 1963
Dunn, Jr., Economic and Social Development, 1973

Easton, A Systems Analysis of Political Life, 1968
Evan. See: Wright *et al.*, 1963
Ewald, Jr., ed., Environment and Change, 1970
————, ed., Environment and Policy, 1970

Fackler. See: Miller *et al.*, 1964
Finer, Road To Reaction, 1946
Forrester, World Dynamics, 1972
Fourastié, The Causes of Wealth, 1961
Fried *et al.*, eds., War, 1969
Friedman, Capitalism and Freedom, 1963
————, Essays in Positive Economics, 1954

Galbraith, The Affluent Society, 1959
————, The New Industrial State, 1967 (2 reviews)
Georgescu-Roegen, The Entropy Law and the Economic Process, 1972
Grace, The Concept of Property in Modern Christian Thought, 1954
Green, Deadly Logic, 1967
Gustavson, The Institutional Drive, 1967

Haas and Whiting, Dynamics of International Relations, 1964
Haavelmo, A Study in the Theory of Economic Evolution, 1955
Halle, The Society of Man, 1967
Hardin, Exploring New Ethics for Survival, 1972
Harris. See: Fried *et al*, 1969
Heilbroner, The Limits of American Capitalism, 1967
Henderson, The Innovative Spirit, 1971
Herzog, The Church Trap, 1969
Hickman and Kuhn, Individuals, Groups, and Economic Behavior, 1956
Hicks, A Theory of Economic History, 1970
————, Value and Capital, 1939
Higgins, What Do Economists Know? 1953
Hitch and McKean, The Economics of Defense in the Nuclear Age, 1961
Hobsbawm, Industry and Empire, 1971
Homans, Social Behavior, 1962
Horowitz, Empire and Revolution, 1969
Hudson, Super Imperialism, 1972

Iklé, Every War Must End, 1972
————, How Nations Negotiate, 1966

Ilchman. See: Uphoff, 1970
Instituto Brasileiro dé Economia da Fundacão Getúlio Vargas, Contribuicões à
    Análise do Disenvolvimento Econômico, 1958

James, The Death of Progress, 1973
Janeway, The Economics of Crisis, 1968
Jewkes, Public and Private Enterprise, 1967
Johnson and Ackerman, The Church as Employer, Money Raiser and Investor,
    1959

Kahn, Thinking About the Unthinkable, 1962
——— and Wiener, The Year 2000, 1968
Kaplan, System and Process in International Politics, 1958
Kuhn, A., The Study of Society, 1964
Kuhn, M. See: Hickman, 1956

La Paix, Recueils de la Societe Jean Bodin, 1964
Lachman, Capital and Its Structure, 1956
Lange, Wholes and Parts, 1966
Lapp, The Logarithmic Century, 1973
Lauterbach, Man, Motives, and Money, 1955
Lave, Technological Change, 1967
Leites and Wolf, Jr., Rebellion and Authority, 1970
Lincoln. See: Padelford, 1964
Lindblom. See: Braybrooke, 1964 and 1969
Linder, The Harried Leisure Class, 1970
Little, A Critique of Welfare Economics, 1951
Lo Bello, The Vatican Empire, 1969
Lorenz, On Aggression, 1967
Lowe, On Economic Knowledge, 1965
Lundberg, E., Business Cycles and Economic Policy, 1958
Lundberg, F., The Rich and the Super-Rich, 1968
Lutz, F. and V., The Theory of Investment of the Firm, 1953

Machlup, The Production and Distribution of Knowledge in the United States,
    1963
Mack, ''Contrasts in Patterns of Flows of Commodities and Funds,'' 1952
Maddison, Economic Growth in the West, 1964
Maddox, The Doomsday Syndrome, 1973
Mamdani, The Myth of Population Control, 1973
March. See: Cyert, 1964
Marcuse, An Essay on Liberation, 1969
Markowitz. See: Brunner, 1952
Mason, ed., The Corporation in Modern Society, 1960
Mazlish, ed., The Railroad and the Space Program, 1966
McCarthy, The Ultimate Folly, 1969
McClelland, College Teaching of International Relations, 1964
McKean. See: Hitch, 1961

McLuhan, The Gutenberg Galaxy, 1965
————, Understanding Media, 1965
Mead, Culture and Commitment, 1970
Meade, The Growing Economy, 1969
Meadows, D. and D. *et al.*, The Limits to Growth, 1972
Means, Pricing Power and the Public Interest, 1962
Medawar, The Future of Man, 1961
Meisel, The Myth of the Ruling Class, 1958
Mendes-France and Ardant, Economics and Action, 1955
Merton, On the Shoulders of Giants, 1966
Mesthene, Technological Change, 1970
Miller *et al.*, eds., Fritz Machlup, Essays on Economic Semantics, 1964
Millis, An End To Arms, 1965
Morgan, Observations, 1969
Morgenthau, Politics Among Nations, 1964
Murphy. See: Fried *et al.*, 1969
Myrdal, Asian Drama, 1968
————, Beyond the Welfare State, 1961
————, An International Economy, 1956

National Bureau of Economic Research, Studies in Income and Wealth, Vol. 13, 1952
Niebuhr, The Structure of Nations and Empires, 1960
Nieburg, In the Name of Science, 1967
Novick, The Careless Atom, 1969
Nygaard, America Prays, 1946

Okun, The Political Economy of Prosperity, 1970
Olson, Jr., The Logic of Collective Action, 1969
Organski, World Politics, 1964

Padelford and Lincoln, The Dynamics of International Politics, 1964
Parsons, Structure and Process in Modern Societies, 1961
———— and Smelser, Economy and Society, 1957
Paton, Shirtsleeve Economics, 1952
Perlo, Militarism and Industry, 1963
Peterson, The Industrial Order and Social Policy, 1973
Platt, Perception and Change, 1971
Polak, The Image of the Future, 1962
Power, with Arnhym, Design for Survival, 1965
Price, The Scientific Estate, 1966

Quandt. See: Thorp, 1960

Rae, American Automobile Manufacturers, 1959
Randall, Economics and Public Policy, 1955
————, A Foreign Economic Policy for the United States, 1955
Ransom. See: Breit, 1973
Rapoport, Strategy and Conscience, 1964

_____ and Chammah, Prisoner's Dilemma, 1966
Rawls, A Theory of Justice, 1973
Report from Iron Mountain, 1968
Robertson, Should Churches Be Taxed? 1969
Robinson, Economic Heresies, 1971
_____, Economic Philosophy, 1963
Roose, The Economics of Recession and Revival, 1954
Röpke, The Social Crisis of Our Time, 1950
Rosenau, ed., International Politics and Foreign Policy, 1964
Rostow, Politics and the Stages of Growth, 1971
Russett, ed., Economic Theories of International Politics, 1969
_____, What Price Vigilance? 1972

Samuelson, Foundations of Economic Analysis, 1948
Samuelsson, Religion and Economic Action, 1962
Schelling, The Strategy of Conflict, 1961
Schleicher, International Relations, 1964
Schneider, Destiny of Change, 1969
Schramm, Responsibility in Mass Communication, 1958
Schultz, The Theory of Measurement of Demand, 1939
Seligman, Most Notorious Victory, 1967
_____, Permanent Poverty, 1968
Shackle, Epistemics & Economics, 1973
_____, A Scheme of Economic Theory, 1967
Sievers, Revolution, Evolution and the Economic Order, 1962
Slichter, The American Economy, 1949
Smelser. See: Parsons, 1957
Solo, Economic Organizations and Social Systems, 1967
Sporn, Technology, Engineering, and Economics, 1969
Stein, The Fiscal Revolution in America, 1970
Stoessinger, The Might of Nations, 1964

Tarshis, The Elements of Economics, 1948
Taylor, The Classical Liberalism, Marxism, and the Twentieth Century, 1960
Thorp and Quandt, The New Inflation, 1960
Thomas. See: Bahr et al., 1973
Tullock, The Organization of Inquiry, 1968

Uphoff and Ilchman, eds., The Political Economy of Change, 1970

Valk, Production, Pricing, and Unemployment in the Static State, 1938
van Dorp, A Simple Theory of Capital, Wages, and Profit or Loss, 1937
Vickers, The Undirected Society, 1960

Walter, Terror and Resistance, 1971
Ward, Space Ship Earth, 1966
Warner, The Corporation in the Emergent American Society, 1963
West, Education and the State, 1966
Whiting. See: Haas, 1964

Wiener, A. See: Kahn, 1968
Wiener, N., The Human Use of Human Beings, 1952
William W. Cook Lectures on American Institutions 1950-51, 1951
Wilson, An Opening Way, 1961
Wolf, Jr. See: Leites, 1970
Woodward, The Human Dilemma, 1973
Wright, D., The Economics of Disturbance, 1948
Wright, Q. et al., eds., Preventing World War III, 1963

Zipf, Human Behavior and the Principle of Least Effort, 1951

VERSE BY TITLE *

Arden House Poetry, 1963
A Ballad of Ecological Awareness, 1972
The Brandywine River Anthology, 1958
The Busted Thermostat, 1952
The Conservationist's Lament; The Technologist's Reply, 1955
COPRED, A Prophecy, 1973
The Ditchley Bank Anthology, 1969
The Feather River Anthology, 1966
The Nayler Sonnets, 1944
New Goals for Society? 1972
The Old Agricultural Lag, 1967
Reflections (on the National Conference on Managing the Environment), 1973
A Shelter for All, 1961
Some Reflections (on the 4th National Study Conference on the Church and
  Economic Life), 1962
Summary (of The Range of Human Conflict: A Symposium), 1966
T. R., 1958
There Is a Spirit. See: The Nayler Sonnets, 1944
X Cantos, 1969

* A selection of Kenneth Boulding's verse is published as a separate volume by
the Colorado Associated University Press, 1975, entitled: Sonnets from the
Interior Life and Other Autobiographical Verse.

INDEX OF NAMES

SUBJECT INDEX